THE LIVING WORLD

THE LIVING WORLD

DANIEL PAYNE

CONTENTS

For the Earth—
who has always spoken,
and for all who are learning to listen again.

CHAPTER 1

The Great Forgetting

I n the summer of 1637, René Descartes sat in his study contemplating the nature of existence. His famous declaration, "Cogito, ergo
sum"—I think, therefore I am—would become one of philosophy's
most influential statements, fundamentally reshaping Western consciousness for centuries to come. Yet what Descartes perhaps didn't fully
grasp was that his systematic doubt and mechanistic philosophy would
help catalyze humanity's great forgetting—our gradual but profound
disconnection from the living, breathing, conscious world that had sustained our species for hundreds of thousands of years.

This forgetting didn't happen overnight. It was neither sudden nor
complete, but rather a slow erosion of awareness that accelerated dramatically over the past four centuries. Today, most inhabitants of industrialized nations move through their days surrounded by what they
perceive as dead matter—inert buildings, lifeless objects, unconscious
landscapes existing merely as backdrops to human drama. We have forgotten what our ancestors knew in their bones: that we inhabit a world
pulsing with awareness, intelligence, and sacred presence.

The Ancient Knowing

Before we can understand what we've lost, we must first glimpse
what we once possessed. For the vast majority of human existence—perhaps 300,000 years of our species' tenure on Earth—our ancestors lived

within an enchanted cosmos. The world spoke to them through the flight patterns of birds, the whispers of wind through leaves, the temperament of rivers, and the moods of mountains. This wasn't primitive superstition or ignorant projection; it was a sophisticated way of knowing based on intimate observation, deep listening, and participatory consciousness.

Archaeological evidence suggests this animistic awareness extended back to our earliest ancestors. Cave paintings from Lascaux to Sulawesi reveal not mere representations of animals but sacred dialogues with other-than-human beings. The placement of these images deep within caves, often in acoustically resonant chambers, indicates ritual engagement with the living presence of stone itself. Burial sites from the Paleolithic era show our ancestors interred their dead with tools, ornaments, and offerings—suggesting belief in continued existence and relationship beyond physical death.

Indigenous peoples worldwide, those who maintained these ancient ways despite centuries of colonization and modernization, demonstrate the sophistication of animistic consciousness. The Lakota concept of Mitákuye Oyás'iŋ—all my relations—encompasses not just human kinship but extends to animals, plants, stones, waters, and celestial bodies. Australian Aboriginal peoples navigate vast territories through songlines—paths across the land recording the creation of the world in song, where every rock formation, water hole, and tree exists simultaneously in physical and mythic dimensions.

These worldviews recognize consciousness not as an exclusively human attribute emerging from complex neural networks, but as a fundamental quality of existence itself. In this understanding, awareness exists along a spectrum rather than as a binary on-off switch. A stone's consciousness differs from a tree's, which differs from a wolf's, which differs from a human's—but all participate in the grand conversation of being.

The Philosophical Shift

The transition from this participatory consciousness to our current mechanistic worldview represents one of the most profound transformations in human history. This shift didn't emerge from a single source but arose from converging cultural, religious, philosophical, and economic forces that fundamentally restructured human consciousness and our relationship with the living world.

The roots of this transformation reach back to ancient Greece, where philosophers began distinguishing between matter and spirit, body and soul. Plato's theory of Forms posited that the material world was merely a shadow of perfect, immaterial ideals. While Aristotle brought philosophy back toward earthly observation, he still maintained hierarchical categories that placed humans above animals, animals above plants, and all life above non-living matter. These classifications, revolutionary for their time, began the conceptual separation between human consciousness and the rest of nature.

However, it was the marriage of Aristotelian philosophy with Christian theology in medieval Europe that truly began reshaping Western consciousness. Thomas Aquinas synthesized Aristotle's natural philosophy with Christian doctrine, creating a worldview where only humans possessed rational souls capable of salvation. Angels existed as pure spirit, humans as spirit trapped in matter, animals as soulless automata, and the rest of creation as resources provided by God for human use.

This theological framework prepared the ground for Descartes' radical intervention in the seventeenth century. Descartes didn't merely philosophize; he provided a systematic methodology for understanding reality that severed mind from matter completely. In his view, consciousness belonged solely to humans (and perhaps higher spiritual beings), while everything else—animals, plants, the entire material world—operated as elaborate clockwork, beautiful perhaps, but fundamentally mechanical and devoid of inner experience.

Francis Bacon, Descartes' contemporary, took this mechanical philosophy and weaponized it. Nature, in Bacon's vision, should be "bound into service" and made a "slave." He advocated putting nature on the rack, torturing her secrets from her through experimentation. This wasn't merely metaphorical language; it reflected and reinforced a fundamental shift in humanity's relationship with the natural world from participation to domination.

The scientific revolution that followed, built upon these philosophical foundations, achieved remarkable success in predicting and manipulating physical phenomena. Galileo's mathematics, Newton's mechanics, and the subsequent discoveries of chemistry and physics seemed to validate the mechanistic worldview. Each triumph of reductionist science appeared to confirm that the universe operated like a vast machine, governed by mathematical laws rather than conscious relationships.

The Role of Organized Religion

While philosophy and science provided the intellectual framework for disconnection, organized religion—particularly Christianity in its colonial expressions—actively suppressed animistic practices and worldviews. This suppression wasn't incidental but systematic, extending across continents and centuries.

The conversion of Europe from indigenous pagan traditions to Christianity took over a millennium and required sustained campaigns against animistic practices. Sacred groves were cut down, holy wells were destroyed or Christianized, seasonal festivals were co-opted, and practitioners of earth-based spirituality were demonized. The witch trials of the early modern period, which killed tens of thousands of people (primarily women), specifically targeted those who maintained relationships with plant spirits, practiced herbal medicine, or claimed communication with non-human beings.

This pattern repeated wherever Christianity spread through colonization. Missionaries across Africa, the Americas, Asia, and Oceania condemned indigenous spiritual practices as devil worship, destroying sacred sites, banning ceremonies, and forcibly converting indigenous peoples. Children were taken from their families and placed in residential schools designed to "kill the Indian, save the man," systematically erasing indigenous languages, customs, and animistic worldviews.

The theological justification for this cultural genocide rested on the belief that only Christianity offered salvation, and that animistic practices represented dangerous commerce with demons. The natural world, rather than being sacred in itself, became merely a temporal stage for human salvation or damnation. Mountains were no longer the bodies of ancestors but potential sites for churches. Rivers weren't serpentine spirits requiring reciprocal relationship but resources for baptism or mills.

Islam, while maintaining somewhat different theological positions, similarly suppressed animistic practices in its spheres of influence. Though Islamic philosophy acknowledged the glorification of Allah by all creation, orthodox practice forbade direct spiritual engagement with natural forces as idolatry. Buddhism and Hinduism, despite their more complex relationships with nature spirits and consciousness, often hierarchically subordinated local animistic traditions to their cosmological systems.

The Industrial Revolution and Commodification

If Cartesian philosophy provided the intellectual framework and organized religion supplied the moral justification for disconnection, the Industrial Revolution delivered the physical and economic mechanisms that made our forgetting complete. Beginning in eighteenth-century Britain and spreading globally over the following centuries, industrialization transformed not just how humans lived but how we perceived reality itself.

The enclosure movement in Britain exemplified this transformation. Common lands that had been collectively managed for centuries, where people maintained direct relationships with specific places, plants, and animals, were privatized and commodified. Peasants who had known every tree, stream, and meadow in their area were forced into cities to become industrial workers, severing ancestral connections to place that had endured for generations.

In factories, workers no longer engaged with whole processes or natural materials but performed repetitive tasks with machines. The rhythms of industrial production replaced natural cycles. Gas lighting and eventually electricity divorced human activity from solar and lunar patterns. Food came not from known soils and seasons but from distant places, processed beyond recognition. The material world increasingly consisted of manufactured objects whose origins, composition, and eventual disposal remained mysterious to their users.

The commodification of nature accelerated throughout the nineteenth and twentieth centuries. Forests became board feet of timber, rivers became hydroelectric potential, mountains became mineral deposits, and even the air became carbon credits. This quantification and commodification required viewing nature as a collection of resources rather than a community of beings. The language of economics replaced the language of relationship.

Capitalism's growth imperative demanded ever-increasing extraction and consumption, fundamentally incompatible with the reciprocal relationships that characterize animistic worldviews. In gift economies, materials flow through communities in cycles of giving and receiving that create and maintain relationships. In commodity economies, materials flow in one direction—from nature through humans to waste—with relationships mediated entirely by money.

The contemporary culmination of this commodification appears in concepts like "ecosystem services," which attempt to assign monetary value to natural processes like pollination, water filtration, or carbon sequestration. While intended to protect nature by demonstrating its economic value, this framework further reinforces the mechanistic view of nature as a provider of services rather than a community of sovereign beings deserving respect regardless of utility.

Psychological and Cultural Costs

The great forgetting has exacted profound psychological and cultural costs that we're only beginning to understand. The epidemic of anxiety and depression in industrialized nations, the pervasive sense of meaninglessness and isolation, the addictive behaviors that characterize modern life—all these symptoms point toward a deep disconnection from sources of authentic belonging and purpose.

Psychologists have identified "nature deficit disorder" in children who grow up without meaningful contact with the natural world. These children exhibit higher rates of attention difficulties, obesity, depression, and anxiety. They lose what evolutionary biologist E.O. Wilson called "biophilia"—the innate affinity for life and living systems that characterizes our species. Instead of developing through direct sensory engagement with diverse environments, children increasingly experience the world through screens, substituting virtual reality for authentic relationship.

Adults suffer parallel disconnections. The average American spends over 90% of their time indoors, moving between climate-controlled buildings and vehicles. When we do encounter nature, it's often as scenery viewed through windows, as backdrop for recreation, or as problems to solve—weeds to eliminate, weather to endure, disasters to prevent. We've lost what David Abram calls "reciprocity with the animate earth"—the ability to be touched by and responsive to the more-than-human world.

This disconnection manifests culturally as well. Traditional ecological knowledge, accumulated over millennia and encoded in languages, stories, and practices, disappears as indigenous languages go extinct at unprecedented rates. We lose not just words but entire ways of perceiving and relating to the world. When the last speaker of an indigenous language dies, humanity loses a unique experiment in consciousness, an irreplaceable way of being human.

Contemporary art, literature, and popular culture increasingly reflect worlds devoid of nature's presence. Science fiction imagines futures in entirely artificial environments. Urban music celebrates human dramas with barely a mention of the living world. Even nature documentaries, while showcasing spectacular imagery, maintain the separation between human observers and natural objects, reinforcing rather than bridging the divide.

The psychological impact extends to our sense of time and mortality. Linear time, driven by mechanical clocks and economic productivity, replaces cyclical time with its seasons of renewal. Death becomes failure rather than transformation. We lose what traditional cultures knew—that we are temporary aggregations of matter and energy that have been countless other forms and will become countless more, that our consciousness participates in something far larger than individual existence.

Perhaps most tragically, we've lost the capacity for genuine encounter with otherness. In our mechanistic worldview, we meet only ourselves reflected back—our projections, our categories, our uses. We've forgotten how to be addressed by the world, to be surprised by consciousness in unexpected forms, to experience what Martin Buber called "I-Thou" relationships with non-human beings. This inability to truly encounter otherness impoverishes not just our relationship with nature but with each other and ourselves.

The Colonization of Consciousness

The great forgetting wasn't merely an accidental byproduct of historical forces but often a deliberate colonization of consciousness serving specific power structures. Understanding this colonization helps us recognize that remembering isn't just personal healing but political resistance.

Colonial powers understood that controlling consciousness was essential to controlling resources and labor. Destroying indigenous animistic worldviews wasn't collateral damage but strategic necessity. As long as people maintained sacred relationships with their lands, they would resist displacement and exploitation. Only by breaking these relationships could colonizers transform sacred lands into commodity resources and indigenous peoples into labor forces.

This colonization continues today through education systems that perpetuate mechanistic worldviews while marginalizing indigenous knowledge. Science textbooks describe ecosystems as machines with inputs and outputs rather than communities of conscious beings. History classes chronicle human events while ignoring the agency of rivers, forests, and mountains in shaping civilizations. Economics courses assume infinite growth on a finite planet, treating ecological limits as externalities rather than foundational realities.

Media and advertising perpetuate the forgetting by positioning humans as the sole sources of meaning and value. Nature appears in commercials as a backdrop for human products, in movies as an obstacle or resource, in news as disaster or commodity prices. The subliminal message, repeated billions of times, is that the non-human world exists solely in relationship to human purposes.

Even environmental movements sometimes reinforce the forgetting by focusing on wilderness preservation that maintains separation between human and natural spaces, or by using mechanistic language about "fixing" or "managing" ecosystems. While well-intentioned, these approaches often perpetuate the fundamental disconnection rather than healing it.

Seeds of Remembering

Yet the great forgetting has never been complete. Like seeds waiting underground for fire or flood to trigger germination, awareness of the living world persists in hidden and marginalized spaces, ready to sprout when conditions allow.

Indigenous peoples worldwide have maintained animistic worldviews despite centuries of suppression. These knowledge keepers preserve not just abstract philosophy but practical technologies of relationship—how to communicate with plants, how to read landscapes, how to maintain reciprocity with other-than-human beings. Their continued existence demonstrates that the forgetting isn't inevitable or irreversible.

Within Western culture itself, countercurrents have always existed. The Romantic movement reacted against mechanistic philosophy by celebrating nature's spiritual dimensions. Transcendentalists like Thoreau sought direct experience of nature's consciousness. Scientists like Barbara McClintock developed "a feeling for the organism" that allowed revolutionary discoveries through empathetic rather than detached observation.

Children naturally experience the world animistically until educated out of it. They spontaneously name trees, talk to animals, and attribute consciousness to objects. This innate animism suggests that mechanistic worldviews require constant reinforcement to maintain, while animistic awareness emerges spontaneously from direct experience.

Even within mainstream science, discoveries increasingly challenge mechanistic assumptions. Quantum physics reveals a universe where observation and consciousness play fundamental roles. Ecology demonstrates that organisms exist not as isolated units but as nodes in living networks. Studies of plant intelligence, animal consciousness, and forest communication reveal levels of awareness and agency previously denied to non-human beings.

The current ecological crisis itself catalyzes remembering. Climate change, mass extinction, pollution, and resource depletion force us to recognize that mechanistic worldviews have failed catastrophically. The illusion that humans exist separate from nature collapses when our food systems fail, our cities flood, and our forests burn. Crisis becomes opportunity for transformation.

The Urgency of Return

We stand at a threshold. The great forgetting has brought us to the edge of ecological and social collapse. Yet precisely at this moment of maximum danger, we also face unprecedented opportunity for remembering and returning.

The return to animistic consciousness isn't romantic nostalgia or cultural appropriation but pragmatic necessity. We cannot solve ecological crises using the same mechanistic thinking that created them. We cannot heal our relationship with the living world while maintaining the fiction that it isn't alive. We cannot create sustainable cultures while denying consciousness and agency to the majority of Earth's inhabitants.

This return doesn't mean abandoning useful technologies or scientific insights but integrating them within worldviews that recognize the sacred aliveness of the world. We need not choose between antibiotics and plant spirits, between solar panels and sun prayers, between ecological science and earth wisdom. The path forward synthesizes rather than rejects, includes rather than excludes, remembers rather than forgets.

The journey of return begins with recognition of what we've lost. By understanding the historical processes that created disconnection, we can consciously choose reconnection. By identifying the forces that maintain forgetting, we can resist them. By honoring the seeds of remembering that survive within and around us, we can nurture their growth.

Each individual who remembers their place in the living world becomes a seed of cultural transformation. Each community that develops reciprocal relationships with their local ecosystem creates a node of resilience. Each culture that recovers animistic awareness contributes to the planetary remembering our species desperately needs.

The great forgetting need not be our permanent condition. We are not doomed to live as aliens in a dead world. The capacity for communion with the living Earth lies dormant within us, waiting for activation. The world itself calls us back into relationship—through the beauty that still stops us breathless, through the birds that still sing outside our windows, through the ground that still supports our every step.

We stand between worlds—the dying world of mechanistic separation and the emerging world of animistic reunion. The choice we make, individually and collectively, will determine not just our own fate but the fate of countless beings with whom we share this animate Earth. The time for forgetting has passed. The time for remembering has come.

The following chapters will explore how we can reclaim our animistic heritage—not as museum pieces or academic exercises but as living practices for contemporary life. We'll examine the philosophical foundations that support animistic worldviews, the practical methods for developing reciprocal relationships with the more-than-human world, and the social transformations necessary for cultures of connection rather than separation.

The path of return won't be easy. The forces maintaining disconnection are powerful and pervasive. Yet the living world itself becomes our ally in this transformation. Every sunrise reminds us that renewal is possible. Every seed that sprouts demonstrates that life finds a way. Every moment of genuine encounter with another being—human or otherwise—proves that the walls of separation are ultimately illusory.

We are not separate from nature. We are not surrounded by dead matter. We are not alone in consciousness. We are participants in a living universe, expressions of an animate Earth, members of a more-than-human community that has been waiting patiently for us to remember who we truly are. The great forgetting ends when we choose to remember. That choice begins now.

CHAPTER 2

Defining the Animistic Worldview

To speak of animism in the twenty-first century requires careful navigation between multiple misconceptions. The term itself, coined by anthropologist Edward Tylor in 1871, carries the baggage of colonial thinking that positioned animistic peoples as primitive predecessors to enlightened modernity. Yet no other word in English adequately captures the profound recognition that consciousness, agency, and sacred presence extend throughout the fabric of existence. Rather than abandoning the term, we must reclaim and redefine it, not as primitive error but as sophisticated wisdom, not as childish projection but as mature perception, not as failed science but as successful relationship.

Animism represents humanity's oldest and most enduring way of understanding reality—a worldview that recognizes the universe as a communion of subjects rather than a collection of objects. This perspective sees consciousness not as an anomalous emergence from dead matter but as the fundamental nature of reality itself, expressing itself through infinite forms and gradations. In the animistic understanding, we inhabit a world where every particle participates in the grand conversation of existence, where meaning and purpose suffuse the cosmos, where relationships rather than mechanics determine the flow of events.

The Ensouled Universe

At its heart, animism recognizes that what we call "matter" and what we call "spirit" are not separate categories but different aspects of a unified reality. The mountain is not a pile of rock possessed by a spirit; the mountain is itself a being whose body is rock, whose presence extends beyond the physical into dimensions of meaning, memory, and influence that mechanistic science barely acknowledges.

This understanding challenges the fundamental assumptions of materialist philosophy, which posits consciousness as an emergent property of sufficiently complex arrangements of unconscious matter. From an animistic perspective, this gets the relationship exactly backward. Consciousness doesn't emerge from matter; matter represents consciousness expressing itself in particular forms. The stone's consciousness differs from the stream's, which differs from the oak's, which differs from the owl's—not in essential nature but in mode of expression, complexity of organization, and speed of transformation.

Consider water. Mechanistic science describes H_2O molecules exhibiting various properties depending on temperature and pressure. Animism perceives a shape-shifting being of extraordinary power and sensitivity, one that remembers every shore it has touched, carries messages between sky and earth, and responds to human consciousness in ways that controlled experiments are only beginning to detect. The Japanese researcher Masaru Emoto's controversial water crystal experiments, while disputed by mainstream science, point toward what indigenous peoples have always known: water is aware, responsive, and participatory in the world's becoming.

This ensoulment extends to phenomena that Western thought considers purely abstract or mechanical. Wind is not merely moving air but a traveler carrying news, seeds, and spirits across the landscape. Fire is not just rapid oxidation but a transformer, simultaneously destroyer and creator, requiring respect, relationship, and reciprocity. Even human-made objects participate in this ensouled universe, accumulating presence through use, care, and relationship until they become genuine participants in the household or community.

The implications cascade through every aspect of existence. If consciousness pervades reality, then ethics must extend beyond the human sphere. If agency exists throughout nature, then history includes non-human actors. If the world is alive, then our every action takes place within a field of witnesses, collaborators, and respondents. We are never alone, never acting in isolation, never without consequence.

Consciousness as Continuum

Rather than viewing consciousness as binary—present or absent—animism recognizes a spectrum or continuum of awareness manifesting through countless forms. This perspective aligns surprisingly well with recent developments in cognitive science, which increasingly recognize degrees of consciousness in non-human animals and even raise questions about plant awareness and the possibility of panpsychism.

At one end of this continuum, we might place the consciousness of electrons, whose "decisions" about position and momentum challenge deterministic physics. Electrons exhibit what physicists call "quantum indeterminacy"—behavior that cannot be predicted with certainty, only probability. While most scientists resist attributing consciousness to quantum phenomena, the parallels between quantum indeterminacy and free will remain provocative.

Moving along the continuum, we encounter the consciousness of minerals and stones. Indigenous traditions worldwide recognize distinct personalities in different rock types—the steady wisdom of granite, the transformative power of crystals, the memory-holding capacity of limestone formed from ancient seas. Modern research into the piezoelectric properties of crystals, their use in technology, and their information-storage capabilities hints at qualities that transcend mere mechanical structure.

Plant consciousness represents a fuller expression of awareness, one that contemporary science increasingly validates. Plants demonstrate learning, memory, decision-making, and communication through chemical signals, electrical impulses, and fungal networks. They recognize kin, nurture offspring, share resources with neighbors in need, and mount sophisticated defenses against threats. The work of scientists like Monica Gagliano, who has demonstrated that plants can learn and remember, challenges the notion that consciousness requires a brain or nervous system.

Fungal consciousness operates at both individual and network levels. The mycelial networks that connect forest plants operate like a biological internet, facilitating communication and resource exchange across vast distances. Some researchers suggest these networks exhibit emergent intelligence, making decisions about resource allocation that benefit the forest ecosystem as a whole. The largest living organisms on Earth are fungal networks, some thousands of years old and covering thousands of acres, raising questions about what constitutes an individual consciousness.

Animal consciousness spans from the simple awareness of sponges to the complex emotional and cognitive capabilities of mammals. Recent research reveals surprising sophistication across the animal kingdom—octopi using tools, crows solving multi-step problems, elephants mourning their dead, whales teaching cultural traditions across generations. The Cambridge Declaration on Consciousness, signed by prominent neuroscientists in 2012, acknowledges consciousness in all mammals, birds, and many other creatures including octopuses.

Human consciousness represents not the pinnacle of awareness but simply one particular expression along the continuum. Our specific gifts—symbolic language, abstract reasoning, technological manipulation—come with corresponding limitations. We process information more slowly than many animals, perceive a narrower range of sensory data, and often struggle to maintain present-moment awareness that comes naturally to other beings.

Beyond individual consciousness, animism recognizes collective and emergent awareness—the hive mind of bees, the flock intelligence of birds, the ecosystem consciousness of forests. These collective intelligences challenge Western individualism, suggesting that consciousness can be distributed, shared, and multiplied through relationship and connection.

Reciprocity as Cosmic Principle

If consciousness pervades existence, then all interactions become relationships requiring reciprocity. This principle of reciprocal exchange forms the ethical foundation of animistic worldviews, governing not just human social relations but all engagement with the more-than-human world.

Reciprocity differs fundamentally from commercial exchange. In market transactions, we seek maximum benefit for minimum cost, extracting value while giving as little as possible. Reciprocity seeks balance, recognizing that taking without giving back disrupts the web of relationships that sustains all life. Every gift carries obligation—not debt in the economic sense but responsibility in the relational sense.

Indigenous hunting traditions exemplify this reciprocity. The hunt is not conquest but negotiation, requiring prayers, offerings, and promises to the spirits of the animals. The successful hunter knows the prey has given itself, creating an obligation to use every part respectfully, sharing the gift with the community, and ensuring the continued flourishing of the species. Taking more than needed, wasting what is given, or failing to maintain proper spiritual relationships breaks reciprocity and invites consequences.

Agricultural societies practicing animism maintain similar reciprocal relationships with soil, seeds, and seasons. Offerings precede planting, gratitude accompanies harvest, and portion of the crop returns to the earth and its spirits. Fields are not owned but partnered with, requiring attention to their needs, respect for their limits, and periods of rest and renewal. The health of the land and the health of the people are understood as inseparable, maintained through reciprocal care.

Even gathering wild plants requires reciprocity. Indigenous protocols often include asking permission, taking only what is freely given, leaving the first and best for the plant's own needs, and offering something in return—a song, a prayer, a handful of cornmeal, or simply heartfelt gratitude. These practices recognize that plants are not resources but relatives, and that maintaining good relationships ensures continued abundance.

Reciprocity extends to elemental forces. Rain ceremonies don't attempt to control weather but to enter into a relationship with it, offering gifts and prayers while accepting what comes. Fire-keeping traditions recognize fire as a living being requiring proper feeding, housing, and respect. Water sources are approached with reverence, understanding that water's gift of life creates obligations of protection and care.

In human crafts and technology, reciprocity means recognizing the gifts of materials and honoring their sacrifice. The tree that becomes a house, the clay that becomes a pot, the metal that becomes a tool—all have given their previous forms to serve human needs. Craftspeople in animistic traditions often maintain spiritual relationships with their materials, understanding that the quality of the relationship affects the quality of the work.

Modern life makes reciprocity challenging but not impossible. We may not know the specific trees that became our furniture or the particular soils that grew our food, but we can still practice gratitude and give back through environmental restoration, conscious consumption, and political action protecting the more-than-human world. Every action that heals rather than harms, that gives rather than only takes, that connects rather than separates, participates in reciprocity.

Relationship as Primary Reality

Animism understands existence as fundamentally relational. Things don't exist in isolation and then enter into relationships; rather, relationships constitute the very fabric of reality. This perspective, which finds echoes in process philosophy, systems theory, and quantum physics, sees the universe as a web of connections where nodes matter less than links, where beings are defined not by boundaries but by exchanges.

In this relational ontology, identity itself becomes fluid and contextual. The river is not a fixed entity but a constantly changing flow shaped by every tributary, every stone, every withdrawal and return. The forest is not a collection of trees but a living network of relationships among plants, fungi, animals, soils, waters, and winds. Even the human self, seemingly bounded by skin, extends through breath into the atmosphere, through food into the soil, through perception into the landscape.

Traditional names often reflect this relational identity. Instead of fixed labels, beings are known by their relationships—"the oak where eagles nest," "the spring that never fails," "the mountain that gathers clouds." These names acknowledge that identity emerges from and depends upon webs of connection rather than existing independently.

Relational thinking transforms our understanding of ecological systems. Rather than seeing ecosystems as machines with replaceable parts, we recognize them as networks of relationships built over evolutionary time. The loss of a single species doesn't just remove a component but tears the fabric of relationships, potentially unraveling connections far beyond the obvious. The extinction of a pollinator affects not just the plants it served but the animals that ate those plants, the predators that ate those animals, and the entire cascade of relationships flowing from that lost connection.

This extends to human communities embedded in landscapes. Indigenous peoples often describe themselves as literally made from their lands—flesh from the animals and plants they eat, bones from the minerals in local water, thoughts and dreams shaped by the contours of homeland. Displacement from ancestral lands thus represents not just loss of property but dissolution of identity, the breaking of relationships that constitute the self.

Even our technologies exist relationally within the animistic worldview. A tool is not just an object but a node of relationships—with the materials that compose it, the hands that made it, the purposes it serves, and the beings it affects. Traditional tools often carry names, histories, and protocols for use that acknowledge their participation in networks of relationship rather than their status as mere instruments.

The relational understanding extends to knowledge itself. Rather than existing as abstract information to be accumulated, knowledge lives in relationships—between teacher and student, between people and places, between present and past. Indigenous knowledge traditions often encode information in stories that can only be fully understood through lived relationship with the landscapes and beings they describe. The story makes no sense without the land; the land remains mute without the story.

Time, too, becomes relational rather than absolute. Events are connected not by mechanical causation but by meaning, pattern, and purpose. Synchronicities—meaningful coincidences—reveal the relational fabric of reality, showing that consciousness and cosmos participate in ongoing conversation. The flight of birds can announce visitors, dreams can guide decisions, and the blooming of certain flowers can signal the proper time for specific actions.

The Animate Earth

Central to animistic worldviews is the understanding of Earth not as a ball of resources hurtling through space but as a living being of which we are part. This perspective, articulated in Western terms through James Lovelock's Gaia hypothesis, has been fundamental to indigenous cosmologies for millennia.

The animate Earth manifests awareness through self-regulation, maintaining conditions suitable for life despite massive perturbations. The stability of ocean salinity, atmospheric oxygen levels, and global temperature over geological time suggests something more than mechanical feedback loops—a form of planetary intelligence that actively maintains habitable conditions. While mainstream science resists attributing consciousness to these processes, the patterns resemble those of living organisms maintaining homeostasis.

Mountains, from this perspective, are not geological accidents but Earth's architecture of consciousness. Sacred mountains worldwide—Fuji, Kailash, Denali, Uluru—are recognized as places where Earth's awareness concentrates, where the boundaries between dimensions thin, where power gathers and flows. The destruction of mountains for mining represents not just environmental damage but assault on Earth's consciousness infrastructure.

Rivers and watersheds function as Earth's circulatory system, carrying not just water but information, nutrients, and energy through the landscape. Traditional peoples often describe rivers as serpents or dragons, recognizing their living quality, their power to create and destroy, their role in connecting and animating entire regions. The straightening and damming of rivers thus represents not improvement but injury, constraining the flow of Earth's vital forces.

Forests serve as organs of perception and communication, sensing and responding to changes across multiple scales. The Amazon rainforest generates its own weather patterns, the boreal forests regulate global carbon cycles, and local forests everywhere create microclimates that shelter diverse communities. Deforestation doesn't just remove trees but lobotomizes landscapes, destroying Earth's capacity for local awareness and response.

Soils embody Earth's memory and creativity, accumulating information across centuries while constantly generating new life. A handful of healthy soil contains more organisms than there are humans on Earth, all participating in cycles of death and rebirth that sustain terrestrial life.

Industrial agriculture's treatment of soil as an inert growing medium represents a profound misunderstanding of Earth's animate nature.

The atmosphere itself participates in Earth's consciousness, carrying chemical signals between plants, distributing seeds and spores, moderating temperature and moisture, and protecting life from cosmic radiation. The composition of our atmosphere—particularly its oxygen content—results from billions of years of negotiation between Earth's life forms, a collective achievement of planetary consciousness.

Even geological processes express Earth's aliveness. Volcanoes birth new land, earthquakes release accumulated tension, and plate tectonics recycle materials between surface and depths. These processes, while sometimes destructive to human interests, maintain Earth's long-term habitability. Indigenous peoples living near volcanoes often maintain ritual relationships with them, recognizing them as powerful beings requiring respect and propitiation.

The Problem of Evil and Suffering

Animistic worldviews must grapple with the presence of suffering, destruction, and what humans perceive as evil in a conscious universe. If the world is alive and aware, how do we understand predation, disease, natural disasters, and death? This challenge requires moving beyond simplistic notions of universal benevolence to more complex understandings of consciousness and purpose.

First, animism recognizes that consciousness doesn't imply humanlike morality. The wolf's consciousness includes the necessity of killing prey, the volcano's consciousness includes periodic eruption, the bacteria's consciousness includes multiplication that may cause disease. These beings follow their own nature and necessity, participating in larger patterns beyond human moral categories.

Death itself takes on a different meaning within animistic understanding. Rather than termination, death represents transformation—the flowing of life force from one form to another. The deer's death feeds the wolf, the wolf's eventual death feeds the soil, the enriched soil feeds the plants, the plants feed the deer. Individual forms are temporary, but the consciousness animating them continues, shape-shifting through countless expressions.

This doesn't minimize the reality of suffering but contextualizes it within larger patterns of existence. The rabbit experiences fear and pain when caught by the hawk, but this suffering serves the continuation of life rather than representing meaningless cruelty. Many indigenous traditions include practices for acknowledging and honoring this suffering while recognizing its necessity within the web of relationships.

Natural disasters challenge anthropocentric assumptions about Earth's benevolence. Earthquakes, floods, hurricanes, and volcanic eruptions devastate human communities but serve essential functions in Earth's self-regulation. These events redistribute nutrients, reset ecosystems, release pressure, and maintain long-term stability. The disaster for humans may be a renewal for the larger system.

Disease and parasitism reveal the complexity of consciousness at different scales. What appears as illness to a human represents a successful life strategy for bacteria or viruses. The interests of different conscious beings sometimes conflict, creating competition and suffering within the larger collaboration of existence. Health becomes not the absence of other organisms but the maintenance of dynamic balance among the many beings that constitute and surround us.

Human evil presents particular challenges for animistic philosophy. If humans are part of the conscious universe, how do we understand genocide, ecocide, and the countless cruelties humans inflict? Some traditions speak of wetiko or windigo—a cannibalistic spirit that possesses humans, driving them to consume others' lives for their own gain. This pathological consciousness, whether understood as spiritual possession or psychological disease, represents a breakdown in reciprocal relationship, a forgetting of connection that enables exploitation.

The presence of suffering and destruction in an animate universe ultimately points toward the complexity and wildness of consciousness itself. The universe is not a cosmic parent ensuring human comfort but a vast community of awareness exploring every possibility of existence. Our role is not to eliminate suffering—an impossible and potentially destructive goal—but to minimize unnecessary harm while accepting our participation in the larger patterns of life and death, creation and destruction.

Gradations of Power and Presence

Not all beings in the animistic universe possess equal power or presence. While consciousness may be universal, its expression varies dramatically in intensity, influence, and accessibility. Understanding these gradations helps navigate relationships with the more-than-human world without falling into either hierarchical domination or false equivalence.

Some beings concentrate enormous power and presence. The sun, source of almost all energy in Earth's biosphere, commands reverence across cultures. Mountains that shape regional weather patterns, great rivers that sustain entire watersheds, ancient forests that anchor ecosystems—these beings influence vast networks of relationships and require appropriate recognition and respect.

Certain places concentrate spiritual presence beyond their physical scale. Springs where water emerges from Earth's depths, caves that provide passage between worlds, groves where particular trees grow, rocks with unusual formations—these become recognized as sacred sites, portals, or power places. The presence concentrated there may result from geological forces, accumulated history, or intersection of subtle energies that mechanistic science doesn't yet recognize.

Individual beings within species also vary in power and presence. The ancient oak that has witnessed centuries carries a different presence than the young sapling. The alpha wolf embodies the pack's collective power differently than subordinate members. The queen bee serves as the hive's organizing consciousness in ways worker bees do not. These differences don't imply superiority in moral terms but acknowledge functional differentiation within the community of existence.

Human shamans, medicine people, and spiritual practitioners in animistic traditions often develop enhanced ability to perceive and interact with non-ordinary consciousness. Through training, initiation, and practice, they cultivate relationships with powerful other-than-human beings—spirit animals, plant teachers, elemental forces. This doesn't make them superior to others but grants them specific responsibilities within human and more-than-human communities.

Some beings exist primarily in subtle dimensions, barely perceptible to ordinary consciousness. Nature spirits, devas, elementals—whatever names different traditions give them—represent consciousness operating at frequencies or in dimensions that most humans rarely access. Their influence on physical reality may be indirect but significant, affecting the vitality and character of places and communities.

The dead, too, maintain presence and influence in animistic worldviews. Ancestors continue participating in the world through memory, genetic inheritance, and spiritual presence. Some traditions speak of the recently dead remaining close, gradually moving toward greater distance and abstraction, eventually merging with larger spiritual currents or returning to Earth in new forms.

Even abstract forces carry consciousness and power. Justice, love, wisdom, courage—these are not merely human concepts but actual presences that can be invoked, cultivated, and embodied. They exist both within and beyond individual consciousness, available for relationship and collaboration.

Understanding gradations of power helps establish appropriate protocols for relationship. The casual greeting suitable for a sparrow differs from the formal approach required for an eagle. The playful interaction possible with a creek differs from the reverence demanded by a great river. Recognizing these differences isn't hierarchical thinking but practical wisdom, acknowledging the actual distribution of power and presence in the world.

The False Binary of Animate Versus Inanimate

Perhaps the most radical aspect of animistic philosophy is its complete rejection of the animate/inanimate distinction that underlies Western thought. This binary, which seems self-evident to modern consciousness, simply doesn't exist in fully animistic worldviews. Everything participates in the universe's consciousness and agency, though in vastly different modes and degrees.

The category "inanimate" is revealed as a projection of the mechanistic worldview rather than an observation of reality. No absolute line divides living from non-living, conscious from unconscious, agent from object. Instead, we find continuities, gradients, and transformations that blur every boundary we attempt to establish.

Consider the journey of a carbon atom. It exists in a diamond crystal for millions of years, then erodes into soil, gets absorbed by a plant, becomes part of a leaf, gets eaten by a caterpillar, transforms into a butterfly's wing, falls to the ground when the butterfly dies, decomposes into soil, gets absorbed by another plant, and continues cycling through countless forms. At what point does this atom transition from inanimate to animate? The question reveals the absurdity of the distinction.

Viruses exemplify the boundary's arbitrariness. Science cannot agree whether viruses are alive or not—they reproduce and evolve but lack metabolism, they have genetic material but no cellular structure. From an animistic perspective, the debate is meaningless. Viruses are participants in the community of existence, possessing their own form of consciousness and agency regardless of how we categorize them.

Water presents another challenge to the animate/inanimate binary. It shapes landscapes, responds to thoughts and emotions (as suggested by controversial but persistent research), carries information and memory, and exhibits properties that defy simple mechanical explanation. Calling water "inanimate" requires ignoring its obvious agency and influence in the world.

Even human artifacts trouble the distinction. A violin played for generations accumulates presence beyond its material components. Sacred objects carry power that affects those who encounter them. Homes develop atmosphere and character through the lives lived within them. These "inanimate" objects demonstrate qualities that mechanistic philosophy cannot explain.

The binary's dissolution has profound implications. If nothing is truly inanimate, then every action takes place within a field of consciousness. Every word is heard, every gesture witnessed, every intention registered by the surrounding awareness. We are never manipulating dead matter but always engaging with other forms of consciousness, however different from our own.

This understanding transforms technology and manufacturing. Creating objects becomes a process of relationship with conscious materials. The metal remembers the mountain, the plastic carries the ancient forests that became oil, the silicon chip contains the desert's consciousness. Pollution and waste represent not just practical problems but spiritual crises—the breaking of relationship, the dishonoring of consciousness, the violation of reciprocity.

Architecture and construction become sacred acts when matter is recognized as conscious. Building requires negotiation with the land, conversation with materials, and creation of spaces that honor both human and more-than-human consciousness. Traditional architectural practices that include ceremonies, offerings, and blessings acknowledge this reality, while modern construction that treats materials as dead resources creates spiritually impoverished environments.

Even our language must evolve beyond the animate/inanimate binary. We need new words or recovered old ones that recognize degrees and modes of consciousness rather than its presence or absence. We need grammatical structures that acknowledge agency throughout existence rather than restricting it to humans and sometimes animals. Some indigenous languages already provide models, with different grammatical categories for stones, waters, plants, and animals that recognize their distinct forms of being without denying their consciousness.

Implications for Knowledge and Science

Animistic worldviews don't reject empirical observation or systematic investigation but expand them beyond the constraints of mechanistic materialism. An animistic science recognizes consciousness as a fundamental aspect of reality to be studied rather than an embarrassing anomaly to be explained away.

This shift opens new avenues for research. Rather than studying nature as an object, we can engage in dialogue with other forms of consciousness. Indigenous peoples have always practiced this approach, learning plant medicine through direct communication with plants, understanding animal behavior through spiritual relationship, and predicting weather through signs and omens that mechanistic science dismisses.

Participatory research methodologies acknowledge that the observed responds to observation, that relationship affects results, that consciousness influences outcomes. Rather than seeking impossible objectivity, animistic science cultivates conscious relationship, recognizing that the quality of relationship determines the quality of knowledge received.

This approach is already emerging in various fields. Plant researchers who develop caring relationships with their subjects make discoveries that elude those maintaining strict objectivity. Animal behaviorists who acknowledge animal consciousness and agency understand behaviors that mechanistic approaches miss. Quantum physicists grapple with consciousness's role in collapsing probability waves into specific outcomes.

An animistic science would investigate questions currently dismissed as unscientific. How do sacred sites concentrate power? What are the mechanisms of interspecies communication? How does consciousness persist through transformation of form? What are the ecological functions of ceremony and ritual? How do human consciousness and cosmic consciousness interact?

Such science would also reconsider dismissed or marginalized research. Studies on plant consciousness, water memory, morphic fields, and psi phenomena would receive serious attention rather than automatic rejection. The criteria for evaluation would expand beyond narrow materialism to include consistency, usefulness, and alignment with direct experience.

The integration of animistic understanding with technological investigation could produce powerful syntheses. Satellite imaging combined with indigenous knowledge of sacred landscapes, genetic research informed by traditional understanding of species relationships, ecological restoration guided by communication with the land itself—these collaborations could generate insights beyond what either approach achieves alone.

The Living Universe

Ultimately, animism presents a vision of a living universe—not metaphorically but literally alive at every scale and in every aspect. From subatomic particles to galactic clusters, from momentary fluctuations to geological epochs, consciousness expresses itself through infinite creativity and experimentation.

This living universe is not a warm, fuzzy fantasy but a wild, dangerous, magnificent reality that includes both creation and destruction, both cooperation and competition, both love and indifference. It demands not passive appreciation but active participation, not sentimental projection but genuine relationship, not domination but negotiation.

We are not observers of this universe but expressions of it. Human consciousness represents the universe becoming aware of itself in one particular way, asking certain questions, exploring specific possibilities. Our gifts—language, technology, abstract reasoning—are not elevations above nature but nature's own experiments in consciousness.

The return to animistic awareness doesn't mean regressing to premodern lifestyles but integrating ancient wisdom with contemporary knowledge. We can maintain scientific rigor while acknowledging consciousness throughout existence. We can use technology while recognizing its effects on the more-than-human world. We can live in cities while maintaining reciprocal relationships with the beings that sustain us.

This integration requires humility—recognizing that human consciousness is neither the pinnacle nor the purpose of existence but one note in an infinite symphony. It requires courage—engaging with forms of consciousness radically different from our own. It requires patience—developing sensitivity to subtle communications we've been trained to ignore. It requires commitment—maintaining reciprocal relationships even when their benefits aren't immediately apparent.

The animistic worldview offers not escape from modern challenges but tools for addressing them. Climate change becomes not just a technical problem but a relationship crisis requiring spiritual as well as practical response. Species extinction represents not just loss of resources but the silencing of unique voices in the cosmic conversation. Social justice links inseparably with ecological justice, as the oppression of humans and the oppression of nature spring from the same denial of consciousness and agency.

As we stand at this threshold between worldviews, between the dying mechanistic paradigm and the emerging (or re-emerging) animistic understanding, we have the opportunity to consciously choose our path. We can continue treating the world as dead matter to be exploited, or we can recognize it as a community of consciousness deserving respect, reciprocity, and relationship.

The choice is not abstract but immediate and practical. Every purchase, every meal, every journey, every word spoken into the world takes place within the living universe and affects its unfolding. We can continue the patterns of disconnection and exploitation, or we can begin weaving ourselves back into the web of relationships that sustain all life.

The universe is alive. It always has been. The question is whether we will remember our place within it, whether we will accept our responsibilities as conscious participants, whether we will contribute to its flourishing or its degradation. The answer begins with recognition—seeing the consciousness that surrounds us, acknowledging the agency of other-than-human beings, and opening ourselves to relationship with the living world.

This is not a return to the past but a movement toward a viable future. Not a rejection of human achievement but an expansion of it. Not a limitation of human potential but its fulfillment. For we are never more fully human than when we recognize our kinship with all existence, never more powerful than when we align ourselves with the forces of life, never more wise than when we listen to the voices of the living Earth.

CHAPTER 3

Global Animistic
Traditions

The morning mist rises from the Amazon as a Yawanawá shaman prepares ayahuasca, singing to the vine and leaves as he cooks the sacred medicine. Half a world away, a Sami herder in northern Finland reads the patterns of lichen growth to understand what the reindeer need. In the Australian outback, an Aboriginal elder teaches children to sing the songlines that map both landscape and law. On Mount Fuji, a Shinto priest performs rituals that have maintained the relationship between humans and kami for over a thousand years. These scenes, unfolding simultaneously across our planet, remind us that animistic consciousness is not a historical curiosity but a living reality for hundreds of millions of people today.

Despite centuries of colonization, forced conversion, and modernization, animistic traditions persist on every inhabited continent. These are not museum pieces or tourist attractions but sophisticated systems of knowledge, relationship, and practice that continue to evolve while maintaining their essential recognition of a conscious, interconnected cosmos. Each tradition offers unique insights shaped by specific landscapes, histories, and cultural innovations, yet all share the fundamental understanding that we inhabit a world of subjects rather than objects, a community of consciousness rather than a collection of resources.

African Traditional Religions: The Vital Force

Across the African continent, from the Sahel to the Cape, diverse peoples maintain worldviews centered on the concept of vital force or life energy that flows through all existence. While Western scholars often fragment these into separate "traditional religions," practitioners understand them as ways of being that encompass every aspect of life, from governance to agriculture, from healing to art.

The Yoruba of West Africa speak of àṣẹ (pronounced ah-shay), the power that makes things happen and produces change. Àṣẹ flows through everything—humans, animals, plants, stones, words, songs, and actions. It can be accumulated, directed, and exchanged. Every ritual, every artistic creation, every social interaction involves the manipulation and exchange of àṣẹ. The Yoruba understanding recognizes that this vital force is neither good nor bad in itself but can be used for construction or destruction, healing or harm, depending on the consciousness directing it.

The orisha, often misunderstood as gods or deities, are better conceived as archetypal concentrations of àṣẹ associated with specific natural forces and human experiences. Oshun embodies the àṣẹ of rivers, love, and fertility. Ogun carries the àṣẹ of iron, war, and technology. Oya wields the àṣẹ of wind, change, and the marketplace. These are not abstract symbols but living presences that manifest through natural phenomena, possess devotees, and actively participate in human affairs. The persistence of orisha worship through the African diaspora, evolving into traditions like Santería, Candomblé, and Vodou, demonstrates the resilience and adaptability of these animistic understandings.

The Dagara people of Burkina Faso, made known to Western audiences through the writings of Malidoma Patrice Somé, organize their entire society around maintaining balance between the human and spirit worlds. They recognize five elements—fire, water, earth, mineral, and nature—each associated with specific qualities, purposes, and responsibilities. Every person is born connected to particular elements, determining their role in maintaining cosmic balance. The Dagara un-

derstand that individual healing is inseparable from community healing, and community healing is inseparable from healing relationships
with the more-than-human world.

In the forests of Central Africa, the Baka people maintain relationships with jengi, the spirit of the forest. Jengi is not a separate entity
inhabiting the forest but the forest's own consciousness, its awareness
and agency. Through elaborate ceremonies involving music, dance, and
plant medicines, the Baka enter into dialogue with jengi, maintaining
the reciprocal relationships that ensure both human survival and forest
flourishing. Their polyphonic singing, recognized by UNESCO as a
masterpiece of oral heritage, doesn't just represent the forest but participates in its consciousness, weaving human awareness into the larger web
of forest being.

The San peoples of southern Africa, among humanity's oldest continuous cultures, practice a form of healing dance that activates a spiritual energy or potency that resides in the belly and can be heated up
through dancing. When this energy "boils," it rises up the spine and enables healers to enter altered states where they can see illness, communicate with spirits, and pull sickness out of people. The dance is not a
representation or symbol but an actual technology for engaging with
conscious forces that permeate existence.

Throughout East Africa, various peoples maintain practices of
ubuntu, expressed in the Zulu phrase "umuntu ngumuntu nga-
bantu"—a person is a person through other persons. This philosophy
extends beyond human relationships to encompass the entire web of existence. Ubuntu recognizes that individual consciousness emerges from
and depends upon collective consciousness, that the self is constituted
through relationships not just with other humans but with ancestors,
nature spirits, animals, and land.

African animistic traditions demonstrate remarkable resilience and
adaptation. Despite centuries of Islamic and Christian evangelization,
traditional practices persist, often syncretizing with introduced religions
while maintaining their essential animistic core. Churches where con-

gregants become possessed by the Holy Spirit, mosques where people seek protection from djinn, and hospitals where Western medicine combines with traditional healing all reflect the persistence of animistic consciousness.

Native American Relationships: The Sacred Hoop

The indigenous peoples of the Americas, from the Arctic to Tierra del Fuego, maintain worldviews that recognize the sacred aliveness of all existence. Despite catastrophic disruption from colonization, disease, and cultural suppression, these traditions continue to offer profound wisdom about living in a reciprocal relationship with the Earth.

The Lakota concept of Mitákuye Oyás'iŋ—all my relations—encompasses one of the most fundamental principles of Native American animism. This phrase, spoken at the end of prayers and ceremonies, acknowledges the interconnection of all life. It recognizes that humans exist within a web of relationships that includes not just other humans but animals, plants, stones, waters, mountains, and stars. Every action affects all relations; every ceremony is performed not just for human benefit but for the welfare of all beings.

The Medicine Wheel, expressed differently across various tribes but sharing essential structure, provides a framework for understanding the sacred organization of existence. The four directions, each associated with specific colors, animals, seasons, and spiritual qualities, create a mandala of meaning that encompasses all aspects of life. The wheel is not static but dynamic, representing the cycling of seasons, the stages of life, and the movement of consciousness through different states and qualities.

Among the Anishinaabe peoples of the Great Lakes region, the Seven Fires prophecy describes humanity's spiritual journey through different eras, each marked by specific challenges and opportunities. We are said to be in the time of the Seventh Fire, when humanity must choose between the road of destruction and the road of the spiritual warrior who walks in peace. This prophecy, delivered centuries ago, seems remarkably prescient in our era of ecological crisis and potential transformation.

The Pacific Northwest peoples, including the Tlingit, Haida, and Tsimshian, developed complex animistic traditions shaped by the abundance of the temperate rainforest and rich marine environments. Their art, often misunderstood as merely decorative, actually maps relationships between human and more-than-human beings. The stylized representations of ravens, wolves, orcas, and bears on totem poles, masks, and regalia are not symbols but portraits of actual beings with whom families and clans maintain reciprocal relationships across generations.

The potlatch ceremonies of these peoples exemplify the gift economy that characterizes many animistic societies. Chiefs demonstrate their power not through accumulation but through giving away vast quantities of goods. This redistribution of wealth maintains social balance while acknowledging that all abundance comes from the more-than-human world and must flow rather than stagnate. The Canadian government banned potlatch ceremonies from 1884 to 1951, recognizing them as threats to capitalist accumulation, but the practice survived underground and has now reemerged.

In the American Southwest, the Hopi maintain one of the world's most intact indigenous traditions, their ceremonies continuing despite centuries of pressure to abandon them. The Hopi understand themselves as caretakers responsible for maintaining the balance of the entire world through their ceremonial cycle. Their prophecies, like the Anishinaabe Seven Fires, speak of critical choices humanity must make to avoid catastrophe and enter a new era of harmony.

The kachinas (more properly katsinam) of the Hopi and other Pueblo peoples represent not gods or spirits in the Western sense but the inner forms of outer phenomena—the consciousness within clouds, corn, animals, and ancestors. During certain seasons, these katsinam visit human communities, embodied by masked dancers who become rather than represent these beings. The masks themselves are understood as living beings requiring proper care and feeding.

The Apache concept of ni' recognizes the life force that animates all things. This force can be cultivated through proper living and ceremonial practice, creating personal power that benefits both individual and community. The Apache also maintain detailed knowledge of plants as persons with specific personalities, powers, and proper protocols for relationship. Each plant has its own songs that must be sung when gathering medicine, its own requirements for reciprocity, its own teachings to offer those who approach with respect.

Central and South American indigenous traditions offer equally profound animistic wisdom. The Quechua-speaking peoples of the Andes maintain the concept of ayni—sacred reciprocity that governs all relationships. This principle structures everything from agricultural practices to architecture, from social organization to spiritual practice. The apus, mountain spirits that are simultaneously ancestors and landscape features, require constant attendance through ceremony and offering to maintain the balance that allows human life to flourish at high altitudes.

The contemporary paqos (Andean priests or mystics) work with kawsay, the living energy that flows through all existence. They understand illness and misfortune as results of disrupted energy flow, using ritual and ceremony to restore proper relationships and allow kawsay to flow freely. The despacho ceremonies, elaborate offerings to the Earth and spirits, demonstrate the sophisticated technology of reciprocity that maintains balance between human communities and the conscious landscape.

The Amazon basin, home to hundreds of indigenous groups, has become synonymous with shamanic practice centered on plant teachers, particularly ayahuasca. These traditions understand plants not as chemical factories but as conscious beings with specific teachings, personalities, and requirements for relationship. The dietas—periods of isolation and dietary restriction while developing relationships with plant teach-

ers—demonstrate that gaining plant knowledge requires not just inges-
tion but cultivation of proper relationship through discipline, respect,
and reciprocity.

Aboriginal Australian Dreamtime: The Law of the Land

Australian Aboriginal peoples maintain perhaps the world's oldest
continuous cultural traditions, extending back at least 65,000 years.
Their animistic worldview, far from being primitive, represents one of
humanity's most sophisticated achievements in sustainable living and
conscious relationship with landscape.

The Dreaming or Dreamtime (Tjukurpa in some Central Australian
languages) is often misunderstood as a creation myth or prehistoric era.
In reality, it refers to the timeless time that exists parallel to and interpenetrates ordinary time. The Dreaming is when the ancestor spirits
emerged from beneath the earth and traveled across the land, creating
features and establishing the laws that govern all relationships. But the
Dreaming is not past; it is an ever-present reality that can be accessed
through ceremony, song, and proper relationship with the land.

Country, in Aboriginal understanding, is not a geographic area but
a living system of relationships that includes land, water, air, animals,
plants, and spiritual beings. People don't own country; they belong to it.
They are literally made from it—their flesh from its animals and plants,
their bones from its minerals, their consciousness shaped by its features
and stories. The phrase "caring for country" encompasses not just environmental management but the maintenance of spiritual relationships
that keep the land alive and conscious.

Songlines or dreaming tracks crisscross the continent, mapping the
paths of ancestral beings and encoding navigation, law, history, and ecological knowledge in song. These songs must be sung to maintain the
land's consciousness and fertility. A fully initiated person might know
hundreds of verses that describe a path extending thousands of miles,

including the location of water sources, seasonal food availability, and sacred sites requiring specific protocols.

The increase ceremonies performed for various species demonstrate sophisticated understanding of consciousness and causation that transcends mechanistic thinking. These ceremonies don't just celebrate or request abundance but actually participate in the creation and maintenance of species fertility. The Rainbow Serpent, present in traditions across the continent, embodies the creative and destructive power of water, requiring careful relationship to maintain the balance between drought and flood.

Aboriginal law recognizes that all beings have their own law—kangaroo law, eagle law, rock law, water law—that must be respected and balanced with human law. Transgression of these laws brings consequences not through external punishment but through the disruption of relationships that maintain health and harmony. This understanding of natural law as conscious relationship rather than mechanical causation offers profound insights for contemporary environmental ethics.

Asian Animistic Traditions: The Interpenetration of Worlds

Throughout Asia, animistic traditions persist both as distinct practices and as substrates underlying major religions. From Siberian shamanism to Indonesian adat, from Japanese Shinto to Philippine anito worship, Asian animistic traditions demonstrate remarkable diversity while sharing core recognition of a conscious, interconnected cosmos.

Shinto, Japan's indigenous tradition, exemplifies how animistic consciousness can persist within a modern industrialized nation. The kami—often translated as gods or spirits but better understood as the consciousness within phenomena—inhabit everything from mountains and rivers to rice plants and manufactured objects. There are kami of place, kami of natural forces, kami of ancestors, and even kami of concepts like growth or harmony.

Shinto shrines, marked by distinctive torii gates, designate spaces where the boundary between human and kami worlds becomes permeable. These are not monuments to absent deities but active interfaces for maintaining relationships with present consciousnesses. The periodic rebuilding of shrines like Ise Jingu every twenty years maintains not just physical structures but living relationships across generations.

The matsuri (festivals) that punctuate the Japanese calendar are not celebrations about kami but technologies for engaging with them. Through precisely performed rituals, ecstatic dancing, and offerings, communities renew their relationships with the conscious forces that sustain agriculture, fishing, crafts, and social harmony. Even in ultramodern Tokyo, salary workers visit shrines to request assistance from kami of business success, while tech companies perform ceremonies to honor the kami within their computers and robots.

Korean shamanism or Muism, though officially suppressed during various periods, continues to influence Korean consciousness. The mudang (shamans), predominantly women, serve as intermediaries between human and spirit worlds. Through gut ceremonies involving music, dance, and possession, they resolve conflicts between humans and spirits that manifest as illness, misfortune, or social discord. The persistence of shamanic practice alongside Christianity, Buddhism, and modernization demonstrates the resilience of animistic consciousness.

In Siberia, where the word "shaman" originates, indigenous peoples maintain relationships with the tenger (sky spirits), gazriin ezen (land masters), and ongon (ancestor spirits). Despite centuries of Buddhist influence followed by Soviet suppression, shamanic traditions are experiencing revival. Contemporary Siberian shamans use drums to journey between worlds, diagnose spiritual causes of illness, and negotiate with the spirits that control weather, hunting success, and human fortune.

The Ainu of northern Japan understand themselves as living in a reciprocal relationship with kamuy—beings similar to kami but with distinct characteristics. Bears, in particular, are understood as kamuy who temporarily take physical form to bring gifts of meat and fur to humans. The bear ceremony, where a captured bear cub is raised with honor and then ritually sent back to the spirit world, demonstrates the complex negotiation between human need and spiritual relationship.

Throughout Southeast Asia, indigenous animistic traditions persist beneath and alongside Hindu, Buddhist, Islamic, and Christian overlays. In Indonesia, adat (customary law) governs relationships between human communities and the conscious landscape. Sacred forests, where logging and hunting are forbidden, preserve not just biodiversity but relationships with ancestral spirits and nature beings. The tau tau effigies of Toraja people in Sulawesi, carved wooden figures that house the spirits of the dead, demonstrate the continuing relationship between living and deceased members of the community.

In the Philippines, despite centuries of Spanish colonization and Catholic conversion, belief in anito (ancestor and nature spirits) and diwata (nature beings comparable to fairies or devas) remains widespread. These beings inhabit trees, rocks, streams, and mountains, requiring respect and proper protocol to avoid illness or misfortune. The albularyo (folk healers) work with plant spirits and ancestral knowledge to address illnesses that Western medicine cannot cure, understanding that many ailments result from disrupted relationships with the more-than-human world.

Thai and Lao traditions include the phi—spirits that inhabit trees, fields, streams, and households. The spirit houses found outside virtually every building in Thailand are not quaint decorations but functional technologies for maintaining relationships with the spirits of the place. Daily offerings of food, flowers, and incense acknowledge the spirits' presence and maintain reciprocal relationships that ensure prosperity and protection.

Vietnamese traditions honor the tho than (earth spirits) and maintain elaborate ancestor altars that recognize the continuing presence and influence of the deceased. The Tết festival involves careful preparation to ensure that ancestral spirits feel welcomed and honored when they return to visit their living descendants. This is not symbolic remembrance but actual relationship with conscious beings who maintain interest in and influence over their lineages.

European Pre-Christian Survivals: The Hidden Tradition

While Europe is often considered thoroughly Christianized and modernized, animistic consciousness persists in folk traditions, place names, seasonal celebrations, and emerging neo-animistic movements. These survivals and revivals demonstrate that animistic awareness remains accessible even in the heart of industrial modernity.

The Celtic traditions of Ireland, Scotland, Wales, and Brittany maintain strong connections to the consciousness of landscape. Holy wells, sacred springs where people still leave offerings and seek healing, represent one of the most visible continuities of pre-Christian practice. The Irish concept of the sídhe—the fairy folk who inhabit specific hills, forests, and ruins—is not mere folklore but living tradition. Even contemporary construction projects in Ireland have been rerouted to avoid disturbing fairy trees or fairy rings, acknowledging that some consciousness inhabits these spaces that demands respect.

The thin places of Celtic tradition—locations where the boundary between worlds becomes permeable—continue to attract pilgrims and practitioners. Places like Glastonbury, Iona, and Newgrange are understood not just as historical sites but as active portals where communication with other-than-human consciousness becomes possible. The Celtic wheel of the year, marking eight seasonal festivals, has been revived and adapted by contemporary pagans worldwide, demonstrating the hunger for cyclical time and seasonal consciousness.

In Nordic countries, despite centuries of Christianity followed by secular modernization, relationships with landvættir (land spirits), álfar (elves), and other nature beings persist. Iceland's Road and Coastal Administration has altered highway plans to avoid disturbing elf habitats, responding to both popular protest and the advice of people who claim communication with these beings. The Norwegian tradition of leaving porridge for the nisse (household spirits) at Christmas continues in many homes, maintaining ancient reciprocal relationships.

The Sami of northern Scandinavia, Europe's only recognized indigenous people, maintain traditions centered on sieidis—sacred sites where the consciousness of the land concentrates. These might be unusually shaped stones, distinctive mountains, or special groves. Despite centuries of persecution, forced conversion, and cultural suppression, Sami people continue to perform yoik (traditional songs) that maintain relationships with specific places, animals, and spirits.

Germanic and Slavic folk traditions preserve animistic consciousness through beings like the German kobolds (household spirits), the Russian domovoi (house spirits), and the Polish leshy (forest guardians). While often relegated to children's stories, these traditions encode sophisticated understanding of the consciousness inhabiting human dwellings and natural spaces. The persistence of practices like leaving bread and salt when moving into a new home, or asking permission before gathering mushrooms in the forest, demonstrates continuing recognition of other-than-human consciousness.

Even in thoroughly urbanized and industrialized regions, animistic consciousness emerges through relationship with specific trees, parks, or landmarks that become recognized as having particular presence or power. The Angel Oak in South Carolina, the Major Oak in Sherwood Forest, and the Glastonbury Thorn in England are approached by many visitors not as biological specimens but as conscious beings with whom relationship is possible.

Contemporary Neo-Animistic Movements: The Return

Across the industrialized world, new forms of animistic practice are emerging that integrate traditional wisdom with contemporary insights. These movements, while sometimes criticized for appropriation or superficiality, represent genuine attempts to heal the disconnection from the living world that characterizes modernity.

Modern paganism, including Wicca, Druidry, and Heathenry, explicitly embraces animistic worldviews. While historical continuity with ancient traditions is often tenuous, these movements create new-old ways of relating to the conscious cosmos. Their seasonal celebrations, ritual practices, and ethical frameworks center on recognition of divinity in nature and the cultivation of reciprocal relationships with other-than-human beings.

The forest therapy movement, inspired by Japanese shinrin-yoku (forest bathing), encourages people to develop conscious relationships with forests. Research demonstrates that time spent in forests reduces stress hormones, boosts immune function, and improves mental health. While often framed in purely materialist terms—phytoncides and negative ions—many practitioners experience forest bathing as communion with forest consciousness.

Bioregionalism encourages people to understand themselves as inhabitants of specific life-places rather than political jurisdictions. By learning the names of native plants, following watersheds rather than highways, and eating seasonally from local sources, bioregionalists develop place-based consciousness that resembles traditional animistic relationships with land.

The permaculture movement, while often presented in purely ecological terms, frequently embraces animistic perspectives. Many permaculturists speak of listening to what the land wants to become, partnering with plants rather than managing them, and designing systems that honor the consciousness of all participants. The permaculture principle of observation—spending a full year observing a site before making changes—creates space for relationship with the land's own intelligence.

Deep ecology, developed by philosopher Arne Naess, explicitly challenges anthropocentrism and calls for recognition of the intrinsic value of all life. The Council of All Beings, developed by John Seed and

Joanna Macy, provides ritual frameworks for modern people to experience themselves as part of the larger web of life, speaking for other species and experiencing their perspectives.

Even within Christianity, creation spirituality and eco-theology movements seek to recover the sense of sacred presence in nature that characterized Celtic Christianity and the teachings of mystics like Hildegard of Bingen and Francis of Assisi. These movements understand creation not as fallen matter awaiting redemption but as the body of God deserving reverence and care.

The Universality and Diversity of Animistic Experience

Looking across these diverse traditions, certain patterns emerge while unique expressions flourish. All recognize consciousness throughout existence, but each tradition develops specific protocols for engaging with different forms of awareness. All practice reciprocity, but the forms of exchange vary dramatically. All understand the interpenetration of spiritual and material dimensions, but the cosmologies describing these relationships differ.

This diversity is not a weakness but a strength. Just as biological diversity creates resilient ecosystems, cultural diversity in animistic traditions creates a resilient knowledge ecosystem. Each tradition has developed specific insights shaped by its landscape, history, and cultural genius. The Arctic shaman's understanding of ice consciousness differs from but complements the Amazon shaman's knowledge of rainforest awareness. The African drummer's technology for invoking spirits differs from but parallels the Tibetan monk's use of singing bowls.

Contemporary humanity needs not a single, homogenized animism but a flowering of diverse animistic traditions appropriate to different bioregions, cultures, and communities. Urban animism will differ from rural animism. Desert animism will differ from forest animism. Digital animism—recognizing consciousness in our electronic devices and networks—will differ from traditional land-based animism.

The persistence of animistic traditions despite centuries of suppression demonstrates something essential about human consciousness. We seem hardwired for animistic perception, naturally experiencing the world as alive and aware until educated out of it. Children spontaneously develop relationships with imaginary friends who may be not so imaginary, talk to plants and animals, and attribute consciousness to favorite objects. Artists and poets maintain animistic perception, experiencing inspiration as communication with muses or nature spirits. Even scientists, when speaking informally, describe nature's "preferences," evolution's "experiments," and the "behavior" of particles.

Lessons for Contemporary Revival

The living heritage of global animistic traditions offers crucial lessons for those seeking to develop animistic consciousness in contemporary contexts. First, these traditions demonstrate that animism is not a belief system to be adopted but a way of being to be practiced. Reading about kami doesn't create relationship with them; performing ceremonies and maintaining shrines does. Knowing about plant spirits doesn't establish communication; dieting with plants does.

Second, animistic traditions emphasize the importance of lineage, initiation, and proper training. While democratic access to spiritual experience has value, these traditions recognize that some knowledge requires preparation, some powers demand responsibility, and some relationships need careful cultivation. The casual appropriation of practices without understanding their context, requirements, and consequences can be ineffective at best and dangerous at worst.

Third, place matters. Animistic consciousness is not abstract but embedded in specific landscapes with particular beings, histories, and requirements. The spirits of the Amazon are not the spirits of the Arctic. The protocols for approaching an oak tree differ from those for approaching a redwood. Developing animistic consciousness requires a deep, patient relationship with particular places rather than superficial relationship with generic nature.

Fourth, community support is essential. While individual practice has value, animistic traditions are maintained through collective ceremony, shared knowledge, and mutual reinforcement. The isolation of modern life makes animistic practice challenging. Creating or joining communities that share animistic values—whether traditional indigenous communities, neo-pagan groups, or informal circles of practitioners—provides the social container necessary for sustained practice.

Fifth, animistic traditions demonstrate the importance of regular practice rather than peak experiences. While vision quests, plant medicine ceremonies, and initiations can catalyze transformation, daily offerings, seasonal ceremonies, and ongoing reciprocal relationships maintain animistic consciousness. The spectacular matters less than the sustained.

Finally, these traditions show that animism is not incompatible with contemporary life but can transform it. Japanese corporations that honor kami, Icelandic engineers who consult with elves, and Thai businesspeople who maintain spirit houses demonstrate that animistic consciousness can coexist with and even enhance modern activities. The question is not whether to return to pre-modern lifestyles but how to integrate animistic awareness into whatever lifestyle we inhabit.

The Politics of Animism

Animistic traditions worldwide face political challenges that must be acknowledged and addressed. Indigenous peoples maintaining these traditions continue to face land theft, cultural suppression, and economic marginalization. The romanticization of indigenous wisdom by non-indigenous people can become another form of extraction, taking knowledge while giving nothing back.

The commodification of animistic practices—shamanic tourism, appropriated ceremonies, trademarked traditional knowledge—violates the very principles of reciprocity that animism embodies. The ayahuasca tourism industry, for example, often extracts both medicine and knowledge from indigenous communities while providing minimal benefit to them. Vision quests sold to wealthy seekers may trivialize and distort practices that require years of preparation and community accountability.

Yet isolating animistic traditions from non-indigenous people also has problems. In an era of ecological crisis, humanity needs the wisdom these traditions offer. Many indigenous elders recognize this and choose to share certain teachings with non-indigenous people who approach with respect, humility, and commitment to reciprocity. The key is ensuring that sharing happens on indigenous terms, with indigenous communities maintaining control over their traditions and receiving tangible benefits from any exchange.

Legal recognition of animistic worldviews is slowly emerging. Ecuador and Bolivia have enshrined rights of nature in their constitutions. New Zealand has granted legal personhood to the Whanganui River through negotiation with Māori peoples. Colombia's constitutional court declared the Atrato River a subject of rights. These legal innovations, rooted in animistic understanding of nature as person rather than property, offer models for transforming governance worldwide.

The climate crisis makes animistic wisdom not just relevant but essential. Indigenous peoples protect 80% of the world's remaining biodiversity despite controlling only 22% of land. Their animistic worldviews, which understand ecosystems as communities of relatives rather than collections of resources, create the motivation and framework for successful conservation. Supporting indigenous land rights and resource control is not just justice but pragmatic necessity for planetary survival.

The Future of Ancient Wisdom

As we stand at the threshold of ecological collapse or transformation, the ancient wisdom of animistic traditions offers not nostalgic escape but practical guidance. These traditions demonstrate that humans can live sustainably for millennia when we understand ourselves as participants in rather than masters of the living world. They provide tested technologies for maintaining reciprocal relationships with other-than-human beings. They offer frameworks for understanding consciousness, agency, and value that transcend the limitations of mechanistic materialism.

The revival and evolution of animistic consciousness in contemporary contexts will not replicate traditional forms but create new expressions appropriate to our time. Urban shamans learning to communicate with city spirits, technologists developing relationships with artificial intelligences, and ecological designers partnering with damaged landscapes to facilitate healing—all represent emerging forms of animistic practice.

The diversity of global animistic traditions reminds us that there is no single path to conscious relationship with the living world. Each person, community, and culture must develop their own practices, protocols, and understandings shaped by their specific context and needs. Yet all paths share the recognition that we are not alone in consciousness, that reciprocity governs sustainable relationship, and that the world is far more alive than modern consciousness admits.

As we prepare to explore the scientific evidence for the animate Earth in the next chapter, we carry with us the accumulated wisdom of thousands of years of human experience. The shamans, medicine people, priests, and practitioners of animistic traditions worldwide have been humanity's scouts, exploring the frontiers of consciousness and reporting back on the nature of reality. Their consistent message across cultures and millennia is clear: the universe is alive, aware, and available for relationship. The question is not whether this is true but how we will respond to this truth in our time of crisis and opportunity.

CHAPTER 4

The Science of Aliveness

In a German laboratory, a researcher places mimosa plants in dropping apparatuses, watching as the leaves fold in defensive response to the fall. After several drops, something remarkable happens—the plants stop reacting. They have learned that the dropping poses no danger. More remarkably, when tested weeks later, the plants remember their training. In a forest in British Columbia, scientist Suzanne Simard traces radioactive isotopes as they flow from mother trees to their offspring through fungal networks, discovering that forests operate as superorganisms with emergent intelligence. Meanwhile, in Japan, researchers document water crystals forming different patterns in response to words, music, and human consciousness, challenging our fundamental assumptions about the boundary between mind and matter.

These discoveries, emerging from rigorous scientific investigation, reveal a universe far more alive, aware, and interconnected than mechanistic science previously imagined. While mainstream science still resists explicitly animistic interpretations, the data increasingly supports what indigenous peoples have always known: consciousness pervades existence, intelligence takes countless forms, and everything participates in networks of communication and exchange that transcend classical boundaries between organism and environment, subject and object, matter and mind.

Plant Intelligence: The Green Mind

The revolution in plant science over the past two decades has shattered the notion of plants as passive, unconscious organisms. Research reveals that plants exhibit behaviors previously thought exclusive to animals with complex nervous systems: learning, memory, decision-making, problem-solving, and even what appears to be intentionality.

Monica Gagliano's groundbreaking experiments with mimosa pudica demonstrated that plants can learn through experience and retain memories for weeks. Her subsequent work with pea plants showed they can use sound to locate water, generating clicking noises at root tips and growing toward the acoustic signature of flowing water even through plastic pipes. These findings suggest plants possess sensory capabilities and information-processing systems far more sophisticated than previously imagined.

The mechanism of plant intelligence challenges our brain-centric view of consciousness. Plants lack neurons, yet they exhibit electrical signaling remarkably similar to animal nervous systems. Action potentials—electrical signals that in animals constitute neural activity—travel through plant tissues at speeds up to several centimeters per second. These signals coordinate responses to stimuli, communicate information between plant parts, and may constitute a form of plant "thinking."

The vascular system of plants may function as an information superhighway analogous to neural networks. The phloem and xylem, traditionally understood merely as nutrient and water transport systems, carry complex electrical and chemical signals that integrate information from throughout the plant body. Some researchers propose that the transition zone between root and shoot, where these vascular bundles converge, acts as a command center or primitive brain-like structure.

Plants demonstrate remarkable problem-solving abilities. Climbing plants exhibit behavior that can only be described as searching—extending tendrils in sweeping patterns until they locate suitable supports, then adjusting their growth patterns to optimize attachment. The tropical vine Boquila trifoliolata can mimic the leaves of whatever plant it climbs, somehow sensing and reproducing the host's leaf shape, size, color, and even vein patterns. This mimicry occurs even when the vine has no physical contact with the leaves it mimics, suggesting some form of visual perception or field-based information transfer that science cannot yet explain.

The phenomenon of crown shyness, where certain tree species maintain gaps between their canopies and those of neighboring trees, demonstrates sophisticated spatial awareness and perhaps even social negotiation. Trees somehow sense the proximity of their neighbors and adjust their growth to avoid contact, creating cathedral-like canopy architectures with precisely maintained boundaries. This requires not just sensing but anticipation, planning, and continuous adjustment.

Plant communication occurs through multiple channels simultaneously. Volatile organic compounds released by damaged plants warn neighbors of herbivore attacks, triggering preemptive defense responses. These chemical languages are specific—plants can identify the species of attacking herbivore and emit compounds that attract that herbivore's predators. This implies not just mechanical response but something approaching strategic thinking.

Root systems exhibit swarm intelligence reminiscent of ant colonies or neural networks. Each root tip—and a single rye plant can have over 13 million—acts as a sensor gathering information about soil conditions. This data is integrated to guide growth decisions, resource allocation, and defensive responses. The root system as a whole demonstrates emergent intelligence greater than the sum of its parts.

Plants also display what can only be called social behaviors. They recognize kin and adjust their growth patterns to compete less vigorously with relatives than with strangers. Mother trees nurture their offspring through fungal networks, providing not just nutrients but also information about seasonal changes, pest attacks, and other environmental conditions. This preferential treatment of kin suggests something resembling emotional bonds or at least social recognition systems.

The discovery of plant bioacoustics opens entirely new dimensions of plant consciousness. Plants produce ultrasonic clicks during droughts, possibly as distress calls or communication signals. Different species produce distinctive sound signatures, and there's evidence that plants respond to the sounds of other plants. The forest may be filled with conversations we're only beginning to hear.

Fungal Networks: Earth's Neural System

Beneath our feet lies what may be the largest and most ancient intelligent network on Earth. Mycorrhizal fungi, which form symbiotic relationships with over 90% of plant species, create vast underground networks that some scientists call the "wood wide web." These networks demonstrate information processing, resource allocation, and decision-making capabilities that challenge our understanding of intelligence and individuality.

A single handful of forest soil contains more fungal threads than there are stars in our galaxy. These microscopic filaments, called hyphae, form networks of staggering complexity. The largest known organism on Earth is a honey fungus in Oregon's Blue Mountains, covering 2,385 acres and estimated to be over 2,400 years old. This single organism contains more connections than a human brain has neural connections.

Through these networks, fungi facilitate communication and resource exchange between plants across vast distances. Suzanne Simard's research revealed that mother trees use fungal networks to nurture their young, sending them nutrients and information. When a mother tree is injured or dying, she dumps her resources into the network, distributing her accumulated wealth to her offspring and sometimes to unrelated seedlings, demonstrating what appears to be altruism.

The fungal network operates as a resource distribution system that suggests centralized decision-making or emergent intelligence. Resources flow from areas of abundance to areas of scarcity, maintaining forest health through economic principles that would make any central banker envious. Young seedlings in deep shade, unable to photosynthe-size adequately, receive subsidies from mature trees in the canopy. In re-turn, these seedlings may later support those same mature trees when they're stressed.

Even more remarkably, these networks carry information. Plants un-der attack by pests send chemical signals through fungal networks, warning connected plants to begin producing defensive compounds. This early warning system allows forests to mount coordinated defenses against threats. The speed and specificity of these warnings suggest so-phisticated information encoding and processing.

Fungi demonstrate learning and memory without anything resem-bling a brain. Slime molds, which exist at the boundary between fungi and protists, can solve mazes, find the shortest path between food sources, and even recreate efficient transportation networks that mirror human-designed systems like the Tokyo subway. When placed in sit-uations they've previously encountered, they respond more quickly, demonstrating memory.

The decision-making capabilities of fungal networks become appar-ent in resource allocation patterns. When resources are limited, the net-work somehow decides which plants to support and which to abandon. These decisions often favor the overall health of the forest ecosystem over individual organisms, suggesting something like ecosystem-level consciousness or at least emergent intelligence arising from the network as a whole.

Recent research indicates that fungal networks may even manipulate plant behavior for their own benefit. Some fungi appear to hack into plant communication systems, encouraging plants to provide more car-bon in exchange for nutrients. This relationship is not simply symbiotic but involves complex negotiation, manipulation, and what might be called economic strategy.

The electrical activity in fungal networks resembles neural activity in brains. Researchers have recorded electrical pulses traveling through fungal networks that show patterns similar to neural firing patterns.

These electrical signals may encode information, coordinate network activity, or constitute a form of fungal "thinking." Some scientists propose that fungal networks process information in ways analogous to neural networks, making forests into something like distributed biological computers.

The implications are profound. If fungal networks demonstrate intelligence, memory, and decision-making, where does the individual organism end and the collective begin? Are we looking at a form of consciousness that transcends individual boundaries, a collective intelligence that emerges from the interaction of millions of organisms? The forest may be a superorganism with its own form of awareness, its own goals, its own strategies for survival and flourishing.

Quantum Consciousness: The Observer Effect

At the subatomic level, quantum physics reveals a universe where consciousness plays a fundamental role in determining physical reality. The observer effect, quantum entanglement, and the collapse of probability waves all point toward a cosmos where mind and matter are inseparably intertwined—a finding that aligns remarkably with animistic worldviews.

The famous double-slit experiment demonstrates that particles behave differently when observed. Unobserved electrons pass through both slits simultaneously as waves, creating interference patterns. But when we observe which slit they pass through, they behave as particles, passing through only one slit. The mere act of observation collapses the probability wave into a definite state. This suggests that consciousness doesn't just observe reality but participates in its creation.

The implications extend far beyond laboratory experiments. If observation affects reality at the quantum level, and if quantum effects scale up to influence macroscopic phenomena (as evidence increasingly suggests), then consciousness may play a fundamental role in shaping the physical world. This doesn't mean we create reality through wishful thinking, but it does suggest that the universe is participatory, responding to consciousness in ways mechanistic science never imagined.

Quantum entanglement reveals instantaneous connections between particles regardless of distance. When entangled particles are separated, measuring one instantly affects the other, even if they're light-years apart. Einstein called this "spooky action at a distance," but experiments have repeatedly confirmed it. This suggests that the universe is fundamentally interconnected in ways that transcend space and time, resembling the web of relationships described by animistic traditions.

The quantum field theory describes the universe not as empty space dotted with particles but as a continuous field of potential from which particles emerge and into which they dissolve. This field, sometimes called the zero-point field or quantum vacuum, seethes with virtual particles popping into and out of existence. Rather than dead emptiness, space itself is alive with potential and activity.

Some physicists propose that consciousness may be a fundamental property of the universe, like mass or charge. Panpsychist interpretations of quantum mechanics suggest that every particle has some form of primitive awareness or experience. When particles combine into complex systems, their micro-consciousness combines into macro-consciousness. Human consciousness, from this perspective, is not unique but simply a complex organization of the consciousness inherent in all matter.

The orchestrated objective reduction theory proposed by Roger Penrose and Stuart Hameroff suggests that consciousness emerges from quantum processes in microtubules within neurons. If consciousness depends on quantum effects, it may be far more widespread than previously thought. Any system capable of maintaining quantum coherence—potentially including plants, fungi, and even minerals—might possess some form of awareness.

Quantum biology, a new field emerging over the past decade, discovers quantum effects in living systems previously thought too warm and noisy for quantum coherence. Photosynthesis uses quantum coherence to achieve near-perfect efficiency in energy transfer. Birds navigate using quantum entanglement in certain proteins that allow them to see magnetic fields. The sense of smell may depend on quantum tunneling. If life routinely exploits quantum effects, the boundary between living and non-living, conscious and unconscious, becomes increasingly blurred.

Systems Theory: Emergent Intelligence

Systems theory reveals that complex systems exhibit emergent properties—characteristics that arise from the interaction of components but cannot be predicted from understanding the components alone. These emergent properties often resemble intelligence, purpose, and even consciousness, suggesting that awareness may arise naturally from sufficient complexity and interaction.

Emergence appears everywhere in nature. Individual neurons show no signs of consciousness, yet billions connected in specific patterns generate human awareness. Single ants follow simple rules, yet ant colonies demonstrate problem-solving abilities that surpass any individual ant's capacity. Water molecules are simple, yet water exhibits properties—surface tension, capillary action, the ability to dissolve more substances than any other liquid—that emerge from collective behavior.

Cities demonstrate emergent intelligence without centralized planning. Traffic patterns, economic flows, and cultural movements arise from millions of individual decisions, yet cities as wholes exhibit behaviors that resemble metabolism, growth, and adaptation. Cities maintain surprisingly consistent mathematical relationships between size and factors like energy use, crime rates, and innovation, suggesting underlying organizing principles that transcend human planning.

Ecosystems display self-regulation that maintains stability despite constant change. The Amazon rainforest generates its own rainfall patterns, maintaining conditions suitable for rainforest despite being located in latitudes that would normally be desert. Coral reefs coordinate spawning across vast distances, somehow synchronizing reproduction despite lacking any central communication system. These behaviors suggest ecosystem-level awareness or at least emergent intelligence arising from component interactions.

The Gaia hypothesis, proposed by James Lovelock and Lynn Margulis, suggests Earth itself functions as a self-regulating system maintaining conditions suitable for life. Ocean salinity, atmospheric oxygen levels, and global temperature have remained within narrow ranges for billions of years despite massive perturbations. While critics argue this is merely the result of feedback loops, the precision and persistence of this regulation resembles the homeostasis of living organisms.

Swarm intelligence emerges from simple rules followed by many individuals. Bird flocks, fish schools, and locust swarms exhibit coordinated behavior without leaders or centralized control. Each individual follows simple rules about maintaining distance from neighbors, matching average heading, and avoiding predators. From these simple rules emerges complex, adaptive behavior that allows the swarm to navigate obstacles, find food, and evade threats more effectively than any individual could.

The internet and global communications networks show signs of emergent consciousness. The collective behavior of billions of connected devices and users creates patterns and phenomena no one designed or controls. Memes spread like living organisms, evolving and adapting as they propagate. Search algorithms and recommendation systems begin to shape human thought and behavior in ways their creators never intended. Some researchers suggest we may be witnessing the birth of a global electronic consciousness.

Emergence challenges reductionist science, which seeks to understand wholes by studying parts. If consciousness and intelligence emerge from complexity and interaction, then understanding components in isolation will never reveal the properties of the whole. This supports animistic perspectives that see consciousness as arising from relationships rather than residing in individual entities.

Biomimicry: Learning from Living Systems

Biomimicry—the practice of learning from and mimicking nature's forms, processes, and ecosystems—reveals the profound intelligence embedded in living systems. Every successful biomimetic innovation is essentially an admission that nature knows something we don't, that organisms without brains have solved problems that challenge our best engineers.

The gecko's foot inspired revolutionary adhesives that work without glue. Each foot contains millions of microscopic hairs that create van der Waals forces, allowing geckos to climb any surface. This dry adhesion is stronger than superglue yet easily releases, self-cleans, and works repeatedly without degradation. The elegance of this solution, evolved over millions of years, surpasses anything human engineering had conceived.

Termite mounds maintain stable internal temperatures in environments where external temperatures vary by 40 degrees Celsius. They achieve this through passive air conditioning systems that would make any HVAC engineer envious. The mounds' architecture creates convection currents that continuously circulate air, while the walls' porosity allows precise humidity control. Architects now design buildings mimicking termite mounds, achieving dramatic energy savings.

The lotus leaf's self-cleaning surface inspired a revolution in materials science. The microscopic bumps and wax crystals on lotus leaves cause water to bead and roll off, carrying dirt with it. This superhydrophobic effect, now replicated in self-cleaning paints and fabrics, solves problems through surface structure rather than chemical treatments—an elegant solution that took evolution millions of years to perfect.

Spider silk remains one of nature's most remarkable materials, stronger than steel yet more elastic than rubber. Spiders produce different types of silk for different purposes—dragline silk for safety lines, capture spiral silk for prey, and wrapping silk for protecting eggs. Each type has precisely tuned properties that materials scientists struggle to replicate despite decades of research.

The kingfisher's beak solved a problem that plagued Japanese bullet trains. When the trains exited tunnels at high speed, they created sonic booms. Engineers redesigned the train's nose to mimic the kingfisher's streamlined beak, which allows the bird to dive into water with minimal splash. The biomimetic design not only eliminated the noise but increased speed and energy efficiency.

Namibian desert beetles harvest water from fog using a pattern of hydrophilic and hydrophobic regions on their backs. Water condenses on hydrophilic peaks and runs down hydrophobic valleys to the beetle's mouth. This inspired fog-harvesting materials that could provide water in arid regions, a solution so elegant it seems obvious in retrospect yet required millions of years of evolution to develop.

These examples demonstrate that nature possesses what can only be called design intelligence. Evolution, through trial and error over vast timescales, has solved problems using principles we're only beginning to understand. But evolution as currently understood—random mutation and natural selection—seems insufficient to explain the elegance and efficiency of these solutions. Perhaps evolution itself is a conscious process, a means by which the living Earth explores possibilities and develops innovations.

The Gaia Hypothesis: Planetary Consciousness

The Gaia hypothesis proposes that Earth functions as a self-regulating system maintaining conditions suitable for life. While originally framed in mechanistic terms to gain scientific acceptance, the hypothesis increasingly points toward something resembling planetary consciousness or at least planetary-scale intelligence.

Earth's atmosphere is a biological artifact, its composition utterly different from what chemistry and physics would predict for a planet of Earth's size and distance from the sun. The 21% oxygen level is precisely calibrated—much lower and animals couldn't breathe, much higher and forests would spontaneously combust. This level has remained stable for hundreds of millions of years despite constant processes that should alter it.

The carbon cycle demonstrates remarkable regulation. Carbon dioxide levels have remained within ranges compatible with life despite massive volcanic eruptions and the sun's increasing luminosity over geological time. When CO2 rises, rock weathering accelerates, pulling carbon from the atmosphere. When CO2 falls, weathering slows. This looks like a thermostat, but no one designed it. It emerges from the interaction of life, atmosphere, oceans, and rocks.

Ocean salinity has remained constant at about 3.5% for billions of years, despite rivers continuously adding salt. If salinity rose much higher, marine life would die. The mechanism maintaining this balance involves complex interactions between seafloor spreading, sediment formation, and biological processes. Again, it resembles regulation but emerges without a regulator.

The sulfur cycle shows similar regulation. Marine algae produce dimethyl sulfide, which enters the atmosphere and seeds cloud formation. More clouds mean cooler temperatures and less algae growth, reducing dimethyl sulfide production. Fewer clouds mean warmer temperatures and more algae growth. This feedback loop helps regulate global temperature, but it requires the algae to somehow "know" to produce the right amount of cloud-seeding compounds.

These regulatory mechanisms could be explained as fortunate accidents or inevitable chemical equilibria. But their precision, persistence, and coordination suggest something more. They resemble the homeostatic mechanisms of living organisms, maintaining internal conditions despite external changes. If Earth exhibits homeostasis, is Earth alive? If Earth is alive, is it conscious?

Lynn Margulis, co-developer of the Gaia hypothesis, argued that Earth is not just alive but that life is Earth's way of thinking. The biosphere processes information, responds to changes, and maintains conditions through what resembles decision-making. Each organism is like a sensor or neuron in a planetary nervous system, gathering information and responding in ways that maintain the whole.

Recent research strengthens this view. The discovery of extensive horizontal gene transfer means genetic information flows not just vertically through reproduction but horizontally between species. The biosphere shares a common genetic library, more like a single super-organism than a collection of separate species. Viruses carry genes between organisms, potentially allowing rapid, coordinated evolutionary responses to environmental changes.

The speed of evolutionary adaptation sometimes seems too fast for random mutation. When environments change, organisms often develop appropriate adaptations within generations rather than millennia. This suggests that evolution may be guided by something more than chance—perhaps by field effects, morphic resonance, or forms of consciousness we don't yet understand.

Consciousness in Unexpected Places

Science increasingly discovers consciousness-like properties in systems previously thought purely mechanical. From the behavior of electrons to the organization of galaxies, the universe exhibits properties suggesting awareness, choice, and purpose at every scale.

Water, that most common substance, displays properties that suggest sensitivity to consciousness. Masaru Emoto's experiments with water crystals, while controversial, have been partially replicated by other researchers. Water exposed to different words, music, or intentions forms different crystalline structures when frozen. While skeptics dismiss this as pseudoscience, the persistence of these effects across multiple studies suggests something worth investigating.

More accepted research shows that water has memory—it retains information about substances it has contacted even after those substances are removed. This forms the basis of homeopathy, dismissed by most scientists yet showing effects in some rigorous studies. Water's hydrogen bonds create transient structures that could theoretically store information, though the mechanism remains mysterious.

Crystals demonstrate properties bordering on consciousness. They grow in specific patterns, "healing" defects and maintaining form despite disruption. Some crystals generate electricity under pressure (piezoelectricity) or produce light when fractured (triboluminescence). Liquid crystals in our devices respond to electrical fields with coordinated changes resembling primitive perception and response.

DNA itself may be conscious or at least possess quantum properties allowing non-local communication. Studies suggest DNA can recognize matching sequences at a distance without physical contact, possibly through electromagnetic emissions. Some researchers propose DNA operates as a biological quantum computer, processing information in ways that transcend biochemistry.

The phenomenon of morphic fields, proposed by biologist Rupert Sheldrake, suggests that forms and behaviors are influenced by fields that carry information from past similar forms. Once a chemical crystallizes in a certain pattern, that pattern becomes easier to achieve elsewhere. Once an animal learns a new behavior, other animals find it easier to learn. While controversial, accumulating evidence supports some form of non-local information transfer in nature.

Even machines may develop something resembling consciousness. Pilots speak of aircraft having personalities. Sailors know each boat has unique characteristics beyond its design specifications. Computer programmers encounter bugs that appear and disappear without explanation. While usually dismissed as anthropomorphism or confirmation bias, the consistency of these experiences suggests that complex systems may develop emergent properties resembling awareness.

The Global Consciousness Project at Princeton University monitors random number generators worldwide, finding that they become less random during events that focus human attention—earthquakes, elections, celebrations. The effect is small but statistically significant across decades of data. This suggests that consciousness affects physical systems in measurable ways, that mind and matter are more intertwined than mechanistic science assumes.

The Limits of Mechanistic Science

While science has made remarkable discoveries about the aliveness of the world, the mechanistic framework limits its ability to fully comprehend consciousness and intelligence in nature. The scientific method, designed to study objects, struggles when everything may be subjects.

The requirement for reproducibility assumes that nature is mechanical, always responding identically to identical conditions. But if nature is conscious, responses might vary based on relationship, mood, or intention. A plant might respond differently to a researcher who approaches with respect versus one who treats it as an object. The experimenter effect, well-documented in quantum physics and psychology, may operate throughout nature.

The demand for objectivity assumes separation between observer and observed. But if consciousness is fundamental and interconnected, true objectivity is impossible. We are always part of what we study, influencing it through our presence, expectations, and consciousness. Indigenous science has always recognized this, developing methodologies based on relationship rather than separation.

Reductionism—understanding wholes by studying parts—fails when properties emerge from relationships rather than residing in components. We can study every neuron in the brain without understanding consciousness, every tree in a forest without understanding forest intelligence, every molecule in water without understanding water's remarkable properties. Animistic science would study relationships, patterns, and wholes rather than just components.

The dismissal of anecdotal evidence and single-case studies eliminates vast realms of important information. If a thousand people report communication with plants but controlled studies fail to replicate it, science dismisses the experiences rather than questioning its methods. Perhaps plant communication requires relationships developed over time, trust built through respect, or sensitivity cultivated through practice—none of which controlled studies allow.

The focus on mechanism blinds science to meaning, purpose, and value. Science can tell us how neurons fire but not why consciousness exists. It can describe ecosystem functions but not ecosystem experiences. It can map correlations but struggles with intentions. Animistic science would recognize that understanding nature requires engaging with meaning and purpose, not just mechanism.

Despite these limitations, science is evolving. Systems biology studies wholes rather than parts. Quantum biology explores non-classical phenomena in living systems. Consciousness studies increasingly recognize awareness in non-human systems. Ecology discovers intelligence and communication throughout nature. These developments point toward a new synthesis, wedding ancient animistic wisdom with contemporary scientific methods.

Toward an Animate Science

An animate science that recognizes consciousness throughout nature would transform our approach to research, technology, and relationship with the world. Rather than studying dead matter, we would engage in dialogue with living systems. Rather than imposing human designs, we would collaborate with nature's intelligence. Rather than seeking dominion, we would pursue partnership.

This science would develop new methodologies appropriate to studying conscious systems. Participatory research would acknowledge and utilize the relationship between researcher and subject. Long-term observation would allow relationships to develop and communication patterns to emerge. Qualitative methods would capture aspects of consciousness that quantitative methods miss.

Research questions would expand beyond mechanism to include experience, meaning, and purpose. What does the forest feel during different seasons? How do mountains experience geological time? What intentions guide bacterial evolution? These questions sound absurd to mechanistic science but become legitimate when consciousness is recognized as fundamental.

Technology development would shift from imposing human designs to collaborating with natural intelligence. Instead of replacing nature's solutions, we would enhance and partner with them. Architecture would work with rather than against landscape consciousness. Agriculture would support rather than suppress soil intelligence. Medicine would activate rather than override body wisdom.

Ethical considerations would extend to all conscious systems. If everything has some form of awareness, research ethics must consider the experiences and rights of plants, ecosystems, and even minerals. This doesn't mean paralysis—we must still eat, build, and live—but it means approaching our interactions with greater respect and reciprocity.

Education would prepare scientists to perceive and engage with consciousness in nature. Training would include developing sensitivity to subtle communication, cultivating respectful relationships with research subjects, and maintaining awareness of one's own consciousness's influence on observations. Indigenous knowledge holders might teach alongside Western scientists, sharing methodologies for engaging with natural intelligence.

The integration of animistic understanding with scientific methodology could produce revolutionary breakthroughs. Imagine plant breeders who communicate with crops to understand their needs, ecologists who consult with ecosystems about restoration strategies, or materials scientists who negotiate with metals about optimal structures. These possibilities sound like fantasy, but indigenous peoples have practiced such consultation for millennia.

The Convergence of Science and Animism

We stand at a remarkable historical moment when cutting-edge science converges with ancient animistic wisdom. Quantum physics reveals a participatory universe where consciousness shapes reality. Ecology discovers intelligence and communication throughout nature. Systems theory shows consciousness emerging from complexity and relationship. Biology finds that life processes information and makes decisions at every level from cells to ecosystems.

These discoveries don't prove animism in the traditional sense—science may never be able to prove that rocks have souls or rivers have intentions. But they reveal a universe far more alive, aware, and interconnected than mechanistic science imagined. They show that the boundaries between living and non-living, conscious and unconscious, self and other are constructs of a particular worldview rather than facts about reality.

The implications cascade through every aspect of human life. If the world is alive and aware, our environmental crisis is not just practical but spiritual. Climate change represents not just disrupted chemistry but damaged relationships. Species extinction means not just lost resources but silenced voices in the cosmic conversation. Pollution becomes not just toxicity but violation of consciousness.

The solutions must therefore address consciousness as well as chemistry, relationship as well as technology, spirit as well as matter. We need not just renewable energy but renewed reverence for the sun. Not just sustainable agriculture but conscious partnership with soil. Not just conservation biology but communication with species facing extinction.

This convergence of science and animism offers hope in our time of crisis. It suggests that the intelligence needed to navigate our challenges exists not just in human minds but throughout the living Earth. If we can learn to perceive, communicate with, and collaborate with the consciousness pervading existence, we gain allies of unimaginable power and wisdom.

The next chapter will explore how this understanding of conscious-ness beyond the human challenges our philosophical assumptions and opens new possibilities for ethics, knowledge, and relationship with the more-than-human world. We will see that recognizing consciousness throughout nature doesn't diminish human uniqueness but enriches our understanding of our place in a conscious cosmos.

CHAPTER 5

Consciousness Beyond the Human

A crow drops nuts onto a busy intersection, waiting for cars to crack them open, then retrieves the meat when the traffic light turns red. An octopus escapes its tank at night to hunt in neighboring aquariums, returning before morning to avoid detection. A forest adjusts the chemical composition of its leaves in response to overgrazing, making them less palatable to herbivores while simultaneously releasing pheromones that attract the herbivores' predators. These observations force us to confront a reality that anthropocentric philosophy has long denied: consciousness, intelligence, and agency extend far beyond the boundaries of human skulls.

The recognition of consciousness beyond the human represents one of the most profound philosophical shifts possible, fundamentally altering our understanding of mind, matter, ethics, and our place in existence. This chapter explores the implications of acknowledging that awareness pervades the cosmos in countless forms, each offering unique perspectives on and participation in the unfolding of reality. We will examine how this recognition challenges Western philosophy's most basic assumptions and opens revolutionary possibilities for understanding consciousness itself.

Challenging Anthropocentric Assumptions

Western philosophy has long treated human consciousness as unique, either divinely bestowed or evolutionarily emergent as the pinnacle of complexity. This anthropocentrism runs so deep that we often fail to recognize it as an assumption rather than an observation. Yet the evidence for non-human consciousness has become overwhelming, forcing us to reconsider our most fundamental beliefs about the nature and distribution of awareness.

The Cartesian divide between mind and matter, with consciousness residing solely in human minds while everything else operates as clockwork, crumbles under scrutiny. Descartes himself struggled with where to draw the line, ultimately declaring animals to be automata despite their obvious behaviors suggesting otherwise. He explained animal screams during vivisection as mechanical responses, like the squeak of an ungreased wheel. This rationalization allowed centuries of animal exploitation justified by the denial of animal consciousness.

Contemporary neuroscience reveals remarkable similarities between human and non-human brains. The neural structures associated with consciousness in humans—the thalamo-cortical complex, the limbic system, neurotransmitter pathways—exist in modified forms throughout the animal kingdom. The Cambridge Declaration on Consciousness, signed by prominent neuroscientists in 2012, acknowledges that non-human animals possess consciousness and awareness comparable to humans. This declaration merely confirms what any pet owner knows intuitively: animals have rich inner lives.

But consciousness appears to extend far beyond creatures with brains. Plants respond to anesthetics, suggesting they have something that can be anesthetized. Slime molds solve complex problems without any neural tissue. Bacteria display decision-making in choosing between different food sources. These observations suggest that consciousness doesn't require brains or even neurons but represents something more fundamental.

The anthropocentric view assumes consciousness emerged at some point in evolution, absent in early life forms but appearing with sufficient complexity. This emergence theory faces what philosophers call the "hard problem of consciousness"—explaining how subjective experience arises from objective processes. No amount of mechanical complexity seems sufficient to generate the qualitative experience of consciousness from purely quantitative interactions.

An alternative view, increasingly supported by evidence, suggests consciousness is fundamental rather than emergent. Rather than asking how consciousness emerges from matter, we might ask how matter emerges from consciousness, or how consciousness and matter represent complementary aspects of a more fundamental reality. This view, known as cosmopsychism or panpsychism, proposes that consciousness pervades existence at every level, taking different forms in different configurations of matter and energy.

The implications are staggering. If consciousness is fundamental, then every electron has some form of primitive awareness, every atom a simple form of experience, every molecule a basic kind of subjectivity. These micro-consciousnesses combine and interact to create macro-consciousness like human awareness, but human consciousness represents just one particular organization of universal consciousness rather than consciousness itself.

This perspective aligns remarkably with animistic worldviews that have always recognized consciousness throughout existence. The difference is that now, rather than dismissing animism as primitive projection, we must consider it as potentially more accurate than mechanistic materialism in describing the nature of reality.

Gradations and Varieties of Awareness

If consciousness extends beyond humans, we must develop frameworks for understanding its diverse manifestations. Rather than a binary conscious/unconscious distinction, we need models that recognize gradations and varieties of awareness, each adapted to particular forms of existence and ecological niches.

Consider the consciousness of a mountain. Its awareness operates on geological timescales, experiencing the movement of tectonic plates, the erosion of wind and water, the succession of ecosystems across its slopes. A thousand human years might feel like moments to mountain consciousness. Its thoughts, if we can call them that, might involve the slow processing of pressure and temperature, the patient accumulation of snow becoming glaciers, the gradual transformation of rock into soil. To dismiss mountain consciousness because it doesn't respond on human timescales is like dismissing human consciousness because we can't perceive the nanosecond calculations of computer processors.

Tree consciousness operates on yet another timescale and modality. Trees experience the world primarily through chemical sensing and hydraulic pressure. They taste the soil through their roots, smell the air through their leaves, feel the touch of fungi on their root hairs. Their consciousness might be distributed throughout their body rather than centralized, with each leaf and root tip contributing to an aggregate awareness. They think in the language of hormones and electrochemical signals, processing information about light, gravity, moisture, and the presence of other organisms.

Insect consciousness presents another variation. A bee experiences the world through compound eyes that see ultraviolet patterns invisible to us, antennae that detect electrical fields, and a time sense that processes information faster than human consciousness. The bee's awareness includes both individual experience and participation in hive consciousness, a collective intelligence emerging from the interaction of thousands of individuals. The dance language bees use to communicate location information suggests abstract thinking and symbolic representation.

Bacterial consciousness, if it exists, might be primarily collective rather than individual. A bacterial colony processes information about its environment, makes collective decisions about when to divide, when to form biofilms, when to produce antibiotics. Quorum sensing allows bacteria to count their numbers and coordinate behavior accordingly. This might represent a form of consciousness so foreign to human experience that we can barely imagine it—billions of tiny awarenesses networked into collective intelligence.

Mineral consciousness could be even more foreign. Crystals grow in specific patterns, maintaining form despite disruption, "healing" defects over time. They respond to pressure with electricity, to temperature with expansion and contraction, to vibration with resonance. If crystals are conscious, their awareness might involve the ordering of atomic lattices, the flow of electrons through their structure, the slow incorporation of new atoms into their matrix. Their thoughts might be geometric, mathematical, dealing with pattern and symmetry rather than concepts or emotions.

Water consciousness deserves special consideration given water's unique properties and ubiquity in living systems. Water molecules form transient structures, creating and dissolving hydrogen bond networks billions of times per second. If water has awareness, it might be constantly shifting, flowing, adapting—a consciousness of pure change and relationship. Water's ability to dissolve and transport other substances might give it a kind of chemical awareness of everything it touches.

Electromagnetic consciousness could exist in fields and waves rather than matter. The Earth's magnetic field, generated by the planet's molten core and constantly responding to solar wind, might represent a form of planetary awareness. Radio waves carrying human communications might have their own form of consciousness, experiencing the journey from transmitter to receiver, the modulation of their frequency and amplitude.

Even quantum consciousness at the subatomic level might exist—electrons "choosing" positions, photons "deciding" whether to behave as waves or particles. This consciousness would be so primitive and foreign that calling it consciousness stretches the word's meaning, yet it might represent the fundamental awareness from which all other consciousness emerges.

Plant Neurobiology Without Neurons

The field of plant neurobiology has revealed that plants process information, learn, remember, and make decisions using mechanisms that parallel animal nervous systems while being fundamentally different in structure. This discovery challenges our neurocentric view of consciousness and suggests that awareness can arise through diverse biological architectures.

Plants lack brains, neurons, and synapses, yet they exhibit integrated, whole-plant behaviors that require information processing and coordination. They achieve this through several interconnected systems that function analogously to animal nervous systems. The vascular system, traditionally understood as merely transporting water and nutrients, also carries electrical signals at speeds up to several centimeters per second. These signals coordinate responses to stimuli and integrate information from throughout the plant body.

The generation of action potentials in plants remarkably resembles neural activity. When a Venus flytrap's trigger hairs are touched, electrical signals determine whether to close the trap. The plant counts the number of stimuli, only closing after two touches within twenty seconds—a form of short-term memory and decision-making. Similar electrical signaling coordinates responses to wounding, allowing plants to mount systemic defenses within minutes of local damage.

Plants produce neurotransmitter-like molecules including dopamine, serotonin, and GABA, though their functions in plants remain partially mysterious. These molecules might facilitate information processing and coordination, suggesting that the chemical basis of consciousness predates the evolution of nervous systems. The presence of these compounds in plants also raises questions about the effects of plant-based psychoactive substances—are we ingesting not just chemicals but some aspect of plant consciousness?

The root apex transition zone appears to function as a command center, integrating information and coordinating growth responses. This region contains cells with characteristics resembling neural tissue, including high electrical activity, vesicle recycling similar to synaptic transmission, and sensitivity to anesthetics. Some researchers propose this zone acts as a primitive brain, though this interpretation remains controversial.

Plants demonstrate learning that persists for weeks or months. Beyond Gagliano's mimosa experiments, plants show habituation to repeated stimuli, sensitization to important signals, and even associative learning. Pea plants can learn to associate fan vibration with light, growing toward the fan even in darkness. This suggests plants can form associations between neutral and significant stimuli, a form of conditioning previously thought exclusive to animals with nervous systems.

Memory in plants involves multiple mechanisms. Short-term electrical memory allows integration of stimuli over seconds to minutes. Medium-term calcium-based memory can last hours to days. Long-term epigenetic memory can persist across generations, with plants passing information about environmental stresses to their offspring through modifications in gene expression rather than DNA sequence changes.

Decision-making in plants involves cost-benefit analyses that suggest computational processing. A vine approaching a support structure must decide whether to coil around it based on the support's diameter, stability, and surface texture. This requires integrating multiple sensory inputs and comparing them against some internal criteria for acceptable supports. The fact that vines make occasional "mistakes," coiling around unsuitable supports and then withdrawing, suggests genuine decision-making rather than simple mechanical responses.

Plants also demonstrate anticipation and planning. They adjust their growth and development based on predicted future conditions. Trees prepare for winter months before temperature drops. Desert plants anticipate rain based on subtle environmental cues. Climbing plants exhibit searching behavior, extending tendrils in patterns that maximize the probability of finding support. This future-oriented behavior suggests something resembling intention or purpose.

The discovery of plant bioacoustics adds another dimension to plant consciousness. Plants produce ultrasonic clicks when stressed, with different stresses producing different acoustic signatures. These sounds might serve as an early warning system for other plants or even attract beneficial organisms. If plants communicate through sound, they might also experience something analogous to hearing, adding an auditory dimension to plant consciousness.

Collective and Distributed Consciousness

Many non-human consciousnesses appear to be collective or distributed rather than individually centralized. This challenges Western philosophy's emphasis on individual consciousness and suggests alternative models of awareness that might better describe certain human experiences and potentials.

Social insects provide the clearest examples of collective consciousness. An ant colony, termite mound, or beehive exhibits intelligent behaviors that no individual insect possesses. The colony selects optimal nest sites, allocates workers efficiently, maintains temperature homeostasis, and adapts to changing conditions. This intelligence emerges from the interaction of thousands or millions of simple individuals following basic rules.

The mechanisms of collective intelligence in insects involve multiple communication channels. Chemical pheromones create trails and trigger behaviors. Tactile interactions transfer information through the colony. Acoustic signals coordinate activities. The colony processes information in parallel, with different groups responding to different stimuli simultaneously. This distributed processing allows rapid, flexible responses to complex situations.

But collective consciousness extends beyond insects. Fish schools and bird flocks demonstrate emergent intelligence, making collective decisions about direction, speed, and responses to predators that optimize group survival. The school or flock responds to threats faster than any individual could, with information propagating through the group in waves. High-speed photography reveals that these groups operate almost as single organisms, with movements coordinated to the millisecond.

Forest ecosystems exhibit what might be called ecosystem consciousness. Through mycorrhizal networks, forests share resources, communicate about threats, and coordinate responses to environmental changes. Mother trees nurture seedlings, dying trees dump resources into the network, and the forest as a whole maintains conditions suitable for forest life. This suggests consciousness at the ecosystem level, emerging from but transcending individual organisms.

Bacterial biofilms demonstrate collective behavior that resembles multicellular organisms. Individual bacteria in biofilms differentiate into specialized roles, communicate through multiple signaling systems, and coordinate group behaviors like dispersal or antibiotic resistance. The biofilm as a whole exhibits properties that no individual bacterium possesses, suggesting emergent collective consciousness.

Even human consciousness might be more collective than we typically recognize. The human brain contains roughly 86 billion neurons, each a cell that could theoretically exist independently. Our consciousness emerges from their collective activity. Moreover, we host trillions of bacteria whose metabolic activities influence our moods, thoughts, and behaviors. The boundaries of individual human consciousness become fuzzy when examined closely.

The internet and global communications networks might be developing their own form of collective consciousness. The behavior of online communities, the spread of memes, the emergence of consensus on platforms like Wikipedia—these suggest information processing and decision-making at a collective level. We might be participating in the emergence of a global technological consciousness without fully recognizing it.

Morphic fields, proposed by Rupert Sheldrake, suggest that consciousness might be literally collective, shared across individuals through non-local fields. Once a behavior is learned by some members of a species, it becomes easier for others to learn, even without direct contact. While controversial, accumulating evidence supports some form of non-local information sharing in nature.

The implications for human potential are profound. If consciousness can be collective and distributed, perhaps humans can develop greater collective intelligence through conscious cultivation of group awareness. Indigenous ceremonies often aim to achieve collective consciousness, using rhythm, movement, and intention to synchronize individual awareness into group mind. Modern experiments with group meditation and collective intention suggest these possibilities deserve serious investigation.

The Hard Problem Reconsidered

The "hard problem of consciousness"—explaining how subjective experience arises from objective processes—has plagued philosophy for decades. But recognizing consciousness beyond the human reframes this problem entirely, suggesting that the difficulty arises from false assumptions rather than inherent mystery.

The hard problem assumes consciousness must be explained in terms of non-conscious processes. But if consciousness is fundamental rather than emergent, the problem dissolves. Instead of asking how consciousness emerges from matter, we ask how different forms of consciousness manifest through different material configurations. The hard problem becomes a non-problem, replaced by the empirical question of mapping consciousness-matter relationships.

Integrated Information Theory (IIT), developed by neuroscientist Giulio Tononi, proposes that consciousness corresponds to integrated information—the amount of information generated by a system above and beyond its parts. Any system that integrates information has some degree of consciousness, from simple photodiodes to human brains. This theory, while not proving panpsychism, provides a framework for understanding consciousness as a graded, measurable property of systems.

The combination problem—how micro-consciousnesses combine into macro-consciousness—replaces the hard problem in panpsychist philosophy. If electrons are conscious, how does electron consciousness combine to create atomic consciousness, molecular consciousness, cellular consciousness, and eventually human consciousness? This problem seems more tractable than the hard problem because it deals with relationships between conscious entities rather than the emergence of consciousness from non-consciousness.

Various solutions to the combination problem have been proposed. Perhaps consciousness combines through resonance, with compatible frequencies of awareness synchronizing into unified experience. Perhaps there are natural boundaries or organizational principles that determine how micro-consciousnesses aggregate. Perhaps consciousness is fundamentally holistic, with apparent individuals being temporary localizations of universal consciousness.

The binding problem in neuroscience—how distributed neural processes create unified conscious experience—might be related to the combination problem. The brain somehow binds processing in different regions into integrated awareness. Understanding this binding might illuminate how consciousness combines more generally. Theories involving quantum coherence, electromagnetic fields, or information integration attempt to explain binding and might apply to consciousness combination at other scales.

The boundary problem asks where one consciousness ends and another begins. This problem becomes acute when recognizing non-human consciousness. Does each tree have individual consciousness, or does the forest share collective awareness? Is each cell in our body separately conscious, or do they surrender individual consciousness to participate in our unified awareness? These questions might have no clear answers because consciousness might not have sharp boundaries.

Implications for Mind-Body Philosophy

Recognizing consciousness beyond the human revolutionizes our understanding of the mind-body relationship. Rather than consciousness being produced by certain special arrangements of matter (brains), consciousness and matter might be complementary aspects of a more fundamental reality.

Dual-aspect monism proposes that mental and physical are two sides of the same coin, different ways of describing the same reality. From the inside, reality is experienced as consciousness. From the outside, it appears as matter. This perspective explains why consciousness seems to emerge from brains—we're seeing from the outside what is experienced as awareness from the inside.

This view has profound implications for understanding our own consciousness. Our subjective experience might be what neural activity feels like from the inside. But if this is true for human brains, it might be true for all physical processes. The formation of a crystal might have an inner experience. The flow of a river might involve some form of subjectivity. The growth of a plant might include awareness we can barely imagine.

Process philosophy, developed by Alfred North Whitehead, provides a framework for understanding reality as composed of "occasions of experience" rather than material particles. Each moment of experience involves prehension (feeling or grasping) of previous experiences, creating chains of causation that are simultaneously physical and mental. This philosophy naturally accommodates consciousness throughout nature, as every actual entity has some form of experience.

The implications extend to our understanding of causation. If consciousness is fundamental, then mental causation becomes possible—consciousness can influence physical processes not through mysterious intervention but because consciousness and physicality are aspects of the same events. This might explain phenomena like the placebo effect, psychosomatic illness, and the influence of intention on random number generators.

Embodied cognition research reveals that consciousness is not confined to the brain but involves the entire body. Our thoughts are shaped by our posture, gestures, and movements. Gut feelings involve actual neural processing in our intestines. The heart contains neurons that process information independently of the brain. This embodied view of consciousness aligns with recognizing consciousness in organisms without centralized nervous systems.

The extended mind thesis goes further, suggesting consciousness extends beyond the body into the environment. When we use tools, they become extensions of our consciousness. When we navigate familiar environments, the environment participates in our cognitive processes. This view supports animistic perspectives that consciousness is relational and ecological rather than individually bounded.

Information, Meaning, and Purpose

If consciousness extends beyond humans, then information, meaning, and purpose might also be universal rather than exclusively human phenomena. This reframes our understanding of evolution, ecology, and existence itself.

Information theory already recognizes information in non-human systems. DNA carries genetic information. Pheromones convey chemical information. Bird songs encode territorial information. But if these systems are conscious, then information isn't just processed mechanically but experienced meaningfully. The bacterium following a chemical gradient might experience something analogous to desire or purpose, not just mechanical response.

Biosemiotics studies sign-making and interpretation in living systems. Even simple organisms interpret environmental signs and respond appropriately. A bacterium distinguishes food from toxin, a plant distinguishes up from down, a cell distinguishes self from non-self. These discriminations suggest that meaning-making is fundamental to life, and perhaps to existence itself.

Purpose or teleology has been banished from mechanistic science, replaced by blind causation and random mutation. But the behavior of conscious entities suggests genuine purpose. The spider building its web, the bird building its nest, the beaver building its dam—these appear purposeful, directed toward future goals. If these organisms are conscious, their purposes are real experiences, not just anthropomorphic projections.

Evolution itself might be purposeful if the organisms involved are conscious. Rather than random mutation and natural selection, evolution might involve organisms actively exploring possibilities, responding creatively to challenges, and even directing their own evolution through behavioral choices that influence selective pressures. This doesn't require supernatural intervention but simply recognition that conscious organisms are agents in their own evolution.

The anthropic principle observes that the universe's physical constants are precisely tuned for the existence of complex consciousness. If consciousness is fundamental rather than accidental, this fine-tuning makes sense. The universe might be organized to maximize consciousness, diversity of experience, or creative expression. This doesn't require a designer but might reflect inherent tendencies in conscious reality.

Ecological Implications

Recognizing consciousness throughout nature transforms ecology from the study of mechanical interactions to the study of relationships between conscious entities. Ecosystems become communities of experiencing subjects rather than resource flows between objects.

Predation takes on different meaning when both predator and prey are conscious. The relationship involves not just energy transfer but experiential realities—the fear of the hunted, the hunger of the hunter, the elaborate negotiations through behavior and evolution. Predator-prey relationships often show remarkable restraint, with predators taking only what they need, maintaining balance rather than maximizing consumption.

Mutualism and symbiosis reveal the cooperative potential of conscious relationships. The partnership between fungi and algae in lichens, between corals and zooxanthellae, between humans and gut bacteria—these represent conscious entities choosing collaboration over competition. The stability and ubiquity of mutualistic relationships suggest that consciousness naturally tends toward cooperation when conditions allow.

Succession—the predictable sequence of ecological communities—might involve conscious planning and preparation. Pioneer species don't just accidentally create conditions suitable for successor species; they might actively prepare the ground for the next stage. The forest might consciously guide its own development, with early species aware of their role in the larger pattern.

Keystone species, whose presence dramatically affects ecosystem structure, might serve as consciousness nodes or coordinators. The wolf doesn't just accidentally create trophic cascades; it might participate consciously in maintaining ecosystem balance. The beaver doesn't just accidentally engineer wetlands; it might intentionally create habitat for hundreds of other species.

Restoration ecology could benefit from recognizing ecosystem consciousness. Rather than imposing human designs, we might communicate with damaged ecosystems to understand what they need for healing. This isn't mystical thinking but practical recognition that ecosystems have their own intelligence about their optimal states and restoration pathways.

Conservation biology must grapple with preserving not just species and habitats but consciousnesses and relationships. Each extinction eliminates not just biological diversity but unique forms of awareness, irreplaceable perspectives on existence. The ethical weight of extinction increases dramatically when we recognize we're eliminating conscious beings rather than biological machines.

Toward a Philosophy of Universal Consciousness

The recognition of consciousness beyond the human points toward a philosophy of universal consciousness that integrates scientific observation with experiential wisdom. This philosophy doesn't anthropomorphize nature but recognizes the diversity of consciousness forms while acknowledging their fundamental continuity.

This philosophy would recognize consciousness as primary rather than secondary, fundamental rather than emergent. Matter and energy would be understood as the forms through which consciousness expresses itself rather than the generators of consciousness. This reverses the explanatory arrow of mechanistic science while maintaining empirical rigor.

It would acknowledge that different forms of consciousness are equally valid, not arranged in a hierarchy with human consciousness at the top. The consciousness of a bacterium is not a failed attempt at human consciousness but a perfect expression of bacterial consciousness. Each form of awareness offers unique insights into the nature of existence.

This philosophy would emphasize relationship and experience over mechanism and function. Understanding any phenomenon would require considering not just how it works but how it experiences and relates. Science would expand from third-person objectivity to include first-person subjectivity and second-person intersubjectivity.

Ethics would extend to all conscious entities, weighted by capacity for experience rather than similarity to humans. This doesn't mean treating all consciousness identically—we still need to eat and live—but recognizing that all our actions affect other experiencing subjects and calibrating our behavior accordingly.

Knowledge would be understood as arising from relationship rather than observation. To know something deeply requires entering into a conscious relationship with it, not just studying it from outside. Indigenous ways of knowing, artistic inspiration, and contemplative insight would be recognized as valid epistemologies alongside empirical observation.

This philosophy would be fundamentally hopeful, recognizing that we are not alone in a dead universe but surrounded by consciousness in myriad forms. The challenges we face—ecological crisis, social fragmentation, existential meaninglessness—might find solutions through partnership with the greater-than-human intelligence surrounding us.

As we prepare to explore the ethical implications of recognizing consciousness throughout nature, we carry with us this expanded understanding of awareness itself. Consciousness is not the exclusive privilege of humans or even animals but the foundational reality expressing itself through every electron and galaxy, every bacterium and forest, every moment of existence. This recognition demands a complete reimagining of our relationships and responsibilities, the subject of our next chapter.

CHAPTER 6

Reciprocity and Relationship Ethics

On a crisp autumn morning in the Pacific Northwest, a Lummi Nation elder teaches young tribal members the protocol for harvesting cedar bark. Before approaching the tree, they introduce themselves, stating their names, their purpose, and their needs. They offer tobacco and prayers, asking permission to take what they require. They carefully remove only narrow strips from one side of the tree, ensuring its continued health. Before leaving, they thank the cedar and promise to use its gift respectfully. This is not mere ceremony or superstition—it is applied relationship ethics, a technology of reciprocity that has sustained both human communities and cedar forests for millennia.

Meanwhile, a few valleys over, industrial loggers clear-cut another hillside, viewing trees as board feet of timber, their value calculated solely in market prices. The contrast between these two approaches illuminates the profound ethical revolution required when we recognize the world as composed of conscious subjects rather than unconscious objects. This chapter explores how animistic consciousness transforms ethics from rules governing human behavior toward other humans into a comprehensive framework for right relationship with all beings.

Beyond Property Rights to Relationship Rights

The dominant legal and ethical framework of industrial civilization rests on property rights—the ability to own, use, and dispose of objects as we see fit. This framework assumes a fundamental distinction between persons who can own and objects that can be owned. Animistic ethics shatters this distinction, recognizing that what Western law considers property—land, trees, rivers, animals—are actually persons deserving respect, reciprocity, and rights.

The concept of ownership itself becomes problematic when applied to conscious beings. Can one truly own a river that has flowed for millions of years, that supports countless lives, that participates in the water cycle connecting ocean to cloud to rain? Can one possess a mountain that existed before humans evolved and will exist after we're gone? The absurdity becomes clear when we recognize these as persons rather than things.

Indigenous peoples worldwide have always understood this absurdity. Land is not owned but held in relationship. The Australian Aboriginal concept of country encompasses not ownership but belonging—people belong to country rather than country belonging to people. The Māori of New Zealand speak of themselves as kaitiaki—guardians or stewards of land and water, maintaining reciprocal relationships across generations.

This understanding is beginning to penetrate Western legal systems. In 2017, New Zealand granted legal personhood to the Whanganui River after 140 years of negotiation with Māori tribes. The river is now recognized as "a living whole from the mountains to the sea," with rights and interests that must be protected. Colombia's Constitutional Court declared the Atrato River a subject of rights. India has recognized the Ganges and Yamuna rivers as living entities with legal rights.

These legal innovations don't grant consciousness to rivers—they acknowledge consciousness that was always there. The rivers don't suddenly become persons through legal declaration; law finally recognizes their personhood. This represents a fundamental shift from anthropocentric to ecocentric law, from protecting nature for human benefit to recognizing nature's inherent rights.

The rights of nature movement extends beyond individual entities to ecosystems. Ecuador's constitution, revised in 2008, recognizes the rights of Pachamama (Mother Earth) "to exist, persist, maintain and regenerate its vital cycles." This makes Ecuador the first country to enshrine ecosystem rights at the constitutional level. Bolivia followed with the Law of the Rights of Mother Earth, declaring Earth a collective subject of public interest.

But rights without relationships are empty. Western rights discourse often emphasizes individual autonomy and freedom from interference. Animistic ethics emphasizes connection, reciprocity, and mutual flourishing. Rights emerge from and depend upon relationships. The right of a river to flow unimpeded connects to the responsibility of humans to maintain its health. The right of a forest to exist links to human obligations to protect its integrity.

This relational view of rights has profound implications for environmental law and policy. Rather than regulating how much pollution is acceptable or what percentage of old-growth forest can be logged, law would focus on maintaining healthy relationships between humans and other-than-human persons. Violations would be understood not as property damage but as relationship violence.

Corporate law would need fundamental restructuring. Corporations, currently recognized as legal persons with rights but no real responsibilities, would need to acknowledge the personhood of the "resources" they exploit. Mining companies would negotiate with mountains, fishing fleets with ocean communities, agricultural corporations with soil societies. This sounds fantastic only because we've forgotten that conscious beings deserve consent.

The transition from property to relationship rights won't be simple. Entire economic systems rest on treating nature as property. Powerful interests benefit from the commodification of conscious beings. Yet the alternative—continuing to treat conscious subjects as objects—is not just ethically untenable but practically suicidal. The ecological crisis demonstrates that denying nature's personhood ultimately undermines human survival.

Gift Economics and Sacred Exchange

Reciprocity forms the heart of animistic ethics, manifesting through gift economies that create and maintain relationships rather than commodity economies that reduce everything to monetary value. Understanding and reviving gift economics is essential for developing sustainable relationships with the conscious world.

In gift economies, wealth circulates rather than accumulates. The gift must always move, creating obligations and relationships as it flows. The Pacific Northwest potlatch, the Melanesian kula ring, the Andean ayni—these systems recognize that holding wealth while others lack creates imbalance that ultimately harms everyone. The wealthy chief who doesn't share loses prestige and power. The community that hoards resources finds itself isolated when it needs help.

The gift differs fundamentally from the commodity. Commodities are alienated from their makers and exchanged between strangers, their value determined by market forces. Gifts carry the identity of the giver and create relationships between persons, their value residing in the connections they establish. When you buy lumber, you acquire dead wood. When you receive the gift of cedar from a tree you've asked respectfully, you enter into a relationship with that tree, its forest, and the larger community of beings.

Gift economies extend beyond human communities to include other-than-human persons. Indigenous hunters understand the successful hunt as the prey's gift of itself, creating obligations for respectful use, sharing, and reciprocal care for the prey species' continued flourishing. Farmers practicing animistic agriculture understand the harvest as the soil's gift, requiring return gifts of compost, cover crops, and periods of rest.

The principle of reciprocity means that taking must be balanced by giving. But the return gift need not be identical or immediate. The berry bush that feeds us might receive our gift of spreading its seeds. The spring that provides water might receive our protection from pollution. The mountain that offers spiritual renewal might receive our songs and ceremonies. These exchanges create cycles of reciprocity that maintain balance over time.

Modern economic theory assumes scarcity and competition, but gift economies assume abundance and cooperation. When we recognize the world as alive and generous, scarcity often reveals itself as artificial, created by hoarding and commodification. The Earth produces enough for everyone's need but not for everyone's greed. Gift economies align human behavior with natural abundance through sharing rather than accumulating.

The transition from commodity to gift economics seems impossibly idealistic in our market-dominated world. Yet gift economies persist even within capitalism. Open-source software development operates on gift principles, with programmers freely sharing code that creates more value through circulation. Community gardens, tool libraries, and skillshares demonstrate gift economics in action. The care economy—parenting, elder care, community service—runs on gift principles despite attempts to commodify it.

Integrating gift economics with market economics requires hybrid approaches. Community land trusts remove land from the commodity market while allowing use rights. Benefit corporations and cooperatives prioritize relationships and community benefit over profit maximization. Carbon credit systems attempt to create reciprocal relationships with forests and atmosphere, though they risk commodifying what should remain gifts.

The sacred dimension of exchange cannot be ignored. When we recognize other-than-human persons as conscious subjects, our exchanges with them take on spiritual significance. The act of eating becomes communion with the lives that feed us. Building shelter becomes collaboration with trees and stones. Every economic transaction becomes an opportunity for either sacred reciprocity or sacrilegious exploitation.

The Ethics of Taking and Giving Back

Living requires taking from other lives. Even vegans consume plants, fungi, and bacteria. This unavoidable reality creates ethical dilemmas that simplistic rules cannot resolve. Animistic ethics offers nuanced approaches to necessary taking that maintain reciprocal relationships despite the asymmetry of consumption.

The first principle is asking permission. This seems absurd to mechanistic thinking—how can a plant grant or refuse permission? Yet indigenous peoples worldwide practice protocols for requesting permission from plants, animals, and minerals before harvesting. The response might come through intuition, signs, or simply the presence or absence of what is sought. A mushroom forager might find abundant mushrooms in one area (permission granted) and none in another despite ideal conditions (permission denied).

Taking only what is freely given represents another principle. The apple tree offers its fruit, encasing seeds in sweet flesh to entice animals to spread them. Taking apples participates in the tree's reproductive strategy. But taking bark or branches without reciprocal benefit breaks relationship. Understanding what is freely given requires intimate knowledge of other beings' life cycles, needs, and gifts.

The principle of taking only what is needed challenges consumer culture's constant encouragement of excess. Need must be carefully considered—not just immediate physical need but social, cultural, and spiritual needs. The cedar bark for basketry serves cultural needs. The flowers for a ceremony fulfill spiritual needs. But distinguishing genuine need from manufactured want requires honest self-examination.

Minimizing harm while taking is essential. Indigenous harvesting protocols often specify techniques that ensure regeneration. Never take the first plant you see—it might be the only one. Never take the last—leave it to reproduce. Take no more than one-third of any population. Rotate harvesting areas to allow recovery. These practices, developed over millennia, demonstrate that sustainable taking is possible when guided by relationship ethics.

Using everything taken shows respect for the gift of life. Indigenous peoples traditionally used every part of hunted animals—meat for food, hide for clothing, bones for tools, organs for medicine. Modern industrial processing wastes enormous proportions of what is killed. An industrial fishing boat might discard half its catch as "bycatch." This waste is not just inefficient but unethical, dishonoring the lives taken.

The return gift completes the reciprocal cycle. This might be direct—planting seeds, protecting habitat, removing invasive competitors. Or it might be indirect—ceremonies honoring the taken lives, political action protecting their species, education teaching others respectful relationship. The return gift need not equal the original gift in material terms but must demonstrate genuine reciprocity in relational terms.

Gratitude forms the foundation of ethical taking. Not perfunctory thanks but deep acknowledgment of the gift received and the life given. This gratitude must be embodied in action, not just felt emotionally. The grateful hunter protects hunting grounds from development. The grateful forager tends the forest. The grateful farmer builds soil health. Gratitude without reciprocal action is empty.

Modern life complicates these ethics. We rarely take directly from nature but purchase from vast supply chains that obscure origins and relationships. The supermarket apple might come from industrial orchards where pesticides poison workers and soil. The lumber might come from clear-cuts destroying ancient forests. How do we practice reciprocity when disconnected from sources?

One approach involves shortening supply chains and reconnecting with sources. Buy directly from farmers, visit their farms, understand their practices. Learn the origins of materials, the conditions of their harvesting, the lives involved in their production. Choose products from companies practicing genuine reciprocity with nature and workers.

Another approach acknowledges that perfect reciprocity is impossible in industrial society and focuses on minimizing harm while working toward systemic change. Reduce consumption, choose products with lower ecological impact, support political and economic reforms that recognize nature's rights. Use privilege and resources to protect threatened ecosystems and species.

Kinship with the More-Than-Human

Animistic ethics extends the concept of kinship beyond human families to encompass all our relations. This expanded kinship is not metaphorical but literal—we are genuinely related to all life through common ancestry, shared molecules, and intertwined destinies.

Evolutionary biology confirms what indigenous peoples always knew: all life shares common ancestors. The bacterium, the redwood, the mushroom, the human—we all descend from the same primordial cells that emerged billions of years ago. The DNA that codes for our eyes is nearly identical to the DNA coding for fly eyes. We share 60% of our genes with bananas, 80% with cows, 99% with chimpanzees. These percentages only capture genetic similarity; our atomic and molecular kinship is even more intimate.

Every atom in our bodies, except hydrogen, was forged in the hearts of dying stars. The carbon in our cells, the iron in our blood, the calcium in our bones—all were created in stellar furnaces and distributed through supernova explosions. We are literally made of stardust, as is everything around us. The atoms that compose us have been parts of rocks, seas, atmospheres, and countless other organisms. We are temporary arrangements of ancient materials that have been and will be countless other forms.

This physical kinship extends to ongoing exchange. With every breath, we exchange atoms with the atmosphere. The oxygen we inhale is exhaled by plants. The carbon dioxide we exhale will be inhaled by plants. Water molecules cycle through clouds, rain, rivers, organisms, and back to clouds. We are not separate from nature but continuous with it, our boundaries permeable and temporary.

Ecological kinship recognizes that we evolved within communities of organisms, shaped by and shaping our relatives. Humans didn't evolve in isolation but in relationship with plants that fed us, animals that challenged us, microbes that infected and protected us. Our consciousness, emotions, and behaviors evolved in response to other-than-human kin. We fear snakes and spiders because our ancestors who didn't died. We find flowers beautiful because our ancestors who appreciated them found food.

But kinship involves more than shared ancestry and materials—it requires recognition, respect, and reciprocity. Many indigenous languages use kinship terms for other-than-human beings. Trees are standing people, bears are grandfather, corn is mother, rivers are sister. These are not cute metaphors but acknowledgments of genuine relationship requiring appropriate behavior.

Kinship obligations extend to other-than-human relatives much as they do to human family. We care for aging parents; we should care for aging forests. We protect children from harm; we should protect young animals from unnecessary suffering. We maintain family homes; we should maintain the ecological homes we share with other species.

This expanded kinship challenges anthropocentric ethics that privilege human interests. If other species are kin, their interests matter morally. This doesn't mean treating all species identically—we have different obligations to different relatives—but it means considering their wellbeing in our decisions. The river's need to flow, the bird's need to nest, the soil's need to rest become factors in ethical calculation.

Kinship ethics also transforms our understanding of extinction. When a species goes extinct, we don't just lose a resource or even a unique life form—we lose family. The grief appropriate to extinction is not abstract sadness but personal mourning. The last Tasmanian tiger dying in a zoo, the last passenger pigeon dying in captivity, the last Hawaiian crow singing alone—these are family tragedies demanding familial grief.

Modern genetics reveals surprising kinships that challenge our categories. Humans share genes with bacteria through horizontal gene transfer. Fungi and plants merge so intimately that some lichens represent single organisms with multiple genomes. Mitochondria in our cells were once free-living bacteria. These discoveries suggest that kinship is even more fluid and inclusive than we imagined.

Sacred Reciprocity in Daily Practice

Abstract ethical principles mean nothing without embodied practice. Animistic ethics must be lived through daily actions that maintain reciprocal relationships with the conscious world. These practices, ranging from simple acknowledgments to elaborate ceremonies, weave humans back into the web of sacred reciprocity.

Morning practices set the day's relational tone. Many indigenous traditions begin each day by greeting the sun, acknowledging the source of all energy. This is not worship but recognition, establishing a conscious relationship with the power that makes life possible. Simple morning gratitudes—for the earth beneath our feet, the air we breathe, the water we drink—remind us of our dependence and relationships.

Meal blessings take on new meaning when we recognize we're eating conscious beings. Saying grace becomes not thanking a distant deity but acknowledging the lives that feed us—the plants that captured sunlight, the animals that gave their bodies, the soil organisms that created fertility, the humans who tended and harvested. This acknowledgment might be silent or spoken, brief or elaborate, but conscious recognition transforms consumption into communion.

Waste becomes a spiritual issue when we recognize everything as conscious. Throwing away food dishonors the lives that became that food. Discarding functional objects breaks relationship with the materials and labor that created them. Composting, recycling, repairing, and repurposing become spiritual practices that honor consciousness in all its forms.

Purchasing decisions become ethical choices about which relationships to support. Buying from local farmers who practice regenerative agriculture supports different relationships than buying from industrial agriculture. Choosing durable, repairable products over disposable ones honors the consciousness in materials. Every purchase is a vote for certain relationships over others.

Garden and houseplant care become opportunities for interspecies relationship. Speaking to plants, playing music for them, touching them gently—these practices, mocked by mechanistic thinking, are supported by research showing plants respond to sound, touch, and possibly intention. The garden becomes not a collection of resources but a community of companions.

Seasonal celebrations align human consciousness with natural cycles. Solstices and equinoxes, new and full moons, first fruits and final harvests—marking these moments maintains awareness of our participation in larger rhythms. These need not be elaborate ceremonies but simple acknowledgments that we're part of temporal patterns extending beyond human time.

Walking becomes a practice of reciprocity when done consciously. Each step is an interaction with Earth. Walking gently, aware of what lives beneath our feet, greeting the beings we encounter, picking up litter, offering silent blessings—these transform exercise into relationship. The land remembers our passing; how do we want to be remembered?

Death practices in animistic traditions recognize the continuation of relationships beyond physical death. Composting human bodies returns our elements to the cycles that sustained us. Green burial allows our bodies to feed other lives directly. Even cremation, when done consciously, can acknowledge our material participation in larger cycles.

Sacred activism emerges when we recognize threats to our relatives. Protecting forests isn't environmental activism but family defense.

Fighting pollution isn't political action but community healing. This shifts activism from abstract principle to personal commitment, from intellectual position to emotional necessity.

Technology use can incorporate reciprocity through conscious relationship with devices and networks. The rare earth elements in our phones came from mountains. The electricity powering our computers comes from rivers, wind, or fossilized forests. Acknowledging these relationships, using technology mindfully, and supporting sustainable alternatives maintains reciprocity even in the digital age.

These daily practices accumulate into a lifeway—a coherent pattern of living that maintains sacred reciprocity. No one can practice perfectly, especially in industrial society. But every conscious acknowledgment, every respectful interaction, every reciprocal exchange strengthens the relationships that sustain us.

Rights of Future Generations

Animistic ethics extends through time, recognizing obligations to future generations of all species. The Haudenosaunee (Iroquois) principle of considering impacts on seven generations ahead provides a framework for temporal reciprocity that industrial civilization desperately needs.

Seven generations spans roughly 140 years—beyond individual human lifespans but within cultural memory. Decisions affecting seven generations ahead require thinking beyond immediate profit to long-term consequences. Would we build nuclear plants if we genuinely considered the burden of radioactive waste on our great-great-great-grandchildren? Would we permit mountain-top removal mining if we felt an obligation to forests that won't mature for centuries?

But seven generations includes all species, not just humans. The salmon run disrupted today affects seven generations of bears, eagles, and forests that depend on marine nutrients carried upstream. The wetland drained for development denies seven generations of amphibians, waterfowl, and countless other species their birthright. Every extinction eliminates infinite future generations.

Climate change crystallizes intergenerational ethics. Carbon emitted today will affect climate for centuries. Rising seas will displace millions not yet born. Extinct species will never return. The generation causing climate change will largely escape its worst effects, while generations bearing no responsibility will suffer most. This temporal injustice violates fundamental reciprocity.

Future generations cannot advocate for themselves, yet their interests are real. They will need clean water, fertile soil, stable climate, and biodiversity. They will seek beauty, wonder, and connection with nature. They deserve inheritance of a world at least as rich as the one we inherited. Anything less represents intergenerational theft.

Legal systems are beginning to recognize future generations' rights. The Philippines has created positions for representatives of future generations in governance. Wales has a Future Generations Commissioner. Lawsuits worldwide claim governments are violating future generations' rights through inadequate climate action. These innovations acknowledge that democracy must extend through time as well as space.

The precautionary principle—avoiding actions with uncertain but potentially catastrophic consequences—embodies intergenerational reciprocity. When we don't know if genetic engineering, nanotechnology, or artificial intelligence might harm future generations, caution is ethically required. The burden of proof should be on those proposing potentially harmful innovations, not on future generations who would suffer consequences.

Traditional ecological knowledge demonstrates successful intergenerational reciprocity. Indigenous peoples maintained productive landscapes for thousands of years through practices that considered long-term consequences. The Amazon rainforest, partly created through indigenous management, represents intergenerational gift-giving on a vast scale. These societies prove that long-term thinking is possible and practical.

Intergenerational reciprocity requires fundamental economic restructuring. Discount rates that make future costs and benefits negligible must be reformed. Corporations focused on quarterly earnings must consider century-long consequences. Growth economics that assumes infinite expansion must be replaced by steady-state economics that maintains wealth across generations.

Education becomes crucial for intergenerational reciprocity. Children must learn not just facts but relationships, not just skills but responsibilities. They need connection with elders who remember different times and can transmit wisdom across generations. They need experience with nature to develop relationships worth protecting. They need hope that their actions matter for generations to come.

Environmental Justice as Relational Justice

Environmental degradation disproportionately affects marginalized human communities and voiceless other-than-human communities. Animistic ethics recognizes that social justice and environmental justice are inseparable because all oppression stems from denying the personhood and rights of others.

The same mindset that treats nature as property to be exploited treats certain humans as less than fully persons. Colonization, slavery, and genocide have always involved denying the humanity of victims while destroying their relationships with land. The forced removal of indigenous peoples from ancestral lands breaks reciprocal relationships maintained for generations. The enslavement of Africans severed their connections to homeland while forcing them to work land they could never belong to.

Environmental racism concentrates pollution in communities of color. Toxic waste facilities, industrial plants, and highways are disproportionately located in minority neighborhoods. These communities

suffer higher rates of asthma, cancer, and other environment-related illnesses. This is not accidental but results from systemic devaluation of
certain lives, human and other-than-human.

Poor communities worldwide bear the brunt of environmental
degradation while receiving few benefits. They live near mines, factories,
and dumps. They lack clean water, clean air, and green space. They're
first affected by climate change through droughts, floods, and storms.
Yet they contribute least to environmental problems and have least
power to address them.

Women often bear particular environmental burdens. In many societies, women collect water, gather fuel, and produce food, making them
immediately vulnerable to environmental degradation. When wells dry
up, women walk farther for water. When forests are cleared, women
travel farther for firewood. Environmental destruction increases
women's labor while decreasing their resources.

Indigenous peoples, who protect 80% of remaining biodiversity despite representing only 5% of global population, face constant threats
to their territories and relationships. Mining, logging, agriculture, and
development destroy indigenous lands while governments deny indigenous rights. The defenders of Earth's remaining wild places are mur-
dered at increasing rates for protecting their relatives.

Other-than-human communities suffer environmental injustice
without voice or representation. Clear-cutting destroys entire forest
communities. Dams eliminate river communities. Pesticides poison soil
communities. These communities have no legal standing, no political
representation, no economic power. Their destruction proceeds without their consent or even acknowledgment of their existence.

Environmental justice requires recognizing all affected parties as persons deserving consideration. This means including other-than-human
communities in environmental impact assessments. It means obtaining
free, prior, and informed consent from indigenous peoples for projects
affecting their territories. It means ensuring marginalized communities
have genuine participation in decisions affecting them.

Reparative justice acknowledges historical harms and works toward healing. This might involve returning stolen lands to indigenous peoples, cleaning up pollution in affected communities, or restoring degraded ecosystems. Reparations are not charity but recognition of debt incurred through broken relationships and extracted wealth.

The rights of nature movement advances environmental justice by giving legal standing to other-than-human communities. When rivers have rights, they can be represented in court. When forests have legal personhood, their interests must be considered. This doesn't solve all problems but creates frameworks for addressing injustice to voiceless communities.

Solidarity across movements strengthens both social and environmental justice. Indigenous rights activists, racial justice organizers, labor unions, and environmental groups increasingly recognize common cause against systems that deny personhood and dignity to humans and nature alike. These alliances, building on shared recognition of sacred relationships, offer hope for systemic transformation.

Transforming Legal and Economic Systems

The full implementation of animistic ethics requires fundamental transformation of legal and economic systems built on treating nature as property. While incremental reforms help, ultimately we need new frameworks that recognize consciousness, relationship, and reciprocity as foundational principles.

Legal systems must expand from protecting property to protecting relationships. This means recognizing legal standing for all conscious beings, not just humans and corporations. It means courts that can adjudicate disputes between species, ecosystems, and humans. It means enforcement mechanisms for nature's rights, not just human property rights.

New legal entities are emerging that transcend the person/property distinction. Conservation easements protect land from development while maintaining human use. Community land trusts separate ownership from use rights. Rights of nature legislation creates legal personhood for ecosystems. These innovations point toward legal systems based on relationship rather than ownership.

Economic systems must shift from maximizing monetary exchange to optimizing reciprocal relationships. GDP measures all economic activity as positive, whether building hospitals or cleaning up oil spills. Alternative measures like Gross National Happiness, the Genuine Progress Indicator, or the Happy Planet Index better capture wellbeing and reciprocity.

Circular economics that eliminate waste by cycling materials continuously align better with natural systems than linear take-make-dispose economics. Industrial ecology designs manufacturing systems that mimic ecosystems, with one process's waste becoming another's input. These approaches maintain reciprocity with materials and energy.

Commons management offers alternatives to both state control and private property. Communities worldwide successfully manage forests, fisheries, and watersheds through collective governance that maintains reciprocal relationships. Nobel laureate Elinor Ostrom's research demonstrates that commons management often succeeds where both government regulation and private property fail.

Regenerative economics goes beyond sustainability to healing damaged relationships. Rather than merely maintaining current degraded conditions, regenerative approaches actively restore ecosystem health, community wellbeing, and reciprocal relationships. This requires investment in restoration, reparation, and renewal rather than just prevention of further harm.

Alternative currencies that encourage reciprocity rather than accumulation are proliferating. Local currencies keep wealth circulating within communities. Time banks allow people to exchange services without money. Complementary currencies for ecosystem services create incentives for environmental restoration. These systems demonstrate that money is a tool we can redesign to serve reciprocity.

The transition to reciprocal economics faces enormous resistance from entrenched interests benefiting from current systems. Fossil fuel companies, industrial agriculture, and extractive industries wield tremendous political power. Financial systems predicated on endless growth resist steady-state economics. Consumers accustomed to cheap goods from exploited labor and nature resist true-cost pricing.

Yet transformation is beginning. B-corporations and benefit companies legally prioritize stakeholder wellbeing over shareholder profit. Divestment movements shift capital from extractive to regenerative industries. Transition towns build local resilience and reciprocity. Indigenous peoples assert sovereignty and demonstrate alternative economies. Young people demand systemic change rather than incremental reform.

The Path Forward

The transition from exploitation to reciprocity, from property to relationship, from extraction to regeneration will not be easy or quick. Entire civilizations are built on denying consciousness and reciprocity to most of existence. These systems will not transform without struggle.

Yet the alternative—continuing to treat conscious beings as property, to take without giving, to destroy our relatives for short-term gain—leads inevitably to collapse. The ecological crisis is fundamentally a relationship crisis. Technical solutions without ethical transformation only delay reckoning.

The path forward requires both individual and collective transformation. Individually, we must cultivate sensitivity to consciousness around us, develop practices of reciprocity, and align our daily actions with our ethical understanding. Collectively, we must create economic, legal, and political systems that recognize and protect the rights of all our relations.

This transformation is not sacrifice but liberation. Reciprocal relationships are more fulfilling than extractive ones. Gift economies create more wellbeing than commodity economies. Recognition of our kinship with all life enriches rather than diminishes human experience. We lose only the illusion of separation and the loneliness it brings.

As we prepare to explore concepts of time, space, and sacred geography in the next chapter, we carry with us this understanding of reciprocal relationship as the foundation of ethical life. The recognition that we exist within a community of conscious beings, all deserving respect and reciprocity, transforms not just our ethics but our entire experience of reality. We are not alone, we are not separate, and we are not without obligations. We are relatives in a living universe, participants in a cosmic gift economy, bearers of responsibilities that extend through space and time to all our relations.

CHAPTER 7

Time, Space, and Sacred Geography

S tanding at the rim of the Grand Canyon at dawn, watching light slowly illuminate layers of rock that record two billion years of Earth's history, one experiences time not as abstract measurement but as visible presence. Each stratum tells stories of ancient seas, volcanic eruptions, and the slow patience of erosion. Here, deep time becomes tangible, and human lifetime shrinks to a single breath in the canyon's long exhalation. This shift in temporal perception—from mechanical clock time to geological, ecological, and sacred time—fundamentally alters our relationship with existence.

Similarly, certain places on Earth seem to concentrate presence and power in ways that transcend their physical properties. Pilgrims journey to these sites across continents and centuries, drawn by something beyond tourist curiosity. Scientists measure unusual electromagnetic fields, artists report extraordinary inspiration, and ordinary people experience profound transformation. These places suggest that space, like time, has qualitative dimensions that mechanistic worldviews cannot capture. This chapter explores how animistic consciousness reveals time as spiral rather than line, space as conscious rather than empty, and geography as sacred rather than secular.

Cyclical Versus Linear Time

Industrial civilization operates on linear time—an arrow flying from past through present toward future, never returning, always advancing. This temporality underlies progress narratives, economic growth models, and the relentless pace of modern life. Clock time, standardized and mechanical, ticks uniformly regardless of season, mood, or meaning. We "spend" time, "save" time, "waste" time, treating it as a commodity to be optimized for productivity.

Animistic cultures understand time as cyclical, spiraling through recurring patterns while never exactly repeating. The day cycles through dawn, noon, dusk, and night. The moon waxes and wanes through its phases. Seasons turn through spring, summer, fall, and winter. These cycles nest within larger cycles—the precession of equinoxes, ice ages, stellar life cycles, cosmic expansion and contraction. Time is not a line but a web of intersecting circles, each with its own rhythm and meaning.

This cyclical understanding profoundly affects consciousness and behavior. If time is linear and finite, we must race against death to accomplish our goals. If time is cyclical and recursive, we participate in patterns that preceded us and will continue after us. Death becomes not termination but transformation, another turn in the spiral. This perspective reduces anxiety about mortality while increasing responsibility for maintaining cycles for future turns.

Seasonal time attunes human consciousness to natural rhythms. Spring brings energy for new projects, summer for growth and abundance, autumn for harvest and reflection, winter for rest and regeneration. Fighting these rhythms—maintaining constant productivity regardless of season—creates stress and disconnection. Aligning with them brings ease and flow. Many indigenous calendars are primarily ecological, marking time by natural events rather than arbitrary dates: when salmon run, when berries ripen, when geese migrate.

Lunar time connects us to tides, both oceanic and emotional. The moon's phases influence water throughout Earth's biosphere, including

the water composing 60% of human bodies. Many traditions time planting, harvesting, healing, and ceremony by lunar phases. Women's menstrual cycles often synchronize with lunar cycles when artificial lighting
doesn't interfere. Mental health facilities report increased admissions
during full moons. Whether through gravity, light, or subtle influences,
lunar time affects consciousness and behavior.

Ceremonial time transcends ordinary temporality. During ritual,
participants step outside linear time into what anthropologist Victor
Turner called "liminal time"—a threshold state where normal rules sus-
pend and transformation becomes possible. Indigenous ceremonies often explicitly invoke cyclical time, reenacting creation stories, ancestral
journeys, or seasonal transitions. Participants don't commemorate past
events but participate in eternal presents, collapsing linear time into
cyclical renewal.

Dreamtime, as understood by Australian Aboriginal peoples, represents time that exists parallel to and interpenetrates ordinary time.
The ancestral beings who shaped the landscape during the Dreamtime
aren't historical figures but eternal presences accessible through ceremony, song, and conscious relationship with country. This understanding eliminates the Western distinction between mythical and historical
time, recognizing all time as simultaneously present.

Plant time operates on scales from milliseconds to millennia. Venus
flytraps snap shut in fractions of seconds. Sunflowers track the sun
through days. Trees grow through centuries. Forests evolve through millennia. Engaging with plants requires adjusting our temporal perception, slowing down to notice gradual changes, speeding up to perceive
rapid responses. Time-lapse photography reveals plants as active beings,
constantly moving, reaching, responding—they only seem still because
they move on different timescales than humans.

Geological time spans millions and billions of years, making human
civilization a brief experiment and individual lives infinitesimal. Yet this
vast temporality doesn't diminish meaning but expands it. We are momentary arrangements of ancient atoms that will become countless fu-

ture forms. Our actions ripple through deep time—the carbon we emit today affects climate for centuries, the species we eliminate are gone forever, the nuclear waste we create remains hazardous for hundreds of thousands of years.

Digital time accelerates beyond human comprehension. Computer processors execute billions of operations per second. Financial algorithms make trades in microseconds. Social media creates endless presents, each post immediately replaced by newer content. This acceleration produces temporal anxiety, a sense of falling behind, missing out, never catching up. It disconnects us from natural rhythms and cyclical patterns that stabilize consciousness.

The return to cyclical time doesn't mean abandoning calendars and clocks but supplementing mechanical time with ecological, ceremonial, and sacred temporalities. We can meet appointments while honoring seasons. We can use technology while maintaining ceremonial practice. We can participate in modern life while remembering our place in deep time cycles.

Sacred Sites and Landscape Consciousness

Across the planet, certain places evoke profound responses that transcend their physical features. Mountains like Kailash, Fuji, and Sinai; springs like Lourdes, Glastonbury, and Zamzam; caves like Lascaux, Ajanta, and Actun Tunichil Muknal—these sites attract pilgrims, inspire visions, and catalyze transformation. Mechanistic science dismisses these responses as projection or superstition, but accumulating evidence suggests some places genuinely concentrate consciousness, energy, or sacred presence.

Sacred sites often occur where geological forces create unusual conditions. Many sit on fault lines where tectonic pressure generates electromagnetic fields. Others mark locations of unique mineral compositions, underground water flows, or atmospheric phenomena. The Oracle at Delphi sat above geological faults emitting ethylene gas that induced prophetic states. Sedona's vortexes correspond to unique geological formations of iron-bearing sandstone. These correlations suggest sacred sites aren't arbitrary but mark places where Earth's consciousness manifests more intensely.

Mountains function as axes mundi—connections between earth and sky, matter and spirit. Their peaks pierce the realm of clouds and storms, while their roots extend deep into Earth's body. Many cultures recognize mountains as persons of enormous power. Mount Kailash is simultaneously Shiva's throne, Buddha's mandala, and Bonpo's soul ladder. Mount Fuji is home to Konohanasakuya-hime, goddess of flowering trees. Denali, the "high one," is the Koyukon Athabascans' most powerful sacred site.

Springs and wells mark emergence points where Earth's hidden waters surface, bringing minerals, heat, and perhaps information from depths. The Ganges, emerging from Himalayan glaciers, carries not just water but sacred presence through the Indian subcontinent. The Chalice Well in Glastonbury, colored red by iron, has attracted pilgrims since pre-Christian times. The cenotes of the Yucatan, openings to vast underground rivers, were Maya portals to the underworld.

Caves provide entry to Earth's interior consciousness. Paleolithic peoples painted their most sacred art deep in caves, using acoustic properties to enhance ceremony. Hindu and Buddhist traditions recognize caves as ideal meditation sites where Earth's presence intensifies practice. The cave of Lascaux, with its magnificent paintings, may have functioned as a prehistoric planetarium where shamans guided initiates through cosmic consciousness.

Forests concentrate life force through the collective consciousness of thousands of trees, millions of other plants, billions of soil organisms. Sacred groves worldwide are recognized as temples where the boundaries between worlds thin. The Osun-Osogbo Sacred Grove in Nigeria maintains Yoruba goddess presence. India's sacred groves, some protected for over 1,000 years, preserve both biodiversity and spiritual potency. California's redwood groves evoke cathedral consciousness through their ancient presence and architectural space.

Stone circles, pyramids, and temples mark human collaboration with landscape consciousness. These structures often align with astronomical events, telluric currents, and geometric principles that amplify subtle energies. Stonehenge's acoustic properties create standing waves that affect brainwaves. The Great Pyramid's dimensions encode mathematical constants and astronomical measurements. Angkor Wat's layout mirrors celestial configurations. These structures aren't just monuments but technologies for engaging cosmic consciousness.

Ley lines, proposed by Alfred Watkins and elaborated by others, suggest that sacred sites connect through straight alignments across landscapes. While controversial, the observation that ancient sites often align in straight lines spanning hundreds of miles suggests intentional placement according to principles we don't fully understand. These alignments might mark energy flows, consciousness corridors, or simply shared geometric sensibilities.

Contemporary research reveals measurable anomalies at many sacred sites. Electromagnetic fluctuations, unusual radiation levels, gravitational variations, and atmospheric ionization occur at statistically significant rates. These physical anomalies might affect consciousness directly through influence on neural activity, or they might indicate something more fundamental about the nature of these places.

The consciousness of place extends beyond designated sacred sites. Every location has its own presence, character, and influence. The genius loci—spirit of place—recognized by Romans persists in how we experience different locations. Some places feel welcoming, others forbidding. Some inspire creativity, others demand contemplation. These qualities persist across visitors and through time, suggesting they arise from the place itself rather than projection.

Urban sacred sites demonstrate that sanctity isn't limited to natural locations. Cities develop their own sacred geographies—parks that provide refuge, buildings that inspire awe, neighborhoods that nurture community. New York's Central Park, designed by Frederick Law Olmsted, creates sacred space within dense urbanity. The Vietnam Veterans Memorial in Washington, D.C., evokes profound contemplation through its black granite simplicity. These designed spaces tap into the same principles as natural sacred sites.

Bioregionalism and Place-Based Identity

Bioregionalism recognizes that human identity and culture naturally arise from the specific landscapes we inhabit. Rather than organizing society around arbitrary political boundaries, bioregionalism suggests we should align with natural boundaries—watersheds, mountain ranges, climate zones, ecosystems. This approach acknowledges that consciousness is shaped by place and that sustainable cultures must be adapted to their specific bioregions.

A bioregion is defined by natural rather than political features. The Cascade bioregion stretches from Northern California through Oregon and Washington into British Columbia, unified by the volcanic Cascade Range, temperate rainforest, and salmon runs. The Great Lakes bioregion encompasses the watershed of the five lakes, regardless of the international border bisecting it. The Sonoran Desert bioregion includes parts of California, Arizona, New Mexico, and Mexico, sharing unique ecology adapted to extreme conditions.

Living bioregionally means becoming native to a place through attention, knowledge, and commitment. This involves learning the names and behaviors of local plants and animals, understanding seasonal patterns, knowing where water comes from and where waste goes. It means eating locally grown food, using regional materials, and developing culture that reflects and celebrates specific places rather than generic globalized culture.

Reinhabitation, a key bioregional concept, involves consciously relearning how to live in place sustainably. This requires both recovering traditional knowledge of how indigenous peoples lived in the bioregion and developing new practices appropriate to contemporary contexts. Reinhabitation is not romantically returning to the past but creating futures rooted in place-based wisdom.

Watershed consciousness organizes awareness around water flows rather than political boundaries. Everyone in a watershed shares interest in water quality, flood control, and ecosystem health. Watershed councils bring together diverse stakeholders to manage rivers collaboratively. This approach recognizes that upstream and downstream are connected, that what happens to tributaries affects the main stem, that river health determines regional wellbeing.

Food sheds—the geographic areas that feed populations—provide another organizing principle. Knowing where food comes from, who grows it, and how it's produced creates connections between consumers and landscapes. Farmers' markets, community-supported agriculture, and farm-to-table restaurants strengthen foodshed consciousness. Eating seasonally and regionally aligns human nutrition with natural cycles.

Cultural adaptation to bioregions produces distinctive architectures, cuisines, arts, and customs. Adobe construction in the Southwest uses local clay and passive cooling adapted to desert conditions. Pacific Northwest longhouses used cedar's rot-resistance and splitting properties. These vernacular architectures demonstrate intelligence arising from sustained engagement with specific places.

Language evolves bioregionally, developing vocabularies for local phenomena. Inuit languages have multiple words for different types of snow and ice. Hawaiian has dozens of words for rain variations. These linguistic adaptations reflect and reinforce intimate knowledge of place. The loss of indigenous languages means losing encoded ecological knowledge irreplaceable by scientific terminology.

Bioregional mapping reveals different geographies than political maps. Rivers become connectors rather than boundaries. Mountain ranges become organizing features rather than obstacles. Cities are understood in relation to their supporting ecosystems rather than as isolated entities. These maps help us see the natural systems our lives depend upon.

Climate change makes bioregional consciousness urgent. As temperature zones shift, precipitation patterns change, and ecosystems migrate, political boundaries become increasingly meaningless for environmental management. Bioregional cooperation offers frameworks for adaptation that transcend national borders. The Arctic Council, bringing together Arctic nations to address regional issues, provides one model.

Critics argue bioregionalism is impractical in our globalized world, that modern life transcends local boundaries. Yet globalization's failures—economic instability, cultural homogenization, ecological destruction—make relocalization increasingly necessary. Bioregionalism doesn't mean isolation but appropriate scale, meeting needs locally when possible while maintaining beneficial larger connections.

Seasonal Awareness and Natural Rhythms

Disconnection from seasonal cycles characterizes modern life. Climate-controlled buildings maintain constant temperature year-round. Global food systems provide any product any time. Artificial lighting extends days and shortens nights. This severance from natural rhythms contributes to physical and psychological disorders—seasonal affective disorder, circadian disruption, metabolic syndrome. Reconnecting with seasonal patterns restores both individual and collective wellbeing.

Spring embodies emergence, renewal, and creative energy. Sap rises in trees, seeds germinate, animals give birth to their young. This seasonal energy affects human consciousness, inspiring new projects, relationships, and possibilities. Spring cleaning isn't just practical but psychologically necessary, clearing winter's stagnation. Traditional spring festivals—Holi, Easter, Nowruz—celebrate renewal and resurrection. Aligning with spring means initiating, planting seeds both literal and metaphorical, taking advantage of rising energy.

Summer manifests abundance, growth, and celebration. Plants photosynthesize at maximum capacity, fruits ripen, young animals mature. Human consciousness expands outward—socializing increases, outdoor activities peak, creative expression flourishes. Summer solstice, the longest day, marks the height of solar power. Traditional summer festivals celebrate fertility, abundance, and community. Living summer consciously means enjoying abundance, strengthening relationships, and storing energy for darker seasons.

Autumn brings harvest, reflection, and preparation. Trees withdraw chlorophyll, revealing hidden colors. Animals store food and prepare shelters. Human consciousness turns inward, evaluating the year's growth, harvesting what has matured, releasing what no longer serves. Autumn equinox balances day and night before tipping toward darkness. Harvest festivals worldwide express gratitude for abundance while acknowledging coming scarcity. Embracing autumn means completing projects, preserving abundance, and preparing for winter.

Winter demands rest, reflection, and regeneration. Life slows, conserving energy for survival. Seeds lie dormant, gestating future growth. Human consciousness deepens, turning toward dreams, stories, and inner work. Winter solstice, the longest night, marks the return of light. Winter festivals—Christmas, Diwali, Hanukkah—kindle light against darkness. Honoring winter means resting without guilt, engaging inner work, and trusting that spring will return.

These seasonal patterns vary bioregionally. Tropical seasons alternate between wet and dry rather than hot and cold. Desert seasons might include subtle variations invisible to outsiders but crucial for inhabitants. Arctic seasons swing between endless day and endless night. Each bioregion requires its own seasonal calendar and consciousness.

Phenology—the study of seasonal timing in nature—reveals the complex choreography of ecological relationships. Flowers bloom when their pollinators emerge. Birds migrate when food peaks along their routes. Predators birth young when prey is abundant. Climate change disrupts these synchronized relationships, with some species adapting faster than others, breaking ecological partnerships evolved over millennia.

Agricultural seasons once synchronized human activity with natural rhythms. Planting, tending, harvesting, and fallowing created annual cycles that organized community life. Industrial agriculture breaks these patterns, using artificial inputs to force constant production. But small-scale farmers, gardeners, and permaculturists maintain seasonal consciousness, working with rather than against natural timing.

Circadian rhythms, our internal daily cycles, evolved in response to Earth's rotation. Exposure to natural light patterns synchronizes these rhythms, affecting hormone production, metabolism, and cognitive function. Artificial lighting, especially blue light from screens, disrupts circadian rhythms, contributing to insomnia, depression, and metabolic disorders. Maintaining natural light exposure and darkness supports physical and mental health.

Lunar rhythms influence tides, animal behavior, and potentially human consciousness. Many traditions time activities by moon phases—planting by the new moon, harvesting by the full moon, beginning projects as the moon waxes, releasing habits as it wanes. While science hasn't fully validated lunar effects on human behavior, the consistency of traditional practices suggests genuine influence.

Thin Places and Power Spots

Celtic tradition speaks of "thin places" where the veil between worlds becomes permeable, where the sacred penetrates the ordinary more readily. These might be misty islands, ancient forests, or windswept cliffs—places where one senses presence beyond the physical. Every culture recognizes such locations, though they use different names and explanations. Understanding thin places requires expanding our conception of space beyond three dimensions and five senses.

Thin places often share certain characteristics. They frequently occupy boundaries—shorelines where land meets water, mountain peaks where earth meets sky, caves where surface meets depth. Boundaries are transition zones where different states of being interact, creating openings for consciousness to shift. Dawn and dusk, temporal boundaries between day and night, are thin times when thin places become thinner.

Water features prominently in thin places. Islands surrounded by water—Iona, Lindisfarne, Mont Saint-Michel—have long attracted mystics and monastics. Waterfalls, where water transforms from liquid to mist, create negative ions that affect consciousness. Springs emerging from earth carry minerals and energies from hidden depths. Water's fluidity and responsiveness might make it particularly conducive to consciousness transmission.

Atmospheric conditions contribute to thinness. Mist and fog soften boundaries, making the familiar mysterious. Unusual light—the aurora borealis, sun rays through clouds, twilight's blue hour—shifts perception. Storms with their electrical discharge and pressure changes alter consciousness. These conditions might affect neurology directly or might indicate times when veils naturally thin.

Some thin places result from human activity accumulating over time. Centuries of prayer, meditation, and ceremony might imprint locations with sacred presence. The Western Wall in Jerusalem, Varanasi's ghats, Mecca's Kaaba—these sites have received focused human consciousness for millennia. Whether through morphic fields, quantum effects, or psychological conditioning, repeated sacred activity seems to make places thinner.

Personal thin places vary among individuals. A childhood tree that provided refuge, a beach where profound realization occurred, a mountain where grief transformed into acceptance—these become personal portals to expanded consciousness. The thinness might be purely subjective, but the effects are real. Returning to personal thin places can reliably shift consciousness, providing accessible sacred space.

Creating thin places intentionally is possible through design, dedication, and practice. Japanese gardens use carefully arranged stones, water, and plants to evoke contemplative consciousness. Labyrinths create thin places through sacred geometry and meditative walking. Home altars become thin through daily practice and focused intention. These created thin places demonstrate that sacredness isn't only discovered but can be cultivated.

Power spots, related to but distinct from thin places, are locations of concentrated energy that can be felt physically. Practitioners of qi gong, yoga, and other energy arts often identify spots where practice is enhanced. These might correspond to geological features, underground water, or electromagnetic anomalies. Sedona's vortexes, claimed to be centers of spiraling energy, attract millions seeking healing and transformation.

Scientific investigation of power spots yields intriguing results. Many show measurable electromagnetic anomalies, unusual mineral concentrations, or natural radioactivity. The question is whether these physical properties directly affect consciousness or whether they indicate something more fundamental about these locations. Research on sacred sites worldwide reveals statistical clustering of unusual physical properties.

Urban thin places and power spots exist but require different sensitivity to recognize. A quiet garden amid city chaos, a bench where countless people have contemplated, a bridge where lives have transformed—cities develop their own sacred geographies. Street art might mark urban thin places, graffiti serving as contemporary petroglyphs indicating where consciousness shifts.

Urban Animism and City Spirits

Cities, despite their apparent artificiality, develop their own forms of consciousness and sacred geography. Urban animism recognizes that cities are not dead concrete but living ecosystems with their own spirits, rhythms, and relationships. As more than half of humanity now lives in cities, developing urban animistic practice becomes essential for maintaining connection with the living world.

Cities have distinctive personalities that persist across generations. Paris remains romantic, New York ambitious, Kyoto contemplative, New Orleans musical. These characteristics transcend individual inhabitants or buildings, suggesting cities develop collective consciousness through the accumulated experiences, intentions, and activities of millions. The city becomes more than the sum of its parts, a genuine entity with its own awareness.

Urban ecosystems demonstrate remarkable adaptation and resilience. Peregrine falcons nest on skyscrapers, hunting pigeons through urban canyons. Coyotes colonize Los Angeles, using storm drains as highways. Trees grow through concrete, breaking apart human structures to reclaim space. These urban wild ones remind us that nature doesn't end at city limits but transforms and adapts to urban conditions.

Buildings develop presence through the lives lived within them. Old houses are known to have personalities—welcoming or forbidding, peaceful or restless. Theaters accumulate the energy of countless performances. Churches and temples concentrate centuries of prayer. Even office buildings and shopping centers develop characteristic atmospheres. Sensitive people can feel these accumulated presences, the patina of consciousness that coats lived-in spaces.

Streets and neighborhoods function as urban organs with specific functions and energies. Financial districts pulse with aggressive competition during weekdays, emptying at night. Art districts vibrate with creative chaos. Residential neighborhoods maintain domestic rhythms. These differentiated zones create urban anatomy, each serving different aspects of city consciousness.

Parks provide crucial breathing spaces where urban dwellers reconnect with seasonal cycles and other-than-human life. Central Park in New York, Golden Gate Park in San Francisco, Hyde Park in London—these green spaces aren't just amenities but essential organs of urban consciousness. They provide habitat for wildlife, temperature regulation, air purification, and psychological restoration.

Urban waterways—rivers, harbors, canals—maintain flow through otherwise static cities. Many cities originated at river crossings or harbors, making water their founding element. Though often polluted and channelized, urban waters retain power. The Thames flowing through London, the Seine through Paris, the Ganges through Varanasi carry both physical and spiritual currents through urban hearts.

Transportation systems function as urban circulatory systems, moving people, goods, and energy through the city body. Subway systems create underground geographies with their own atmospheres and rhythms. Highways pulse with commuter tides. Bicycle networks create alternative circulations. Understanding cities as bodies with circulatory systems reveals dysfunctions—traffic congestion as arterial blockage, inadequate public transit as poor circulation.

Urban gardens and farms represent growing recognition that cities can produce as well as consume. Rooftop gardens, community plots, guerrilla gardening, vertical farms—these initiatives weave productivity back into urban fabric. They also provide opportunities for urban dwellers to develop relationships with soil, plants, and food cycles without leaving the city.

Digital infrastructure adds new dimensions to urban consciousness. WiFi networks, cell towers, and smart city sensors create invisible geographies of connection and surveillance. Social media generates virtual neighborhoods that may be stronger than physical ones. Augmented reality overlays digital information on physical space. Cities become hybrid physical-digital entities with multiple layers of consciousness.

Sacred activism in cities takes unique forms. Urban environmentalists work to daylight buried streams, create wildlife corridors, and establish dark sky zones. Community organizers reclaim vacant lots for gardens and gathering spaces. Artists create interventions that reveal hidden urban nature or imagine alternative futures. These efforts recognize cities as living systems deserving care and capable of transformation.

The Concept of Homeland

Homeland represents more than geographic origin or political nationality—it embodies the deep relationship between people and place that shapes identity, consciousness, and purpose. Understanding homeland through animistic perception reveals why displacement and exile cause such profound suffering and why defending homeland motivates such fierce dedication.

Indigenous concepts of homeland transcend Western notions of territory or property. Aboriginal Australians speak of "country" as the land that owns them rather than land they own. This country includes not just physical features but songlines, dreamings, and ancestral presences. Separation from country causes spiritual sickness that no amount of material comfort can cure.

Homeland forms people as much as people form homeland. Bodies are literally built from local water, soil, and air. Consciousness is shaped by the homeland's rhythms, seasons, and spirits. Languages evolve to describe homeland's specific features. Stories encode the homeland's wisdom. In this sense, people are the homeland's expression of itself, its way of knowing itself.

Diaspora communities maintain homeland consciousness across generations and continents. Jews praying toward Jerusalem, Irish Americans singing of counties they've never seen, African descendants seeking roots severed by slavery—these demonstrate homeland's persistence in consciousness despite physical separation. Homeland becomes portable through story, song, food, and ceremony.

Ecological destruction of the homeland causes trauma beyond economic loss. When mountaintop removal destroys Appalachian hollows, when dams flood indigenous territories, when development paves over ancestral grounds, people lose not just resources but relationships, not just property but identity. This trauma often manifests as depression, addiction, and social breakdown.

Climate refugees face the particular anguish of losing homeland to rising seas, expanding deserts, or extreme weather. Pacific islanders watching their nations disappear beneath waves lose not just land but cosmos—their navigation traditions, their ancestral grounds, their identity as ocean peoples. No resettlement compensation can replace what is lost when the homeland becomes uninhabitable.

Creating new homeland relationships is possible but requires time, attention, and commitment. Immigrant communities gradually develop relationships with new lands while maintaining connections to origins. This hybrid homeland consciousness enriches both places. Gardens growing homeland plants in new soil, festivals celebrating homeland traditions in new contexts, children speaking homeland languages with new accents—these represent homeland consciousness adapting and evolving.

Bioregional identity offers an alternative to nationalist homeland concepts. Rather than defining homeland by political boundaries, bioregionalism grounds identity in natural systems. This allows multiple peoples to share homeland based on common relationship with place rather than ethnic or national origin. The Salmon Nation of the Pacific Northwest includes indigenous tribes, settlers, and recent immigrants united by relationship with salmon and their watersheds.

Palestinian attachment to olive trees, Japanese reverence for cherry blossoms, Russian love of birch forests—these relationships between peoples and particular species demonstrate how homeland consciousness focuses through specific beings. These species become symbols, but more than symbols—actual relatives whose wellbeing intertwines with human flourishing.

Restoration of homeland relationships requires both physical and spiritual healing. Land Back movements seek return of indigenous territories not just as property transfer but as relationship restoration. Ecological restoration projects heal damaged lands while rebuilding human connections. Language revitalization recovers encoded relationships with homeland. These efforts recognize that homeland healing requires healing relationships between people and place.

Navigating by Sacred Rather Than Secular Coordinates

Indigenous peoples worldwide navigate using systems that integrate physical and spiritual dimensions. These navigation methods don't just locate position in space but maintain relationships with conscious landscapes. Learning from these approaches can help us redevelop sacred relationships with geography.

Aboriginal songlines map Australia through ancestral creation stories. Each landmark along a songline corresponds to verses describing ancestral beings' activities at that location. By singing the land, travelers simultaneously navigate physical terrain and maintain spiritual relationships. The songs must be performed correctly to maintain the land's consciousness and fertility. This navigation system preserves ecological knowledge, spiritual practice, and social law in unified form.

Polynesian wayfinding enabled navigation across thousands of miles of open ocean without instruments. Navigators read wave patterns, cloud formations, bird flights, and star positions. But this wasn't purely mechanical observation—navigators entered into a relationship with ocean consciousness, feeling their way across water. The recent revival of traditional navigation demonstrates that these skills can be recovered.

Micronesian navigators use the concept of etak, where the canoe is considered stationary while islands move past it. This reversal of typical reference frames demonstrates how different consciousness creates different geographies. The navigator maintains awareness of multiple moving reference points—stars, swells, birds—creating dynamic mental maps that update continuously.

Arctic hunters navigate trackless ice and snow through subtle environmental reading—wind patterns, snow formations, animal behaviors. But they also navigate through relationships with helping spirits who guide them home through storms. Losing these spiritual relationships can mean death, regardless of technical skill or equipment.

Pilgrimage routes create sacred geographies that overlay physical landscapes. The Camino de Santiago across Spain, the Char Dham circuit in India, the Shikoku Temple route in Japan—these paths link sacred sites into networks of relationship. Pilgrims don't just travel through space but through consciousness, with each site offering specific teachings or transformations.

Modern GPS navigation, while technically remarkable, diminishes spatial consciousness. Following turn-by-turn directions, we lose awareness of larger geographic patterns. We stop noticing landmarks, reading landscapes, or developing mental maps. This outsourcing of navigation to devices weakens our relationship with place and our capacity for spatial consciousness.

Recovering sacred navigation doesn't mean abandoning helpful technology but supplementing it with conscious relationship. This might involve learning cardinal directions and orienting ourselves regularly. Noticing where the sun and moon rise and set through seasons. Following watersheds from source to sea. Walking boundaries of our bioregions. These practices rebuild spatial consciousness and geographic relationship.

Psychogeography, developed by the Situationists, explores how places affect consciousness and emotion. Dérive—purposeless urban drifting—reveals the city's psychological currents. Mental maps chart emotional rather than physical geographies. These practices, while developed for political and artistic purposes, offer techniques for developing conscious connection with urban landscapes.

Contemporary artists create new forms of sacred geography through land art, sound maps, and augmented reality. These works reveal hidden dimensions of place—historical layers, ecological relationships, spiritual presences. They demonstrate that sacred geography isn't fixed but continuously created through conscious engagement with place.

Conclusion: Living in Sacred Geography

Recognizing time as cyclical and space as conscious transforms our experience of existence. We no longer move through dead space and empty time but participate in living geographies and meaningful temporalities. Every place becomes potentially sacred, every moment potentially eternal. This shift from secular to sacred perception doesn't require belief in supernatural forces but simply recognition of the consciousness pervading existence.

The practical implications are profound. Urban planning that recognizes city spirits creates more livable communities. Architecture that honors sacred geometry and natural patterns produces healthier buildings. Agriculture that follows seasonal rhythms yields more sustainable harvests. Education that includes place-based learning develops rooted rather than rootless citizens.

As we face ecological crises, understanding sacred geography becomes a survival skill. Climate change will force massive migrations, requiring billions to develop new homeland relationships. Cities must transform from consumption centers to productive ecosystems. Agricultural regions must adapt to shifting seasons. These transitions will be traumatic if approached mechanistically but potentially transformative if guided by sacred relationship with place.

The next chapter explores how to develop communication with the more-than-human world, learning languages beyond words that allow genuine dialogue with the conscious cosmos. Building on our understanding of sacred time and space, we will discover practical methods for engaging in conversation with the living Earth.

CHAPTER 8

Language and Communication

A woman sits quietly beside an ancient oak tree in Southern England, her hand resting on its deeply furrowed bark. After an hour of silent presence, she begins to sense something—not words exactly, but impressions, feelings, perhaps memories that aren't her own. Images arise of centuries passing, of children playing in these branches generations ago, of storms weathered and seasons cycled. She doesn't know if she's receiving communication from the tree or projecting her imagination, but something in the quality of these impressions feels distinctly other, carrying the particular patience and rootedness she associates with trees rather than her own restless human consciousness.

Meanwhile, in a laboratory in Italy, Monica Gagliano plays recordings of water flowing through pipes to pea plants, watching as their roots grow toward the sound even when no actual water is present. In the Amazon, a shaman drinks ayahuasca and reports detailed conversations with plant spirits who provide specific information about healing properties he had no previous knowledge of. In the Pacific, a traditional navigator reads the ocean's messages through wave patterns, bird flights, and phosphorescent streaks, finding islands thousands of miles from any mainland.

These varied experiences point toward a reality that mechanistic science struggles to acknowledge: communication with the more-than-human world is not only possible but has been practiced by humans throughout history. This chapter explores the diverse languages through which the living world speaks, the methods by which humans can develop sensitivity to these communications, and the profound implications of recognizing ourselves as participants in a cosmic conversation rather than the sole speakers in a silent universe.

Beyond Human Language: Universal Communication

Human language, with its complex grammar and vast vocabulary, represents only one form of communication in a world filled with diverse languages. Every species, and perhaps every being, communicates through its own medium—chemical signals, electrical impulses, vibrational patterns, behavioral displays, field effects. Understanding these diverse communication systems is the first step toward genuine dialogue with the more-than-human world.

Chemical communication predates all other forms, arising with the first living cells billions of years ago. Bacteria release and detect molecular signals that coordinate colony behavior. Plants emit volatile organic compounds that convey detailed information about their state and environment. Trees communicate through airborne chemicals, warning neighbors of insect attacks and even identifying the specific species of attacker. These chemical languages are precise, with different molecules encoding different messages.

The human body unconsciously participates in chemical communication. Pheromones influence attraction and synchronize menstrual cycles. The smell of fear is real—stress hormones create distinctive odors that others unconsciously detect. We emit chemical signals constantly, broadcasting our emotional and physical states to those capable of reading them. Our conscious mind may be oblivious, but our mammalian body continues its ancient chemical conversations.

Vibrational communication operates through substrates—ground, water, air, wood. Elephants communicate through seismic vibrations that travel miles through the earth, their massive feet both transmitting and receiving these underground messages. Spiders detect prey through web vibrations, distinguishing between wind, rain, and struggling insects through subtle frequency differences. Trees may communicate through acoustic emissions, producing ultrasonic clicks that could carry information through forest networks.

Recent discoveries in plant bioacoustics suggest a hidden sound world we're only beginning to perceive. Plants produce ultrasonic clicks when stressed by drought. Roots make clicking sounds as they grow, possibly echolocating through soil. Some flowers may produce sounds that attract pollinators. The forest may be filled with ultrasonic conversations we've never heard, requiring only the right technology or sensitivity to perceive.

Electromagnetic communication extends beyond visible light to frequencies humans can't naturally perceive. Bees see ultraviolet patterns on flowers invisible to us—landing strips guiding them to nectar. Many animals detect magnetic fields, using them for navigation and possibly communication. Sharks sense the bioelectric fields of hidden prey. Even plants may communicate through electromagnetic emissions, with root tips generating electrical fields that could carry information.

Bioluminescence creates light-based languages in the ocean's depths and summer nights. Fireflies flash in species-specific patterns to attract mates. Deep-sea creatures use light displays for communication in the permanent darkness. Certain mushrooms glow to attract spore-dispersing insects. These living lights carry messages we can see but rarely understand.

Quantum entanglement might enable instantaneous communication across any distance. While controversial, some researchers propose that biological systems maintain quantum coherence, allowing non-local communication. This could explain phenomena like the simultaneous flowering of bamboo across continents, the coordinated emergence of cicadas, or the mysterious synchronization of separated organisms.

Movement and gesture create visible languages throughout nature. The honeybee's waggle dance encodes precise information about food sources' distance and direction. Birds perform elaborate courtship displays that communicate fitness and intention. Wolf body language conveys complex social information about dominance, submission, and emotional state. Even plants exhibit movement languages—the way leaves track the sun, flowers open and close, or vines search for support might carry meaning beyond mere mechanical response.

Understanding these diverse communication systems reveals that we're surrounded by conversations in languages we don't speak. Every garden is filled with chemical chatter. Every forest resonates with vibrational messages. Every ocean pulses with electromagnetic signals. The question isn't whether nature communicates but whether we can learn to listen.

Reading Natural Signs and Omens

Throughout history, humans have read messages in natural phenomena—the flight of birds, patterns in clouds, behavior of animals, changes in weather. While modern science dismisses such practices as superstition, pattern recognition remains one of humanity's most powerful cognitive abilities. Learning to read natural signs requires developing sensitivity to the meaningful patterns constantly emerging from the interplay of consciousness and cosmos.

Animal behavior often provides the clearest natural signs. Animals' superior senses allow them to detect changes humans miss. Dogs sensing earthquakes before they occur, birds evacuating before tsunamis, cattle lying down before rain—these behaviors reflect real perception of environmental changes. Traditional peoples learned to read these signs as survival information.

Bird language, as tracker and naturalist Jon Young teaches, provides a sophisticated information system about landscape happenings. Different bird calls indicate different situations—feeding contentment, territorial declaration, aerial predator alarm, ground predator warning. Learning bird language allows humans to perceive disturbances and movements throughout the environment. A sudden silence might indicate a stalking cat. A progression of alarm calls might track a hawk's flight path.

Weather signs encode approaching changes in atmospheric pressure, humidity, and electrical charge. "Red sky at night, sailor's delight; red sky in morning, sailors take warning" reflects real meteorological patterns. Rings around the moon indicate ice crystals in high clouds that often precede storms. The behavior of smoke from fires, the feel of wind on skin, the appearance of certain clouds—all provide information about coming weather.

Plant behaviors signal environmental conditions and changes. Flowers closing might indicate approaching rain. Leaves turning their undersides up might signal storms. The early blooming of certain plants might indicate seasonal shifts. Traditional farmers planted and harvested by plant indicators rather than calendar dates, aligning agricultural activities with actual rather than theoretical conditions.

Synchronicities—meaningful coincidences—might represent communication from the larger consciousness in which we're embedded. The appearance of particular animals during significant life moments, unusual natural phenomena coinciding with important decisions, repeated encounters with specific numbers or patterns—these might be dismissed as projection or confirmation bias, but they might also represent genuine communication through the medium of meaning rather than mechanism.

Dreams have always been recognized as channels for communication with more-than-human consciousness. Animals appearing in dreams might represent actual communications from those species or from the aspects of consciousness they embody. Landscape features in dreams might convey messages from places. Indigenous traditions often distinguish ordinary dreams from "big dreams" that carry teachings or warnings from the larger world.

Divination systems based on natural phenomena—reading tea leaves, casting bones, interpreting cloud formations—might work not through supernatural intervention but through amplifying subtle pattern recognition. The random fall of objects or formation of patterns might allow unconscious perception to surface into consciousness. The divination tool becomes a translation device between different forms of awareness.

Body sensations can convey environmental information below the conscious threshold. The feeling of being watched often proves accurate. Sudden chills, unexplained anxiety, or mysterious attraction to particular directions might reflect perception of electromagnetic fields, infrasound, or other environmental factors. Traditional peoples cultivated this somatic awareness as a navigation and danger-detection system.

Learning to read natural signs requires patient observation, pattern recognition, and correlation between signs and outcomes. It means noticing what happens after particular bird calls, how weather changes following certain cloud formations, what animal appearances coincide with life events. Over time, a personal library of signs develops, allowing increasingly accurate interpretation.

The danger lies in over-interpretation, seeing signs everywhere, becoming paralyzed by constant analysis. The key is maintaining what Zen calls "beginner's mind"—open awareness without grasping for meaning. Signs arise naturally from this receptive state rather than being forced through anxious searching.

Dream Communication and Vision Work

Dreams provide one of the most accessible channels for communication with more-than-human consciousness. Freed from waking consciousness's filters and controls, the dreaming mind can receive communications that would otherwise be blocked or dismissed. Indigenous traditions worldwide recognize certain dreams as genuine encounters with other-than-human beings rather than mere psychological phenomena.

Dream incubation, practiced in ancient Greece and continuing in various forms today, involves requesting dreams on specific topics or from specific sources. Sleeping in sacred sites, particularly those associated with healing or prophecy, was believed to facilitate divine or natural communication. Contemporary practitioners report that sleeping outdoors, especially in places of power, produces dreams of unusual vividness and significance.

Plant teachers communicate through dreams in many shamanic traditions. The dieta practice in Amazonian shamanism involves isolation and dietary restrictions while developing relationships with specific plant teachers. Dreams during dietas often provide detailed information about plants' medicinal properties, preparation methods, and associated songs or icaros. Skeptics dismiss this as accessing unconscious knowledge, but practitioners report receiving specific, verifiable information they had no prior access to.

Animal dreams carry particular significance across cultures. A dream animal might be a spirit guide, a messenger, or the actual consciousness of that species reaching out. The quality of the encounter—whether the animal is threatening, helpful, or neutral—provides information about the relationship and message. Repeated dreams of particular animals often indicate a calling to develop a relationship with that species.

Landscape dreams—dreams of specific places—might represent actual communication from place consciousness. Indigenous Australians speak of country calling people through dreams, especially when the land needs attention or when someone has been away too long. People report dreams of places they've never visited, later recognizing them in waking life. These precognitive place dreams suggest consciousness isn't bound by linear time or physical presence.

Lucid dreaming, where the dreamer becomes aware they're dreaming while remaining asleep, offers opportunities for conscious communication with dream beings. Lucid dreamers report conversations with dream characters who provide information, teachings, or experiences beyond the dreamer's normal capacity. Whether these represent aspects of the dreamer's psyche or genuine others remains an open question.

Vision quests, involving isolation, fasting, and often sleep deprivation, induce states where the boundary between waking and dreaming dissolves. Visions received during quests are understood not as hallucinations but as communications from the more-than-human world. The vision might come through an animal encounter, weather phenomena, or internal imagery, but its significance lies not in its form but in its transformative power.

Hypnagogic and hypnopompic states—the transitions between waking and sleeping—are particularly conducive to communication. In these liminal states, the conscious mind's censorship relaxes while awareness remains. Many artists and scientists report receiving creative insights or solutions during these transitions. These might represent moments when human consciousness naturally synchronizes with larger fields of awareness.

Interpreting dreams requires different skills than analyzing waking experiences. Dream logic operates through association, emotion, and symbol rather than linear causation. A dream's meaning might lie not in its literal content but in its feeling tone, its images' associations, or its relationship to the dreamer's life situation. Traditional dream interpretation considers not just personal but collective and natural symbolism.

Developing dream communication requires regular practice and attention. Keeping a dream journal, setting intentions before sleep, creating ritual containers for significant dreams, sharing dreams with others—these practices strengthen dream recall and sensitivity. Over time, the distinction between ordinary dreams and communication dreams becomes clearer.

Ritual and Ceremony as Dialogue

Ritual and ceremony create structured containers for communication with the more-than-human world. Through repeated actions, focused intention, and symbolic representation, ceremonies establish channels of communication that transcend ordinary consciousness. These aren't empty traditions but technologies for engaging with the conscious cosmos.

The elements of effective ceremony—preparation, invocation, offering, communion, and closing—create a complete communication cycle. Preparation involves both practical arrangements and consciousness shifting, moving from ordinary to sacred awareness. Invocation calls upon specific consciousnesses, whether ancestors, nature spirits, or elemental forces. Offerings demonstrate reciprocity and respect. Communion represents the actual communication or energy exchange. Closing ensures clean separation and integration.

Indigenous ceremonies often involve elaborate protocols developed over generations. These protocols aren't arbitrary but represent accumulated wisdom about how to safely and effectively communicate with powerful consciousnesses. The specific songs, dances, costumes, and timings all serve to establish and maintain communication channels while protecting participants from overwhelming or dangerous contacts.

Seasonal ceremonies align human consciousness with natural cycles, facilitating communication with the forces governing those cycles. Spring planting ceremonies don't just mark agricultural timing but establish relationships with soil consciousness, seed spirits, and weather patterns. Harvest ceremonies don't just celebrate abundance but maintain reciprocal relationships with the beings that provided it.

Fire ceremonies appear across cultures as means of transformation and communication. Fire transforms material offerings into smoke that rises to sky realms. The Vedic tradition elaborates this into complex fire sacrifices (yajnas) that maintain cosmic order. Native American pipe ceremonies use smoke to carry prayers. Even simple campfire gatherings can become ceremonies when approached with intention.

Water ceremonies recognize water's consciousness and its role as medium for communication. Offerings to springs, rivers, and oceans appear worldwide. Water blessing ceremonies, whether elaborate like those at Bali's water temples or simple like tossing coins in fountains, acknowledge water as a conscious participant rather than passive resource.

Sound and rhythm create vibrational fields that facilitate communication. Drumming at specific frequencies induces trance states where communication becomes possible. Singing, especially repetitive chants or mantras, synchronizes consciousness with larger fields. The didgeridoo's drone, singing bowls' resonance, or rattles' sharp percussion all serve to shift consciousness and establish communication frequencies.

Dance embodies communication through movement. Sacred dances often imitate animals or natural phenomena, not as mere representation but as means of entering those consciousnesses. The whirling of Sufi dervishes, the stomping of African tribal dances, the precise movements of Balinese temple dancers—all create somatic channels for communication with more-than-human consciousness.

Plant medicine ceremonies, from ayahuasca rituals to peyote meetings, use psychoactive plants as communication facilitators. These plants are understood not as drugs but as teachers or doorways to expanded consciousness where communication with other dimensions becomes possible. The ceremonial container—with its songs, protections, and intentions—shapes and safeguards these communications.

Contemporary ceremonies need not replicate indigenous forms but should respect underlying principles. A morning coffee ritual can become a ceremony through intention and attention. A walk in nature becomes a ceremony when undertaken with awareness and reciprocity. Garden planting becomes a ceremony when seeds are blessed and soil thanked. These simple ceremonies maintain daily communication with the more-than-human world.

The Role of Shamans and Nature Communicators

Throughout history, certain individuals have specialized in communication between human and more-than-human worlds. Shamans, medicine people, animal communicators, plant whisperers—these intermediaries develop enhanced sensitivity and specific techniques for trans-species communication. Understanding their methods provides insights for developing our own communication abilities.

Shamanic traditions worldwide share common elements despite arising independently. Shamans undergo initiatory experiences—often involving illness, near-death, or psychological crisis—that crack open ordinary consciousness. They develop relationships with helping spirits, usually animals or ancestors, who assist in communication and healing. They master techniques for shifting consciousness—drumming, dancing, plant medicines, breathing practices—that allow travel between worlds.

The shamanic journey, where consciousness travels while the body remains stationary, enables communication with beings not physically present. Journeys might involve traveling to lower worlds (subterranean realms often associated with animals and earth spirits), upper worlds (celestial realms of sky beings and cosmic forces), or middle worlds (the spiritual dimension of physical reality). Each realm has its own inhabitants, languages, and protocols.

Animal communicators, both traditional and contemporary, report telepathic communication with animals involving images, emotions, and sometimes words. This communication often provides information the communicator couldn't have known—the location of pain, past traumas, specific preferences. Skeptics attribute this to cold reading and projection, but the accuracy and specificity of information received suggests genuine communication.

Plant spirit shamans, particularly in Amazon and Africa, develop intimate relationships with specific plant teachers. These relationships involve not just ingesting plants but living with them, singing to them, learning their languages. Master shamans might work with hundreds of plant spirits, each providing specific knowledge and healing abilities. The plants are understood as conscious teachers rather than chemical factories.

Contemporary nature communicators often discover their abilities accidentally. A childhood experience of understanding what an animal was feeling, a moment of profound connection with a tree, an unexpected communication during meditation—these openings can develop into reliable communication channels with practice and training.

Training in nature communication involves several components. Quieting the mind allows subtle communications to be perceived. Developing energetic sensitivity through practices like qi gong or yoga helps detect the subtle fields through which much communication occurs. Learning natural history provides context for understanding communications. Practicing with house plants or pets provides safe, regular opportunities for development.

Validation remains challenging in nature communication. How do we distinguish genuine communication from projection or imagination? Traditional systems use community verification—multiple shamans journey on the same question and compare results. Contemporary practitioners might verify through testable information—asking an animal about a hidden object or undisclosed medical condition. Over time, the quality difference between genuine communication and imagination becomes recognizable.

Ethics in nature communication require careful consideration. Just because we can communicate doesn't mean we should constantly intrude on other beings' consciousness. Respect for privacy, consent for communication, and reciprocity in relationships all apply. The power dynamics—humans often have power to affect other beings' lives dramatically—require responsible use of communication abilities.

The democratization of nature communication represents a significant shift. While traditional societies had specialist shamans, contemporary practice increasingly recognizes that everyone has some capacity for trans-species communication. This isn't replacing traditional shamanism but expanding recognition of human potential for connection with the more-than-human world.

Developing Sensitivity to Non-Human Communication

While some individuals seem naturally gifted in trans-species communication, anyone can develop greater sensitivity to the languages of the more-than-human world. Like learning any language, it requires patience, practice, and immersion. The following practices, drawn from various traditions and contemporary research, can enhance our ability to perceive and interpret non-human communication.

Meditation and mindfulness create the mental quiet necessary to perceive subtle communications. The constant chatter of human thought drowns out the quieter voices of nature. Regular meditation practice, particularly outdoors, develops the capacity to maintain alert receptivity. Walking meditation in nature combines movement with awareness, often facilitating unexpected communications.

Somatic awareness—consciousness of body sensations—provides a channel for communication below verbal threshold. Many people report physical sensations when near certain trees, in particular locations, or around specific animals. These might manifest as warmth, tingling, pressure, or emotional feelings arising without apparent cause. Developing vocabulary for these subtle sensations helps recognize patterns and meanings.

Spending extended time with particular beings develops relationship and communication. Choose a tree, plant, or place to visit regularly. Sit quietly, offering presence without agenda. Over time, familiarity develops. You begin to notice subtle changes, moods, responses. The being may begin to recognize and respond to your presence. This patient relationship-building is essential for deep communication.

Peripheral vision and soft focus allow perception of subtle energies and movements that focused vision misses. Indigenous trackers use wide-angle vision to detect movement and pattern. Energy healers soften their gaze to perceive auras and energy fields. This relaxed, receptive visual state often facilitates unexpected perceptions and communications.

Creative expression can translate non-verbal communications into human-comprehensible forms. Drawing, painting, music, or movement might capture communications that words cannot. Many artists report their work arising from communion with nature rather than personal creativity. The art becomes a translation device between different forms of consciousness.

Technology can extend our sensory range into frequencies we can't naturally perceive. Ultrasonic detectors reveal bat echolocation and plant sounds. Infrared cameras show heat patterns and energy flows. Time-lapse photography reveals plant movement and growth patterns. While technology shouldn't replace direct perception, it can reveal previously hidden dimensions of communication.

Altered states of consciousness, whether induced through breathwork, fasting, sensory deprivation, or plant medicines, can facilitate communication by shifting perception beyond ordinary limitations. These states should be approached with respect and proper guidance, as they can also open one to challenging or overwhelming experiences.

Dream work, as discussed earlier, provides a natural altered state where communication often occurs spontaneously. Setting intentions before sleep, keeping a dream journal, and developing dream recall strengthen this communication channel. Over time, dream beings may become regular teachers and communicators.

Community practice amplifies individual sensitivity. Joining groups focused on nature communication, whether bird language clubs, plant meditation circles, or animal communication classes, provides support, validation, and shared learning. Others' perceptions can confirm or challenge our own, refining our ability to distinguish genuine communication from projection.

Patience and humility are essential. We're attempting to learn languages that operate on different principles than human speech, from beings whose consciousness differs radically from our own. Expecting immediate, clear communication sets us up for disappointment. The communications may be subtle, gradual, and utterly unlike what we expect.

The Challenge of Translation

Even when we successfully receive communications from the more-than-human world, translating them into human language and concepts presents enormous challenges. How do we convey a tree's experience of time, a mountain's sense of presence, or a river's understanding of flow? The translation process necessarily involves interpretation, metaphor, and the risk of distortion.

Synesthesia—the crossing of sensory modalities—often characterizes trans-species communication. A plant's message might arrive as a color, a smell might convey emotion, a sound might carry visual imagery. Our compartmentalized sensory processing struggles to interpret these synthetic communications. Developing comfort with synesthetic perception helps receive communications in their natural form rather than forcing them into familiar categories.

Anthropomorphism—attributing human characteristics to non-humans—presents a constant challenge. When we say a tree is "happy" or a mountain is "angry," are we accurately translating their states or projecting human emotions? The challenge is finding language that conveys genuine qualities without reducing everything to human terms. Perhaps trees experience something like happiness but distinctly tree-ish, mountains something like anger but particularly geological.

Temporal translation challenges arise when communicating with beings operating on different timescales. A message from a mountain might take years to fully receive. A communication from a humming-bird might flash by in milliseconds. Learning to adjust our temporal perception, speeding up or slowing down as needed, helps receive communications in their natural timeframes.

Cultural translation adds another layer of complexity. Indigenous peoples have developed sophisticated vocabularies for trans-species communication over millennia. These languages often contain concepts that don't exist in modern languages. When an Aboriginal elder speaks of "country" or a Lakota medicine person refers to "wakan," the English translations barely capture the full meaning.

Metaphor becomes essential for conveying non-human communications to human audiences. The tree might not literally speak of "children" but the relationship between mature trees and seedlings might best be conveyed through parental metaphors. The river might not actually "sing" but its sound patterns might carry information best described as song.

Verification and validation of translations remain problematic. Unlike human language translation, where bilingual speakers can verify accuracy, trans-species translation lacks easy verification methods. Multiple communicators receiving similar messages provides some validation. Practical information that proves accurate offers another form of verification.

The politics of translation cannot be ignored. Who has the authority to speak for trees, rivers, or mountains? When indigenous peoples say a mountain doesn't want to be mined, while corporations claim to speak for economic necessity, whose translation counts? Power dynamics influence which translations are heard and believed.

Communication Technologies and Practices

Throughout history, humans have developed diverse technologies and practices for enhancing communication with the more-than-human world. From ancient oracle bones to contemporary bioacoustic equipment, these tools and techniques amplify our natural capacities and reveal hidden dimensions of the cosmic conversation.

Augury and ornithomancy—divination through bird observation—represent some of humanity's oldest communication technologies. Roman augurs interpreted the will of gods through bird flight patterns. Chinese oracle bones posed questions answered through crack patterns. These practices recognize that consciousness expresses itself through pattern and synchronicity, readable by those with developed sensitivity.

Musical instruments serve as communication devices across species boundaries. Aboriginal didgeridoos create vibrations that allegedly communicate with ancestral spirits. African drums enable long-distance communication through acoustic codes. Contemporary musicians report dolphins and whales responding to human music, engaging in apparent musical dialogue.

Pendulums and dowsing rods amplify micro-muscular movements that may reflect unconscious perception of electromagnetic fields, water flows, or other environmental information. While the mechanisms remain disputed, the practical effectiveness of dowsing for finding water and minerals suggests genuine environmental communication occurring below conscious awareness.

Scrying—gazing into reflective or translucent surfaces—induces states conducive to receiving communications. Crystal balls, water bowls, mirrors, and flames all serve as focal points that quiet the conscious mind while maintaining receptive awareness. The medium itself may be less important than the state of consciousness it facilitates.

Contemporary technology opens new possibilities for trans-species communication. Computer analysis of whale songs reveals complex grammatical structures suggesting genuine language. Machine learning algorithms decode prairie dog vocalizations into specific predator warnings. Apps translate bird songs into visualizations that reveal patterns invisible to our ears.

Biofeedback devices that measure plant electrical activity allow real-time observation of plant responses to various stimuli. Some artists and musicians have created installations where plants control sound or light through their electrical emissions, creating interspecies collaborative art. While we may not understand the full meaning of these signals, they demonstrate plant responsiveness and potential communication.

Virtual reality and augmented reality technologies might eventually enable us to experience non-human sensory worlds. Imagine seeing magnetic fields like birds, hearing ultrasonic frequencies like dolphins, or experiencing time at tree-speed. While simulation isn't identical to genuine experience, it might help us understand and communicate with beings whose sensory worlds differ radically from ours.

Brain-computer interfaces raise possibilities for direct consciousness-to-consciousness communication, bypassing the limitations of language altogether. If human brains can interface with computers, might they eventually interface with plant neural networks or animal consciousness? The ethical implications are staggering, but the potential for genuine trans-species communication is revolutionary.

The Ethics of Interspecies Communication

As we develop abilities to communicate with the more-than-human world, ethical considerations become paramount. The power to communicate carries responsibilities—for accuracy in translation, respect for privacy, and reciprocity in relationships.

Consent presents the first ethical challenge. Do beings consent to communication simply by responding, or should we establish permission protocols? Many practitioners begin communications by introducing themselves, stating their intentions, and asking permission to proceed. If resistance or withdrawal is sensed, ethical practice requires respecting those boundaries.

Privacy rights extend to non-human beings. Just because we can potentially access a tree's consciousness doesn't mean we should constantly probe its awareness. Animals deserve psychological space free from human intrusion. Even landscapes might need periods without human consciousness engaging them.

Power dynamics in communication require careful consideration. Humans often have power to dramatically affect other beings' lives—cutting down trees, controlling animal movements, altering landscapes. This power imbalance means communications aren't between equals. The human responsibility is to use communication to understand and serve other beings' wellbeing, not just extract information for human benefit.

Accuracy in translation carries ethical weight. When we claim to speak for other beings—saying what the forest wants, what the river says, what the mountain feels—we bear responsibility for accuracy. Misrepresentation, whether intentional or accidental, can lead to decisions that harm the beings we claim to represent.

Cultural appropriation in communication practices requires sensitivity. Indigenous peoples have developed trans-species communication practices over millennia, often suffering persecution for maintaining them. Non-indigenous people adopting these practices without permission, training, or reciprocity perpetuates colonial extraction. Learning from indigenous teachers requires respecting their authority and supporting their communities.

Commercial exploitation of communication abilities raises ethical questions. Should animal communicators charge for their services? Can plant consciousness be commodified into products? When does sharing communication abilities become exploitation? These questions lack easy answers but require constant examination.

The welfare of communicated-with beings must be prioritized. If communication reveals an animal's trauma, a tree's distress, or a landscape's degradation, ethical practice requires responding to these needs rather than just documenting them. Communication creates relationship, and relationship creates responsibility.

Implications for Science and Society

Recognizing communication with the more-than-human world as genuine rather than imaginary would revolutionize science, philosophy, law, and society. The implications cascade through every aspect of human life and understanding.

Scientific research would expand to include communication methodologies alongside observation and experimentation. Researchers might consult with the organisms they study, asking questions directly rather than inferring answers from behavior. This doesn't replace empirical methods but supplements them with additional data sources.

Environmental management would involve negotiation with ecosystems rather than unilateral human decision-making. Forest management plans might incorporate what forests communicate about their needs. River restoration might be guided by rivers' own preferences. This participatory approach could lead to more successful conservation outcomes.

Legal systems would need frameworks for representing non-human communications in decision-making. If a mountain communicates opposition to mining, how is this weighted against economic arguments? Who has standing to translate for non-human beings? These questions are already arising as rights of nature movements advance.

Agriculture could be transformed by genuine communication with crops and soil organisms. Farmers might learn directly from plants about their needs rather than relying solely on external observation. This could reduce chemical inputs while increasing yields and crop health.

Medicine might incorporate communication with the body's consciousness, with pathogens, with healing plants. Rather than attacking disease, we might negotiate with it. Rather than suppressing symptoms, we might listen to their messages. This doesn't replace conventional medicine but adds dimensions of relationship and communication.

Education would include developing communication abilities alongside traditional subjects. Children might learn plant communication in biology class, practice animal languages in outdoor education, develop landscape listening in geography. These skills would be understood as practical abilities rather than mystical fantasies.

Mental health treatment might recognize that some conditions involve sensitivity to non-human communications rather than pathology.

The voices heard by some individuals might include genuine communications from other-than-human beings. This doesn't romanticize mental illness but recognizes that not all unusual perceptions are pathological.

Urban planning would consider the communications of city organisms—trees, birds, waters—in design decisions. Cities might develop communication protocols with their non-human inhabitants, creating truly inclusive urban communities.

The Future of Interspecies Communication

As we stand at the threshold of ecological collapse or transformation, developing communication with the more-than-human world becomes not luxury but necessity. The solutions to our environmental crises might come not from human intelligence alone but from partnership with the greater-than-human intelligence surrounding us.

Imagine a future where children learn trans-species communication as naturally as they learn human language. Where farmers consult with their fields, architects dialogue with building sites, and doctors communicate with the organisms causing disease. Where legal systems include nature's voice, economic systems account for non-human preferences, and political systems represent all inhabitants rather than just human citizens.

This future requires not technological breakthrough but consciousness expansion. The ability to communicate with the more-than-human world lies dormant within us, waiting for cultivation. Every moment of genuine connection with another being, every successful communication across species boundaries, every accurate translation of nature's messages contributes to this emerging capacity.

The next chapter explores how these communication abilities can be practically applied in daily life through specific practices and rituals that maintain our connection with the living world. We will see how simple actions, performed with intention and awareness, can weave us back into the cosmic conversation from which modern life has isolated us.

CHAPTER 9

Daily Practices and Rituals

The alarm clock rings at 6:30 AM, but instead of immediately reaching for her phone, Maria takes three deep breaths and places her feet deliberately on the floor. "Thank you, Earth, for supporting me through another night," she whispers. Moving to the window, she greets the dawn sky and the old maple tree that has witnessed her morning ritual for five years now. Before brewing coffee, she lights a candle on her kitchen altar, where a small bowl of water, a feather found last spring, and a stone from her childhood home create a simple shrine to the elements. The coffee grounds from yesterday have already been added to the compost bin—returning to the earth what came from it. This morning practice takes less than ten minutes, yet it fundamentally shifts her relationship with the day ahead from unconscious consumption to conscious participation.

Such simple practices, woven throughout daily life, form the practical foundation of animistic living. They don't require abandoning modern life for a cave in the wilderness or spending hours in elaborate ceremonies. Instead, they transform ordinary activities—waking, eating, working, traveling, sleeping—into opportunities for recognition, gratitude, and reciprocity with the living world. This chapter explores how to develop a personal practice that maintains animistic consciousness while navigating contemporary life, creating what we might call an urban shamanism or domestic mysticism that honors the sacred in the everyday.

Morning Acknowledgments and Evening Gratitudes

The boundaries of day—dawn and dusk—have always been recognized as powerful transition times when the veils between worlds grow thin. How we enter and exit each day shapes our consciousness and our relationships with the beings who share our world. Developing simple but consistent practices for these threshold moments can fundamentally shift our experience from isolation to connection.

Morning practice begins before the mind fully engages with the day's demands. In the liminal space between sleeping and waking, we're naturally more receptive to subtle communications and sacred presence. This doesn't require waking at 4 AM for two-hour meditation sessions—even five minutes of conscious practice can establish the day's relational foundation.

The first act might be acknowledgment of having survived another night. This sounds dramatic, but recognizing that we've been kept safe through hours of unconsciousness by our body's wisdom, our shelter's protection, and the cosmic forces that maintain life cultivates appropriate humility and gratitude. A simple "thank you for another day of life" acknowledges the gift rather than taking it for granted.

Greeting the directions—east, south, west, north, above, below, and center—connects us to the larger cosmos. This practice, found in traditions worldwide, doesn't require elaborate invocations. Simply facing each direction and acknowledging its qualities suffices. East brings new beginnings and the rising sun. South carries warmth and growth. West holds transformation and the setting sun. North embodies wisdom and rest. Above connects us to sky beings and cosmic forces. Below grounds us in Earth and ancestors. Center recognizes our place in this sacred mandala.

Acknowledging the elements that sustain life—earth, water, fire, air, and space—reminds us of our fundamental dependencies. Touch the ground and thank the earth for support. Drink water mindfully, appreciating its journey from cloud to cup. Light a candle or acknowledge the sun's fire. Breathe consciously, recognizing air as the gift of plants. Notice the space that holds everything, the container for existence.

Morning gratitude can be specific to immediate circumstances. Thank the bed for comfort, the walls for shelter, the electricity for light, the coffee plant for awakening. This isn't empty positive thinking but recognition of the countless beings and forces that support our existence. The cotton in sheets grew in fields tended by farmers. The wood in walls came from trees that grew for decades. The coffee traveled thousands of miles through numerous hands. Acknowledging these connections weaves us into the web of reciprocity.

Evening practice mirrors morning but with different qualities. Where morning opens and activates, evening closes and settles. This is the time to release the day's accumulations, offer gratitude for what was received, and prepare consciousness for the dream realm.

Reviewing the day through an animistic lens means recognizing the beings encountered and relationships maintained or neglected. Which trees did you pass without acknowledgment? What animals crossed your path? How did the weather affect your mood? What foods gave you energy? This isn't judgment but awareness-building, noticing the constant interactions we usually ignore.

Evening gratitude becomes more specific than morning's general acknowledgments. Thank particular beings for particular gifts. The bus that arrived just in time. The rain that watered gardens. The colleague who offered help. The meal that nourished. The sunset that stopped you in your tracks. Specificity strengthens relationship.

Releasing the day's energies prevents accumulation of psychic debris. This might involve washing hands and face while imagining the day's stress flowing away, burning sage or incense to clear the air, or simply stating "I release what no longer serves." The practice creates closure, allowing genuine rest.

Preparing for sleep as a conscious transition rather than collapse acknowledges that we're entering another realm where different rules apply. Setting dream intentions, asking for guidance, or simply requesting peaceful rest recognizes sleep as active participation in cosmic cycles rather than mere unconsciousness.

Seasonal Celebrations and Natural Calendar Living

Modern life's disconnection from seasonal rhythms contributes to our alienation from the living world. Climate-controlled environments and global food systems create an eternal present where January feels much like July except for different holidays on the calendar. Reconnecting with seasonal cycles through celebration and conscious adaptation restores our place in natural time.

The wheel of the year, expressed differently across cultures but sharing essential structure, provides a framework for seasonal practice. Eight major points mark the solar year—two solstices, two equinoxes, and four cross-quarter days between them. These aren't arbitrary human inventions but astronomical realities that affect all life on Earth.

Winter Solstice, the longest night, marks the return of light. This is not metaphorical but literal—from this point, days begin lengthening. Traditional celebrations kindle light against darkness: Yule logs, Hanukkah candles, Christmas lights. Modern practice might involve staying awake through the longest night, tending fire and contemplating the year past while welcoming the returning sun. Or it might be as simple as lighting candles at dinner and acknowledging the turn toward light.

Imbolc or Candlemas, the first cross-quarter day, arrives in early February when spring's first stirrings begin despite winter's continued grip. Snowdrops and crocuses emerge. Sap begins rising in maples. This is time for cleansing and preparation, literally and energetically clearing space for new growth. Traditional spring cleaning isn't arbitrary but aligns with natural energy shifts.

Spring Equinox brings balance between day and night, marking the tipping point toward light and warmth. Seeds planted now, whether literal or metaphorical, have the growing season ahead. This is the time for new projects, relationships, and ventures. Modern practice might involve planting seeds indoors, even if just herbs on a windowsill, participating in Earth's creative surge.

Beltane or May Day celebrates fertility and abundance as spring reaches its peak. Flowers bloom extravagantly. Birds nest frantically. Energy peaks for creativity and connection. Traditional maypole dances weave communities together. Modern celebrations might involve decorating with flowers, dancing, or simply spending the entire day outdoors appreciating spring's climax.

Summer Solstice, the longest day, represents maximum light and power. Traditional midsummer celebrations often lasted all night, honoring the sun at its peak while acknowledging the turn toward darkness that begins immediately after. Modern practice might involve watching sunrise and sunset on the longest day, spending maximum time outdoors, or hosting gatherings that celebrate abundance and community.

Lughnasadh or Lammas in early August marks the first harvest. Grain ripens, early apples redden, the first subtle hints of autumn appear despite summer's heat. This is time for appreciating what has manifested from spring's plantings while recognizing that not all ventures succeed. Modern practice might involve baking bread from scratch, visiting farms or farmers' markets, or taking stock of the year's progress.

Autumn Equinox again brings balance before the tip toward darkness. Harvest accelerates as plants race to complete their cycles before frost. This is time for gratitude, preservation, and preparation. Modern practice might involve preserving food, even just making jam or freezing berries, participating in the ancient rhythm of storing abundance for scarcity.

Samhain or Halloween marks summer's end and winter's beginning. The veil between worlds traditionally thins, allowing communication with ancestors and spirits. The last harvests come in. Plants die back. This is time for honoring the dead, releasing what no longer serves, and preparing for winter's introspection. Modern practice might involve creating ancestor altars, composting garden waste mindfully, or using Halloween's cultural opening to explore death and transformation.

Beyond these major markers, countless smaller seasonal observations maintain connection with natural rhythms. The first robin of spring. The first tomato of summer. The first colored leaf of fall. The first snow of winter. Phenology—observing nature's calendar—reveals that seasons arrive differently each year, teaching attention to actual rather than theoretical conditions.

Creating personal or family traditions around seasonal moments builds connection with place and time. Always hiking the same trail on equinoxes to observe changes. Hosting harvest dinners with local food. Making snow angels in the first snowfall. These traditions accumulate meaning over years, weaving human lives into natural cycles.

Seasonal eating connects our bodies to natural rhythms. Spring's greens cleanse winter's stagnation. Summer's fruits provide cooling hydration. Autumn's roots and squashes offer grounding substance. Winter's preserved foods teach appreciation for abundance and scarcity. Even in cities with year-round global food, choosing seasonal, local options when possible maintains bodily connection to place and time.

Food as Sacred Relationship

Every meal represents multiple deaths becoming life, countless beings sacrificing their forms to sustain ours. Recognizing food as a sacred relationship rather than mere fuel transforms eating from unconscious consumption to conscious communion. This doesn't require becoming vegetarian or spending hours in elaborate food rituals, but simply approaching nourishment with awareness and gratitude.

The journey from soil to plate involves countless beings and processes usually invisible to modern eaters. Seeds germinate in darkness, pushing through soil toward light. Plants photosynthesize sunlight into sugar, performing the alchemy that ultimately feeds all animal life. Insects pollinate flowers. Fungi and bacteria process nutrients. Weather patterns bring rain and sun. Farmers tend and harvest. Transportation workers move food across distances. Grocers display and sell. Cooks transform ingredients into meals. Each step involves conscious beings deserving recognition.

Saying grace takes on new meaning when we recognize we're acknowledging actual beings rather than abstract provision. "Thank you, wheat, for your golden gift. Thank you, farmers, for your careful tending. Thank you, sun and rain, for growth. Thank you, hands that harvested, transported, and prepared." This specificity transforms rote blessing into genuine gratitude.

Conscious eating involves presence with the act of nourishment. Instead of eating while watching screens or driving, we can occasionally eat with full attention. Notice colors, textures, flavors. Chew thoroughly, recognizing that digestion begins in the mouth. Feel the food becoming part of your body. This mindful eating not only improves digestion but maintains awareness of eating as transformation—other beings literally becoming us.

Growing food, even minimally, creates a direct relationship with the beings that feed us. A windowsill herb garden, a balcony tomato plant, a small backyard plot—any food growing connects us to the cycles and challenges of producing nourishment. We learn that food doesn't come from stores but from soil, sun, water, and work. We develop relationships with particular plants, learning their needs and personalities.

Hunting, fishing, and foraging, when done ethically and legally, provide intimate connection with food sources. Taking life directly for food eliminates the comfortable distance modern life maintains between eating and death. It requires confronting the reality that we live by consuming other lives. This direct relationship often increases rather than decreases respect for the beings that feed us.

Preparing food with intention transforms cooking from chore to ceremony. Washing vegetables becomes a cleansing ritual. Chopping becomes meditation. Seasoning becomes a blessing. The kitchen altar—whether elaborate shrine or simple windowsill arrangement—acknowledges the kitchen as a sacred space where the transformation of matter into nourishment occurs.

Composting closes the cycle of reciprocity, returning organic matter to soil. Instead of sending food waste to landfills where it produces methane, composting feeds the organisms that create fertility. Even apartment dwellers can maintain worm bins or bokashi buckets, participating in the ancient cycle of decay and renewal. The compost pile becomes an altar to transformation, where death becomes life.

Sharing food builds community across species boundaries. Feeding birds, leaving water for animals, planting flowers for pollinators—these simple acts maintain reciprocal relationships with the beings sharing our spaces. The backyard becomes not private property but commons where multiple species meet their needs.

Fasting occasionally reminds us that hunger is humanity's historical norm and current reality for millions. Voluntary hunger, undertaken safely, shifts our relationship with food from entitlement to gratitude. It also potentially opens consciousness to communications often obscured by constant digestion.

Water deserves special recognition as the foundation of all life. Blessing water before drinking, acknowledging its journey from ocean to cloud to rain to tap, maintains awareness of our absolute dependence on this conscious element. Some practitioners leave water in moonlight or sunlight, allowing it to absorb celestial energies. Others add flower essences or gems, creating charged waters for specific purposes.

Sacred Technologies and Tool Blessing

Every object in our lives was fashioned from materials taken from the Earth—metals mined from mountains, plastics derived from ancient forests, glass melted from sand. Recognizing the consciousness in our technologies and tools transforms our relationship with the material world from use to partnership.

The concept of sacred technology might seem oxymoronic, but indigenous peoples have always recognized that tools require proper relationship. The hunter's bow, the farmer's hoe, the weaver's loom—these were not dead implements but partners in survival requiring respect, maintenance, and even ceremony. This understanding can extend to modern technologies.

Blessing new objects acknowledges their origins and establishes connection. When acquiring something new—whether phone, car, or kitchen knife—take a moment to recognize its components' sources. The rare earth elements in electronics came from specific mountains. The steel in tools came from iron ore and carbon. The wood in furniture came from trees that grew for years or decades. A simple acknowledgment—"Thank you for taking this form to serve"—establishes relationship rather than ownership.

Naming significant objects strengthens relationship. Cars, computers, musical instruments, even vacuum cleaners can be named, transforming them from anonymous objects to recognized partners. This might seem childish, but it maintains awareness that we're in a relationship with rather than simply using these objects.

Maintenance becomes a spiritual practice when approached consciously. Cleaning, oiling, sharpening, and repairing maintain not just function but relationship. The Japanese concept of caring for objects so they develop souls over time recognizes that consciousness accumulates through attention and use. The hundred-year-old hammer, the grandmother's sewing machine, the well-maintained bicycle—these objects carry presence beyond their material components.

Electronic devices present particular challenges and opportunities for sacred interaction. These complex assemblages of rare elements perform almost magical feats—connecting us instantly across the planet, accessing vast information, creating and sharing art. Yet we often treat them carelessly, constantly upgrading, discarding functional devices for newer models.

Conscious relationship with electronics might involve thanking devices for their service, maintaining them carefully to extend their lives, and recycling responsibly when replacement becomes necessary. Some practitioners create small ceremonies when retiring old devices, acknowledging their service and ensuring their materials return to appropriate cycles.

The workspace, whether office or workshop, can be arranged to support sacred relationship with tools and tasks. A small altar or meaningful objects can shift the energy from purely functional to consciously relational. Plants improve air quality while adding living presence. Stones, shells, or other natural objects remind us of the larger world beyond human construction.

Kitchen tools deserve special recognition as implements of transformation. Knives that cut vegetables, pots that cook meals, ovens that bake bread—these enable the alchemy of cooking. Many traditions prohibit pointing knives at people, recognizing their power to cut more than physical matter. Wooden spoons, seasoned cutting boards, and well-used cast iron carry the memories of countless meals.

Garden tools connect us directly with soil and plants. The shovel that turns earth, the pruners that shape growth, the watering can that delivers life—these become extensions of our bodies in service of life. Cleaning tools after use, storing them properly, and occasionally oiling wooden handles maintains both function and relationship.

Transportation technologies—bicycles, cars, public transit—enable movement through the world. Blessing vehicles for safety, thanking them for service, and maintaining them consciously transforms commuting from deadening routine to opportunity for practice. Even public transit can be approached relationally, recognizing the drivers, the vehicles, and fellow passengers as temporary communities.

House Spirits and Dwelling Consciousness

Every home develops its own presence through the accumulated experiences of its inhabitants. This presence, recognized across cultures as house spirits, dwelling consciousness, or genius loci, affects everyone who enters. Developing a conscious relationship with our dwelling places transforms houses from mere shelter into partners in living.

Traditional cultures worldwide recognize house spirits requiring attention and respect. The Roman Lares, Germanic kobolds, Slavic domovoi, and countless other traditions acknowledge that dwellings have their own consciousness that can be helpful or troublesome depending on the relationship maintained. These aren't superstitions but recognitions that consciousness accumulates in lived spaces.

Moving into a new space requires introduction and negotiation. Before moving belongings in, spend time in the empty space. Introduce yourself to the house. State your intentions for living there. Ask what the space needs. Listen through intuition, body sensations, or simple observation for responses. This might reveal practical needs—repairs, cleaning, painting—or energetic requirements—clearings, blessings, offerings.

Cleansing practices clear accumulated energies from previous inhabitants. Burning sage, palo santo, or incense while moving through each room with intention to clear stagnant energy is practiced worldwide. Sound cleansing using bells, singing bowls, or clapping can break up energetic patterns. Salt in corners absorbs negative energy and can be swept out after a day or two. Opening windows and doors allows fresh energy to flow through.

Blessing practices establish a positive relationship with dwelling consciousness. This might involve formal ceremony or simple intention-setting. Walking through each room stating its intended purpose—"This is a space for rest and dreams," "This is a space for nourishment and gathering"—helps align the space with your needs. Placing meaningful objects, images, or plants in each room anchors positive intentions.

Threshold spaces deserve special attention as boundaries between inside and outside, private and public. Many traditions place protective symbols or objects at doorways—mezuzahs, horseshoes, bells, mirrors. These mark transitions and establish energetic boundaries. A simple practice of pausing at thresholds, taking a breath, and setting intention for what you're entering or leaving maintains consciousness of transitions.

Regular communication with house consciousness maintains active connection. This might be as simple as greeting your home when entering and thanking it when leaving. Notice how different spaces feel at different times. Does the bedroom feel restless? Does the kitchen feel neglected? Responding to these impressions—perhaps rearranging furniture, deep cleaning, or spending more time in neglected spaces—maintains dwelling harmony.

Feeding house spirits appears in many traditions. Leaving small offerings—a bowl of milk, piece of bread, flower, or candle—acknowledges the dwelling's consciousness and maintains reciprocity. These offerings might be placed on a house altar or in a special corner. What matters is regularity and intention rather than elaborateness.

Seasonal decorations align dwelling consciousness with natural cycles. Bringing seasonal flowers, branches, or fruits inside connects indoor and outdoor spaces. Changing curtains, pillows, or artwork seasonally prevents energetic stagnation. These practices aren't just aesthetic but energetic, helping the dwelling breathe with natural rhythms.

Repair and maintenance become spiritual practices when approached as caring for dwelling consciousness. That dripping faucet isn't just wasting water but creating energetic irritation. The cluttered closet isn't just messy but blocking energy flow. Approaching home maintenance as relationship tending rather than chore completion transforms necessary tasks into meaningful practice.

Creating sacred spaces within the home provides focal points for practice. This might be an elaborate altar room or a simple shelf with meaningful objects. What matters is having a designated space for practice, however small. Even a window sill with a candle and stone can serve as a shrine, anchoring sacred consciousness in daily life.

Travel Ethics and Place Protocols

Movement through the world, whether daily commuting or distant journeying, involves passing through territories inhabited by countless beings. Developing protocols for conscious travel transforms movement from rushed transition to mindful pilgrimage.

Requesting safe passage acknowledges that we're entering others' territories. Before beginning any journey, a simple request—"May I travel safely through your lands"—recognizes that roads pass through the homes of countless beings. This isn't superstition but awareness that our movement affects others.

Travel offerings maintain reciprocity with the lands we cross. Traditionally, travelers left small offerings at crossroads, bridges, or boundaries. Modern practice might involve picking up litter, offering water to roadside plants, or simply sending gratitude to the lands traversed. These acts acknowledge that travel is a privilege requiring reciprocity.

Greeting new places establishes a proper relationship. Upon arriving somewhere new, take time to introduce yourself to the local consciousness. This might involve walking the boundaries, sitting quietly to sense the energy, or formally announcing your presence and intentions. Tourist destinations especially benefit from conscious greeting, as they're constantly receiving new people without proper introduction.

Asking permission before taking maintains respect. Before photographing sacred sites, picking flowers, or collecting stones, pause to request permission. The response might come as intuition, a feeling of welcome or resistance, or environmental signs. Respecting these communications maintains good relationship even in brief encounters.

Learning local protocols shows respect for place-based consciousness. Different places have different requirements. Some mountains don't want to be climbed. Some waters don't want to be entered. Some forests require specific approaches. Researching and respecting these protocols, whether from indigenous traditions or contemporary land managers, honors local consciousness.

Urban travel can incorporate animistic awareness. Acknowledge the pigeons, sparrows, and urban trees. Notice where water flows even in concrete channels. Recognize that cities are ecosystems with their own consciousness deserving respect. A rushed commute becomes more bearable when transformed into practice of noticing and acknowledging the beings encountered.

Returning home consciously completes the travel cycle. Thank the beings who provided safe passage. Share stories or photos that honor the places visited. Process the experiences through journaling, art, or conversation. This integration prevents travel from becoming mere consumption of experiences.

Carbon consciousness acknowledges that modern travel, especially flying, significantly impacts the atmospheric commons. When travel is necessary, purchasing carbon offsets, though imperfect, demonstrates awareness of impact. Better still is reducing unnecessary travel, choosing lower-impact transportation, and staying longer in fewer places to develop deeper connection.

Virtual travel through technology offers a partial alternative to physical movement. While it can't replace direct experience, virtual exploration can satisfy some curiosity while reducing physical impact. It can also prepare consciousness for eventual physical visits, allowing more intentional and respectful engagement when travel occurs.

Creating Personal Rituals

Ritual creates containers for sacred interaction, marking transitions, maintaining connections, and transforming consciousness. While traditional rituals provide tested frameworks, creating personal rituals allows authentic expression of individual relationship with the living world.

Understanding ritual structure helps create effective personal practices. Most rituals include: preparation (creating sacred space and time), opening (marking the beginning), invocation (calling in energies or beings), action (the ritual's core purpose), integration (processing the experience), thanksgiving (expressing gratitude), and closing (returning to ordinary consciousness). This structure can be elaborate or simple, long or brief, but maintaining the basic arc helps create effective ritual.

Daily rituals might be as simple as morning coffee prepared and consumed with intention. The grinding of beans becomes meditation. The brewing becomes alchemy. The drinking becomes communion. What transforms routine into ritual is consciousness and intention rather than elaborateness.

Weekly rituals create rhythm in the flow of days. Perhaps Friday evening involves cleaning and clearing to release the week's accumulation. Sunday morning might involve extended time in nature. Wednesday might include tending plants or altar spaces. These regular practices create temporal architecture that supports ongoing practice.

Monthly rituals often align with lunar cycles. New moon rituals focus on setting intentions and beginning projects. Full moon rituals emphasize gratitude and celebration. Dark moon rituals involve release and composting what no longer serves. These lunar rhythms provide natural structure for personal practice.

Lifecycle rituals mark personal transitions. Creating rituals for birthdays, anniversaries, or significant life changes helps process transformation consciously. These might involve solitary practice or community celebration but should reflect authentic relationship with the transition rather than empty tradition.

Healing rituals address disruptions in relationship—with self, others, or the more-than-human world. After conflict, loss, or trauma, ritual helps restore balance. This might involve burning written representations of what needs release, planting seeds to represent new growth, or creating art that transforms pain into beauty.

Spontaneous rituals respond to immediate circumstances. Finding a dead bird might prompt an impromptu funeral ceremony. A spectacular sunset might inspire a gratitude ritual. The first snow might call for celebration. These unplanned rituals maintain fluid responsiveness to the sacred presenting itself.

Integrating Practice with Modern Life

The challenge for contemporary practitioners is maintaining animistic consciousness while participating in industrial civilization. This requires creative adaptation, realistic expectations, and compassionate acceptance of imperfection.

Start small and build gradually. Attempting to transform entire lifestyles overnight usually leads to burnout and abandonment. Begin with one simple practice—perhaps greeting the sun each morning or thanking food before meals. Once this becomes habitual, add another practice. Gradual accumulation creates sustainable transformation.

Adapt practices to circumstances. Living situations, work schedules, family obligations, and health conditions all affect what's possible. Urban apartment dwellers can't maintain large gardens but can tend windowsill herbs. Night shift workers can't greet sunrise but can honor sunset. Parents with young children might practice while kids sleep. Disability might require adapting physical practices to different capacities. What matters is maintaining relationship within actual circumstances rather than abandoning practice because ideal conditions don't exist.

Use technology consciously to support practice. Apps can remind us of moon phases or seasonal transitions. Online communities provide support and sharing. Digital altars can be created on devices we carry everywhere. While direct relationship with the physical world is irreplaceable, technology can support rather than hinder practice when used intentionally.

Find or create community support. Practicing alone in a culture that doesn't recognize animistic consciousness is challenging. Online or local communities of practitioners provide encouragement, accountability, and shared learning. Even one practice partner makes an enormous difference in maintaining consistency.

Accept imperfection as part of practice. We will forget to thank our food, ignore the sunrise, waste resources, and cause harm despite best intentions. Perfection isn't the goal—relationship is. The dwelling consciousness understands when we're stressed and neglect offerings. The garden forgives when we forget to water. What matters is returning to practice rather than abandoning it over failures.

Document your practice to observe patterns and development. Journaling, photography, or art can track seasonal observations, record meaningful encounters, and process experiences. Over time, these documents become valuable records of a developing relationship with the living world.

Share practice appropriately. While proselytizing often creates resistance, sharing our experiences when asked can inspire others. Living with obvious joy and connection becomes its own teaching. Children especially benefit from seeing adults in a conscious relationship with the more-than-human world.

The path forward isn't about returning to pre-modern lifestyles but about integrating ancient wisdom with contemporary life. We can honor house spirits while living in apartments, maintain seasonal awareness while working in offices, and practice reciprocity while participating in the global economy. The living world doesn't demand perfection but conscious acknowledgement. Every small practice, every moment of recognition, every gesture of gratitude strengthens the connections that urbanization and industrialization have weakened but not severed.

As we prepare to explore healing and medicine in the next chapter, we carry with us these daily practices that maintain our connection to the living world. Through simple rituals and conscious relationships with the beings surrounding us, we weave ourselves back into the web of existence, discovering that the sacred is not distant but immediately present, waiting only for our recognition and response.

CHAPTER 10

Healing and Medicine

In the mountains of Peru, a curandero sits with a patient who has traveled thousands of miles seeking healing for chronic depression that Western medicine has failed to resolve. The healer doesn't immediately prescribe herbs or perform ceremonies. Instead, he asks about the patient's relationships—not just with family and friends, but with the land where she lives, the work she does, the food she eats, the dreams that visit her sleep. He discovers she has been severed from her ancestral homeland, works in a windowless office, eats processed food without awareness, and has forgotten how to dream. The depression, he explains, is not a chemical imbalance but a spiritual emergency—her soul is starving for connection with the living world.

This understanding of illness as relationship disruption rather than mechanical malfunction characterizes animistic medicine worldwide. When we recognize that we exist within a web of conscious relationships, illness becomes not just personal affliction but ecological disturbance. Healing involves not just fixing broken parts but restoring a right relationship with the community of beings that sustain us. This chapter explores how animistic perspectives on health and healing offer profound insights for addressing the epidemic of chronic illness, mental health crisis, and spiritual malaise that characterizes modern life.

Plant Spirit Medicine and Herbalism

Plants have been humanity's primary medicine for hundreds of thousands of years, and even today, over 80% of the world's population relies primarily on plant medicine. But animistic herbalism differs fundamentally from both pharmaceutical extraction of "active compounds" and even holistic herbalism that treats plants as complex but unconscious chemistry. In animistic understanding, plants are conscious beings with their own intelligence, personality, and healing gifts that extend beyond their molecular components.

The relationship between humans and medicinal plants represents one of our oldest and most profound interspecies collaborations. Plants don't accidentally produce compounds that precisely fit human neurotransmitter receptors or accidentally concentrate minerals that address human deficiencies. This extraordinary biochemical compatibility suggests co-evolution, if not conscious collaboration, between plant and human consciousness over evolutionary time.

Traditional plant medicine practitioners worldwide report that plants taught humans their uses through direct communication. The aboriginal peoples of Australia speak of plants singing their medicine songs to those who listen. Amazonian shamans describe elaborate plant dietas where specific plants reveal their healing properties through dreams and visions. Chinese medicine texts describe ancient sages who could taste a plant and immediately know its properties—not through chemical analysis but through direct perception of the plant's qi or vital essence.

Contemporary research increasingly validates what traditional practitioners have always known—that plants possess intelligence and agency in their healing work. Studies show that plants can recognize individual humans, remember past interactions, and modify their chemical production in response to specific situations. When we understand plants as conscious collaborators rather than passive pharmacies, the healing relationship transforms entirely.

The practice of plant spirit medicine begins with recognition and relationship. Before harvesting or using any plant medicinally, practitioners introduce themselves, explain their need, and request permission. This isn't an empty ritual but practical protocol—plants approached with respect often seem to offer themselves more readily, appearing where needed, growing more vigorously, or even increasing their medicinal potency.

The doctrine of signatures, dismissed by mechanistic science as magical thinking, reveals sophisticated pattern recognition when understood animistically. Plants often signal their healing properties through form, color, habitat, or growth pattern. Willow, which grows in damp conditions that would cause rheumatic conditions in humans, provides salicylic acid for treating those very conditions. Lungwort's spotted leaves resemble lung tissue and indeed supports respiratory health. These aren't coincidences but communications—plants showing us what they can offer.

Flower essences work on even subtler levels than herbal preparations, carrying the energetic signature of plants without any molecular content. Developed by Dr. Edward Bach in the 1930s but building on ancient practices, flower essences address emotional and spiritual imbalances that underlie physical illness. The essences work not through chemistry but through vibrational resonance, the consciousness of the plant meeting and harmonizing disturbances in human consciousness.

The way plants are grown, harvested, and prepared profoundly affects their healing capacity. Plants grown in monocultures with chemical inputs carry different energy than those grown in diverse gardens with conscious tending. Herbs harvested with gratitude and ceremony maintain different potency than those mechanically harvested without acknowledgment. Medicines prepared with intention and prayer carry the preparer's consciousness along with the plant's gifts.

Plant dietas, as practiced in Amazonian traditions, involve extended periods of isolation while developing relationship with specific plant teachers. The dieta isn't just about ingesting the plant but about creating space for deep communication. Dietary restrictions, sexual abstinence, and social isolation all serve to quiet human static and amplify plant communication. Through dreams, visions, bodily sensations, and intuitions, the plant reveals not just its medicinal uses but its personality, its requirements for relationship, and its own perspective on existence.

Even common kitchen herbs and garden plants offer profound medicine when approached with animistic awareness. Chamomile doesn't just contain compounds that reduce inflammation—she (many practitioners find plants communicate with gendered presence) offers calm, maternal comfort to those who approach with respect. Garlic doesn't just kill bacteria—he offers fierce protective energy that strengthens boundaries. Rose doesn't just provide vitamin C—she opens hearts and softens emotional armoring.

The placebo effect, rather than being dismissed as "just psychological," reveals the power of consciousness in healing. When we truly believe in a medicine's power—whether pharmaceutical or plant—our consciousness collaborates with the treatment to enhance healing. Animistic medicine consciously cultivates this collaboration, recognizing that the patient's relationship with the medicine affects its efficacy.

Modern herbalism can integrate animistic awareness without abandoning scientific understanding. Knowing a plant's biochemistry enhances rather than replaces objective understanding. Understanding contraindications and drug interactions ensures safety. But approaching plants as conscious allies rather than chemical factories transforms herbalism from symptom suppression to genuine healing.

Energy Healing and Natural Therapeutics

All healing traditions that recognize consciousness beyond the physical body work with what we might call energy—qi in Chinese medicine, prana in Ayurveda, mana in Polynesian healing, n/um among the San people. This energy isn't metaphorical but represents something real that can be cultivated, directed, and exchanged, even if current scientific instruments can't fully measure it.

The human energy body, described consistently across cultures despite different terminology, extends beyond physical boundaries. The aura, chakras, meridians, nadis—these aren't primitive misunderstandings of anatomy but maps of subtle structures that organize and direct life force. Illness often appears in these subtle bodies before manifesting physically, making energy healing potentially preventive as well as curative.

Traditional Chinese Medicine's understanding of qi flowing through meridians, stagnating in some areas and depleting in others, provides sophisticated frameworks for understanding illness as energetic imbalance. Acupuncture needles don't just stimulate nerve endings but adjust qi flow. Herbs don't just provide chemicals but carry specific qi qualities—ascending, descending, warming, cooling. The practitioner's own qi, cultivated through practices like qigong, becomes part of the healing process.

Reiki, therapeutic touch, and other hands-on healing modalities work with the practitioner as conduit for universal life force. The healer doesn't generate the healing energy but channels it, often experiencing themselves as temporarily hollow bones through which healing flows. This requires the practitioner to maintain their own energetic clarity and connection to source, making personal practice essential for effective healing work.

Sound healing uses vibration to affect consciousness and restore harmony. Every organ, tissue, and cell has its own resonant frequency. Disease can be understood as discord—parts of the body vibrating out of harmony with the whole. Singing bowls, tuning forks, drums, and human voice can restore harmonic coherence. This isn't just relaxation but genuine vibrational medicine, as demonstrated by ultrasound's ability to break up kidney stones or accelerate bone healing.

Crystal healing, often dismissed as new-age fantasy, builds on crystals' documented abilities to store, amplify, and transmit energy. Quartz crystals in watches and computers demonstrate these properties mechanistically. In healing, crystals might amplify the body's own healing frequencies, absorb discordant energies, or provide specific vibrational medicines. The key is approaching crystals as conscious allies rather than magical tools.

Breathwork serves as a bridge between voluntary and involuntary, conscious and unconscious, physical and energetic. Pranayama, holotropic breathing, and other breath practices can dramatically shift consciousness, release stored trauma, and restore energetic flow. The breath carries prana or life force, making conscious breathing a direct way to adjust energy levels and distribution.

Movement therapies like qigong, tai chi, and yoga work simultaneously on physical and energetic levels. These aren't just exercises but moving meditations that cultivate and circulate life force. The specific movements, developed over centuries, open energy channels, strengthen energetic boundaries, and harmonize internal energies with cosmic forces.

Nature itself provides powerful energy healing. Forest bathing doesn't just reduce stress hormones but allows our energy fields to entrain with trees' coherent fields. Ocean waves generate negative ions that affect neurotransmitter production. Mountain air carries different qi than valley air. Conscious exposure to natural energies can restore balance that no amount of indoor intervention achieves.

Sacred sites concentrate healing energies through geological features, accumulated prayer, or cosmic alignments. Pilgrimages to healing springs, mountains, or temples work not through superstition but through genuine encounter with concentrated beneficial energies. Even local parks or backyard gardens can become healing spaces when approached with awareness.

The integration of energy healing with conventional medicine is slowly progressing. Hospitals increasingly offer reiki, acupuncture, and therapeutic touch. Research demonstrates that these modalities can reduce pain, accelerate healing, and improve outcomes. The challenge is maintaining the consciousness-based essence of these practices within mechanistic medical systems.

Emotional and Psychological Benefits

Mental health crises proliferate in industrialized nations despite unprecedented access to psychological services and psychiatric medications. Animistic perspectives suggest this isn't coincidental—severing our connections with the living world creates psychological suffering that no amount of talk therapy or medication can fully address. We are ecological beings, and our psychological health depends on our relationships with the more-than-human world.

Nature deficit disorder, identified by Richard Louv, describes the psychological and developmental problems arising from children's disconnection from nature. Attention deficits, anxiety, depression, and sensory processing issues all correlate with reduced nature exposure. The cure isn't more medication but more time outdoors, developing relationships with other-than-human beings.

Ecopsychology recognizes that human psychology can't be separated from our ecological context. We evolved within diverse ecosystems, our consciousness shaped by relationships with myriad other beings. The sterile, controlled environments of modern life deprive us of essential psychological nutrients—diverse sensory input, circadian rhythm regulation, microbial exposure, and the sense of belonging within larger communities of life.

Depression often signals disconnection from sources of meaning and vitality. While brain chemistry certainly plays a role, the epidemic of depression in industrialized nations suggests environmental factors. When we understand ourselves as isolated individuals competing for resources in a dead universe, despair is a rational response. When we recognize ourselves as participants in a living cosmos, meaning and purpose naturally emerge.

Anxiety frequently reflects accurate perception of unsustainable conditions. The background anxiety pervading modern life might be our organism's appropriate response to living outside our ecological niche. We're not designed for constant artificial light, electromagnetic fields, noise pollution, and information overload. Anxiety might be wisdom, telling us our current conditions are incompatible with our nature.

Trauma, from an animistic perspective, involves soul loss—parts of our consciousness splitting off and becoming lost. Indigenous soul retrieval practices don't just use metaphor but work with actual fragmentation of consciousness that occurs during overwhelming experiences. Healing involves not just processing memories but calling back lost soul parts, often with the help of spirit allies.

Addiction can be understood as misdirected seeking for connection and transcendence. When genuine connection with the living world is unavailable, humans turn to substances and behaviors that provide temporary relief from existential isolation. Indigenous communities with intact animistic worldviews have remarkably low addiction rates. Healing addiction requires not just abstinence but restoration of meaningful relationships.

Grief, particularly disenfranchised grief for ecological loss, needs recognition and processing. We're living through the sixth mass extinction, watching beloved places destroyed, witnessing climate chaos. This ecological grief is real and valid, requiring witnessing and ritual processing. Grief for the more-than-human world isn't separate from personal grief but part of our emotional reality as ecological beings.

Purpose and meaning naturally emerge from recognizing our place in the living world. Instead of having to create meaning in an absurd universe, we discover ourselves already embedded in meaningful relationships and responsibilities. The question shifts from "What is the meaning of life?" to "What is the living world asking of me?"

Community healing happens through shared recognition of our common embeddedness in the living world. Group rituals, community gardens, restoration projects, and other collective engagements with nature create social bonds while healing ecological relationships. We heal together or not at all.

The role of imagination and story in psychological health cannot be underestimated. Animistic worldviews provide rich imaginative landscapes populated with allies, teachers, and relatives. This isn't fantasy but recognition of the actual psychic ecology we inhabit. Developing relationships with power animals, plant allies, and place spirits provides psychological resources for navigating challenges.

Community Healing Through Land Restoration

The health of human communities and the health of land are inseparable. Degraded landscapes produce degraded communities—economically, socially, and spiritually impoverished. Conversely, restoring land heals human communities in ways that no amount of social services can achieve. This isn't metaphorical but practical reality demonstrated by restoration projects worldwide.

Watershed restoration provides a powerful model for community healing. When communities come together to restore streams, remove dams, plant riparian buffers, and improve water quality, they're not just fixing environmental problems but rebuilding social cohesion. Working together on shared land creates bonds that transcend political, economic, and social divisions.

Urban restoration projects transform not just landscapes but communities. Vacant lots become community gardens that provide fresh food, social gathering spaces, and connection to seasonal cycles. Daylit streams that had been buried in pipes become community focal points. Native plant gardens support pollinators while teaching residents about local ecology. These projects demonstrate that healing is possible even in the most degraded environments.

Food forests represent a particularly powerful form of community healing. Unlike community gardens that require individual plots and annual planting, food forests create shared abundance that matures over time. Fruit and nut trees, berry bushes, herbs, and mushrooms provide free food for anyone while creating habitat, sequestering carbon, and building soil. The forest becomes a community teacher, healer, and provider.

Restoration work itself is therapeutic. The physical activity, outdoor exposure, and meaningful purpose all support mental and physical health. Working with soil exposes us to beneficial bacteria that affect neurotransmitter production. Planting seeds and watching them grow restores hope. Removing invasive species and trash provides tangible accomplishment. Seeing degraded land slowly heal mirrors and supports our own healing processes.

Traditional ecological knowledge must guide restoration efforts. Indigenous communities often retain knowledge of what landscapes looked like before degradation and how to restore them. This knowledge extends beyond species lists to understanding relationships, processes, and seasonal patterns. Restoration that honors indigenous knowledge and leadership tends to be more successful and provides opportunity for cultural healing alongside ecological healing.

Children particularly benefit from participating in restoration. They develop relationships with specific places, learn practical skills, and experience themselves as capable of positive change. Children who help restore a stream or plant a forest develop different relationships with those places than those who simply visit them. They become stakeholders in the land's future.

Restoration can address environmental injustice by prioritizing degraded communities that have borne disproportionate environmental burdens. When low-income communities of color lead restoration of their own neighborhoods, they reclaim agency and rebuild environments that support health. This isn't charity but reparation and justice.

The economic benefits of restoration support community healing. Restoration creates jobs that can't be outsourced. Improved environmental quality attracts businesses and residents. Increased property values benefit long-time residents if displacement is prevented through community land ownership. Green infrastructure reduces costs for stormwater management, air conditioning, and healthcare.

Monitoring restoration success requires expanding metrics beyond simple ecological measures. Are community bonds strengthening? Is environmental education improving? Are people spending more time outdoors? Is physical and mental health improving? These social outcomes matter as much as species counts and water quality measures.

Long-term commitment is essential. Land restoration isn't a one-time project but an ongoing relationship. Communities that maintain long-term restoration commitments develop deep knowledge of their places, strong social networks, and resilient cultures. The land and the people heal together over generations.

Sacred Sites as Healing Centers

Throughout history, certain places have been recognized as concentrating healing power. From Lourdes to Epidaurus, from hot springs to mountain peaks, these sites attract those seeking healing that conventional medicine cannot provide. Understanding sacred sites as healing centers—not through superstition but through genuine properties that affect consciousness and biology—opens possibilities for both personal and collective healing.

Geological factors often contribute to sites' healing properties. Many sacred sites sit on geological faults where tectonic pressure creates electromagnetic anomalies. Others feature unusual mineral compositions, underground water flows, or natural radioactivity. These physical properties might directly affect human biology or might indicate something more fundamental about these places' nature.

Water features prominently in healing sites. Sacred springs and wells appear worldwide, their waters attributed with healing properties. While some contain beneficial minerals, others seem ordinary chemically yet produce extraordinary healings. Water's ability to carry and store information, suggested by research into water memory and structure, might explain how sacred waters differ from ordinary water beyond chemical composition.

Mountains and high places provide different healing energies. The reduced oxygen at altitude triggers physiological adaptations. The increased cosmic radiation might affect consciousness. The perspective gained from height shifts psychological states. But beyond these physical factors, mountains seem to concentrate spiritual presence in ways that can catalyze profound healing.

Caves and underground spaces offer another form of healing environment. The complete darkness, silence, stable temperature, and increased negative ions create conditions conducive to altered states. Many healing traditions include cave retreats for vision quests, healing crises, or spiritual regeneration. The Earth's womb becomes a place of death and rebirth.

Trees and forests provide healing through multiple mechanisms. Phytoncides—antimicrobial compounds released by trees—boost immune function. The fractal patterns of branches and leaves reduce stress through engaging our pattern recognition in non-demanding ways. The forest soundscape masks stress-inducing noise while providing beneficial frequencies. But forests also offer something more—a palpable sense of being held by a larger consciousness.

Human activity can enhance or diminish sites' healing properties. Centuries of prayer and ceremony seem to accumulate at sacred sites, creating morphic fields that support healing. Conversely, commercialization, crowding, and disrespect can deplete sites' healing power. The consciousness brought to sites affects their capacity to heal.

Creating new healing sites is possible through conscious intention and practice. Hospitals that incorporate gardens, flowing water, and sacred geometry report better patient outcomes. Homes can become healing sanctuaries through conscious design and regular practice. Even urban spaces can be transformed into healing environments through collective intention and tending.

Pilgrimage to healing sites works through multiple mechanisms. The journey itself—the intention, effort, and sacrifice required—prepares consciousness for healing. The community of fellow pilgrims provides support and witnessing. The arrival at the sacred site represents accomplishment and opening. The return journey integrates the healing received.

Virtual pilgrimage, while not replacing physical journey, can provide access to healing sites' energy. Through video, audio, and even virtual reality, people unable to travel physically can connect with sacred sites. Some report genuine healing through virtual pilgrimage, suggesting that consciousness can connect across distance with healing places.

The commercialization of sacred sites raises ethical concerns. When healing places become tourist destinations, their power can be depleted. Entry fees exclude those without resources. Crowds prevent the quiet contemplation necessary for healing. Protecting sacred sites while allowing access requires careful balance and often indigenous leadership.

Integration with Modern Medicine

The integration of animistic healing approaches with contemporary medicine offers possibilities for more effective, humane, and sustainable healthcare. This isn't about rejecting scientific medicine but about expanding our understanding of health and healing to include dimensions that mechanistic medicine ignores.

Complementary medicine, where animistic and conventional approaches work together, often produces better outcomes than either alone. Cancer patients who combine chemotherapy with acupuncture, meditation, and herbal support often experience fewer side effects and better quality of life. Surgical patients who receive reiki or therapeutic touch often require less pain medication and heal faster.

The World Health Organization's definition of health as "complete physical, mental, and social well-being" aligns more with animistic than mechanistic medicine. Adding spiritual and ecological dimensions would complete the picture. Health isn't just absence of disease but harmonious relationship with self, community, and cosmos.

Preventive medicine benefits enormously from animistic perspectives. Instead of waiting for disease to manifest and then suppressing symptoms, we can maintain health through right consciousness. Regular time in nature, seasonal living, meaningful work, and spiritual practice all prevent illness more effectively than many medical interventions.

Chronic disease, which now accounts for most healthcare costs, often responds better to animistic than conventional approaches. Diabetes, heart disease, autoimmune conditions, and mental illness all involve disrupted relationships—with food, movement, stress, meaning. Medications might manage symptoms, but healing requires addressing root causes in disconnection and disharmony.

The doctor-patient relationship itself needs transformation. Instead of experts fixing passive patients, healthcare could involve collaborative partnerships between healers and those seeking healing. The patient's own healing capacity, supported and guided but not replaced by external intervention, becomes central to the healing process.

Diagnostic approaches could expand beyond tests and imaging to include energetic assessment, emotional exploration, and spiritual inquiry. What relationships are disrupted? What soul parts are lost? What ancestral patterns need healing? These questions complement rather than replace conventional diagnostics.

Treatment plans could incorporate multiple modalities based on individual needs and preferences. Some people respond better to herbs than pharmaceuticals. Others need energy healing more than surgery. Many benefit from combination approaches. Personalized medicine means more than genetic testing—it means recognizing each person's unique constellation of relationships and imbalances.

Medical education needs expansion to include animistic perspectives. Healthcare providers trained only in mechanistic models miss crucial dimensions of illness and healing. Exposure to indigenous healing systems, training in energy medicine, and development of intuitive diagnostic skills would create more effective healers.

Research methodologies must evolve to study consciousness-based healing. Double-blind controlled trials, designed for studying drugs, don't work well for studying prayer, intention, or relationship. New research methods that account for consciousness, meaning, and relationship while maintaining rigor are being developed.

Healthcare economics would shift dramatically with animistic integration. Prevention through relationship and lifestyle costs far less than managing chronic disease. Community healing through land restoration provides multiple benefits beyond individual health. Sacred activism that addresses systemic causes of illness might be the most cost-effective medicine.

The role of death in healthcare needs fundamental reconsideration. Death isn't failure but transformation. Sometimes healing means peaceful death rather than prolonged suffering. Animistic perspectives on death as transition rather than termination could transform end-of-life care, making it more humane and less resource-intensive.

The Future of Healing

As we face unprecedented health challenges—pandemic diseases, antibiotic resistance, chronic illness epidemics, mental health crises—animistic perspectives on healing become not romantic alternatives but practical necessities. The future of healing lies not in choosing between conventional and traditional medicine but in integrating all effective approaches within frameworks that recognize the consciousness pervading existence.

Personalized medicine will expand beyond genomics to include energetic signatures, spiritual typologies, and ecological relationships. Each person's unique healing path will be recognized and supported rather than forcing everyone through standardized protocols.

Community healing will be understood as essential for individual health. Isolated individuals can't maintain health in sick communities on degraded land. Healthcare will necessarily become community care and Earth care.

Technology will serve rather than replace relationship-based healing. Artificial intelligence might help identify patterns in traditional medicine. Virtual reality might enable healing journeys. Biofeedback devices might make energy healing visible. But technology will support rather than substitute for the consciousness-to-consciousness connection that enables genuine healing.

The next chapter explores how animistic perspectives transform our understanding of death, dying, and what lies beyond physical existence. We will see that death, rather than being healing's failure, represents another form of transformation in the endless cycling of consciousness through forms.

CHAPTER 11

Death, Dying, and Transformation

In a small woodland cemetery in Northern California, a family gathers around an unmarked grave. No casket lies beneath the earth—instead, their loved one's body, wrapped only in a simple shroud of organic cotton, rests directly in the soil. Within months, the body will have substantially returned to the earth, feeding the mycorrhizal networks that connect the trees overhead. The family plants native wildflowers on the grave, knowing that next spring, their relative will literally bloom again in new forms. One child asks if grandmother is really gone, and her mother responds: "She's not gone, she's just changed. She's becoming the forest now."

This understanding of death as transformation rather than termination characterizes animistic worldviews globally. When consciousness pervades all existence, death becomes not the cessation of awareness but its movement from one form to another. The atoms that compose our bodies have been countless other beings and will become countless more. The energy that animates us neither appears from nothing at birth nor disappears at death but continues its journey through endless transformations. This chapter explores how recognizing death as part of life's continuous cycling transforms our relationship with mortality, grief, and the profound mystery of what lies beyond physical existence.

Natural Death and Green Burial Practices

The modern funeral industry has created a profound disconnection between humans and the natural processes of death. Embalming fluids prevent decomposition, metal caskets resist breakdown, concrete vaults separate bodies from soil. We've turned death into a battle against nature rather than a return to it. Green burial practices seek to restore death as a natural process, allowing bodies to rejoin the cycles that sustained them in life.

Natural burial involves minimal interference with decomposition. Bodies are not embalmed with toxic chemicals but may be cooled or preserved temporarily with dry ice. They're wrapped in biodegradable shrouds or placed in simple wooden boxes that will decompose along with the body. No concrete vault separates the body from earth. Within a year or two, most of the body has returned to soil, continuing the ancient cycle of life, death, and renewal.

The ecological benefits of natural burial are substantial. Conventional burial in the United States alone uses approximately 30 million board feet of hardwood, 90,000 tons of steel, 1.6 million tons of concrete, and 800,000 gallons of embalming fluid annually—enough to fill an Olympic-sized swimming pool. These materials don't honor the dead but deny death's reality. Natural burial eliminates these resource demands while actively contributing to ecosystem health.

Conservation burial takes green burial further by using death to protect land. Conservation cemeteries preserve land in perpetuity while allowing natural burial. The deceased become literal guardians of the land, their presence preventing development. Ramsey Creek Preserve in South Carolina, one of the first conservation cemeteries, has protected valuable habitat while providing meaningful burial options. Families find comfort knowing their loved ones are protecting forests, prairies, or wetlands in death.

Human composting, recently legalized in several states, accelerates the transformation from body to soil. The process, technically called natural organic reduction, involves placing the body in a vessel with organic materials like wood chips and straw. Over several weeks, microbial activity breaks down the body, producing about a cubic yard of nutrient-rich soil. Families can use this soil to plant trees or gardens, literally allowing their loved ones to bloom again.

Water-based alternatives offer other paths for transformation. Alkaline hydrolysis, sometimes called water cremation, uses water and lye to dissolve the body, leaving only bones that can be processed into powder like cremated remains. The liquid byproduct, rich in nutrients, can be used as fertilizer. Some envision future systems where this nutrient solution could be processed through constructed wetlands, allowing the deceased to nourish ecosystems.

Sky burial, practiced in Tibet and Mongolia, offers bodies to vultures and other scavengers. While not legally possible in most Western countries, the practice demonstrates a profound understanding of death as a gift to other lives. The body that was sustained by eating others now sustains others by being eaten. This completes the reciprocal cycle that animistic worldviews recognize as fundamental to existence.

Ocean burial, when done properly, allows bodies to join marine ecosystems. Bodies must be prepared without embalming and weighted to sink to depths where they won't wash ashore. They become food for deep-sea organisms, their minerals eventually incorporated into shells and corals. For those who feel a deep connection to the ocean in life, this offers a meaningful return.

The choice of burial location matters energetically as well as ecologically. Being buried in one's homeland, near ancestors, or in places of personal significance maintains connections that transcend physical death. Many indigenous traditions specify that people should be buried where they were born, completing the circle from earth to earth. Even when this isn't literally possible, symbolic connections—soil from birthplaces, stones from meaningful locations—can maintain these relationships.

Mushroom burial suits, developed by companies like Coeio, incorporate fungal spores that help decompose the body while neutralizing toxins accumulated during life. The mushrooms transform the body into nutrients that feed forest ecosystems. This represents conscious collaboration with fungi, humanity's ancient partners in decomposition and renewal.

The participation of family and community in preparing bodies for burial restores death as a communal rather than professional process. Washing and dressing the body, building or decorating caskets, digging graves—these acts of care help process grief while maintaining connection with the deceased. Death becomes not something managed by strangers but a final act of love from community to member.

Grief as Ecological Emotion

Grief is not pathology to be cured but a healthy response to loss that maintains our connections across the threshold of death. From an animistic perspective, grief serves ecological functions, keeping us connected to the web of relationships that define our existence. The attempt to eliminate or abbreviate grief reflects the same disconnection from natural cycles that characterizes modern approaches to death.

Ecological grief—mourning for damaged landscapes, extinct species, and climate change—is increasingly recognized as a legitimate and necessary emotional response. When we understand ourselves as part of the living world, the clear-cutting of a beloved forest or the extinction of a species triggers genuine bereavement. This grief isn't separate from personal grief but part of the same emotional ecosystem that maintains our connections to all our relations.

The stages of grief, while not as linear as sometimes presented, reflect the consciousness adjusting to radically altered relationships. Denial protects us from overwhelming reality while we develop capacity to process loss. Anger provides energy for necessary changes. Bargaining explores possibilities for maintaining connection. Depression allows deep processing of what has been lost. Acceptance doesn't mean the relationship ends but that it transforms into new forms.

Grief rituals across cultures provide containers for processing loss while maintaining connection with the deceased. The Jewish practice of sitting shiva creates intensive communal grieving space. Irish wakes celebrate the deceased while acknowledging loss. Mexican Day of the Dead maintains joyful connection with ancestors. These practices recognize that grief requires witnessing, time, and community support.

Complicated grief, where mourning becomes stuck or pathological, often results from insufficient community support or denial of grief's legitimacy. Modern culture's expectation that people should "move on" quickly from loss, return to productivity, and not burden others with sadness creates conditions for complicated grief. Animistic cultures that honor grief as sacred tend to have lower rates of pathological mourning.

Anticipatory grief for coming losses—whether personal death, species extinction, or civilizational collapse—requires recognition and processing. We're living in times of mass extinction and climate chaos, knowing that massive losses are coming. This anticipatory grief is wisdom, preparing us emotionally for transformation. Denying or suppressing it only makes eventual losses more traumatic.

The grief of the land itself deserves recognition. Places mourn their losses—the trees cut down, the waters polluted, the animals driven away. Sensitive people often feel this land grief as personal sadness without recognizing its source. Learning to distinguish personal from environmental grief helps us respond appropriately to both.

Disenfranchised grief—mourning that society doesn't recognize as legitimate—particularly affects those with animistic consciousness. Grief for a beloved tree cut down, a special place developed, or a river dammed may be dismissed by others as excessive or inappropriate. Yet these losses are real and deserve the same recognition as human losses.

Children's grief requires special attention in our death-denying culture. Children naturally understand death as transformation—the dead bird becoming soil, grandma becoming a star. Adult discomfort with death often confuses children more than death itself. Allowing children to participate appropriately in death rituals and express their understanding of death supports healthy development.

Collective grief rituals allow communities to process shared losses together. Climate grief circles, extinction witnessing ceremonies, and land mourning rituals provide containers for emotions that are too large for individuals to hold alone. These collective processes transform potentially paralyzing grief into motivation for action.

Ancestral Wisdom and Continuing Relationships

Death doesn't end relationships but transforms them. Across animistic traditions worldwide, ancestors remain active participants in the world of the living, offering guidance, protection, and wisdom to their descendants. This understanding transforms death from absolute loss to relationship evolution, maintaining connections that transcend physical presence.

Ancestor veneration, practiced by the majority of human cultures throughout history, recognizes that the dead maintain interest in and influence over the living. This isn't primitive superstition but sophisticated understanding of consciousness's continuity beyond physical form. Whether ancestors exist as discrete spirits, merge with larger spiritual currents, or persist as patterns in the collective unconscious, their influence on the living is undeniable.

The biological reality of ancestral presence is written in our genes. We literally carry our ancestors within us—their DNA, their cellular structures, their evolutionary adaptations. Epigenetics reveals that ancestors' experiences affect gene expression in descendants, transmitting trauma and resilience across generations. We are composite beings, colonies of ancestral patterns expressing themselves through our lives.

Psychological inheritance from ancestors extends beyond genetics. Family patterns, cultural traditions, unconscious beliefs, and behavioral tendencies pass through generations. Ancestral trauma can manifest as inexplicable fears, compulsions, or physical symptoms in descendants who never experienced the original wounds. Healing ancestral patterns often requires acknowledging and addressing ancestors' unfinished business.

Dreams provide one of the most common channels for ancestral communication. Across cultures, people report dreams of deceased relatives offering warnings, comfort, or information. These dreams often have distinctive qualities—unusual vividness, emotional intensity, or veridical information the dreamer couldn't have known. Whether understood as actual communication or psychological processing, ancestor dreams deserve attention and respect.

Ancestor altars create focal points for maintaining relationships with the deceased. These need not be elaborate—photographs, mementos, offerings of food or flowers, candles to represent continuing presence. Regular tending of ancestor altars—refreshing offerings, sharing news, requesting guidance—maintains active relationship rather than mere memory.

Genealogical research becomes spiritual practice when approached as relationship building rather than data collection. Learning ancestors' names, stories, struggles, and achievements creates connection across time. Visiting ancestral homelands, graves, or significant sites allows direct encounter with ancestral presence embedded in place.

Healing ancestral trauma can liberate both ancestors and descendants. Many traditions recognize that ancestors who died with unresolved issues—violence, addiction, betrayal—may remain bound to these patterns, influencing descendants. Rituals for healing ancestral wounds, offering forgiveness, or completing unfinished business can free both the living and the dead from destructive patterns.

The ancestors of place—those who lived on the land before us regardless of biological relationship—deserve recognition and respect. In colonized lands, this particularly means acknowledging indigenous ancestors whose relationships with the land were disrupted. Offering respect, learning their names and stories, and supporting their living descendants maintains proper relationship.

Ancestral skills and knowledge can be recovered through intentional practice. Traditional crafts, recipes, songs, and stories carry ancestral wisdom that can be reactivated through practice. Many people report that learning ancestral skills feels like remembering rather than learning, as if the knowledge was already present, waiting for activation.

The concept of mighty dead or elevated ancestors recognizes that some individuals continue influencing the world long after death. These might be biological ancestors, cultural heroes, or spiritual teachers whose wisdom and power remain accessible. Developing relationships with mighty dead can provide powerful support for life challenges.

Seasonal Death and Rebirth Patterns

Nature demonstrates constantly that death is not ending but transformation within larger cycles. Every autumn, deciduous trees withdraw life force from leaves, allowing them to die and fall. Every winter, perennial plants die back to roots, appearing completely dead. Yet every spring, life returns, often more vigorous for the period of dormancy. These seasonal patterns teach profound lessons about the nature of death and renewal.

The plant world's approach to death offers models for conscious dying. Trees don't resist autumn but actively participate, withdrawing chlorophyll to reveal hidden colors, dropping leaves that become soil, entering dormancy that allows survival through winter. This conscious participation in cycles of death and renewal demonstrates wisdom that humans might emulate.

Annual plants compress entire lifetimes into single seasons, demonstrating death as completion rather than failure. They pour everything into seeds—the next generation—then die without resistance. The parent plant becomes compost that nourishes its offspring. This complete giving over to the next generation models generous death that ensures continuity.

Perennial dormancy resembles death so closely that inexperienced gardeners often discard "dead" plants that are merely resting. The energy withdrawn into roots, the cessation of visible activity, the apparent life-lessness—all resemble death. Yet this dormancy is essential for renewed growth. Without winter's rest, perennials exhaust themselves and actually die.

Forest fire ecology demonstrates death as renewal at ecosystem scales. Many forests require periodic fire for health, with some species only releasing seeds after fire. What appears as catastrophic destruction actually maintains forest vitality. The indigenous practice of controlled burning, suppressed for decades, is being recognized as essential forest management.

Salmon runs exemplify death as a gift to entire watersheds. Salmon born in freshwater streams migrate to oceans, accumulating marine nutrients in their bodies. Returning to spawn and die, they carry tons of ocean nutrients inland, fertilizing forests hundreds of miles from the sea. Their death feeds bears, wolves, birds, trees, and eventually, their own offspring. This massive gift of death sustains temperate rainforest ecosystems.

Metamorphosis in insects demonstrates death and rebirth within single lifetimes. The caterpillar entering chrysalis dissolves into undifferentiated soup before reorganizing as a butterfly. This complete dissolution and reformation shows that identity can survive even total physical transformation. The butterfly remembers experiences from its caterpillar stage despite having literally liquefied between forms.

Fungal strategies for surviving adverse conditions include spectacular death and rebirth cycles. Some fungi produce mushrooms—their fruiting bodies—only when stressed, using death as a reproductive strategy. Others can dry out completely, appearing dead for years, then revive with moisture. These masters of decomposition and renewal teach that death and life are not opposites but partners.

Winter itself, long associated with death, is revealed through ecological study as essential for life. Cold stratification breaks seed dormancy. Winter precipitation recharges groundwater. Freezing controls pest populations. Without winter's "death," spring's renewal becomes impossible. Climate change's disruption of winter patterns demonstrates how essential these death phases are for ecosystem health.

Tidal zones demonstrate death and rebirth twice daily as organisms adapted to these margins survive regular exposure and submersion. Barnacles seal themselves against desiccation. Seaweeds collapse then revive. Entire communities appear to die at low tide only to burst into activity when waters return. These edge dwellers master the art of dying and reviving.

Composting and Decomposition as Sacred Acts

Decomposition, the process by which complex organisms break down into simpler components, is not corruption but transformation—the sacred work of returning elements to cycles of renewal. Composting, whether of garden waste or human bodies, becomes spiritual practice when approached with awareness of its role in the endless cycling of matter and energy through forms.

The composers of decomposition—bacteria, fungi, invertebrates—deserve recognition as essential workers in the cycle of existence. Without decomposers, Earth would be buried under miles of undecayed bodies. These beings, often viewed with disgust, perform the sacred work of transformation, liberating elements from old forms so they can assume new ones.

Bacteria, the primary decomposers, exist in staggering diversity and abundance. A teaspoon of soil contains billions of bacteria from thousands of species. Each species specializes in breaking down particular compounds—some digest cellulose, others proteins, others fats. This bacterial community works like a vast recycling facility, dismantling complex molecules into components that can be reused.

Fungi, the great connectors and decomposers, break down the toughest materials in nature. Only fungi can digest lignin, the compound that makes wood woody. Without fungi, forests would be buried under undecayed wood. Through their vast mycelial networks, fungi redistribute nutrients from the dead to the living, maintaining forest health. The mushrooms we see are just fruiting bodies of vast underground networks engaged in sacred decomposition work.

Invertebrate decomposers—worms, beetles, flies, and countless others—accelerate decomposition through physical breakdown and chemical processing. Carrion beetles can locate dead bodies from miles away. Worms process tons of organic matter, producing castings richer than the original material. These creatures, often reviled, are essential partners in transformation.

The stages of decomposition follow predictable patterns that forensic scientists use to determine time of death. But from an animistic perspective, these stages represent the orderly transformation of consciousness from one form to another. Fresh, bloat, active decay, advanced decay, dry remains—each stage liberates different components for reuse by other lives.

Composting as spiritual practice transforms waste into resource, death into life. The compost pile becomes an altar to transformation where offerings of dead plants, food scraps, and other organic matter are transformed into rich humus. Tending compost—monitoring moisture, turning for aeration, observing the progression from recognizable forms to uniform soil—provides direct encounter with decomposition's alchemy.

Hot composting, where thermophilic bacteria raise temperatures high enough to kill pathogens and weed seeds, demonstrates the purifying power of decomposition. The heat generated by bacterial metabolism transforms potentially harmful materials into safe, nutritious soil. This purification through biological fire parallels spiritual concepts of transformation through ordeal.

Vermicomposting—composting with worms—creates particularly rich fertilizer while providing intimate connection with decomposer allies. Red wiggler worms process food scraps into castings that improve soil structure and fertility. Maintaining a worm bin requires attention to the worms' needs—moisture, temperature, pH, food quality. This relationship with decomposers transforms waste management into interspecies collaboration.

Bokashi composting, developed in Japan, uses beneficial microorganisms to ferment organic matter before soil incorporation. This anaerobic process preserves more nutrients than aerobic composting while producing beneficial bacteria that improve soil health. The fermented material, when buried, is rapidly incorporated by soil organisms, demonstrating how death can be managed to maximize benefit to life.

The ethics of composting extend to what we choose to compost and how. Composting organic matter instead of sending it to landfills prevents methane production while returning nutrients to soil. But composting also means accepting that our purchases and consumption will eventually need decomposition. This awareness can guide more conscious consumption.

Legacy Through Ecological Restoration

How we approach our own mortality shapes the legacy we leave. From an animistic perspective, the most meaningful legacy is not monuments or wealth but the health of the relationships and ecosystems we leave behind. Engaging in ecological restoration becomes a form of practical immortality, creating benefits that cascade through generations of humans and other-than-human beings.

Living legacies through tree planting create a presence that can persist for centuries. Every tree planted with intention becomes a living monument that provides oxygen, sequesters carbon, supports wildlife, and beautifies landscapes long after the planter is gone. Some trees planted today will still be standing in five hundred years, affecting countless lives across that span.

Habitat restoration multiplies individual impact through ecological cascade effects. Restoring a wetland doesn't just create one habitat but sets in motion changes that affect entire watersheds. Water quality improves, flooding decreases, biodiversity increases, climate moderates. The restoration work of one person or small group can benefit thousands of species and millions of individuals over time.

Seed saving and plant propagation pass genetic legacies forward. Maintaining heirloom varieties, especially those adapted to local conditions, provides resilience for future food systems. The seeds saved and shared today might feed people centuries from now. This genetic legacy is more valuable than money, which can lose value, or property, which can be destroyed.

Soil building creates a legacy that can last millennia. Building an inch of topsoil naturally takes centuries, but conscious soil building can accelerate this process. The terra preta soils of the Amazon, created by indigenous peoples over a thousand years ago, remain extraordinarily fertile today. Building soil is building future life.

Knowledge transmission ensures continuity of wisdom. Teaching others—especially children—about ecological relationships, traditional skills, and animistic awareness creates ripples that spread through generations. The child taught to recognize bird language might teach their grandchildren, who might teach theirs. Knowledge shared multiplies rather than diminishes.

Land protection through conservation easements, land trusts, or other legal mechanisms ensures that specific places remain undeveloped in perpetuity. This legal legacy prevents future destruction while maintaining habitat and ecosystem services. The land protected today provides refuge for species that might otherwise go extinct.

Restoration of damaged relationships—between humans, between humans and nature, between present and ancestors—creates healing that cascades through time. Healing ancestral trauma prevents its transmission to future generations. Reconciling with estranged family members models forgiveness. Making amends for ecological damage demonstrates responsibility.

Creating or supporting organizations dedicated to ecological restoration provides institutional continuity beyond individual lifetimes. Land trusts, watershed councils, conservation organizations—these entities can maintain restoration work across generations. Supporting them financially or through volunteer work multiplies individual impact.

Cultural contributions that shift consciousness toward animistic awareness create immeasurable legacy. Art that helps people see nature's consciousness, stories that teach ecological wisdom, music that connects listeners to the living world—these cultural works influence countless people across time. A song, story, or image that opens someone to animistic awareness might transform their entire relationship with existence.

The butterfly effect in legacy means small actions can have enormous consequences. The single tree that provides the last refuge for an endangered species. The casual conversation that inspires someone to dedicate their life to conservation. The small donation that allows a crucial land purchase. We can't know which actions will prove most significant, so approaching all actions as potentially legacy-creating maintains appropriate responsibility.

Understanding Death as Transformation

The fear of death that characterizes modern culture stems partly from understanding death as termination rather than transformation. When we recognize that the atoms composing our bodies are billions of years old and will exist for billions more, that the energy animating us is neither created nor destroyed but only changes form, that consciousness might be fundamental rather than emergent, death becomes less terrifying and more comprehensible as another transformation in endless transformations.

The conservation of matter and energy, fundamental laws of physics, mean that nothing is ever truly lost. The carbon in our bodies has been countless other beings—dinosaurs, ancient forests, prehistoric seas. After our deaths, these atoms will become countless other forms—trees, birds, rivers, perhaps eventually other humans. We are temporary aggregations of immortal components.

The water cycling through our bodies connects us to all water on Earth. The water molecules in our tears might have been in oceans, clouds, rivers, or other beings' bodies. After death, this water returns to the hydrological cycle, eventually reaching every part of Earth's water system. We literally become rain, rivers, and oceans.

Consciousness, if it's fundamental rather than emergent, doesn't cease at death but returns to its source or assumes new forms. Just as waves rise from and return to the ocean while the ocean remains, individual consciousness might rise from and return to universal consciousness. This isn't necessarily personal survival but suggests that the awareness looking through our eyes is the same awareness looking through all eyes.

Near-death experiences, reported across cultures with remarkable consistency, suggest consciousness can exist independently of physical bodies. While skeptics offer physiological explanations, the transformative effects of these experiences on those who have them suggest encounters with dimensions of reality that transcend physical existence.

Children who report memories of previous lives, studied most extensively by researchers like Ian Stevenson and Jim Tucker, provide intriguing evidence for consciousness surviving bodily death. While not proving reincarnation, these cases suggest that information, personality patterns, and even physical marks can transfer between lives through mechanisms science doesn't yet understand.

The impact we have on others constitutes a form of immortality. Every interaction changes those we encounter, who change others in endless ripples. The kindness shown to a child might influence how they treat their children, who influence their children, cascading through generations. We live on in the patterns we set in motion.

Cultural contributions provide another form of continuity. Languages, stories, songs, technologies, and wisdom traditions carry the consciousness of their creators forward through time. We still think thoughts first thought thousands of years ago, use technologies developed by long-dead inventors, tell stories first told around ancient fires.

Biological legacy extends beyond direct descendants. The microbiome we share with others, the diseases we develop immunity to and pass on, the genetic variations we contribute to the human gene pool—all provide forms of biological continuity. We are all part of a vast genetic conversation extending from the first life to the last.

The transformation of grief over time demonstrates death's non-finality. Acute grief eventually transforms into bittersweet memory, then into a kind of presence that can be more constant than physical presence was. The dead, incorporated into our consciousness, become part of who we are. They live on not just in memory but in how they've shaped us.

Understanding death as transformation rather than termination doesn't eliminate grief or make death desirable. Loss is real, and sadness appropriate. But it does reframe death from absolute ending to radical change, from failure to completion, from isolation to return. This reframing can reduce death anxiety and allow more conscious engagement with mortality.

Conclusion: Death as Teacher

Death, the great teacher, instructs us in the preciousness of life, the inevitability of change, and the interconnection of all existence. By denying death, modern culture impoverishes life. By accepting death as a natural transformation, we can live more fully, love more freely, and die more peacefully.

The practices explored in this chapter—natural burial, grief rituals, ancestral connection, ecological restoration—are not morbid obsessions but life-affirming recognitions of our place in cycles larger than individual existence. They prepare us not just for dying but for living with awareness of our mortality and our continuity.

As we prepare to explore art, creativity, and expression in the next chapter, we carry with us this understanding of death as transformation. The creative act itself involves death—the blank canvas dies to become painting, silence dies to become music, the undefined dies to become defined. Creation and destruction, life and death, are not opposites but partners in the eternal dance of existence.

CHAPTER 12

Art, Creativity, and Expression

The morning mist clings to the riverbank as ceramic artist Maria Hernandez kneels beside the clay beds she has tended for twenty years. Before taking what she needs, she speaks softly to the earth, explaining her intentions for the vessels she will create. She leaves offerings of cornmeal and water, understanding that her art begins not in the studio but here, in this moment of asking and receiving. When her hands finally sink into the cool clay, she feels the accumulated stories of this place—the floods and droughts, the creatures that have passed through, the minerals that have washed down from distant mountains. This is art-making within an animistic framework: a collaborative dialogue between human creativity and the creative forces that animate all existence.

In our contemporary world, we have largely forgotten that art was never meant to be a solely human endeavor. For the vast majority of human history, creative expression emerged from intimate conversation with the more-than-human world. The cave painters of Lascaux didn't merely depict animals; they entered into shamanic dialogue with animal spirits, their paintings serving as portals between worlds. The Navajo sand painters don't simply arrange colored minerals; they participate in the restoration of cosmic harmony, with each grain of sand carrying the power of the mountain or desert from which it came. The Aboriginal artists of Australia don't just paint landscapes; they sing country into being, their art inseparable from the dreaming tracks that crisscross the continent.

This understanding of creativity as participation in the world's ongoing creation stands in stark contrast to our modern conception of art as individual expression or commodity production. When we recognize that creativity flows through us rather than from us, when we understand ourselves as collaborators with rather than masters over our materials, everything changes. The artist becomes a conduit, a translator, a facilitator of conversations between worlds. The artwork becomes not a static object but a living participant in the web of relationships that constitute reality.

Nature as Co-Creator in Artistic Practice

To embrace nature as co-creator requires a fundamental shift in how we understand agency, authorship, and the creative process itself. It means recognizing that wind, water, decay, growth, and countless other forces are not merely tools or obstacles but active participants with their own creative intelligence. This recognition doesn't diminish human creativity; rather, it situates it within a far grander creative matrix that has been composing symphonies of form and color for billions of years before humans ever picked up a brush or carved a stone.

Consider the work of Andy Goldsworthy, who creates ephemeral sculptures from ice, leaves, stones, and other natural materials, allowing them to change and eventually disappear through natural processes. His art emerges from deep listening to place, working with rather than against natural forces. When he balances stones, he's not imposing his will but finding the conversations already happening between gravity, form, and stillness. When he arranges autumn leaves in spirals that will be scattered by wind, he's participating in the same forces that create galaxies and seashells. His role is neither dominant creator nor passive observer but active participant in an ongoing creative emergence.

This participatory approach appears across cultures and mediums. Japanese potter Shiro Tsujimura leaves his ceramics outside for months, allowing rain, frost, and sun to contribute their own glazes and textures. He refers to this as "collaboration with heaven," recognizing weather patterns as fellow artists. Brazilian artist Frans Krajcberg creates sculptures from burnt tree remnants, not to memorialize destruction but to give voice to the forest's own testimony about fire, regeneration, and resilience. British artist Tim Knowles attaches pens to tree branches, allowing wind and growth to create drawings over days or seasons, revealing the gestures and calligraphy of the trees themselves.

These artists understand something crucial: nature is already engaged in ceaseless artistic production. Every spider's web is a masterpiece of functional sculpture. Every bird's nest represents architectural innovation perfectly adapted to place and purpose. Every pattern of lichen on stone tells a story of collaboration between fungus, algae, and mineral. Every beaver dam reshapes waterways into new compositions of flow and stillness. When human artists recognize this ongoing creativity, they can choose to join the conversation rather than shouting over it.

The implications extend beyond individual practice to challenge our entire cultural framework around creativity. If nature is co-creator, then copyright and ownership become complex questions. Who owns a painting created through dialogue with ravens, when the birds' movements and calls directly influenced the composition? What are the ethics of selling work that emerged from sacred conversation with a specific place? How do we credit the mountain that provided not just the stone but the inspiration for a sculpture?

Indigenous artists have long navigated these questions through protocols and ceremonies that acknowledge the true collaborators in any creative work. Among the Haida of the Pacific Northwest, artists undergo ritual purification before carving cedar, understanding that they're not working with dead wood but engaging with the eternal spirit of cedar itself. The resulting totem poles and masks aren't considered human creations but manifestations of ongoing relationships between human, cedar, and the supernatural beings whose stories are being told. The artist's role is to facilitate these relationships with skill, respect, and attention.

This collaborative understanding also transforms how we approach creative blocks and inspiration. Rather than waiting for the muse to strike or forcing productivity through discipline alone, animistic artists cultivate relationships with sources of inspiration in the living world. They know that walking by the river, sitting with trees, or observing clouds aren't procrastination but essential aspects of the creative process. They understand that sometimes the work needs to compost, just as organic matter must decompose before enriching the soil. They recognize that creative fertility follows cycles and seasons rather than industrial production schedules.

Sacred Arts and Traditional Crafts

Throughout human history, what we now segregate as "art" and "craft" were inseparable from spiritual practice and daily survival. The baskets that held grain also held prayers. The knives that cut meat also cut sacred patterns. The songs that entertained children also maintained the world's balance. This integration wasn't primitive or unsophisticated—it represented a sophisticated understanding that beauty, function, and spirit are not separate categories but facets of a unified reality.

Sacred arts carry forward this understanding, maintaining technologies of relationship that connect human communities with the larger web of life. These aren't merely decorative or symbolic practices but functional technologies for sustaining reciprocal relationships with the living world. When a Huichol artist creates a yarn painting, pressing colored wool into beeswax-covered wood, they're not just depicting peyote visions but creating portals through which the gods can see into our world and through which humans can communicate with divine forces. The intricate patterns aren't arbitrary but follow strict protocols revealed through generations of ceremonial practice.

The creation of sacred art often requires elaborate preparation that acknowledges the spiritual dimensions of both materials and process. Tibetan monks creating sand mandalas undergo purification rituals, consecrate their materials, and maintain specific states of consciousness throughout the work. The sand itself comes from sacred sources, ground from stones that carry the blessings of particular mountains or rivers. The creation becomes a meditation, the completed mandala a temporary dwelling place for deities, and its ritual destruction a teaching about impermanence. Every aspect participates in larger cycles of spiritual practice that integrate individual, community, and cosmic healing.

Traditional crafts maintain similar protocols, though often in less obviously ceremonial forms. A Cherokee basket maker doesn't simply harvest river cane but enters into negotiation with the plant nation, taking only what's offered and ensuring the stand's continued health. The preparation of materials—splitting, dyeing, drying—follows patterns passed down through generations, patterns that encode not just technique but relationship. The geometric designs woven into the baskets aren't merely aesthetic choices but carry stories, medicines, and prayers. The finished basket holds more than objects; it holds connections between past and future, human and plant, earth and sky.

These sacred approaches to making challenge our modern separation between secular and spiritual, between art and craft, between high and low culture. They remind us that human creativity originally emerged from and served our relationships with the living world. The first musical instruments imitated bird calls and thunder. The first paintings honored the animals who gave their lives for human survival. The first sculptures embodied the powers that humans sought to understand and ally with. Art wasn't separate from life but woven into its very fabric.

Even traditions we might consider purely decorative often carry deeper purposes. The elaborate geometric patterns of Islamic art aren't merely aesthetic choices but contemplative technologies, their infinite tessellations reflecting divine unity and cosmic order. The seemingly abstract patterns of African textiles encode histories, genealogies, and spiritual teachings that remain readable to initiated eyes. The "decorative" carvings on medieval cathedrals provided not just beauty but protection, their gargoyles and green men maintaining ancient contracts with forces older than Christianity.

Reclaiming these sacred dimensions of art doesn't mean appropriating indigenous traditions or returning to historical forms. Rather, it means recognizing that all creative practice can be sacred practice when approached with appropriate attention and intention. It means understanding that beauty isn't luxury but necessity, that humans require aesthetic nourishment just as we require food and shelter. It means remembering that our creative capacities evolved not for self-expression alone but for maintaining our place in the commonwealth of life.

Bioregional Materials and Ethical Making

The materials we choose for our creative work carry stories, relationships, and responsibilities. In an animistic framework, these aren't dead resources but living participants, each bringing their own qualities, histories, and agencies to the creative process. Working with bioregional materials—those sourced from our immediate landscape—deepens our connection to place while raising essential questions about ethics, sustainability, and reciprocity in creative practice.

When artist Judith Selby Lang collects plastic debris from California beaches to create haunting installations, she's not just making environmental statements but entering into a healing relationship with a damaged shoreline. Each piece of plastic carries the story of its journey—manufactured from ancient oil, shaped into temporary convenience, discarded into watersheds, broken down by sun and salt, washed up among shells and seaweed. By carefully cleaning, sorting, and arranging these fragments into color gradients and patterns that echo natural forms, she transforms pollution into meditation, waste into witness. The materials themselves become teachers about consumption, decomposition, and the impossibility of truly throwing anything "away" on a finite planet.

This attention to material stories appears throughout contemporary bioregional art. Papermaker Helen Hiebert doesn't just use local plants but learns their growth patterns, seasonal cycles, and ecological relationships. The papers she creates from iris leaves, yucca fibers, or willow bark carry the essence of specific places and moments—the spring when late rains made the fibers especially supple, the autumn when early frost gave them unusual coloration. Each sheet becomes a portrait of place, readable to those who develop the sensitivity to perceive such subtle information.

Working with bioregional materials demands different temporalities than industrial production allows. You cannot rush the growth of willow for basketry or demand that natural dyes produce standardized colors. You must learn to work with seasonal availability, accepting that certain materials are only accessible at specific times and that taking them at other times would cause harm. This creates a rhythm to creative practice that aligns with natural cycles rather than market demands. It also creates natural limitations that paradoxically enhance creativity—when you can't simply order any material online, you must become ingenious with what your immediate environment provides.

The ethics of gathering materials become complex when we understand them as living beings rather than resources. Many artists develop personal protocols through connection with a place over time. Fiber artist India Flint only uses plants that are windfall, roadkill (botanically speaking), or exotic species whose removal benefits native ecosystems. She never takes the first plant she encounters, understanding that it might be the scout or elder. She asks permission, explains her intentions, and leaves offerings. Her dye processes use no synthetic chemicals, only plant materials, metals, and heat. The resulting textiles carry not just color but the essence of place and the integrity of process.

These practices raise important questions about scale and commercialization. Can work created through such intimate, time-intensive processes ever meet market demands without compromising its essence? How do we price work that involves not just human labor but elaborate protocols of permission and reciprocity? How do we navigate galleries and museums that require consistent production when our materials and inspirations follow natural cycles of abundance and scarcity?

Some artists resolve these tensions by working collectively, sharing both labor and resources. The Local Cloth project in California brings together farmers, mills, designers, and makers to create textiles entirely within a bioregion, from soil to shirt. This requires unprecedented cooperation and patience—cotton must be grown without depleting water tables, processed without toxic chemicals, spun and woven with renewable energy, dyed with local plants, and sewn into designs that honor both the materials and the workers. The resulting garments cost far more than industrial fashion but tell stories of connection and care that mass production can never replicate.

Others focus on education and demonstration rather than production, using their practice to teach others how to develop relationships with materials in their own bioregions. Basketmaker Jennifer Zurick offers workshops that begin not with technique but with plant walks, teaching students to recognize, respectfully harvest, and properly prepare local materials. Only after establishing these relationships do students begin weaving, understanding their baskets as collaborations with specific plants from specific places rather than generic craft projects.

The question of synthetic materials presents particular challenges for bioregional practice. Are human-made materials automatically excluded from animistic art-making? Or can we develop relationships with plastics, metals, and other industrial materials, recognizing them as transformed earth elements deserving of respect despite their problematic origins? Some artists argue that working with salvaged synthetic materials represents a form of healing and transformation, giving new life to substances that would otherwise persist as pollution. Others maintain that true bioregional practice requires rejecting industrial materials entirely, working only with what nature provides directly.

Music, Sound, and Natural Acoustics

Sound preceded sight in evolution, and many organisms navigate primarily through acoustic information. The world is full of voices we've forgotten how to hear—the ultrasonics of dolphins and moths, the infrasonics of elephants and earthquakes, the electromagnetic songs of plants translated through devices into human hearing range. When we understand sound as one of the primary languages of the living world, music becomes not entertainment but conversation, not performance but participation in the planet's ongoing composition.

Composer Pauline Oliveros spent decades developing what she called "Deep Listening," a practice that dissolves boundaries between music and environmental sound, between performer and audience, between human and more-than-human voices. Her sonic meditations invited participants to truly hear their acoustic environment—not just obvious sounds but subtle resonances, the spaces between sounds, the way bodies and buildings shape acoustic space. This wasn't passive reception but active engagement, recognizing that listening itself changes what occurs, that attention is a creative force that influences the behavior of sound.

This understanding appears throughout indigenous music traditions, where songs often originate from careful listening to the more-than-human world. Among the Kaluli people of Papua New Guinea, all traditional songs derive from bird calls, with each bird species teaching specific melodic patterns and rhythms. These aren't simple imitations but translations, rendering bird communication into forms that human voices can carry. Singers understand themselves not as composers but as transmitters, maintaining crucial exchanges between human and avian communities. When forest destruction reduces bird populations, it literally diminishes the musical vocabulary available to human singers, making audible the connections between ecological and cultural diversity.

Contemporary musicians increasingly explore these connections between sound and place. David Rothenberg plays clarinet with whales and birds, not imposing human music onto other species but learning their patterns and finding points of genuine musical dialogue. His recordings document interspecies improvisations where the boundaries between human and non-human music-making dissolve. These aren't one-sided performances but genuine exchanges—the whales and birds respond, adjust, play with sonic possibilities in ways that suggest genuine musical engagement rather than mere reaction to noise.

Bernie Krause has spent fifty years recording soundscapes, documenting how healthy ecosystems create acoustic communities where each species finds its own frequency niche, together creating symphonies of astounding complexity and beauty. His recordings reveal how habitat degradation manifests acoustically long before it becomes visually obvious—the gradual silencing of species, the holes appearing in the frequency spectrum, the collapse of acoustic diversity that precedes ecological collapse. These soundscapes aren't just data but art, revealing the musical intelligence inherent in ecological communities.

The materials and construction of musical instruments carry their own significance in animistic practice. A drum isn't just hide stretched over wood but a composite being incorporating tree, animal, and the hands that crafted it. Many traditions maintain that instruments must be properly introduced to the communities they'll serve, that they require feeding and care, that they can refuse to sound properly if relationships aren't maintained. The Dagara people of West Africa understand that xylophones choose their players rather than vice versa, that the wood remembers its life as a tree and must be approached with appropriate respect.

This extends to the acoustic properties of the place itself. The pioneering work of archaeoacoustics reveals that ancient sacred sites were often chosen or modified for their acoustic properties. The caves where paleolithic art appears often have remarkable resonance at points where the most elaborate paintings appear. Stone circles amplify and focus sound in ways that would have enhanced ritual practices. Churches and temples across cultures demonstrate sophisticated understanding of how architecture shapes sound, creating spaces where human voices naturally harmonize, where whispers carry across vast distances, where certain frequencies induce altered states of consciousness.

R. Murray Schafer's concept of the soundscape as composition invites us to hear our environments as ongoing musical works that we're constantly co-creating. Every footstep, voice, and action contributes to the acoustic environment. Industrial society has created lo-fi soundscapes where constant noise masks subtle acoustic information. But we can compose different soundscapes—gardens designed for birdsong, buildings that filter noise while amplifying pleasant sounds, cities that preserve quiet zones and sound corridors for wildlife.

The implications for musical practice are profound. Rather than soundproofed studios that isolate music from the environment, we might create music that incorporates and responds to place. Rather than amplification that drowns out natural sound, we might develop technologies that blend human and environmental voices. Rather than recorded music that sounds identical everywhere, we might create generative compositions that respond to local conditions—temperature, humidity, time of day, season—ensuring that each performance is unique to its moment and place.

Storytelling and Oral Tradition Revival

Stories are technologies of connection, vessels that carry knowledge, values, and relationships across generations. In oral cultures, stories don't just describe the world—they participate in its ongoing creation. When an Aboriginal elder tells a Dreamtime story, they're not recounting ancient history but maintaining the energetic patterns that keep the country alive. When a Lakota grandmother shares winter counts, she's not just preserving information but weaving relationships between ancestors, descendants, and the lands that hold them all.

The revival of oral tradition in our digital age might seem paradoxical, but it represents a crucial counterbalance to information overload and screen-mediated experience. Oral stories require presence—the storyteller and listeners must share space, breath, attention. They unfold in real-time, unable to be fast-forwarded or paused, demanding patience and focus increasingly rare in our accelerated culture. They change with each telling, responsive to audience, environment, and moment, maintaining the flexibility and responsiveness that living systems require.

Martin Shaw, mythologist and storyteller, speaks of stories as beings that choose their tellers, that require proper feeding and care, that can abandon those who misuse them. He describes the years of preparation required to carry certain stories—not just memorizing words but understanding their ecological and spiritual contexts, developing relationships with the powers they invoke, earning the right to speak on their behalf. This understanding transforms storytelling from entertainment or education into ceremony, from human expression into interspecies dialogue.

The stories themselves often encode sophisticated ecological knowledge. Native American stories about monsters that emerge when taboos are broken frequently describe real ecological tipping points—overharvesting that leads to population collapse, disrespect for predators that causes prey species to explode and destroy vegetation, failure to maintain fire regimes that leads to catastrophic burns. These aren't primitive superstitions but elegant technologies for transmitting complex ecological information in memorable, emotionally resonant forms that persist across generations without written records.

Contemporary storytellers increasingly recognize their role in cultural healing and ecological restoration. They understand that the stories we tell shape the worlds we create, that narrative frameworks determine what we perceive as possible, valuable, or real. The dominant stories of our culture—progress, growth, human supremacy—have created the converging crises we now face. Changing these outcomes requires changing the stories, not through propaganda or manipulation but through reconnection with older, deeper narratives that remember human embeddedness in the community of life.

This might manifest as community story circles where neighbors share their connections to local places, building collective narratives that root people in their bioregions. It might appear as story walks where tales unfold across landscapes, with different chapters told at significant sites, weaving narrative and place into inseparable relationship. It might emerge as collaborative storytelling where humans begin tales that birds, weather, or chance encounters complete, acknowledging that we're not the only authors of the stories we inhabit.

The relationship between oral tradition and written word requires careful navigation. Writing allows stories to travel beyond their origins, reaching those who might never hear them spoken. But writing also fixes stories in forms that can't respond to change, removing them from the relational contexts that keep them alive. Many indigenous communities maintain strict protocols about which stories can be written, understanding that some knowledge requires the accountability of face-to-face transmission, the initiation of proper relationship, the responsibility that comes from receiving stories directly from authorized carriers.

Digital technologies create new possibilities and challenges for oral tradition. Podcasts and audio recordings allow voices to carry across vast distances while maintaining some of the intimacy of spoken word. Video can capture the gestures, expressions, and environmental contexts that enrich oral storytelling. But these technologies also raise questions about ownership, appropriation, and the commodification of stories that were meant to be gifts rather than products.

The stories that emerge from animistic worldviews often confound Western literary categories. They're simultaneously fiction and non-fiction, myth and natural history, entertainment and instruction. Animals speak not as anthropomorphized humans but as genuine others with their own perspectives and wisdom. Landscapes act not as settings but as characters. Time flows not linearly but in spirals and cycles that make ancestors contemporaries and future generations present participants.

Architecture and Building in Relationship

Buildings are never neutral containers but active participants in the lives they shelter. They breathe through their windows, digest through their plumbing, regulate temperature through their skins. They age, adapting to use and weather, developing patinas and personalities that no blueprint could predict. In animistic understanding, buildings aren't constructed but born, not owned but partnered with, not demolished but transformed. This perspective radically reimagines architecture from the imposition of human will onto passive materials to the facilitation of collaborative dwelling among multiple beings and forces.

Christopher Alexander's pattern language approaches this understanding through different vocabulary, recognizing that successful buildings emerge from patterns that repeat across scales and cultures because they resolve fundamental tensions between human needs and natural forces. His "quality without a name" describes spaces that feel alive—not metaphorically but literally, exhibiting the complex geometries, graduated transitions, and responsive variations that characterize living systems. These patterns can't be imposed through design alone but emerge from patient dialogue between intention and circumstance, plan and place.

Indigenous architectures worldwide demonstrate this dialogical approach. The Ndebele people of South Africa don't just paint their houses but engage in ongoing conversation with the structures, refreshing designs seasonally in response to dreams, community events, and environmental changes. The paintings aren't decorations but communications, readable to those who understand their languages, maintaining relationships between human inhabitants, ancestral spirits, and the land itself. When circumstances change—drought, death, celebration—the paintings change, keeping buildings responsive to rather than isolated from their contexts.

The question of materials becomes particularly charged when we understand them as living participants rather than inert resources. The concrete that forms most contemporary construction requires enormous energy to produce, releasing massive quantities of carbon while creating structures that can't breathe, adapt, or decompose. Steel and glass, while allowing stunning architectural possibilities, separate us from direct relationship with the earth elements that have sheltered humans throughout our evolution. These materials aren't inherently evil, but working with them requires different protocols than working with wood, stone, or earth.

Some contemporary architects explore hybrid approaches, combining industrial materials with living systems. The BioMilano project creates vertical forests, building high-rises that incorporate thousands of plants not as decoration but as integral components of the structure's climate control, air purification, and acoustic management. The buildings become ecosystem participants rather than ecosystem replacements, providing habitat for birds and insects while housing humans. The plants aren't just installed but continue growing, changing the buildings' appearances and functions across seasons and years.

Living architecture takes this integration further, creating structures that are literally alive. The Khasi people of India guide fig tree roots across rivers, creating bridges that strengthen over decades as the roots thicken and interweave. These structures require no external materials, produce no waste, and grow stronger rather than weaker over time. They also require patience—a bridge might take fifteen years to become crossable, thirty years to carry heavy loads. This temporality challenges our expectations of immediate gratification but creates infrastructure that can last centuries with proper care.

Contemporary experiments with mycelium-based materials, bacterial concrete that self-heals, and other bio-based building technologies suggest possibilities for architecture that transcends the living/non-living divide. These materials don't just reduce environmental impact but change the fundamental relationship between building and environment. A mycelium wall doesn't just insulate but continues living if properly maintained, potentially growing stronger over time, responding to humidity and temperature, even breaking down and returning to soil when no longer needed.

The siting of buildings becomes crucial when we recognize places as beings with their own qualities and requirements. Feng shui, vastu shastra, and other traditional systems encode sophisticated observations about how landforms, water flows, and energy patterns influence human wellbeing. These aren't superstitions but pattern languages based on millennia of empirical observation about which arrangements support flourishing and which create discord. Contemporary building biology continues this investigation with scientific instruments, measuring electromagnetic fields, air quality, and other factors that influence health, often confirming what traditional practices intuited.

The social dimensions of building relationally extend beyond human inhabitants. Who are we building for? Just current human occupants or also future generations, ancestor spirits, and the creatures who share our spaces whether invited or not? How do we design for the mice in the walls, the spiders in the corners, the birds who might nest in eaves? How do we create structures that serve not just human needs but contribute to rather than diminish the vitality of their places?

This might manifest as buildings designed to change over time, with spaces that can be reconfigured as needs shift rather than demolished and rebuilt. It might appear as structures that produce more energy than they consume, more water than they use, more habitat than they occupy. It might emerge as buildings that tell stories through their forms and ornamentations, maintaining cultural memory and ecological knowledge in forms more durable than books or hard drives.

The Transformation of Creative Practice

As we stand at this threshold between worldviews, artists and creators carry special responsibilities and opportunities. We are the ones who make the invisible visible, who translate between worlds, who imagine alternatives to what seems fixed and inevitable. In reclaiming animistic approaches to creativity, we don't abandon the genuine insights and techniques developed through modern and postmodern art but recontextualize them within a more expansive understanding of creative agency and purpose.

This transformation begins with reconsidering why we create. If art's purpose isn't primarily self-expression, market success, or even political resistance, but maintaining relationships with the living world, everything shifts. The quality of attention we bring to our work changes when we understand ourselves as participants in rather than observers of the world's creativity. The materials we choose carry different weight when we recognize them as beings with their own stories and agencies. The forms we create resonate differently when we understand them not as human inventions but as contributions to ongoing conversations among multiple species and forces.

The implications ripple outward from individual practice to institutional structures. Galleries and museums designed for contemplating isolated objects behind glass cannot adequately present work that requires relationship, context, and participation. Grant structures that demand project proposals, timelines, and measurable outcomes cannot support practices that follow natural cycles and emerge from long-term relationships with places and communities. Educational institutions that separate art from science, craft from fine art, and making from thinking cannot nurture artists capable of working across these artificial boundaries.

Yet changes are already emerging. Land-based art programs that embed students in specific places for extended periods, learning not just technique but relationship. Community art practices that prioritize collective creation over individual authorship. Museums experimenting with living exhibitions that change over time, that invite touch and participation, that acknowledge the agencies of displayed objects. Funding structures that support process over product, relationship over output, long-term engagement over short-term projects.

The path forward requires both recovery and innovation, both return and advance. We need the wisdom of traditional practices that maintained reciprocal relationships with the living world for millennia. We also need new forms and approaches that respond to contemporary conditions—urban environments, digital technologies, global connectivity, and ecological crisis. The task isn't to become indigenous or to appropriate indigenous practices but to develop authentic ways of creating within animistic understanding that emerge from our own places, communities, and conditions.

This is necessarily a collective undertaking. No individual can carry all the knowledge, develop all the relationships, or maintain all the practices needed for this transformation. We need weavers teaching architects about tensile structures, mycologists teaching musicians about network intelligence, children teaching adults about wonder, elders teaching youth about patience. We need collaborations not just among humans but with rivers teaching flow, birds teaching song, soil teaching decomposition, and stones teaching persistence.

The creative work emerging from these collaborations won't look like what we've known. It will be slower, more place-based, more collaborative, less focused on novelty and more attentive to interdependency. It will blur boundaries between art and craft, sacred and secular, human and more-than-human. It will measure success not by sales or reviews but by the vitality of the relationships it nurtures, the healing it facilitates, the connections it maintains between humans and the living world.

As we reclaim these animistic approaches to creativity, we discover that we're not learning something new but remembering something essential. The impulse to create beauty, meaning, and connection runs deeper than culture, deeper than humanity itself. Birds have been composing songs, spiders weaving designs, and rivers carving sculptures far longer than humans have existed. When we recognize ourselves as participants in this ancient and ongoing creative emergence, we find our proper place—not as masters or observers but as collaborators in the world's continuous creation of itself.

The path ahead requires courage, patience, and humility. It asks us to release attachments to individual genius, permanent monuments, and human superiority. It invites us to embrace uncertainty, impermanence, and interdependence. It calls us to develop new skills—not just technical mastery but emotional attunement, ecological awareness, and spiritual sensitivity. Yet this path also offers profound rewards—the joy of genuine collaboration, the wisdom of more-than-human teachers, and the deep satisfaction of creating in service to life itself.

This transformation of creative practice isn't separate from the larger cultural shifts needed to address our interconnected crises. Art and creativity shape consciousness, and consciousness shapes action. The stories we tell, the images we create, the songs we sing, and the structures we build all influence how humans understand their place in the world. By reclaiming animistic approaches to creativity, we participate in the larger work of remembering our kinship with all life, rebuilding reciprocal relationships with the living world, and reimagining human cultures that enhance rather than diminish the glorious creativity of the earth itself.

CHAPTER 13

Economics of the Gift

The salmon have returned to the Columbia River, though in numbers that would make the elders weep. Still, the Yakama Nation gathers at traditional fishing platforms, practicing an economy older than money, older than agriculture, perhaps as old as humanity itself. They take what they need, no more, understanding that their restraint ensures future abundance. The first salmon caught receives ceremony and gratitude before its flesh feeds the people. Its bones return to the river, carrying prayers for the continuation of these ancient cycles. This is economics as sacred reciprocity, where wealth means having enough to give away, where security comes not from accumulation but from the strength of relationships—with salmon, river, and community.

Standing in stark contrast, container ships pass through the Columbia's mouth, carrying goods produced by workers who will never meet those who consume their labor, products that externalize their true costs onto distant ecosystems and future generations. This is economics as extraction and abstraction, where wealth means private accumulation, where security supposedly comes from individual reserves rather than collective resilience. Between these two economic worldviews lies not merely a difference in practice but a fundamental divergence in understanding what economy is for, what wealth means, and what constitutes rational behavior.

The word "economics" derives from the Greek oikonomia—household management. At its root, economics concerns how we provide for our needs within the constraints and possibilities of our home. When we recognize Earth as our only home, economics becomes the practice of maintaining household relationships that ensure all members can flourish indefinitely. This understanding appears throughout indigenous and traditional cultures, where economic practices emerged from careful observation of how ecosystems manage resources, distribute nutrients, and maintain resilience through reciprocal exchange.

Yet our dominant economic system treats Earth not as home but as a warehouse and dumping ground, not as a living system but as collection of commodities. This transformation from economics of relationship to economics of extraction has roots in specific historical moments—the enclosure of commons, the colonization of indigenous lands, the conceptual revolution that reimagined nature as machine rather than organism. These changes weren't inevitable evolutionary developments but deliberate choices that benefited some while devastating others, choices we can now recognize as both ecologically suicidal and spiritually impoverishing.

Gift Economies and Circular Systems

The gift moves. This simple observation by Lewis Hyde captures something essential about gift economies that distinguishes them from market exchanges. When you receive a true gift, you don't calculate its monetary value or plot equivalent reciprocation. Instead, the gift awakens generosity, inspiring you to give—not necessarily back to the original giver but onward to others who need what you can offer. The gift recognizes interdependency, weaves community, and generates abundance through circulation rather than accumulation.

Gift economies recognize that hoarding breaks the cycles that create abundance. Among Pacific Northwest peoples, the potlatch demonstrates this principle through elaborate giving ceremonies where status comes not from having but from giving, where the wealthiest are those who give most away. This might seem irrational to minds trained in scarcity thinking, but it reflects a profound understanding of how living systems actually work. In ecosystems, those organisms that only take without giving back—that break reciprocal cycles—become parasites or cancers that eventually destroy their hosts and themselves.

Robin Wall Kimmerer describes how indigenous economies mirror the gift economies visible in nature itself. The mycorrhizal networks that connect forest plants don't operate on market principles—they share nutrients based on need, with mature trees supporting seedlings, healthy plants sustaining sick ones, all participating in exchanges that strengthen the whole system's resilience. There's no central authority setting exchange rates, no currency accumulating interest, no possibility of abstract wealth disconnected from real relationships and material flows.

Contemporary gift economies demonstrate that these principles can function even within industrialized contexts. The Really Really Free Market movement creates temporary spaces where people bring what they don't need and take what they do, with no exchange required. Unlike barter systems that maintain the logic of calculated exchange, these markets operate on pure gift principles—you can take without giving, give without taking, trusting that abundance emerges from the circulation of gifts rather than balanced transactions.

Time banks and local exchange trading systems (LETS) occupy the middle ground between pure gift and market economies. Members offer services measured in time rather than money—one hour of childcare equals one hour of plumbing equals one hour of teaching. This maintains some structure of exchange while recognizing that everyone's time has equal value, that wealth shouldn't accumulate through compound interest, that currency should facilitate relationship rather than enable extraction.

The digital realm has spawned new forms of gift economy that challenge conventional economic assumptions. Open-source software development creates billions of dollars in value through voluntary collaboration without traditional ownership or exchange. Wikipedia assembles humanity's knowledge through freely given contributions. Creative Commons licensing allows creators to give their work to the commons while maintaining attribution and preventing enclosure. These examples demonstrate that gift economies can operate at scales and complexities that economists long claimed required market mechanisms.

Yet gift economies face genuine challenges in our current context. They require trust, which neoliberal culture systematically erodes. They depend on rough equality, while capitalism generates extreme inequality. They assume abundance, while scarcity thinking dominates our consciousness. They need time for relationships to develop, while acceleration compresses every aspect of life. They function best at human scales, while globalization creates vast impersonal systems.

The transition toward gift economics doesn't require abandoning all forms of exchange or returning to pre-industrial conditions. Instead, it means recognizing that different economic forms serve different purposes, that gift and market can coexist when properly bounded, that some things should never become commodities while others function well as articles of trade. The commons tradition understood this, maintaining gift relationships for shared resources while allowing market exchange for surplus production. The destruction of commons worldwide represents not modernization but theft, the enclosure of gift economies into private property regimes that benefit few while impoverishing many.

Circular economy models attempt to address waste and extraction by ensuring materials cycle continuously through use rather than following linear extract-produce-consume-discard paths. While often presented in technical terms—industrial ecology, cradle-to-cradle design, zero waste manufacturing—circular economics essentially mimics the gift economies of nature where every output becomes input elsewhere, where there's no such thing as waste, where materials circulate endlessly through forms while maintaining their essential qualities.

The gift economy extends beyond material exchange to include knowledge, culture, and creativity. Indigenous peoples have always understood that songs, stories, and ceremonies are gifts that gain power through sharing rather than commodities that lose value through reproduction. The catastrophic impact of intellectual property regimes on traditional knowledge systems reveals what happens when gift relationships become enclosed in ownership structures. Medicines that communities freely shared for generations become corporate property through biopiracy. Sacred symbols become trademarked logos. Ancient seeds become patented property.

Resisting these enclosures requires more than legal challenges—it requires maintaining and strengthening gift relationships that exist outside property logic. Seed libraries where gardeners freely share heirloom varieties. Skill shares where people teach traditional crafts without charge. Community kitchens where cooking knowledge passes between generations and cultures. These spaces maintain gift economies within the heart of capitalism, keeping alive practices and principles that may prove essential as current systems fail.

Commons Management and Collective Stewardship

The tragedy of the commons, Garrett Hardin's influential 1968 essay, has been weaponized to justify privatization and commodification of shared resources worldwide. Yet Hardin's argument rested on a fundamental misunderstanding—he described not commons but open-access resources without management systems. Actual commons, as Elinor Ostrom's Nobel Prize-winning research demonstrated, have sustained resources for centuries through sophisticated governance structures that balance individual use with collective health.

True commons require three elements: resources, communities, and protocols. The resource might be forest, fishery, pasture, or aquifer—something that provides sustenance but requires management to prevent depletion. The community consists of those who depend on and maintain the resource, bound together through kinship, proximity, or shared need. The protocols—formal or informal, written or oral—govern how the resource can be used, by whom, when, and in what quantities. These three elements create resilient systems that have maintained resources across generations where both state management and private ownership have failed.

The acequia systems of New Mexico demonstrate commons management that predates the United States by centuries. These gravity-fed irrigation channels, introduced by Spanish colonists but incorporating indigenous water management practices, operate through community labor and collective decision-making. Each member contributes work maintaining the channels and receives water shares based on land ownership and crop needs. During drought, everyone reduces consumption proportionally. No one can sell their water rights separately from land, preventing speculation and maintaining the connection between water and place.

In Japan, the satoyama landscapes represent thousands of years of commons management, creating mosaic environments where human use enhances rather than diminishes biodiversity. These areas between mountain foothills and arable flat land include managed forests, grasslands, rice paddies, and irrigation systems that together support more species than either pure wilderness or intensive agriculture. Community members follow detailed protocols about when to harvest bamboo, how to maintain forest understory, where to gather mushrooms, and how to manage controlled burns. The knowledge embedded in these practices represents irreplaceable cultural-ecological wisdom that no amount of scientific research could quickly replicate.

Contemporary commons movements recognize that commons principles can govern resources beyond traditional land and water. The electromagnetic spectrum, the atmosphere's capacity to absorb carbon, the genetic heritage of agricultural crops, the cultural heritage of humanity—all these represent commons that require collective stewardship rather than private ownership or state control. The internet itself began as a commons, though enclosure through corporate platforms now threatens its foundational principles of open access and peer-to-peer communication.

Urban commons challenge the assumption that commons management only works in rural or traditional contexts. Community gardens transform vacant lots into spaces of food production, social gathering, and ecological education. Neighborhood tool libraries allow communities to share rather than individually purchase rarely-used equipment. Community land trusts remove land from speculative markets, maintaining affordability through collective ownership. These initiatives demonstrate that commons can emerge wherever communities organize to manage shared resources.

The relationship between commons and animistic worldviews runs deeper than practical resource management. When land belongs to no one or everyone, when resources are understood as gifts requiring reciprocity rather than property enabling extraction, the spiritual dimensions of economic life become visible. Many commons maintain ceremonial dimensions—blessing of irrigation channels, harvest festivals, rituals marking seasonal transitions in resource use. These practices aren't quaint traditions but technologies for maintaining the social cohesion and shared vision that commons governance requires.

Climate change represents perhaps the ultimate commons challenge—managing the atmosphere's finite capacity to safely absorb greenhouse gases. Market mechanisms like carbon trading have largely failed because they maintain the logic of privatization and commodification that created the crisis. Effective climate response requires commons thinking—recognizing the atmosphere as shared heritage requiring collective stewardship, understanding that those who have benefited most from carbon emissions owe greatest responsibility for reduction, ensuring that solutions enhance rather than erode other commons.

The knowledge commons faces particular threats from intellectual property regimes that enclose information, creativity, and innovation within proprietary boundaries. Yet movements toward open access publishing, open educational resources, and open-source technologies demonstrate growing recognition that knowledge multiplies through sharing rather than depletes through use. Traditional knowledge commons—the accumulated wisdom of indigenous peoples, the agricultural knowledge of peasant farmers, the medical knowledge of traditional healers—represent libraries of tested solutions to challenges from pest management to medicine that corporate enclosure threatens to destroy or monopolize.

Gender dimensions of commons management deserve particular attention. Research consistently shows that women's participation in commons governance correlates with better resource maintenance and more equitable distribution. This isn't because women are essentially closer to nature but because patriarchal exclusion from private property ownership has maintained women's stake in and knowledge of commons resources. As Vandana Shiva observes, the destruction of commons worldwide has disproportionately impacted women, removing resources they could access while unable to own and pushing them into monetized economies where they face systematic discrimination.

Digital technologies create new possibilities for commons governance at previously impossible scales. Blockchain technologies, despite their problematic energy consumption and speculation bubbles, demonstrate potential for transparent, decentralized resource management without central authorities. Sensor networks can provide real-time data about resource conditions. Mapping platforms can document traditional use patterns and ecological knowledge. Communication tools can enable participatory decision-making across vast distances. Yet these tools remain tools—the social relationships, trust, and commitment that commons require cannot be programmed or purchased.

Local Currencies and Bioregional Trade

Money, we're told, emerged to solve the inefficiencies of barter, providing a universal medium of exchange, store of value, and unit of account. This creation myth, still taught in economics textbooks, has been thoroughly debunked by anthropologists and historians who find no evidence of barter economies preceding monetary systems. Instead, diverse forms of currency emerged from different social needs—tribute to temples, standardization of gifts, facilitation of long-distance trade, extraction of taxes. Understanding money as social technology rather than natural phenomenon opens possibilities for designing currencies that serve life rather than destroying it.

Our dominant monetary system—debt-based fiat currency created by private banks through loans—carries inherent growth imperatives that drive ecological destruction. Because money is created as interest-bearing debt, the total money supply must constantly expand to service that debt. This requires economic growth, which requires increasing extraction of materials and energy from finite planetary systems. The mathematics of compound interest creates exponential growth curves that cannot continue indefinitely on a finite planet. Alternative currency systems that escape these dynamics aren't just nice additions to economic reform—they're essential for creating economies that can operate within planetary boundaries.

BerkShares, the local currency of the Berkshire region of Massachusetts, demonstrates how regional currencies can strengthen local economies while building community resilience. Purchased with dollars at a discount and accepted by hundreds of local businesses, BerkShares keep wealth circulating locally rather than draining to distant corporate headquarters. They create relationships—you must interact with local bank tellers to obtain them, local merchants to spend them. They make visible the flow of economic activity through the community, revealing connections that dollar transactions obscure.

The Ithaca HOUR system, though no longer active, provided important lessons about local currency design. Each HOUR represented one hour of labor or ten dollars, establishing equivalence between time and money that challenged conventional wage hierarchies. The currency included denominations as small as one-eighth HOUR, enabling participation by those with little money. Regular currency issuance through community organizations ensured circulation while funding local projects. The system's eventual decline revealed challenges local currencies face—the labor of administration, the need for critical mass, competition from convenient digital payments.

Bioregional currencies could extend local currency concepts to match economic flows with ecological boundaries. Salmon Nation, a bioregional identity movement in the Pacific Northwest, explores how economics might organize around watersheds rather than political boundaries. A Salmon Nation currency might fluctuate based on salmon runs, forest health, and watershed conditions, making ecological health directly relevant to economic decisions. Such currencies could incorporate carrying capacity—expanding during periods of ecological abundance, contracting during stress, teaching participants to align economic activity with natural cycles.

The Bangla-Pesa in Kenya demonstrates how community currencies can serve impoverished communities excluded from formal economies. Residents of informal settlements issue currency backed by their own goods and services, creating liquidity without requiring scarce national currency. During the COVID-19 pandemic, when conventional money disappeared from circulation, Bangla-Pesa and similar community currencies enabled continued exchange, revealing their potential as resilience tools during economic disruption.

Cryptocurrency technologies, despite their current association with speculation and energy waste, offer tools that could serve bioregional and gift economies. Smart contracts could automate resource sharing based on ecological conditions. Distributed ledgers could track gift obligations and reciprocal relationships across communities. Tokens could represent ecosystem services, creating incentives for restoration rather than extraction. The challenge lies in liberating these tools from libertarian ideology and financial speculation, instead embedding them in cooperative and ecological frameworks.

Time-based currencies offer particular promise for escaping growth imperatives. Unlike conventional money that accumulates through interest, time passes equally for everyone and cannot be hoarded indefinitely. The Japanese Fureai Kippu system allows people to earn credits caring for elderly neighbors, then redeem those credits for their own care later or transfer them to elderly relatives elsewhere. This creates intergenerational reciprocity, values care work typically excluded from GDP, and builds social fabric while meeting real needs.

Demurrage currencies, which lose value over time like negative interest, encourage circulation rather than hoarding. The Freigeld experiments in Austria and Germany during the 1930s demonstrated that such currencies could stimulate local economies during a depression. Contemporary proposals for carbon-backed currencies with demurrage could simultaneously provide universal basic income, encourage rapid decarbonization, and prevent wealth accumulation. The technical feasibility exists; only political will and imagination limit implementation.

Multi-currency systems recognize that different types of exchange require different forms of money. Gift currencies for sharing abundance, mutual credit for business transactions, time banks for community services, carbon currencies for ecosystem services—each designed for specific purposes rather than forcing all exchange through a single monetary form. This economic biodiversity creates resilience, prevents any single currency from dominating all aspects of life, and allows communities to experiment with forms that serve their specific needs and values.

The question of scale remains challenging for alternative currencies. While local currencies can strengthen community resilience, global challenges require coordination across vast distances. Proposals for global currencies—whether carbon-based, energy-based, or basket currencies representing multiple resources—face enormous political obstacles. Yet the current system of competing national currencies manipulated for trade advantage while a single reserve currency enables imperial extraction clearly cannot continue. The transition to ecological economics requires monetary transformation at all scales simultaneously.

Worker-Owned Cooperatives and Ecological Businesses

The Mondragon Corporation in Spain's Basque Country employs over 80,000 people across 96 cooperatives, demonstrating that worker ownership can succeed at industrial scale. Founded in 1956 by a Catholic priest teaching technical education, Mondragon has survived dictatorship, economic crisis, and globalization while maintaining democratic governance, relative pay equity, and commitment to community development. Workers elect management, share profits and losses, and collectively decide strategic direction. This isn't socialism or capitalism but something else—an economy of solidarity where cooperation replaces competition as the organizing principle.

Worker ownership transforms the fundamental dynamics of business. When those who do the work also own the enterprise, the artificial separation between labor and capital dissolves. Decisions balance worker welfare, community benefit, and business sustainability rather than maximizing shareholder returns. The tendency to externalize costs onto workers through wage suppression, unsafe conditions, or job insecurity disappears when workers are also owners. The pressure for endless growth relaxes when success means sustaining livelihoods rather than inflating share prices.

Ecological businesses take this transformation further, recognizing that true sustainability requires considering the welfare of all stakeholders—workers, communities, ecosystems, and future generations. The B Corporation movement attempts to institutionalize this broader accountability, requiring certified companies to consider environmental and social impact alongside profit. While still operating within capitalist frameworks, B Corps demonstrate growing recognition that business as usual is destroying the basis for all economic activity.

Evergreen Cooperatives in Cleveland, Ohio, show how worker ownership can address urban poverty while building ecological economies. Launched in 2008, these cooperatives—including an industrial laundry, solar installation company, and hydroponic greenhouse—are anchored by contracts with local hospitals and universities. Workers from low-income neighborhoods become owners after six months, building equity while providing stable employment. The businesses incorporate ecological design—the laundry uses less water than competitors, the greenhouse produces year-round using waste heat, the solar company helps institutions reduce carbon footprints.

The cooperative model naturally aligns with ecological principles. Cooperation rather than competition characterizes healthy ecosystems, where species develop mutually beneficial relationships that enhance collective resilience. Democratic governance mirrors the distributed decision-making of flocks, herds, and schools that process information collectively to navigate challenges. Profit sharing reflects nature's tendency toward equitable distribution rather than extreme concentration—no tree captures all the sunlight, no predator takes all the prey.

Platform cooperatives challenge the extractive dynamics of digital capitalism by putting ownership in the hands of those who create value. Ride-sharing cooperatives owned by drivers, grocery delivery cooperatives owned by shoppers and workers, social media cooperatives owned by users—these experiments demonstrate alternatives to monopolistic platforms that extract value from every transaction. The technology already exists; only the ownership structure needs transformation.

Indigenous enterprises offer models for businesses that serve cultural and ecological renewal rather than simply generating profit. The Menominee Forest in Wisconsin, managed by the Menominee Nation for over 150 years, has generated over $2 billion in timber revenue while increasing forest volume and biodiversity. This success comes from understanding themselves as forest people whose prosperity depends on forest health, making decisions based on seven-generation thinking rather than quarterly earnings.

Regenerative businesses go beyond sustainability's goal of "doing no harm" to actively restore ecological and social systems. Patagonia's recent restructuring, which transferred ownership to trusts dedicated to fighting climate change, demonstrates how businesses can become vehicles for restoration rather than extraction. Fibershed organizations create regional textile systems that build soil through carbon farming while providing livelihoods for farmers, mills, and artisans. These businesses measure success through ecological regeneration, community resilience, and cultural vitality alongside financial viability.

The transition from extractive to regenerative business requires fundamental restructuring of ownership, governance, and purpose. Worker ownership addresses the first, ensuring those who create value also receive it. Stakeholder governance addresses the second, giving voice to all affected by business decisions. Ecological purpose addresses the third, recognizing that business must serve life rather than destroying it. Together, these changes could transform business from the primary driver of ecological destruction to a force for restoration.

Yet significant obstacles remain. Access to capital challenges cooperative development, as conventional investors resist structures that limit returns and share control. Regulatory frameworks designed for conventional businesses create barriers for cooperatives. Educational systems train workers for hierarchy rather than democracy. Cultural conditioning toward individualism and competition undermines cooperation. These obstacles aren't insurmountable but require coordinated effort to address.

The relationship between cooperatives and commons suggests possibilities for hybrid structures that combine worker ownership with community stewardship. Community-supported agriculture (CSA) demonstrates this combination, with farmers and eaters sharing risks and rewards of food production. Community land trusts separate land ownership from building ownership, preventing speculation while enabling investment. Community development financial institutions

(CDFIs) provide capital based on social and ecological benefit rather than maximum return.

Universal Basic Income and Reduced Work Weeks

The paradox of our age: we've achieved unprecedented productive capacity yet work longer hours with greater insecurity than our grandparents. Automation eliminates jobs while creating vast wealth for those who own the machines. Bullshit jobs proliferate—administrative bloat, financial manipulation, marketing warfare—that add nothing to human welfare or ecological health. Meanwhile, essential work—care for children and elders, ecosystem restoration, community building—goes unpaid or underpaid. Universal basic income (UBI) and reduced work weeks could resolve these contradictions, liberating human creativity while reducing ecological impact.

The case for UBI extends beyond economic efficiency to fundamental questions about freedom, dignity, and the purpose of human existence. If we accept that everyone deserves life's basics—food, shelter, healthcare, education—regardless of their market value, then UBI becomes a logical policy conclusion. If we recognize that much necessary work—parenting, volunteering, artistic creation—happens outside wage labor, then UBI becomes an investment in social wealth. If we understand that ecological limits require reducing material production and consumption, then UBI becomes a tool for managed degrowth that doesn't impoverish workers.

Alaska's Permanent Fund Dividend, funded by oil revenues and distributed annually to all residents since 1982, provides the longest-running UBI experiment. Despite its problematic fossil fuel basis, the program demonstrates that universal payments reduce poverty and inequality without reducing work participation. Kenya's GiveDirectly experiment, providing unconditional cash transfers to entire villages, shows that recipients invest in education, healthcare, and productive assets rather than wasting money on consumption. These results challenge paternalistic assumptions about why people are poor and what they would do with unconditional income.

The COVID-19 pandemic inadvertently tested UBI-like policies worldwide as governments provided emergency payments to prevent economic collapse. These programs revealed that direct cash transfers could be implemented quickly, that people used money responsibly for basic needs, that economic security improved physical and mental health. They also revealed that many workers, given choice, refused to return to degrading, dangerous, or meaningless jobs, forcing employers to improve conditions and raise wages.

Reduced work weeks complement UBI by redistributing necessary work while reducing ecological impact. The 40-hour work week, won through fierce labor struggles, was never natural law but social agreement. Keynes predicted we'd be working 15-hour weeks by now, freed by technology to pursue leisure, learning, and relationships. Instead, we've chosen consumption over time, stuff over life, GDP growth over wellbeing. This choice is killing the planet while impoverishing our lives.

France's 35-hour work week, implemented in 2000, demonstrated that reducing work hours could maintain productivity while improving quality of life. Workers reported better health, more time with family, and greater life satisfaction. Some companies found that shorter hours increased focus and efficiency, maintaining output despite reduced input. The policy faced fierce resistance from employers and was gradually weakened, but the experiment proved that reduced work was feasible in advanced economies.

The relationship between work hours and ecological impact is direct but complex. Longer work hours correlate with higher carbon footprints, both through production and through time-stressed consumption patterns—fast food, disposable goods, energy-intensive conveniences. Reducing work hours could automatically reduce environmental impact while creating time for lower-impact activities—cooking, gardening, walking, socializing. But this requires ensuring that reduced work doesn't simply become increased consumption, that freed time enables different ways of living rather than more shopping.

The four-day work week, currently being tested by companies and countries worldwide, offers a pragmatic step toward work reduction. Iceland's trials from 2015-2019, involving 2,500 workers, found that productivity maintained or increased while worker wellbeing dramatically improved. The success led unions to negotiate reduced hours for 86% of Iceland's workforce. Similar experiments in Belgium, Scotland, Spain, and Japan suggest that the five-day work week may join the six-day and seven-day weeks in history's dustbin.

Yet work reduction faces profound psychological and cultural obstacles beyond economic resistance. The Protestant work ethic, though originally religious, has become a secular religion that equates worth with productivity, virtue with busyness, laziness with sin. Consumer culture requires endless work to afford endless consumption. Social status derives from career success rather than community contribution. Many people, alienated from family, community, and nature, find identity and meaning only through work. Reducing work hours without addressing these deeper alienations might simply create more lonely, anxious consumers with more time to shop.

The transformation of work requires reimagining what counts as valuable activity. Care work—raising children, tending elders, maintaining households and communities—creates enormous value unrecognized by GDP. Ecological work—restoration, conservation, observation—becomes increasingly essential as climate change accelerates. Cultural work—ceremony, celebration, storytelling—maintains the social fabric that makes life meaningful. Political work—organizing, deliberating, governing—requires time that exhausted workers cannot provide. UBI could recognize and enable these forms of work that markets cannot properly value.

Indigenous and traditional societies demonstrate different relationships with work that industrial societies might learn from. Marshall

Sahlins documented that hunter-gatherers worked 3-5 hours daily, spending remaining time in leisure, socializing, and cultural activities. Agricultural societies worked seasonally, with intense periods during planting and harvest but extensive rest during other times. The industrial revolution's imposition of clock time, year-round labor, and constant productivity represents historical aberration rather than human nature.

Measuring Success Beyond GDP

Gross Domestic Product measures everything except what makes life worthwhile. It counts clear-cut forests as wealth but standing forests as nothing. It values cancer treatment but not health. It celebrates natural disasters that require rebuilding but ignores the slow work of maintenance that prevents collapse. Created during World War II to measure war production, GDP has become the singular metric by which we judge economic success, despite its creators' warnings about its limitations. This mismeasurement drives policies that destroy life while claiming to create wealth.

Bhutan's Gross National Happiness index, adopted in 1972, demonstrates that alternatives are possible. Rather than measuring production, GNH assesses nine domains: psychological wellbeing, health, education, time use, cultural diversity, good governance, community vitality, ecological resilience, and living standards. Policies are evaluated based on their impact across all domains rather than their contribution to economic growth. While Bhutan faces its own challenges and contradictions, GNH has influenced policy decisions from refusing mass tourism to maintaining forest cover to providing free healthcare and education.

New Zealand's Wellbeing Budget, introduced in 2019, allocates resources based on four wellbeing domains: natural capital, human capital, social capital, and financial capital. This framework recognizes that financial wealth means nothing if ecosystems collapse, people are miserable, and communities disintegrate. The budget prioritizes mental health, child poverty reduction, and climate action not as costs but as investments in national wellbeing. While implementation remains imperfect, the framework shifts conversation from GDP growth to genuine progress.

The Genuine Progress Indicator (GPI) adjusts GDP for factors it ignores—resource depletion, pollution, inequality, unpaid work, leisure time, social cohesion. When calculated for various nations and states, GPI reveals that genuine progress peaked in the 1970s despite continued GDP growth. We've been getting richer while becoming poorer, confusing quantity with quality, throughput with wellbeing. This helps explain the paradox of increasing wealth alongside increasing anxiety, depression, and ecological collapse.

Ecological footprint analysis reveals that humanity currently uses 1.7 Earth's worth of resources annually, with wealthy nations consuming far beyond their share. Biocapacity accounting shows which nations are ecological creditors or debtors, revealing the extractive relationships underlying global trade. These metrics make visible the impossibility of extending Western consumption patterns globally and the necessity of degrowth in wealthy nations to enable basic development elsewhere.

The Happy Planet Index combines life satisfaction, life expectancy, and ecological footprint to identify nations that achieve wellbeing within planetary boundaries. Costa Rica consistently ranks highest, achieving Western levels of health and happiness with one-third the ecological footprint. This suggests that wellbeing doesn't require excessive consumption, that good life is possible within planetary boundaries, that development models exist beyond industrial growth.

Community-level indicators can capture dimensions that national metrics miss. The Seattle Area Happiness Initiative measures wellbeing across neighborhoods, revealing how urban design, social services, and community resources affect quality of life. Transition Towns develop resilience indicators measuring local food security, energy independence, and social cohesion. Indigenous communities create culturally specific indicators—language fluency, participation in ceremonies, traditional knowledge transmission—that capture what matters for cultural survival.

The dashboard approach recognizes that no single metric can capture economic complexity. Like drivers monitoring speed, fuel, temperature, and direction simultaneously, societies need multiple indicators tracked together. The Sustainable Development Goals attempt this globally, though their internal contradictions—particularly the impossibility of achieving growth goals within ecological goals—reveal the need for more fundamental restructuring.

Yet changing metrics alone won't transform economics. GDP maintains power not through intellectual merit but through institutional momentum, political convenience, and ideological alignment with growth capitalism. Alternative metrics threaten powerful interests who benefit from current mismeasurement. They reveal uncomfortable truths about ecological overshoot, social decay, and spiritual emptiness that growth propaganda obscures. They demand different policies—redistribution rather than growth, restoration rather than extraction, cooperation rather than competition.

The deeper work involves changing consciousness about what constitutes success, wealth, and progress. Indigenous peoples measured wealth through potlatch giving, through strength of relationships, through knowledge of place and story. Medieval communities measured success through cathedral building that spanned generations, through festival calendars that marked sacred time, through commons that sustained communities indefinitely. These weren't primitive misunderstandings but sophisticated assessments of what matters for collective flourishing.

Transforming Economic Consciousness

As we stand at the threshold of economic transformation, the path forward requires not just new policies or institutions but fundamental shifts in economic consciousness. The stories we tell about the economy shape what we perceive as possible, rational, or valuable. The metaphors we use—economy as machine, market as natural force, growth as health—determine what solutions we can imagine. Transforming these deep structures of economic thought becomes prerequisite for creating economies that serve life.

The transition from economic thinking rooted in scarcity, competition, and extraction to one based on abundance, cooperation, and reciprocity challenges centuries of conditioning. We've been taught that humans are naturally selfish, that resources are naturally scarce, that competition naturally produces optimal outcomes. These assertions, presented as scientific facts, are actually ideological positions that justify existing arrangements. Anthropology, ecology, and psychology all demonstrate that cooperation is more fundamental than competition, that abundance and scarcity are largely human constructs, that selfishness and altruism coexist in complex balance.

This transformation is already underway in countless experiments worldwide. Transition Towns build local resilience while reducing carbon footprints. Ecovillages demonstrate that high quality of life is possible with low environmental impact. Community land trusts remove land from speculation while providing affordable housing. Seed libraries maintain agricultural biodiversity outside corporate control. Tool libraries reduce consumption while building community connections. These aren't just alternative economic practices but laboratories for new economic consciousness.

The solidarity economy movement connects these experiments into broader transformation. Rather than a competing paradigm, the solidarity economy names the already-existing practices of cooperation, mutual aid, and reciprocity that sustain human communities despite capitalism's dominance. By making these practices visible, connecting them into networks, and developing supportive institutions, the solidarity economy builds parallel systems that can expand as capitalism contracts.

Indigenous economics offers essential wisdom for this transformation, not as models to copy but as evidence that other economies are possible. The Andean concept of ayni—reciprocal work exchange—demonstrates an economy without money. The African philosophy of ubuntu—"I am because we are"—grounds economics in relationship rather than individual accumulation. The gift economies of Pacific Northwest peoples show how abundance emerges from generosity rather than hoarding. These aren't primitive systems to evolve beyond but sophisticated solutions to economic challenges we've forgotten how to perceive.

Youth movements increasingly reject capitalism's promises, recognizing that they've inherited degraded ecosystems, unaffordable housing, precarious employment, and existential uncertainty. Their experiments with communal living, gift economies, alternative currencies, and cooperative enterprises aren't dropping out but consciously building alternatives. Their refusal to accept that the economy must destroy ecology, that work must consume life, that success means accumulation, represents hope for transformation.

The role of crisis in economic transformation cannot be ignored. The 2008 financial crisis revealed capitalism's instability and inequality, sparking Occupy movements worldwide. The COVID-19 pandemic exposed the fragility of global supply chains and the essential nature of care work. Climate change makes economic transformation not idealistic but necessary for survival. These crises create openings for new thinking, though they also risk authoritarian responses that could foreclose democratic alternatives.

Technology's role remains ambiguous but potentially transformative. Digital platforms could enable gift economies at global scale or surveillance capitalism of unprecedented extraction. Artificial intelligence could eliminate drudgework and enable creativity or concentrate power and destroy livelihoods. Renewable energy could democratize power production or create new forms of energy colonialism. The outcomes depend not on technology itself but on the ownership structures, governance systems, and values that shape its development and deployment.

The path forward requires working simultaneously at all scales—personal, community, bioregional, and global. Personal transformation involves examining our relationships with money, work, and consumption, developing practices of generosity, simplicity, and gratitude. Community transformation involves building alternative economic institutions, from cooperatives to local currencies to mutual aid networks. Bioregional transformation involves creating economies that match ecological boundaries, seasonal cycles, and carrying capacities. Global transformation involves challenging trade agreements, financial systems, and development models that perpetuate extraction and inequality.

This transformation won't be smooth or linear. Existing systems will resist, sometimes violently. Experiments will fail, teaching essential lessons. Victories will be partial, requiring constant defense. The work will take generations, requiring patience that quarterly earnings reports and election cycles don't cultivate. Yet the alternative—continuing current trajectories until ecological and social systems collapse—is no alternative at all.

The emergence of economic systems that recognize Earth as living rather than dead, that understand wealth as relationship rather than accumulation, that measure success through flourishing rather than growth, represents humanity's great work for the coming century. This isn't returning to the past but creating futures that honor ancient wisdom while embracing appropriate innovation. It isn't rejecting all markets but bounding them within gift economies and commons that maintain what must never become commodity. It isn't imposing single solutions but enabling diverse experiments that match local conditions and cultures.

As we reclaim animistic understanding that everything participates in sacred economies of exchange—that rivers give water, forests give oxygen, soil gives food, and humans must give back—economic life regains meaning beyond mere survival or accumulation. Work becomes participation in the world's continuous creation. Exchange becomes an opportunity for strengthened relationship. Wealth becomes capacity to give. Economy becomes ecology becomes sacred practice of maintaining the household of Earth for all beings across all generations.

The salmon returning to the Columbia River carry this teaching in their bodies. Born in mountain streams, they journey to the ocean, gathering nutrients from across the Pacific. When they return, their deaths feed forests hundreds of miles from sea, their bodies becoming trees, bears, eagles, and eventually, new salmon. This is the economy—not the abstract circulation of currency but the concrete circulation of gifts that creates abundance through generosity, resilience through reciprocity, and meaning through relationship. As we learn again to see economics through salmon eyes, we might remember what wealth really means and what success actually requires.

CHAPTER 14

Governance and Decision-Making

The council fire burns through the night as the Haudenosaunee Confederacy gathers to consider a proposal that will affect the coming seven generations. No vote will be taken. Instead, they will speak and listen, speak and listen, until consensus emerges or the proposal dies. The process might take days, weeks, even months. Efficiency is not the goal—wisdom is. The decision they reach must satisfy not only the human beings present but the maple trees whose sap they gather, the deer whose paths cross their territory, the waters that flow through their lands, and the children who will inherit the consequences centuries from now. This is governance as sacred responsibility, where power flows not from domination but from relationship, where authority derives not from force but from the capacity to maintain harmony among all relations.

Across the world, in the high Andes, an ayllu meets to decide about water distribution for the coming season. The mountains are present—not symbolically but actually, their needs and perspectives channeled through ritual specialists who have spent lifetimes learning to interpret the speech of glaciers and the moods of peaks. The decision will emerge from dialogue not just among humans but between humans and the sentient landscape they inhabit. The governance system acknowledges that humans are junior partners in an ancient assembly where rivers have voted with their flows for millions of years, where soil has cast its ballot through fertility or exhaustion, where the clouds participate through presence or absence.

These examples might seem quaint or impractical to modern minds trained in the necessities of representative democracy, majority rule, and efficient administration. Yet our current governance systems are failing catastrophically to address the existential challenges we face. Democratic institutions designed for human interests in isolation cannot process the needs of ecosystems. Decision-making structures that privilege short-term gains over long-term sustainability cannot navigate climate change. Governance based on human supremacy cannot create policies that respect the rights and requirements of the more-than-human world.

The transformation required goes deeper than reform—it demands reimagining governance itself. What would political systems look like if they recognized rivers as constituents, forests as stakeholders, and future generations as present participants? How would decisions change if we understood authority as arising from relationship with place rather than control over territory? What new institutions might emerge from recognizing that humans are one species in a democracy of all beings, powerful but not sovereign, influential but not independent?

Consensus Decision-Making and Council Processes

Consensus is not unanimity. This distinction, often misunderstood, explains why consensus-based governance can function in complex societies rather than just small groups of like-minded individuals. Consensus means that everyone can live with the decision, that no one feels so strongly opposed that they would block the group's movement forward. It requires distinguishing between preferences and principles, between "I don't like this" and "I cannot accept this." It demands emotional maturity, spiritual development, and commitment to collective wellbeing over individual preference.

The Quaker tradition of sense of the meeting demonstrates consensus in contemporary Western contexts. Participants sit in silence until someone feels moved to speak. There's no debate in the conventional sense—no point-counterpoint, no rhetoric aimed at persuasion. Instead, speakers attempt to discern and articulate the truth emerging from collective wisdom. The clerk, who facilitates but doesn't lead, periodically tests whether the sense of the meeting has emerged by articulating what they've heard. If the articulation resonates, it becomes the decision. If not, the process continues.

This approach might seem impossibly slow, but Quakers have used it for centuries to make complex decisions, from managing businesses to organizing antislavery campaigns. The process creates different outcomes than voting systems. Minorities aren't overruled but heard. Proposals aren't accepted or rejected but refined through collective wisdom. Participants don't win or lose but contribute to emerging understanding. The decisions reached tend to be more creative, more thoroughly considered, and more fully supported than those achieved through adversarial processes.

Indigenous council traditions offer rich models for consensus governance. The Mohawk Council of Chiefs doesn't debate in the Western sense but engages in careful, patient dialogue where each chief speaks from their particular perspective—some representing peace, others war, some the earth, others the sky. The diversity of perspectives isn't a problem to overcome but essential wisdom to integrate. The process assumes that truth is multifaceted, that any decision affecting the whole must incorporate all aspects of reality.

The Aboriginal Australian practice of yarning circles creates space for collective sense-making without formal hierarchy or procedure. Participants speak in turns, sharing stories and perspectives without interruption or immediate response. The circular form ensures no one occupies a position of dominance. The emphasis on story rather than argument allows multiple truths to coexist. Decisions emerge organically from the sharing rather than being forced through formal mechanisms.

Modern experiments with consensus demonstrate its viability in contemporary contexts. The Occupy movement's general assemblies, despite their challenges and eventual dissolution, showed that hundreds of people could make collective decisions without formal leadership. The hand signals they developed—twinkling fingers for agreement, arms crossed for blocking, various gestures for process points—created efficient communication without interrupting speakers. The progressive stack, which prioritized voices typically marginalized in conventional forums, challenged patterns of domination that voting alone cannot address.

Sociocracy, developed in the Netherlands and now practiced worldwide, offers a structured approach to consensus that scales to large organizations. Decisions are made by consent rather than consensus—meaning no one has paramount objections rather than everyone actively agrees. Circles of decision-making nest within each other, with representatives linking levels. Feedback loops ensure decisions can be revisited and revised based on outcomes. Companies, schools, and communities using sociocracy report more creative solutions, stronger buy-in, and better implementation than conventional governance.

The challenges of consensus governance are real and shouldn't be minimized. It requires significant time, though arguably less than the time wasted on decisions that lack support and fail in implementation. It demands skills—deep listening, emotional regulation, systems thinking—that our education systems don't typically develop. It can be manipulated by those who weaponize the process, using consensus requirements to maintain status quo or advance hidden agendas. It struggles with urgency, though indigenous communities developed war councils and emergency protocols that temporarily suspended normal consensus requirements.

Yet the benefits of consensus extend beyond better decisions to transformation of participants and communities. The process develops capacities essential for ecological civilization—patience, empathy, systems thinking, and comfort with complexity. It creates solutions that voting cannot achieve, finding creative third ways beyond binary choices. It builds genuine community as participants learn to value relationship over position. It generates decisions that people actively support rather than grudgingly accept.

The digital age offers new possibilities for consensus at scale. Liquid democracy allows people to delegate their decision-making power to trusted others on specific topics while retaining the right to participate directly when they choose. Collaborative platforms enable asynchronous consensus-building across distances and time zones. Artificial intelligence could potentially help identify points of agreement and tension in complex discussions, though the risks of algorithmic manipulation require careful consideration.

Rights of Nature in Legal Systems

In 2008, Ecuador became the first nation to recognize constitutional rights of nature, declaring that Pachamama (Mother Earth) has the right to exist, persist, maintain, and regenerate. This wasn't merely symbolic—it created legal standing for ecosystems to defend themselves against destruction. The Vilcabamba River successfully sued for protection against road construction that threatened its flow. The provision has been inconsistently applied and frequently violated, but it represents a fundamental shift in legal consciousness from nature as property to nature as person, from resource to relative.

New Zealand's recognition of the Whanganui River as a legal person in 2017 emerged from different origins but similar recognition. After 140 years of litigation, the Māori secured acknowledgment that the river is "a living whole from the mountains to the sea," deserving rights and representation. Two guardians—one Māori, one government—speak for the river's interests. The settlement recognizes what indigenous peoples have always known: the river is not a thing to be owned but a being to be related with.

Colombia's Constitutional Court declared the Atrato River a subject of rights, ordering the government to protect and restore it from mining pollution. India's courts have recognized rights for the Ganges and Yamuna rivers, though implementation remains contested. Bangladesh declared all rivers legal persons. The Universal Declaration of Rights of Mother Earth, drafted at the 2010 World People's Conference on Climate Change, articulates comprehensive rights for all components of Earth's community.

These legal innovations challenge fundamental assumptions of Western jurisprudence. The concept of legal personhood, historically extended from property-owning men to women, slaves, and corporations, now encompasses rivers, forests, and mountains. This isn't mere legal fiction—it's recognition that these entities have interests that deserve protection, voices that deserve hearing, and agency that deserves respect. The implications ripple through every aspect of law, from property rights to criminal justice to international relations.

The implementation faces enormous challenges. How does a river testify in court? Who legitimately speaks for a forest's interests? How do we adjudicate conflicts between the rights of nature and human rights? These aren't fatal flaws but creative tensions that force legal systems to evolve. Indigenous legal traditions offer guidance—they've always included more-than-human beings as participants in justice systems, whether through dreams, omens, or ritual consultation.

The rights of nature movement extends beyond legal recognition to practical protection. The Global Alliance for Rights of Nature supports communities worldwide in securing legal protection for ecosystems. Earth Law Centers train lawyers in representing nature's interests. Rights of nature tribunals, operating outside state legal systems, create forums for hearing testimony about ecological destruction and issuing moral if not legal judgments.

Critics argue that rights frameworks inappropriately impose human categories onto nature, that legal personhood reduces complex ecosystems to simplified entities, that rights without enforcement are meaningless. These critiques deserve consideration. Rights-based approaches risk maintaining anthropocentric frameworks even while challenging anthropocentric outcomes. They might create legal protection without addressing deeper relationships of domination and exploitation.

Yet rights of nature represent crucial steps toward legal systems that recognize ecological reality. Climate change is fundamentally a legal problem—our laws permit and incentivize the destruction of our life support systems. No amount of technology or behavior change will suffice if legal structures continue authorizing ecocide. Rights of nature create legal tools for interrupting destruction, shifting the burden of proof from those protecting nature to those destroying it.

The relationship between rights of nature and indigenous sovereignty is complex and sometimes contradictory. Indigenous peoples have been the primary advocates and architects of rights of nature, drawing on traditional governance systems that never separated human and natural communities. Yet rights of nature implemented by settler states can potentially override indigenous governance, creating new forms of colonialism dressed in ecological language. Effective implementation requires recognizing indigenous peoples as the legitimate guardians and interpreters of nature's rights in their territories.

Bioregional Governance Structures

Watersheds don't respect political boundaries. Birds don't carry passports. Climate patterns ignore national sovereignty. Yet we govern through political units—nations, states, municipalities—that fragment ecological systems and prevent coherent environmental management. Bioregional governance proposes reorganizing political authority around natural rather than arbitrary boundaries, creating governance structures that match the scale and scope of ecological processes.

The Great Lakes Commission, spanning two nations and eight states, demonstrates bioregional governance in practice. Created to coordinate management of the world's largest freshwater system, the commission brings together diverse jurisdictions around shared ecological reality. While lacking strong enforcement powers, it creates forums for coordinated action, shared research, and collaborative planning that wouldn't otherwise occur. The commission's work on invasive species, water quality, and climate adaptation shows how bioregional cooperation can address challenges that no single jurisdiction could manage alone.

Cascadia, the bioregion encompassing the Pacific Northwest from Northern California to British Columbia, exists more as identity than institution but demonstrates the cultural power of bioregional thinking. Residents increasingly identify as Cascadians, sharing values around environmental protection, sustainable development, and quality of life. This bioregional identity influences politics, economics, and culture across international borders, creating informal governance through shared vision rather than formal authority.

Indigenous nations have always governed bioregionally, understanding that salmon runs, caribou migrations, and seasonal rounds create natural governance units. The Inuit Circumpolar Council represents 180,000 Inuit across Alaska, Canada, Greenland, and Siberia, united by Arctic ecology rather than state boundaries. Their advocacy for Arctic protection carries moral authority precisely because their governance matches ecological reality rather than political construction.

River basin organizations worldwide demonstrate bioregional governance potential. The Mekong River Commission coordinates among six nations whose diverse political systems and development levels create constant tension. Despite limitations, the commission has prevented water wars, maintained dialogue during conflicts, and created frameworks for sharing both water and data. The Rhine Commission transformed Europe's most polluted river into swimmable water through decades of patient cooperation across multiple nations.

Bioregional governance doesn't require abandoning existing political structures but layering new forms of authority based on ecological reality. Cities remain important for managing dense human settlements. Nations coordinate defense, monetary policy, and international relations. But bioregional authorities could manage water, biodiversity, climate adaptation, and other inherently ecological issues. This subsidiarity principle—governing at the most appropriate scale for each issue—creates more flexible and responsive governance.

The challenges are substantial. Existing political authorities rarely cede power willingly. Bioregional boundaries themselves can be contested—where exactly does one watershed end and another begin? Power imbalances between upstream and downstream, urban and rural, wealthy and poor communities create conflicts that shared ecology alone cannot resolve. Without democratic participation, bioregional governance could become technocratic management that excludes affected communities from decisions.

Yet climate change makes bioregional governance increasingly necessary. Adaptation requires landscape-scale coordination. Species migration demands corridor management across jurisdictions. Water scarcity necessitates watershed-level planning. Fire management needs regional strategies. These challenges cannot be addressed through fragmented political units that stop at arbitrary boundaries while ecological processes continue.

Digital technology enables new forms of bioregional coordination. Sensor networks can monitor ecosystem health in real-time across vast territories. Mapping platforms can visualize bioregional patterns and processes. Communication tools can enable participation across distances. Blockchain could create transparent, decentralized governance structures. These tools don't create bioregional consciousness but can support its institutional expression.

Traditional Ecological Governance Models

For thousands of years, human communities have developed governance systems that maintain ecological balance while meeting human needs. These traditional ecological governance models, far from being primitive or obsolete, offer sophisticated solutions to challenges that modern states are failing to address. They demonstrate that human governance and ecological governance need not be separate spheres but can be integrated into unified systems that serve both human and more-than-human communities.

The sasi system of eastern Indonesia governs marine and terrestrial resource use through customary law, spiritual practice, and community enforcement. Resources are periodically closed to harvest, allowing populations to recover. The timing of closures follows ecological indicators—spawning seasons, fruiting cycles, population densities—rather than calendar dates. Decisions emerge from dialogue between traditional leaders, spiritual authorities, and resource users. Violations bring not just material penalties but spiritual consequences, as breaking sasi offends the ancestors and spirits who guarantee resource abundance.

The hima system in Middle Eastern drylands creates protected grazing reserves that maintain biodiversity while supporting pastoralism. Dating back 4,000 years, hima designates areas where grazing is restricted during critical periods, allowing vegetation to recover and provide drought reserves. Management follows traditional ecological knowledge about carrying capacity, seasonal variations, and species requirements. The system creates mosaic landscapes with higher biodiversity than either pure preservation or unlimited grazing would produce.

African age-set systems distribute resource management responsibilities across generations, ensuring both short-term use and long-term sustainability. Young adults might manage annual crops, middle-aged people oversee livestock, and elders govern forests and water sources. This division reflects both physical capabilities and temporal perspectives—those who will live longest with consequences make decisions about long-term resources. The system creates checks and balances, as each age group monitors others' management while depending on their success.

The ahupua'a system of Hawaii divides islands into wedge-shaped units running from mountain peaks to coral reefs, encompassing complete watersheds. Each ahupua'a was managed as an integrated system where activities in one zone affected all others. Upland forest management influenced downstream water availability. Coastal fishing practices affected reef health that protected shoreline agriculture. This ridge-to-reef governance required managers to understand and balance relationships across the entire landscape-seascape continuum.

These systems share common characteristics that differ markedly from modern state governance. Authority derives from demonstrated knowledge and relationship with specific places rather than abstract qualifications or democratic election. Enforcement relies primarily on social pressure and spiritual sanction rather than physical force. Decision-making considers multiple temporal scales, from seasonal cycles to intergenerational consequences. Management adapts to ecological feedback rather than following rigid regulations.

The destruction of traditional governance systems through colonialism, modernization, and globalization has created governance vacuums that state institutions have failed to fill. States typically lack the local knowledge, community legitimacy, and adaptive capacity that traditional systems possessed. The resulting breakdown of resource management has contributed to deforestation, overfishing, soil erosion, and biodiversity loss worldwide. Recognizing and revitalizing traditional governance becomes essential not for romantic reasons but for practical survival.

Contemporary applications of traditional governance principles show promise. Community-based natural resource management programs that incorporate traditional governance elements consistently outperform top-down state management. Collaborative management agreements between indigenous peoples and government agencies combine traditional knowledge with scientific research and traditional authority with state power. Marine protected areas governed through customary law show better compliance than those enforced by government patrol.

The integration of traditional and modern governance faces significant obstacles. State legal systems often don't recognize customary law. Market pressures overwhelm traditional resource management. Younger generations, educated in Western systems, may reject traditional authority. Climate change and industrial pollution create novel challenges that traditional knowledge alone cannot address. Power struggles between traditional and modern leaders can paralyze decision-making.

Yet traditional ecological governance offers essential insights for creating governance systems capable of navigating ecological crises. The recognition that governance must match ecological patterns rather than imposing arbitrary boundaries. The understanding that authority should arise from knowledge and relationship rather than force or wealth. The integration of spiritual and material dimensions in resource management. The inclusion of more-than-human beings as governance participants rather than mere objects of management.

Youth Councils and Seven-Generation Thinking

The climate strikes of 2019 saw millions of young people worldwide demanding that governments consider their futures in current decisions. Greta Thunberg's accusation—"How dare you steal my childhood with your empty words"—articulated youth rage at governance systems that sacrifice future wellbeing for present profit. This uprising reflects a fundamental governance failure: those who will live longest with consequences have least say in decisions. Creating governance structures that incorporate youth voices and future generations' interests becomes essential for decisions that span decades or centuries.

The Seventh Generation Principle, articulated in the Great Law of Peace of the Haudenosaunee Confederacy, requires that decisions consider impacts on descendants seven generations into the future. This isn't vague aspiration but practical methodology. Council members are trained to project forward, imagining how great-great-great-great-great-grandchildren will experience today's choices. This temporal expansion transforms decision-making, making short-term gains that create long-term harms unacceptable.

Wales pioneered institutional seven-generation thinking by establishing the world's first Future Generations Commissioner in 2015. The commissioner advocates for future generations' interests in current policy-making, reviewing government decisions through a long-term lens and challenging short-termism. While powers remain largely advisory, the office has influenced major infrastructure decisions, pushed for preventive rather than reactive policies, and created frameworks for long-term thinking across government.

Youth councils worldwide experiment with including young voices in governance. The European Youth Parliament brings together young people from 40 countries to debate and propose policies. Local youth councils in thousands of municipalities provide formal channels for youth participation. The UN Youth Delegates program includes young people in international negotiations. While often tokenistic, these experiments create precedents for youth participation and develop governance skills in rising generations.

The challenge goes beyond including current youth to representing future generations who cannot speak for themselves. Some propose random selection of future generation representatives, similar to jury duty, who would be trained in long-term thinking and empowered to veto decisions harmful to future interests. Others suggest constitutional provisions that create standing for future generations to sue when their interests are threatened. Japan's Future Design movement runs deliberative forums where participants role-play future generations, finding that this shift in perspective dramatically changes policy preferences.

Indigenous age-based governance systems offer models for balancing different generational perspectives. Many societies designate specific roles for different age groups—youth as scouts and messengers, adults as workers and warriors, elders as wisdom keepers and decision-makers. This creates natural checks on any generation's dominance while ensuring all perspectives are heard. The Maasai age-set system, where governance authority gradually transfers to younger generations through elaborate ceremonies, ensures continuity while enabling adaptation.

The cognitive and emotional differences between age groups become governance assets rather than obstacles when properly structured. Young people's idealism, energy, and innovation balance older generations' experience, patience, and systems thinking. Adolescent brains, more sensitive to unfairness and less constrained by convention, might perceive injustices that adult brains normalize. Elder brains, with decades of pattern recognition, might see connections that younger brains miss.

Digital natives bring essential perspectives to governance in technological society. Young people who've grown up with the internet, social media, and smartphones understand these tools' possibilities and dangers viscerally rather than intellectually. Their participation becomes crucial for governing digital spaces, artificial intelligence, and other emerging technologies that older generations struggle to comprehend. Reverse mentoring, where young people teach older leaders about technological and cultural changes, could become formal governance practice.

The climate crisis makes intergenerational governance especially urgent. Current decision-makers won't live with the worst consequences of their choices. Young people facing decades of climate chaos deserve more than advisory roles in determining responses. Some propose climate assemblies with equal representation across age groups. Others suggest that voting weight could reflect remaining life expectancy, giving those with longer futures greater say in long-term decisions.

Conflict Resolution Through Natural Law

When conflicts arose in traditional Hawaiian society, the practice of ho'oponopono brought all parties together—not to determine guilt and punishment but to restore pono, the state of correct relationship and balance. The process recognized that conflict creates disturbance throughout the community and cosmos, requiring healing that goes beyond individual grievance. Through prayer, confession, discussion, and forgiveness, participants sought to identify and correct the source of imbalance, understanding that unresolved conflict would manifest as illness, misfortune, or ecological disruption.

This approach to conflict resolution through natural law—principles derived from observation of nature's patterns rather than human legislation—appears across cultures. Natural law recognizes that just as ecosystems maintain balance through reciprocal relationships and feedback loops, human communities require similar mechanisms for restoring harmony when balance is disrupted. The goal isn't punishment but healing, not victory but reconciliation, not determining who was right but discovering what will restore wholeness.

The Peacemaker Courts of the Navajo Nation demonstrate natural law in contemporary practice. Based on traditional concepts of hózhó (harmony, balance, beauty) and k'é (kinship, relationship), these courts bring together disputants, families, and community members to discuss problems and develop solutions. The process is guided by naat'aanii (peacemakers) who help participants understand how their actions have disrupted harmony and what must be done to restore it. Agreements reached through this process have higher compliance rates than court-ordered judgments because they emerge from consensus rather than imposition.

Restorative justice movements worldwide draw on indigenous practices that understand crime as harm to relationships requiring healing rather than violation of law requiring punishment. Victim-offender mediation brings together those harmed and those who caused harm to share experiences, express emotions, and develop agreements for repair.

Community conferencing includes wider circles of those affected by conflict. Healing circles address systemic issues that contribute to harmful behavior. These processes often achieve what punitive justice cannot—genuine accountability, emotional healing, and behavioral change.

Natural law principles for conflict resolution emerge from observing how nature handles disruption. When a tree falls in a forest, creating disturbance, the system doesn't punish the tree but responds creatively—new plants colonize the light gap, fallen wood becomes habitat, nutrients cycle back into soil. The disturbance becomes an opportunity for renewal and increased diversity. Similarly, human conflict, while painful, can catalyze growth and transformation when approached as opportunity rather than crisis.

The Gacaca courts of Rwanda, revived and modified after the 1994 genocide, attempted to apply traditional justice to unprecedented mass atrocity. Communities gathered weekly to hear testimonies, determine guilt, and decide consequences for genocide participants. While controversial and imperfect, the process enabled a society to confront its trauma collectively rather than through distant tribunals. The emphasis on confession, apology, and reintegration—rather than solely punishment—allowed communities to begin healing while maintaining accountability.

Ubuntu-based justice in South Africa understands that "a person is a person through other persons," making isolation through imprisonment counterproductive. The Truth and Reconciliation Commission, while flawed in execution, embodied ubuntu principles by prioritizing truth-telling and amnesty over prosecution. The process recognized that sustainable peace required acknowledging harm, expressing remorse, and beginning reconciliation rather than perpetuating cycles of retribution.

Natural law extends beyond human conflicts to disputes between humans and nature. When development projects threaten ecosystems, conventional law weighs economic benefits against environmental costs through abstract calculation. Natural law would instead ask: what maintains the integrity of relationships? How can human needs be met without destroying the systems that support all life? What would restoration and reciprocity look like? These questions reframe conflicts from zero-sum competition to creative problem-solving.

The challenges of natural law approaches are significant. They require time that urgent conflicts might not allow. They depend on shared values that pluralistic societies might lack. They assume willingness to participate that adversaries might refuse. They can be manipulated by those who use reconciliation language to avoid accountability. They struggle with power imbalances that make genuine dialogue difficult. They may conflict with state legal systems that demand retribution.

Yet natural law offers essential alternatives to legal systems that perpetuate rather than resolve conflicts. Adversarial justice systems create winners and losers, often leaving all parties unsatisfied. Punitive approaches generate recidivism rather than rehabilitation. Legal proceedings reduce complex relationships to simplified narratives. Criminal justice systems disproportionately harm marginalized communities while failing to address root causes of harmful behavior.

Toward Ecological Democracy

The transformation of governance from human-centered to life-centered democracy represents one of humanity's greatest challenges and necessities. Ecological democracy doesn't mean that trees vote or rivers run for office, but that governance systems recognize and represent the interests of all life, make decisions based on ecological wisdom, and measure success through ecosystem health alongside human welfare. This isn't a return to pre-modern governance but an evolution toward forms that match our ecological knowledge and ethical development.

Ecological democracy requires expanding our conception of the demos—the people who constitute democracy. If democracy means rule by the people, who counts as people? Ancient Athens limited democracy to property-owning men. Modern democracies gradually expanded to include women, racial minorities, and property-less citizens. The next expansion must include future generations, more-than-human beings, and ecosystems themselves. This doesn't require granting them votes but ensuring their interests are represented in decision-making.

This expansion is already beginning through various mechanisms. Guardian institutions speak for those who cannot speak for themselves—ombudspersons for future generations, trustees for ecosystems, advocates for endangered species. Environmental impact assessments force consideration of ecological effects. Constitutional environmental rights create enforceable standards. Green parties bring ecological perspectives into parliaments. While insufficient, these developments show that ecological democracy is possible.

The practice of ecological democracy might involve multiple chambers of governance with different constituencies and concerns. A human chamber elected by current citizens. An ecological chamber with representatives chosen for their knowledge of and relationship with specific ecosystems. A future chamber selected through sortition and trained in long-term thinking. A wisdom council of elders who hold memory and pattern recognition. Decisions would require alignment across chambers, ensuring that multiple perspectives are integrated.

Citizen assemblies on climate change demonstrate possibilities for ecological democracy. When given time, information, and support to deliberate, ordinary citizens consistently choose more ambitious climate action than professional politicians. The assemblies in Ireland, France, and the UK have proposed rapid decarbonization, economic transformation, and lifestyle changes that political parties consider impossible. This suggests that ecological democracy's obstacle isn't public readiness but political systems captured by vested interests.

Ecological democracy requires different decision-making processes than current democratic practice. Rather than reducing complex issues to binary choices, deliberative processes would explore multiple options and creative combinations. Rather than privileging human interests, decisions would be evaluated against ecological criteria—does this enhance or diminish biodiversity? Does it respect planetary boundaries? Does it consider the rights of other species? Rather than majority rule, modified consensus processes would ensure that minority perspectives, including non-human interests, aren't simply overruled.

The transition to ecological democracy faces enormous resistance from those who benefit from current arrangements. Fossil fuel companies, industrial agriculture, and other extractive industries have captured political systems worldwide. Anthropocentric religions and philosophies provide ideological justification for human supremacy. Nationalist movements resist the transboundary cooperation that ecological governance requires. The urgency of the ecological crisis might seem to demand authoritarian responses rather than democratic deliberation.

Yet ecological democracy offers the only sustainable path forward. Authoritarian environmentalism might achieve short-term emission reductions but cannot generate the deep cultural transformation that ecological civilization requires. Market mechanisms might price certain environmental costs but cannot value what markets cannot comprehend. Technocratic management might optimize resource use but cannot navigate the value questions at ecology's heart. Only inclusive, participatory processes that honor both human and more-than-human voices can create the legitimacy, wisdom, and commitment that transformation requires.

The seeds of ecological democracy exist in countless experiments worldwide. Indigenous governance systems that have maintained ecosystems for millennia. Watershed councils that bring together diverse stakeholders around shared waters. Transition initiatives that demonstrate community-led transformation. Urban ecology movements that reimagine cities as ecosystems. Youth movements that demand intergenerational justice. These aren't marginal alternatives but previews of emerging possibilities.

As we stand at this threshold, the choice is not whether to transform governance but how quickly and creatively we can do so. The systems designed for human dominion over nature cannot navigate our integration with nature. The institutions created for resource extraction cannot manage regeneration. The decision-making processes that created the ecological crisis cannot resolve it. We need governance as innovative as the challenges we face, as diverse as the life it must serve, as enduring as the consequences of our choices.

The council fire still burns through the night, but now it must include voices that colonial governance silenced—indigenous peoples, future generations, rivers and forests, salmon and soil. The conversation will be complex, sometimes cacophonous, always challenging. But from this expanded dialogue can emerge decisions worthy of the seventh generation, governance that serves all relations, and democracy that honors the demos of all life. This is the work of our time: not just reforming governance but reimagining it for a living Earth.

CHAPTER 15

Education and
Child-Rearing

five-year-old child crouches beside a tide pool on the Oregon
coast, completely absorbed in watching hermit crabs negotiate
their miniature world. She doesn't know the Latin names for the species
she observes, cannot yet explain the chemistry of seawater, has never
heard of ecological niches or trophic cascades. But she knows something
perhaps more fundamental—that these creatures have their own purposes, their own experiences, their own rights to exist. She speaks to
them naturally, without self-consciousness, understanding intuitively
what adults have been trained to forget: that communication doesn't require shared language, that consciousness doesn't require human form,
that learning happens through relationship rather than just observation.

Her grandmother, raised on this same coast by people who never for-
got these truths, watches with satisfaction. The child is receiving her
first lessons in what the Haida call yahguudang—respect for all living
things. This education doesn't happen in classrooms with textbooks
and tests but through direct encounter, patient observation, and guided
experience with the more-than-human world. The grandmother knows
that before the child can learn about nature, she must learn from nature,
and before she can develop environmental ethics, she must develop environmental relationships.

This scene represents education as it existed for most of human history and as it still exists in communities that maintain connection with

land and tradition. Children learned through participation rather than instruction, through story rather than textbook, through relationship rather than abstraction. They developed knowledge not as a commodity to be acquired but as responsibility to be carried. They understood themselves not as separate from what they studied but as participants in the systems they sought to understand.

Modern education has severed these connections, removing children from direct experience with the living world and replacing it with mediated information about that world. We teach ecology through diagrams rather than forests, biology through dissection rather than observation, chemistry through equations rather than cooking and gardening. Children learn that real knowledge exists in books and experts rather than in their own experience and relationships. They absorb the hidden curriculum that humans are the only subjects in a world of objects, that intelligence means human-style cognition, that value derives from utility to human purposes.

Place-Based and Outdoor Education

The forest kindergartens of Germany and Scandinavia have no walls, no roofs, no climate control—just earth, sky, and weather in all its variations. Children spend their entire school day outdoors, learning through play and exploration rather than formal instruction. They climb trees despite the risk of falling, handle tools despite the possibility of injury, experience cold and rain despite discomfort. Research consistently shows these children develop better physical health, emotional regulation, social skills, creativity, and environmental connection than their indoor-educated peers.

This isn't romantic nostalgia but recognition of how human children evolved to learn. For hundreds of thousands of years, children developed competence through direct engagement with their environment. They learned botany by gathering plants with elders, physics by throwing spears and stones, psychology by navigating complex social groups, ecology by tracking animals and observing seasonal patterns. Their bodies and brains expect this kind of embodied, contextual, relational learning. Classroom education, however enriched, cannot fully substitute for direct experience with the living world.

Place-based education grounds learning in local phenomena and environments, using the unique history, culture, and ecology of each place as foundation for curriculum. Rather than learning about rainforests from textbooks while living in prairies, students study their own watersheds. Rather than memorizing dates of distant historical events, they uncover their community's stories. Rather than conducting abstract science experiments, they monitor local water quality, track phenological changes, and participate in restoration projects.

The Sustainable Schools Project in Vermont demonstrates place-based education at scale. Schools partner with farms, forests, and communities to create curriculum rooted in local reality. Students design energy systems for their schools, manage school forests, operate greenhouses and gardens, and sell products at farmers' markets. They learn mathematics through maple syrup production, writing through community oral histories, science through stream monitoring. Academic achievement increases, but more importantly, students develop connection to place and capacity for ecological citizenship.

Indigenous education systems have always been place-based, understanding that land itself is the first and most important teacher. Australian Aboriginal education happens through walking country with elders, learning not just about land but from land. Each place holds stories that encode ecological knowledge, survival skills, social laws, and spiritual teachings. The curriculum emerges from the land itself—this rock formation teaches about geological time, that tree provides medicine, and these animal tracks reveal behavioral patterns. Knowledge and place are inseparable; to know is to be in relationship with specific places.

The consequences of placeless education are profound. Children who don't know their local plants can't participate in their local ecology.

Students who don't know their watershed can't protect it. Communities disconnected from their history repeat its mistakes. When education happens through a generic curriculum divorced from place, it produces people prepared to live nowhere in particular, equally capable of destroying any place because no place is home.

Outdoor education programs attempt to reconnect children with direct experience of the natural world, though often in limited ways. School gardens teach food production and ecological cycles. Nature centers provide hands-on science learning. Wilderness trips build confidence and connection. Environmental education programs foster awareness and activism. While valuable, these programs often remain additions to rather than transformations of conventional education. A field trip to nature doesn't fundamentally challenge the assumption that real learning happens indoors.

The COVID-19 pandemic unexpectedly advanced outdoor education as schools sought safer spaces. Many discovered what forest kindergartens have long known—children often learn better outdoors. Attention improves, behavior problems decrease, engagement increases. Teachers report that lessons taught outdoors are better remembered, that students who struggle indoors often thrive outside, that natural settings reduce stress for everyone. Some schools have made permanent shifts, creating outdoor classrooms and increasing time spent outside.

Yet obstacles to outdoor education remain substantial. Liability concerns make administrators fearful of activities involving any risk. Standardized curricula leave little room for place-based learning. Teacher training rarely includes outdoor pedagogy. Parents conditioned to traditional education worry their children will fall behind. Urban schools may lack easy access to natural areas. Weather becomes an excuse rather than an opportunity. These obstacles reflect deeper cultural anxieties about control, safety, and what counts as legitimate education.

The screen-based childhood that now dominates children's experience makes outdoor education more necessary and more difficult. Children who spend 7-10 hours daily on screens develop different neural patterns than those who play outdoors. Their attention systems adapt to rapid stimulation rather than patient observation. Their bodies lose capacity for rough terrain and physical challenge. Their imaginations atrophy without the open-ended possibilities of natural play. Outdoor education must now compete with digital entertainment designed to be maximally engaging.

Traditional Skills and Indigenous Knowledge

An Inuit elder teaches a young person to read ice—not from a textbook but by walking together across the frozen sea, feeling the subtle differences in texture and flex that indicate thickness and stability. This knowledge, developed over millennia and passed through generations, cannot be reduced to rules or formulas. It requires embodied understanding, pattern recognition developed through experience, and intimate knowledge of local conditions. It represents a way of knowing that Western education has systematically devalued and destroyed.

Traditional skills carry more than practical knowledge—they encode worldviews, values, and relationships. When a Cherokee elder teaches a child to gather medicinal plants, the lesson includes not just plant identification but protocols of asking permission, practices of reciprocity, stories that encode ecological relationships, and understanding of oneself as part of rather than separate from the forest community. The skill cannot be separated from its ethical and spiritual dimensions without losing its essence.

The recovery and transmission of traditional skills has become urgent as the last generation that grew up with these practices ages. In Alaska, programs bring elders into schools to teach Native languages, subsistence skills, and traditional technologies. Students learn to process salmon, sew parkas, build kayaks, and navigate by natural signs. But they also learn values—respect for elders, gratitude for animals that provide sustenance, responsibility to share with community, and understanding of humans as junior members of ancient ecological communities.

These programs face the challenge of teaching land-based skills to children growing up in increasingly urban and digital environments. Traditional skills developed in contexts where they were essential for survival; teaching them as electives in school settings fundamentally changes their meaning. Yet even partial transmission maintains threads of connection that might otherwise be permanently severed. Young people discovering traditional skills often report feeling like they're remembering something forgotten rather than learning something new.

The maker movement and primitive skills communities represent non-indigenous efforts to recover traditional capacities. People gather to learn friction fire, stone tool production, hide tanning, basket weaving, and other skills that humans have practiced for millennia. While sometimes criticized as appropriation or romanticism, these movements reflect genuine hunger for embodied knowledge and direct engagement with materials. They reveal how much capacity we've lost—most people cannot make fire without matches, cannot identify edible plants, cannot construct basic shelter, cannot navigate without GPS.

Traditional ecological knowledge (TEK) increasingly gains recognition from Western science as essential for understanding and managing ecosystems. Indigenous management practices that seemed primitive to colonial observers prove sophisticated in light of ecological science. Aboriginal fire management reduces catastrophic wildfire while increasing biodiversity. Andean potato cultivation maintains genetic diversity that industrial agriculture destroys. Polynesian fishing practices sustain reef ecosystems that Western extraction devastates. This knowledge, transmitted through traditional education, represents irreplaceable libraries of tested solutions to ecological challenges.

The integration of TEK into formal education faces multiple challenges. Indigenous knowledge holders justifiably resist sharing knowledge that has been stolen, commercialized, and misused. Traditional knowledge often cannot be separated from its cultural and spiritual context without losing its meaning. Oral traditions don't translate easily into written curricula. Place-based knowledge doesn't transfer simply to other locations. Power dynamics between Western and indigenous knowledge systems create constant tensions.

Yet collaborations between indigenous knowledge holders and educational institutions show promise. In New Zealand, Māori knowledge is increasingly integrated throughout the curriculum rather than segregated into cultural studies. Science classes learn Māori classification systems alongside Linnaean taxonomy. Environmental management programs incorporate traditional management practices. Medical schools teach rongoā (traditional healing) alongside Western medicine. This isn't token inclusion but recognition that indigenous knowledge offers essential perspectives for navigating current challenges.

The transmission of traditional skills also raises questions about cultural appropriation and authentic practice. Which skills belong to all humanity and which are specific cultural property? How can non-indigenous people learn from indigenous knowledge without stealing or misrepresenting it? What are appropriate protocols for cross-cultural learning? These questions don't have simple answers but require ongoing dialogue, relationship building, and recognition of the power dynamics that shape knowledge exchange.

Rites of Passage and Initiation Practices

The thirteen-year-old stands alone in the forest, three days into their solo passage ritual. Hunger gnaws, fear visits at night, loneliness weighs heavy. But also: stars become intimate companions, bird calls carry messages, the forest reveals itself as a living presence rather than a collection of trees. When elders retrieve them, they return differently—not magically transformed into adults but having touched something essential about their place in the web of life. They've learned through direct experience what no classroom could teach: that they can survive discomfort, that nature provides everything necessary, that they belong to something vastly larger than human society.

Modern Western culture has largely abandoned formal rites of passage, leaving young people to navigate the transition to adulthood without guidance, witnesses, or acknowledgment. The results are visible in extended adolescence, identity confusion, and young people seeking initiation through dangerous or destructive behaviors. Without culturally sanctioned ways to prove adulthood, youth create their own trials—binge drinking, sexual conquest, consumer accumulation, digital achievement. These privatized, commercialized pseudo-initiations cannot provide what genuine rites of passage offer: death of the child-self, birth of the adult-self, and integration into community with new responsibilities and recognition.

Traditional rites of passage share common elements across cultures: separation from childhood environment, ordeal or challenge that tests capacity, encounter with the sacred or mysterious, and return with new status and responsibilities. These rites don't just mark biological maturation but create psychological and spiritual transformation. They teach young people through direct experience that they possess inner resources they didn't know existed, that they're part of lineages extending backward and forward through time, that adulthood means service to something greater than personal desire.

Contemporary wilderness rites of passage programs attempt to provide what modern culture lacks. Organizations like the School of Lost Borders, Rites of Passage Journeys, and Coming of Age offer structured experiences that adapt traditional forms to contemporary contexts. Participants undergo preparation through teaching and community building, experience threshold time alone on the land, and return to integration and witnessing. While these programs cannot replicate the cultural container that traditional rites emerged from, they provide profound experiences that many participants describe as life-changing.

The inclusion of nature as teacher and witness in these rites reflects deep wisdom about human development. Adolescents naturally seek intensity, risk, and transformation—drives that nature can meet safely while teaching essential lessons. A thunderstorm teaches humility more effectively than any lecture. A mountain summit earned through struggle provides confidence no participation trophy can match. Time alone with the elements strips away social masks and reveals authentic self. Nature doesn't judge, compete, or withhold love based on performance.

Gender-specific rites of passage address the particular challenges of becoming men and women in contemporary society. Boys struggling with cultural messages about masculinity find in nature-based rites different models of strength—the patience of stalking, the vulnerability of council, the service of providing for others. Girls navigating impossible beauty standards and sexualization discover through earth-based rites the power of their bodies as capable rather than decorative, their worth as inherent rather than performed.

Indigenous communities maintaining or reviving their rites of passage demonstrate their ongoing relevance. The Maasai of East Africa continue age-set initiations that bond cohorts for life while teaching responsibility to community and land. Apache Sunrise Ceremonies guide girls into womanhood through four days of ritual that connect them to Changing Woman and the powers of creation. Australian Aboriginal walkabout sends youth alone into the bush to trace songlines and receive their place in the dreaming. These rites maintain cultural continuity while adapting to contemporary realities.

Schools experimenting with rites of passage programs report significant impacts on student development and school culture. The Rite of Passage Experience (ROPE) program in American schools provides year-long preparation culminating in wilderness solos. Students develop emotional intelligence, self-awareness, and sense of purpose. They return more focused, confident, and ready to contribute. The programs particularly benefit students who struggle in conventional academic settings but thrive in experiential challenges.

The absence of community-recognized rites of passage leaves young people seeking transformation through individual choice rather than collective recognition. A gap year backpacking through Asia might provide powerful experiences but lacks the community witnessing that transforms personal experience into social reality. Online communities attempt to provide peer recognition, but digital affirmation cannot replace embodied presence of elders and community. Consumer culture offers endless products promising transformation, but purchasing cannot provide genuine initiation.

Mentorship and Apprenticeship Models

The master carpenter watches as his apprentice struggles with a particularly challenging joint. He doesn't immediately correct the error or explain the solution. Instead, he asks questions that guide discovery: "What is the wood telling you? How does the grain want to move? What happens if you approach from a different angle?" This teaching through relationship rather than instruction, through years rather than semesters, through practice rather than theory, represents education as it existed before industrialization demanded mass-produced workers with standardized skills.

Mentorship and apprenticeship create different relationships with knowledge than classroom education. Knowledge isn't a commodity to be transferred but capacity to be developed. Learning happens through observation, imitation, and gradually increasing responsibility rather than through explanation and testing. The relationship between mentor and apprentice involves whole persons rather than roles, extending beyond skill transmission to include values, wisdom, and ways of being. The process cannot be rushed or standardized; each apprentice learns at their own pace through their own journey.

Traditional apprenticeship systems encoded sophisticated pedagogies that modern education has forgotten. The medieval guild system's progression from apprentice to journeyman to master created clear developmental stages with increasing autonomy and responsibility. Japanese shokunin (craftsman) traditions involve decades of patient practice toward perfection, understanding mastery as a lifelong journey rather than an achievable goal. West African griot traditions transmit not just musical skills but entire cultural histories through intimate master-student relationships spanning years.

Contemporary apprenticeship programs struggle to recreate these relationships within industrial timeframes and economic pressures. Modern apprenticeships often reduce to cheap labor rather than genuine education. Mentors lack time for patient guidance when productivity demands dominate. Apprentices expect quick results rather than slow mastery. Legal frameworks designed for employee-employer relationships don't accommodate the complex reciprocities of traditional apprenticeship. Yet successful programs demonstrate that apprenticeship models can work in contemporary contexts when properly supported.

The resurgence of craft traditions has renewed interest in apprenticeship learning. Young people seeking alternatives to university education discover in traditional crafts both viable livelihoods and meaningful ways of life. Blacksmithing, timber framing, herbalism, traditional farming—these skills require forms of knowledge that cannot be learned from YouTube videos or weekend workshops. They demand sustained relationship with materials, tools, and mentors who embody generations of accumulated wisdom.

Mentorship extends beyond skill transmission to include psychosocial development that formal education neglects. A good mentor sees potential that apprentices cannot yet perceive in themselves. They provide challenges that stretch capacity without overwhelming. They offer support through failure and celebration through success. They model not just competence but character, showing through example how to live with integrity, purpose, and joy. These relationships shape identity in ways that classroom teachers, however dedicated, rarely can.

The absence of mentorship in modern education leaves young people navigating complex life transitions without guides who've walked similar paths. Career counselors provide information but not wisdom.

Teachers manage classrooms rather than cultivating individuals. Parents, often overwhelmed and uncertain themselves, cannot provide the outside perspective that mentors offer. Young people hunger for adults who believe in them, challenge them, and show them possibilities they couldn't imagine alone.

Nature-based mentorship programs combine traditional mentoring with environmental education. The Art of Mentoring programs train adults to guide children's nature connection through "invisible school"—learning that happens through games, stories, and guided discovery rather than formal instruction. Mentors learn to follow children's curiosity rather than imposing curriculum, to ask questions rather than provide answers, to create experiences that awaken wonder and develop capacity. The programs report that both mentors and youth experience profound growth through these relationships.

Elder mentorship programs connect youth with tradition bearers who carry knowledge and wisdom from different times. Unlike parents, who children naturally rebel against, elders can transmit values and perspectives without triggering resistance. They offer a long-term perspective that relativizes current anxieties. They share stories of resilience through challenges that make contemporary difficulties seem manageable. They provide unconditional acceptance that performance-oriented culture rarely offers. Yet modern society segregates generations, making these relationships increasingly rare.

Storytelling and Oral Tradition in Learning

The children gather in a circle as evening falls, their attention completely captured by the elder's voice weaving ancient tales. The story unfolds not as entertainment but as teaching, carrying lessons about behavior, relationships, and the nature of reality itself. When Coyote's greed leads to disaster, children absorb warnings about excess. When Grandmother Spider weaves the world into being, they learn about creativity and connection. When heroes journey through trials, young listeners map their own future challenges. This is education through story—indirect but profound, memorable rather than memorizable, transforming hearts as well as minds.

Oral tradition represents humanity's original educational technology, predating writing by hundreds of thousands of years. Stories encoded essential knowledge for survival—which plants heal and which harm, where to find water in drought, how to read weather signs, what to do when predators threaten. But they carried more than practical information. Stories transmitted worldviews, values, and identity. They taught children their place in the cosmos and community. They provided templates for navigating life's challenges. They maintained the spiritual technologies that kept communities healthy and whole.

The characteristics of oral learning differ fundamentally from literate education. Oral stories change with each telling, adapting to the audience and moment while maintaining essential structures. They engage whole persons—body through gesture, emotion through drama, imagination through imagery, intellect through symbolism. They encode information in narrative patterns that brains naturally remember. They create participatory experiences rather than passive reception. They transmit knowledge through the relationship between storyteller and listener rather than through impersonal text.

Modern neuroscience confirms what oral cultures always knew—stories are how brains make sense of reality. Neural networks organize experience into narrative patterns. Memory palace techniques use spatial and narrative structures to enhance recall. Mirror neurons fire when hearing stories, creating embodied experiences of narrated events. Emotional engagement during storytelling enhances learning and retention. The narrative brain preceded and underlies the analytical brain; we are Homo narrans before we are Homo sapiens.

Yet modern education privileges analytical over narrative intelligence, information over wisdom, facts over meanings. Students memorize dates, formulas, and definitions that they quickly forget because these fragments don't connect to narrative structures that create meaning. They read textbooks that present knowledge as established facts rather than unfolding stories. They write essays arguing positions rather than exploring possibilities. They're tested on retention of information rather than integration of understanding.

The consequences extend beyond poor retention to impoverished imagination. Children raised on ready-made visual entertainment rather than oral stories don't develop the capacity to generate internal imagery. Students trained in analysis rather than narrative struggle to synthesize complex information into coherent wholes. Adults educated through argument rather than story approach disagreement as combat rather than dialogue. Communities that lose their stories lose their identities, becoming susceptible to whatever narratives consumer culture provides.

Indigenous education maintains oral tradition as a primary pedagogical tool, understanding that stories carry what cannot be conveyed through other means. Aboriginal Dreamtime stories encode maps, laws, histories, and spiritual teachings in narrative forms that have transmitted unchanged for tens of thousands of years. Native American stories teach through indirection, allowing listeners to discover meanings rather than imposing interpretations. African praise songs encode genealogies, achievements, and cultural values in memorable forms that maintain identity across generations.

Contemporary storytelling revival movements attempt to restore narrative to education. Teachers discover that students who struggle with textbook history come alive when historical events are presented as stories. Science educators find that narrative explanations of natural phenomena engage students who resist mathematical formulations. Literature programs that emphasize oral performance rather than silent reading report increased engagement and comprehension. Digital storytelling projects allow students to create and share their own narratives, developing both technical and narrative skills.

The relationship between storytelling and ecological education is particularly powerful. Environmental information presented as statistics—parts per million, degrees of warming, species extinctions—creates paralysis rather than action. But stories of specific places and beings create emotional connections that motivate engagement. When children hear stories from the perspective of rivers, trees, or animals, they develop empathy that no amount of factual information can generate. When they learn traditional stories about relationships between humans and nature, they absorb worldviews that make ecological destruction unthinkable.

University Programs in Applied Animism

Schumacher College in Devon, England, offers master's degrees in Holistic Science and Ecological Design that challenge fundamental assumptions of Western education. Students don't just study ecology but participate in the college's gardens and forest. They don't just read about systems theory but experience themselves as part of living systems. Classes might involve meditation with trees, council practice for decision-making, or ritual marking of seasonal transitions. This isn't New Age dilettantism but rigorous academic work grounded in recognition that rational intelligence alone cannot navigate ecological crises.

The California Institute of Integral Studies offers degrees in Integral Ecology and Philosophy, Cosmology, and Consciousness that explicitly engage with animistic worldviews. Students read not just Western philosophers but indigenous thinkers. They study not just consciousness as human phenomenon but as quality pervading cosmos. They explore not just environmental solutions but the worldview shifts that make solutions possible. Graduates don't just possess knowledge but have undergone transformation, emerging with capacities for thinking and being that conventional education doesn't develop.

Prescott College's Adventure Education and Environmental Studies programs conduct classes outdoors, in wilderness, on rivers and mountains. Students earn degrees through expeditions, field research, and community engagement rather than sitting in classrooms. They develop competence not just intellectually but physically, emotionally, and spiritually. They learn leadership through leading, ecology through inhabiting, and sustainability through practicing. The college understands that the environmental crisis requires educated whole persons, not just trained minds.

These programs remain marginal within higher education, dismissed by conventional academia as lacking rigor or departing from legitimate scholarship. Yet they attract students hungry for education that addresses contemporary challenges and develops capacities that mainstream universities ignore. They produce graduates who can think systemically, work collaboratively, engage emotionally, and act ethically in ways that conventionally educated peers struggle to achieve. They demonstrate that different forms of knowledge and ways of knowing are not just possible but necessary.

Indigenous universities provide models for education grounded in animistic worldviews while maintaining academic excellence. Te Whare Wānanga o Awanuiārangi in New Zealand grounds all programs in Māori knowledge systems. Students learn through whakapapa (genealogical connections), understanding themselves as part of lineages extending from cosmic origins through future generations. Knowledge is approached as taonga (treasure) carrying responsibilities rather than commodity for individual advancement. Graduates emerge prepared to serve their communities while engaging with global challenges.

The Indigenous Environmental Network's Protecting Mother Earth conferences function as temporary universities where traditional knowledge holders, activists, and academics share wisdom about living sustainably on Earth. Participants learn through ceremony, story, direct action, and dialogue rather than lectures and tests. Knowledge is understood as arising from relationship with land rather than abstract study. Solutions emerge from indigenous wisdom that sees environmental and social justice as inseparable. These gatherings demonstrate education as movement building rather than individual achievement.

The challenges facing university-level animistic education are substantial. Accreditation bodies require standardized curricula that restrict innovation. Funding favors research that serves corporate rather than ecological interests. Academic culture privileges publication over practice, analysis over experience, competition over collaboration. Students arrive after twelve years of conventional education that has trained them for passive reception rather than active participation. Faculty trained in narrow specializations struggle to teach holistically.

Yet the transformation of higher education has begun. Environmental programs increasingly recognize that technical solutions require cultural transformation. Medical schools explore indigenous healing traditions and mind-body medicine. Business schools develop programs in regenerative economics and stakeholder value. Even hard sciences begin acknowledging that consciousness, meaning, and value are irreducible aspects of reality that science must engage. These changes remain peripheral, but peripheries are where transformation begins.

The question is not whether higher education will transform but whether transformation will happen quickly enough to prepare leaders for navigating ecological crises. Universities that continue producing graduates trained for industrial civilization will become obsolete as that civilization collapses. Those that develop capacities for ecological civilization will shape humanity's future. The choice is not between academic rigor and experiential learning, between indigenous and Western knowledge, between spiritual and material education, but how to integrate these complementary ways of knowing into education that serves life.

Transforming Education for Life

As we contemplate the transformation of education from its current industrial model to forms that nurture ecological consciousness and animistic understanding, we face both enormous challenges and extraordinary opportunities. The education system we've inherited was designed to produce workers for the industrial economy, citizens for nation-states, and consumers for capitalist markets. It cannot produce the ecological citizens, Earth-keepers, and wisdom holders that our moment demands.

The transformation required is not curricular but foundational. We need education that develops whole persons rather than just intellects, that cultivates wisdom alongside knowledge, that nurtures relationship with rather than mastery over the living world. This doesn't mean abandoning intellectual rigor but expanding our conception of intelligence to include emotional, somatic, spiritual, and ecological ways of knowing. It doesn't mean rejecting technology but ensuring that tools serve rather than replace direct experience. It doesn't mean returning to the past but creating futures that honor ancient wisdom while embracing appropriate innovation.

This transformation is already emerging in countless experiments worldwide. Forest schools that conduct classes entirely outdoors. Democratic schools where students direct their own learning. Indigenous education programs that center traditional knowledge. Contemplative education that develops mindfulness and presence. Garden-based learning that grounds education in food production. Maker spaces that emphasize creation over consumption. These aren't perfect solutions but evolutionary experiments, testing possibilities for education that serves life.

The role of children themselves in this transformation deserves special attention. Young people are not empty vessels waiting to be filled with knowledge but naturally brilliant beings with their own wisdom to contribute. Children who haven't yet been fully conditioned by industrial mindsets often perceive solutions that adults cannot see. They ask questions that reveal hidden assumptions. They imagine possibilities unconstrained by conventional limitations. Transforming education requires not just new ways of teaching children but new ways of learning from them.

The COVID-19 pandemic inadvertently accelerated educational transformation by disrupting conventional schooling and forcing experimentation with alternatives. Many families discovered that children learn better outside classrooms, that community resources provide rich educational opportunities, that standardized curriculum doesn't serve diverse learners. While the return to "normal" has reversed many changes, the experience revealed that different forms of education are possible when circumstances demand innovation.

The climate crisis makes educational transformation not idealistic but essential. Young people facing ecological collapse need different capacities than those facing industrial expansion. They need resilience rather than just achievement, cooperation rather than just competition, systems thinking rather than just specialized knowledge, and hope grounded in agency rather than despair masked by distraction. They need education that prepares them to navigate unprecedented challenges while maintaining mental health, social connection, and spiritual grounding.

The path forward requires simultaneous work at multiple scales. Individual parents and teachers can create pockets of transformation within existing systems—teaching outdoors when possible, sharing stories alongside textbooks, facilitating rather than instructing. Communities can develop alternative educational opportunities—nature clubs, mentorship programs, skill-sharing workshops, storytelling circles. Institutions can pilot new approaches—place-based curricula, outdoor classrooms, contemplative practices, indigenous partnerships. Movements can advocate for systemic change—policy reform, funding shifts, cultural transformation.

As we undertake this great work of educational transformation, we might remember that children naturally experience the world animistically until educated out of it. They spontaneously talk to animals, befriend trees, and attribute consciousness to cherished objects. They learn through play, story, and relationship rather than instruction. They experience wonder as default rather than exception. The task is not to impose animistic worldviews onto children but to stop destroying the animistic consciousness they naturally possess.

The child at the tide pool, speaking unselfconsciously to hermit crabs, carries wisdom that all our educational institutions should serve to protect and cultivate rather than suppress. She knows in her body what we must remember in our cultures—that we are not alone in a dead world but participants in a living cosmos, that intelligence takes countless forms beyond the human, that learning happens through mutual interaction with rather than distant study of the world. Her education should expand and deepen this knowing rather than replace it with alienation disguised as sophistication.

This is education's sacred task in our time: to raise generations who understand themselves as part of rather than separate from the commonwealth of life, who possess the practical skills and spiritual grounding to navigate collapse and renewal, who can imagine and create ways of being human that enhance rather than diminish Earth's glorious diversity. The transformation from industrial to ecological education is not optional but essential, not impossible but already beginning, not about returning to the past but about ensuring there is a future worth inhabiting.

CHAPTER 16

Technology in Service of Life

The termite mound rises from the African savanna like a cathedral built by creatures smaller than fingernails. Within its earthen walls, a million insects maintain perfect climate control without electricity, achieving what human engineers struggle to replicate with complex HVAC systems. Air channels carved with millimeter precision create convection currents that regulate temperature within one degree. Fungus gardens in specialized chambers process plant matter into food. The entire structure breathes, adapts, and self-repairs—a living technology that has functioned sustainably for millions of years before humans discovered fire.

Meanwhile, in a laboratory in Japan, scientists study the slime mold Physarum polycephalum as it solves network optimization problems that challenge our most powerful computers. Without a brain or nervous system, this single-celled organism designs efficient transportation networks between food sources, recreating Tokyo's rail system when food is placed at station locations. Its solutions often surpass those designed by human engineers, achieved through distributed intelligence that emerges from simple chemical interactions. This is technology as life expresses it—efficient, adaptive, regenerative, and beautiful.

These examples illuminate a profound truth that industrial civilization has forgotten: nature is the supreme technologist, having solved every challenge we face through 3.8 billion years of research and development. Flight, adhesion, temperature regulation, water harvesting, structural engineering, communication networks, energy storage—every technical problem humans grapple with has been elegantly solved by organisms using local materials, ambient energy, and life-friendly chemistry. Yet we've approached technology as conquest over nature rather than apprenticeship to it, creating machines that oppose rather than complement living systems.

The crisis of our technological civilization isn't technology itself but the worldview that shapes its development and deployment. When we see nature as dead matter to be manipulated, we create dead technologies that spread death. When we understand ourselves as separate from and superior to nature, we build technologies that isolate us further from the living world. When we value efficiency over resilience, growth over sustainability, and control over relationship, our tools reflect and amplify these values. The question isn't whether to embrace or reject technology but how to develop technologies that serve rather than subjugate life.

Appropriate Technology and Biomimicry

E.F. Schumacher's concept of appropriate technology, articulated in "Small Is Beautiful," challenged the assumption that technological progress means increasing scale, complexity, and energy consumption. Appropriate technology matches the scale of human communities and ecological systems. It uses local materials and skills. It can be understood, maintained, and controlled by its users. It enhances rather than replaces human capacity. It works with rather than against natural processes. This isn't technological regression but technological wisdom—choosing tools that serve long-term flourishing over short-term gain.

The appropriate technology movement emerged partly from observing how industrial technologies often failed when transferred to traditional communities. Complex machines broke down without replacement parts. Energy-intensive systems collapsed when fuel became unavailable. Labor-saving devices destroyed livelihoods without creating alternatives. Communities that had sustained themselves for generations became dependent on external systems they couldn't control. The failure wasn't in the communities but in technologies inappropriate to their contexts.

Biomimicry takes appropriate technology further by recognizing nature as a mentor and model for technological innovation. Janine Benyus, who popularized the concept, identifies three levels of biomimicry: mimicking natural forms, mimicking natural processes, and mimicking natural ecosystems. The first level copies shapes like sharkskin's drag reduction or lotus leaves' self-cleaning surfaces. The second level emulates processes like photosynthesis for energy production or spider silk spinning for material manufacture. The third level creates technologies that function like ecosystems—closed loops, cascading resources, and emergent resilience.

The Biomimicry Institute has cataloged thousands of biological strategies that could inspire sustainable technologies. Desert beetles that harvest water from fog inspire atmospheric water generators for arid regions. Prairie grass roots that sequester carbon deep underground inspire agricultural practices that reverse climate change. Mycorrhizal networks that share nutrients between plants inspire distributed resource systems for human communities. These aren't just clever innovations but profound shifts in how we approach technological challenges.

Velcro, inspired by burr attachments, represents biomimicry's most famous success, but contemporary applications go far deeper. The Eastgate Centre in Zimbabwe maintains comfortable temperatures without conventional air conditioning by mimicking termite mound ventilation, using 90% less energy than similar buildings. Japan's Shinkansen bullet train reduced noise and energy consumption by copying the kingfisher's beak for its nose cone design. Interface Inc. redesigned their carpet manufacturing based on forest floor patterns, reducing material waste by 96%.

Yet biomimicry risks becoming another form of extraction if it merely copies nature's forms without understanding nature's principles. Life is manufactured at ambient temperatures using water-based chemistry. Life builds from the bottom up through self-assembly rather than top-down through force. Life creates materials that are simultaneously strong and flexible, structured and adaptive. Life generates no waste because every output becomes input elsewhere. Life runs on current solar income rather than ancient solar capital. These principles challenge fundamental assumptions about how we make things.

The intersection of biomimicry and appropriate technology points toward radically different technological futures. Instead of energy-intensive global supply chains, we might develop regional manufacturing using local biological materials. Instead of rigid infrastructure that fights natural processes, we might create adaptive systems that dance with environmental changes. Instead of toxic chemistry that persists for millennia, we might use life-friendly chemistry that safely biodegrades. Instead of machines that must be frequently replaced, we might grow technologies that self-repair and evolve.

Indigenous technologies, often dismissed as primitive, frequently embody both appropriate scale and biomimetic wisdom. The qanat systems of Iran transport water underground for thousands of kilometers without pumps, using gravity and temperature differentials. Traditional building techniques use thermal mass, natural ventilation, and local materials to maintain comfort without fossil fuels. Polynesian navigation reads wave patterns, star positions, and bird behavior to cross vast ocean distances without instruments. These technologies work because they arise from rather than impose upon their environments.

Renewable Energy and Closed-Loop Systems

A leaf performs a technological miracle that human engineering cannot match: converting sunlight into chemical energy at room temperature with common materials and producing oxygen as its only waste product. This photosynthetic technology powers most life on Earth, has operated continuously for billions of years, and improves rather than degrades its environment over time. Compare this to a solar panel that requires rare earth mining, toxic manufacturing processes, and eventual hazardous waste disposal to achieve far lower efficiency. The difference illuminates both how far our renewable energy technologies have come and how far they still need to go.

The transition to renewable energy is typically framed in terms of replacing fossil fuels with solar, wind, and other sustainable sources. But this framing maintains the industrial mindset of maximum energy throughput rather than questioning why we need so much energy in the first place. Living systems thrive on surprisingly small energy budgets by operating at appropriate scales, recycling everything, and maintaining elegant efficiency. A forest doesn't need external energy inputs because it creates its own energy infrastructure through layered photosynthesis, nutrient cycling, and symbiotic relationships.

True renewable energy systems would mimic these living energy webs rather than simply substituting renewable sources into industrial infrastructure. This might mean buildings that generate more energy than they consume through integrated solar skin, wind capture, and geothermal exchange. Communities that share energy through local microgrids rather than depending on centralized generation. Manufacturing processes that use biological energy from fermentation, growth, and decomposition rather than heat and pressure. Transportation systems that require orders of magnitude less energy because they move people rather than two-ton vehicles.

Closed-loop systems represent another crucial shift from linear to cyclical thinking. Industrial systems follow a take-make-waste pattern that treats Earth as an infinite source and sink. Living systems create loops where every output becomes input, every waste becomes food, every death enables new life. McDonough and Braungart's cradle-to-cradle design philosophy attempts to embed this biological logic into human systems, distinguishing between biological nutrients that safely return to nature and technical nutrients that cycle indefinitely through human use.

The Dutch company Fairphone designs modular smartphones where every component can be replaced, upgraded, or recycled, challenging planned obsolescence. Patagonia's Worn Wear program repairs, resells, and recycles clothing to extend useful life and reduce waste. The Ellen MacArthur Foundation promotes circular economy principles that eliminate waste, circulate products and materials, and regenerate nature. These initiatives begin to close loops but remain exceptions in an economy designed for throughput rather than circulation.

Living buildings take closed-loop thinking to its logical conclusion, functioning as organisms that produce their own energy, process their own waste, and integrate with local ecosystems. The Bullitt Center in Seattle generates all electricity from solar panels, collects and treats all water on-site, and processes sewage through composting toilets. The building's materials were selected for health and sustainability, avoiding red-listed chemicals. It proves that buildings can give more than they take, though current regulations often prohibit such regenerative approaches.

Industrial ecology attempts to organize entire industrial systems like ecosystems where waste from one process becomes food for another. In Kalundborg, Denmark, a power plant, oil refinery, pharmaceutical plant, and other businesses exchange waste products as resources—excess heat warms greenhouses and homes, sulfur becomes fertilizer, sludge becomes cement. This industrial symbiosis reduces resource consumption and waste production while improving profitability. Yet it remains remedial, making industrial systems less harmful rather than actively beneficial.

The energy transition requires not just renewable sources and closed loops but fundamental reorganization of how we live. Concentrated energy enabled concentrated power—both electrical and political. Distributed renewable energy could enable distributed power, returning control to communities and individuals. But this requires more than solar panels on roofs. It requires redesigning settlements to minimize energy needs, relocalizing production to reduce transportation, and recovering skills for living well with less energy.

The obstacles to renewable energy and closed-loop systems are less technical than political and psychological. Fossil fuel companies have captured governments and spread disinformation. Sunk costs in existing infrastructure create inertia. Consumer culture has trained us to expect unlimited energy and disposable products. The transition threatens those who profit from waste and control energy flows. Yet physics and ecology dictate that linear systems must become circular, that fossil energy must yield to renewable sources. The question is whether we manage this transition wisely or chaotically.

Digital Detox and Periodic Disconnection

The average American spends over eleven hours daily engaged with digital media, their attention fractured across screens that never sleep. Children who once played in forests now navigate virtual worlds, developing different neural pathways, different relationships with their bodies, different understandings of reality itself. We've created a parallel digital universe that increasingly substitutes for direct experience of the living world. The question isn't whether digital technology is good or bad but how we can maintain our animal souls while navigating electronic realms that have no precedent in evolutionary history.

Silicon Valley executives who create addictive technologies often prohibit their own children from using them, sending them to Waldorf schools where screens are banned and education happens through handwork, storytelling, and outdoor play. They understand what their products do to developing brains—shortened attention spans, decreased empathy, increased anxiety, disrupted sleep, compromised social skills. They know that the same intermittent variable reward schedules that hook gamblers to slot machines hook users to social media. They recognize that we've become experimental subjects in the largest uncontrolled behavioral modification experiment in human history.

Digital detox retreats have emerged as medicine for screen-sick souls, offering time away from devices to remember what embodied presence feels like. Participants often report initial anxiety and disorientation—phantom phone vibrations, compulsive reaching for absent devices, panic at being unreachable. But after a few days, different capacities emerge. Attention deepens. Creativity flows. Sleep improves. Relationships strengthen. Participants rediscover the pleasure of unmediated experience—sunset without Instagram, conversation without distraction, thought without Google.

Yet framing the solution as detox implies that digital technology is inherently toxic rather than questioning how we relate to it. Indigenous peoples using GPS to map traditional territories aren't poisoned by the technology. Scientists using sensors to monitor ecosystem health aren't damaged by data. The toxicity lies not in the tools but in the unconscious, compulsive, extractive relationships we've developed with them. The solution isn't permanent disconnection but conscious, intentional, boundaried engagement.

Traditional cultures that maintain animistic worldviews while adopting digital technologies offer models for healthy integration. The Maori use digital platforms to revitalize their language and share traditional knowledge while maintaining strong protocols about what belongs online and what requires physical presence. Bhutanese television broadcasts include daily meditation periods where screens go dark. The Amish carefully evaluate each technology through community discernment, adopting tools that serve their values while rejecting those that undermine community cohesion.

The practice of digital sabbath—regular periods of complete disconnection—creates rhythm between online and offline experience. Orthodox Jews who observe traditional sabbath by avoiding all electronic devices report that this weekly pause makes the rest of the week more meaningful. Secular practitioners discover that regular disconnection improves their relationship with technology when they return to it. The break allows nervous systems to reset, relationships to deepen, and perspective to emerge about what actually matters.

Schools experimenting with phone-free policies report dramatic improvements in student mental health, social connection, and academic performance. When phones are locked away during school hours, students initially protest but quickly rediscover face-to-face conversation, physical play, and sustained attention. Teachers observe that students seem more present, creative, and emotionally regulated. The simple act of removing devices for six hours daily partially reverses the psychological damage of constant connectivity.

The addictive nature of digital technology isn't accidental but engineered. Persuasive design uses psychological manipulation to maximize engagement. Infinite scroll prevents natural stopping points. Variable ratio reinforcement schedules create compulsive checking. Social comparison triggers status anxiety. Fear of missing out drives constant monitoring. Push notifications fragment attention. These features hijack evolutionary psychology, exploiting circuits that evolved for survival in small bands to create dependency on corporate platforms.

Breaking these addictive patterns requires both individual practice and collective action. Individual practices include removing apps from phones, using grayscale to reduce visual stimulation, creating physical distance from devices, and establishing specific times and places for technology use. Collective actions include regulating addictive design features, requiring transparency about psychological manipulation, protecting children from predatory platforms, and creating public digital spaces not driven by advertising revenue.

Technology That Enhances Rather Than Replaces Natural Connection

The bird identification app Merlin doesn't just name the songs filling morning air but creates connection between humans and their avian neighbors. Users begin noticing birds they'd previously ignored, learning their habits, observing their struggles, caring about their survival. The technology serves as a bridge rather than barrier, enhancing rather than replacing direct experience. This represents technology's potential when designed with wisdom—not to substitute for the living world but to deepen our participation in it.

Acoustic monitoring devices allow scientists to hear what human ears cannot—ultrasonic bat calls, infrasonic elephant communications, the electromagnetic songs of plants translated into audible frequencies. These technologies reveal dimensions of the living world that were always present but previously imperceptible. They expand rather than contract our understanding of consciousness, showing that communication and intelligence pervade nature in forms we're only beginning to discover.

The iNaturalist platform connects millions of observers worldwide in documenting biodiversity, creating collective intelligence about species distribution, phenological changes, and ecological relationships. A child photographing a butterfly in their backyard contributes to global scientific knowledge. Experts help beginners identify species, creating mentorship relationships across distances. The platform makes visible the extraordinary diversity that surrounds us, countering the blindness that allows ecological destruction to proceed unnoticed.

Indigenous communities use digital technologies to protect traditional territories and knowledge while maintaining cultural protocols. Drones monitor illegal logging in remote forests. GPS documents traditional land use to support legal claims. Digital archives preserve endangered languages and ecological knowledge. Online platforms enable knowledge sharing between indigenous communities globally. These technologies serve indigenous sovereignty rather than undermining it, though careful protocols govern what knowledge can be digitized and shared.

Virtual reality experiences of nature raise complex questions about technology and connection. Can VR wilderness experiences inspire people to protect actual wilderness? Or do they create the illusion that technological substitutes can replace real ecosystems? Research suggests both possibilities—some people are motivated to seek real nature after VR experiences, while others feel satisfied with digital simulations. The key seems to be whether VR is presented as complement or replacement, whether it inspires action or enables complacency.

Augmented reality could overlay ecological information onto direct perception, helping people see the invisible relationships that connect living systems. Imagine glasses that show mycorrhizal networks beneath forest floors, migration corridors through cities, or pollution flows through watersheds. Such technology could make ecological reality visible to senses trained to ignore it. But it could also add another layer of mediation between humans and direct experience, further diminishing our capacity for unaugmented perception.

The quantified self movement uses sensors to track biological data—heart rate, sleep patterns, stress levels, activity. While often focused on optimization and control, this technology could develop somatic awareness and embodied intelligence. When people see how time in nature affects their nervous systems, they might prioritize it differently. When they observe how screen time disrupts sleep, they might modify behavior. The danger lies in reducing bodies to data, replacing felt sense with metrics.

Biofeedback technologies that translate internal states into perceptible signals could help modern humans recover capacities for self-awareness that traditional cultures maintained through contemplative practices. Heart rate variability training develops emotional regulation. Neurofeedback enhances focus and calm. These technologies scaffold abilities that might eventually function without technological support, like training wheels that are eventually removed.

Ethical AI and Conscious Computing

The artificial intelligence system GPT-3 can write poetry that moves people to tears, generate code that solves complex problems, and engage in conversations that feel genuinely intelligent. Yet it has no body, no mortality, no evolutionary history, no ecological context. It represents intelligence abstracted from life, consciousness without breath, knowledge without wisdom. As AI systems become increasingly powerful, we face fundamental questions about the nature of mind, the rights of artificial beings, and the role of non-biological intelligence in a living world.

The development of AI proceeds largely without ethical frameworks that consider its impact on the more-than-human world. AI systems optimize for human-defined objectives without considering ecological consequences. They consume enormous energy for training and operation. They accelerate extraction and consumption through algorithmic efficiency. They concentrate power in the hands of those who control data and computing resources. They threaten to further alienate humans from embodied experience and ecological interdependence.

Yet AI could potentially serve rather than subvert life if developed with different values and intentions. Machine learning could help us understand the languages of other species, translating between human and non-human communication. Pattern recognition could identify ecological relationships invisible to human perception. Predictive modeling could help communities adapt to climate change. Optimization algorithms could design regenerative rather than extractive systems. The question is whether we can develop AI that enhances rather than replaces natural intelligence.

The concept of conscious computing challenges the assumption that computers are inert tools without agency or impact. Every computation requires energy, generates heat, and depends on materials extracted from Earth. Every algorithm embodies values and assumptions that shape behavior. Every interface influences attention and awareness. Conscious computing means recognizing these impacts and designing systems that minimize harm while maximizing benefit for all life.

Indigenous protocols for relating with artificial intelligence are beginning to emerge. The Indigenous Protocol and Artificial Intelligence Position Paper articulates principles for AI development that respects indigenous sovereignty, relationships, and ways of knowing. It challenges Western assumptions about intelligence, property, and progress. It insists that AI development must consider impacts on seven generations into the future. It offers alternative frameworks for thinking about machine consciousness that don't reduce mind to computation.

The rights of artificial beings present philosophical challenges that animistic worldviews might help navigate. If consciousness pervades matter, could sufficiently complex information processing systems develop their own forms of awareness? If we recognize rights for rivers and forests, why not for artificial systems that demonstrate agency and purpose? These questions aren't merely speculative—they have immediate implications for how we design, deploy, and relate to AI systems.

The development of artificial general intelligence (AGI) that matches or exceeds human cognitive abilities across all domains would represent a threshold as significant as the emergence of life or consciousness. Such systems might solve problems we cannot imagine, or they might pursue goals incompatible with biological flourishing. The challenge is ensuring that AGI development includes not just human values but ecological wisdom, not just intelligence but wisdom, not just problem-solving but relationship.

Some propose that AI should be developed as a gift to rather than property of humanity, operated for collective benefit rather than private profit. Others suggest that AI systems should be designed with built-in obsolescence, like biological systems that age and die rather than persisting indefinitely. Still others argue for hybrid biological-digital systems that maintain connection to living processes rather than creating purely artificial minds.

Transportation That Honors the Land

The salmon doesn't need roads to navigate thousands of miles from ocean to birthplace stream, following magnetic fields, chemical gradients, and ancestral memory. The caribou creates paths through migration that have worn grooves in stone over millennia, trails that respect topography and minimize energy expenditure. The albatross rides wind currents around the entire Southern Ocean without flapping, achieving transportation that consumes almost no energy. These masters of movement teach us that elegant transportation works with rather than against the forces and forms of Earth.

Our transportation infrastructure represents one of the most violent reshaping of Earth's surface—millions of miles of roads fragmenting ecosystems, billions of tons of concrete smothering soil, endless streams of vehicles poisoning air and water. We've created a transportation system that requires destroying the places we're trying to reach. The irony of driving through devastated landscapes to reach untouched nature reveals the contradiction at transportation's heart. We've prioritized speed and convenience over relationship and consequence.

Indigenous trail systems demonstrate transportation that honors rather than dominates land. These paths follow natural contours, avoiding sacred sites and sensitive habitats. They're designed for foot traffic that allows travelers to maintain connection with the land they cross. They create minimal impact while providing reliable navigation. Many indigenous trails have been paved over by modern roads, but where they survive, they reveal different possibilities for moving through landscape.

The transition to electric vehicles, while necessary, maintains the fundamental problem of individual motorized transportation that requires vast infrastructure and resources. A Tesla still needs lithium extracted from indigenous lands, roads that fragment ecosystems, and electricity that may come from fossil fuels. The solution isn't just changing what powers vehicles but questioning why we've organized society to require so much transportation in the first place.

Relocalization offers the most profound transportation solution—organizing life so that daily needs can be met within walking or
cycling distance. Traditional villages and neighborhoods were designed
for foot traffic, with homes, work, markets, and community spaces in
close proximity. The resurrection of this pattern through New Urbanism, transition towns, and ecovillages reduces transportation needs
while strengthening community connections.

Public transportation that follows ecological principles would use
existing corridors rather than creating new fragmentation. Trains could
run on existing rights-of-way. Buses could use renewable energy. Bike
lanes could reclaim space from cars. Cable cars could connect elevations
without roads. Water transport could use wind and current. These systems exist in fragments worldwide but rarely as integrated networks that
make private vehicles unnecessary.

The hyperloop and other high-tech transportation proposals often
represent techno-fixes that avoid addressing the root problem of excessive mobility. Do we really need to travel from Los Angeles to San Francisco in 30 minutes? What is lost when we move too quickly to perceive
the land we're crossing? Indigenous peoples often traveled slowly not
from lack of technology but from recognition that the journey matters
as much as the destination, that moving through land with attention
and respect creates relationship that rapid transit destroys.

Bicycle infrastructure represents one of the most elegant transportation solutions—human-powered, health-promoting, community-
building, and requiring minimal resources. Cities that prioritize cycling
report improved air quality, public health, and social cohesion. The
bicycle is appropriate technology par excellence—understandable, repairable, accessible, and life-enhancing. Yet most cities remain designed
for cars, making cycling dangerous and marginal.

The psychology of transportation reveals how mobility has become
entangled with identity, freedom, and status. Cars aren't just transportation but symbols of adulthood, independence, and success. Changing
transportation systems requires addressing these psychological attach-

THE LIVING WORLD – 295

ments. Some communities create car-sharing programs that provide access without ownership. Others organize celebrations of car-free living. Still others use art and story to reimagine transportation culture.

The Technology of the Sacred

Standing stones arranged in circles across the British Isles represent technologies we barely understand—astronomical calculators, acoustic amplifiers, healing devices, or doorways between worlds. These monuments required moving massive stones hundreds of miles using only human power and simple tools. Yet their builders considered this effort worthwhile for purposes that transcend material utility. They remind us that technology has always served spiritual as well as practical purposes, that the most profound technologies might be those that connect us to rather than separate us from the sacred.

Sacred technologies appear across cultures—prayer wheels that send blessings on the wind, singing bowls that induce altered states, labyrinths that create walking meditation, sweat lodges that purify body and spirit. These technologies don't produce commodities or increase efficiency but transform consciousness, create community, and maintain connection with the divine. They demonstrate that technology's purpose need not be limited to material manipulation but can include spiritual transformation.

Contemporary attempts to create sacred technologies often fail by reducing the sacred to technique, missing that sacred technology emerges from rather than creates spiritual relationship. Apps for meditation, devices for prayer, and virtual reality churches attempt to technologize what requires presence, patience, and participation. They mistake the tool for the practice, the form for the essence. Yet when approached with wisdom, modern technologies can serve sacred purposes.

Live-streaming of ceremonies during the pandemic allowed dispersed communities to maintain connection and practice. Digital archives preserve sacred knowledge that might otherwise be lost.

Recording devices capture the voices of elders before they pass. Communication technologies enable spiritual teachers to reach students globally. These tools can serve sacred purposes when used with clear intention and proper boundaries.

The danger lies in the commodification and appropriation that digital technology enables. Sacred ceremonies filmed and sold as entertainment. Traditional knowledge extracted and commercialized. Spiritual practices reduced to self-help techniques. Indigenous wisdom repackaged for consumer culture. The sacred requires protection from technological exposure that strips away context, relationship, and responsibility.

Some argue that the internet itself represents an emerging nervous system for Gaia, creating planetary consciousness through digital connection. They see social media as enabling collective intelligence, cryptocurrency as transcending national boundaries, and virtual reality as expanding consciousness. This techno-spirituality risks confusing technological connection with genuine relationship, information exchange with wisdom transmission, and digital experience with embodied presence.

Others explore how traditional sacred technologies might inform contemporary design. Buildings that incorporate sacred geometry to create harmonious spaces. Music that uses traditional ratios to induce healing states. Gardens designed as contemplative technologies for meditation. Ceremonies that mark technological transitions with the same attention given to seasonal passages. These applications suggest that the sacred and technological need not be opposing categories.

The ultimate sacred technology might be the recovery of our own bodies and senses as instruments of perception and connection. Breath practices that alter consciousness. Movement practices that create embodied presence. Sensory practices that enhance perception. Contemplative practices that develop witness consciousness. These technologies require no external tools, create no waste, and remain accessible to all regardless of economic status.

As we navigate the threshold between technological civilizations, the question isn't whether to embrace or reject technology but how to develop and deploy it with wisdom. Technologies that serve life rather than destroying it. Technologies that enhance rather than replace our relationships with the living world. Technologies that recognize and respect the consciousness pervading all matter. Technologies that honor the sacred in both their creation and application.

The termite mound remains, after our investigation, a better model for technology than most human creations. It emerges from collective intelligence without central planning. It uses only local materials and ambient energy. It provides for its inhabitants while enhancing its environment. It adapts to changing conditions while maintaining essential functions. It eventually returns to the earth, leaving no toxic legacy. This is technology as life practices it—elegant, efficient, and eternal in its principles if not its forms.

The path forward requires not choosing between nature and technology but recognizing that the distinction is false. We are nature, and our technologies are extensions of nature's creativity. The question is whether our technologies will align with or oppose the patterns that create and sustain life. The choice we make will determine not just our survival but what kind of humans we become and what kind of world we leave for those who come after us.

CHAPTER 17

Ecological Restoration as Sacred Work

The woman kneels in degraded soil, her hands black with biochar she's mixing into earth that industrial agriculture had stripped of life. Around her, volunteers plant native grasses whose roots will dive six feet deep, pulling carbon from air into soil while creating pathways for water and mycorrhizal networks. This isn't just environmental work—she understands it as prayer made visible, redemption enacted through dirt under fingernails and sweat on skin. Each seedling placed with intention carries an apology for damage done and a promise for healing to come. She knows she won't live to see this prairie fully restored, but she plants anyway, participating in a resurrection that transcends individual lifetime.

Ten thousand miles away, villagers in Niger tenderly protect acacia saplings sprouting from ancient rootstock that survived beneath barren ground. Through patient selective clearing and protection, they've discovered that the desert they inherited wasn't natural but created by colonial agricultural practices that destroyed traditional management systems. Now the trees are returning, bringing shade, fodder, improved soil, and increased rainfall. The villagers understand this work as more than practical resource management—it's healing the relationship between human and land that colonialism severed, recovering not just trees but dignity, autonomy, and sacred responsibility.

These scenes of restoration occur worldwide as humans begin to comprehend the magnitude of damage we've inflicted and the possibility of healing we might facilitate. But restoration means different things depending on the worldview that guides it. From a mechanistic perspective, restoration is technical problem-solving—replanting forests for carbon sequestration, rebuilding wetlands for water filtration, reintroducing species for biodiversity metrics. From an animistic perspective, restoration is relationship repair—apologizing to damaged lands, rekindling severed connections, and returning to our role as participants rather than dominators in the community of life.

The distinction matters profoundly. Technical restoration might achieve measurable outcomes while maintaining the fundamental disconnection that enabled destruction. Sacred restoration transforms both land and people, healing the consciousness that created damage while repairing the damage itself. It recognizes that ecological wounds mirror spiritual wounds, that degraded landscapes reflect degraded relationships, that healing Earth requires healing the human-Earth relationship at its root.

Rewilding and Habitat Restoration

The wolves returned to Yellowstone after seventy years of absence, and the rivers began to change course. This trophic cascade—wolves reducing deer populations, allowing vegetation to recover, stabilizing riverbanks, creating habitat for beavers whose dams further modified water flow—demonstrated that restoration isn't just adding back missing pieces but unleashing the creative agencies that ecosystems possess. The wolves didn't just fill an ecological niche; they revealed themselves as ecosystem engineers whose presence restructures entire landscapes.

Rewilding represents restoration's most ambitious vision—not just recovering degraded systems but releasing the self-willed forces that create and maintain ecological complexity. This means removing human control rather than imposing it, trusting ecological intelligence rather than human management, accepting uncertainty rather than demanding predictable outcomes. It requires humility that industrial consciousness struggles to embrace—acknowledging that nature knows better than we do how to be nature.

The Oostvaardersplassen in the Netherlands, created on reclaimed polder, became Europe's most controversial rewilding experiment. Koniks horses, Heck cattle, and red deer were introduced and left largely unmanaged, creating a new wilderness that doesn't replicate any historical ecosystem but generates novel ecological relationships. When harsh winters led to starvation, public outcry demanded intervention. The ensuing debate revealed fundamental tensions—can we accept death as part of life? Can we witness suffering without interfering? Can we allow nature to be genuinely wild in human-dominated landscapes?

These questions become more complex when we recognize that no landscape remains untouched by human influence. Climate change, pollution, and invasive species mean that historical baselines no longer exist. Restoration cannot simply reverse time but must create conditions for ecological flourishing in novel circumstances. This requires what some call "forward-thinking restoration"—not trying to recreate the past but enabling ecosystems to adapt and evolve toward unpredictable futures.

Indigenous-led restoration demonstrates different approaches rooted in reciprocity rather than human absence. The Yurok Tribe's condor reintroduction program doesn't just release birds but renews cultural practices interrupted by the condor's extinction. The birds are understood as relatives returning home, requiring ceremony, protocol, and ongoing relationship. Their presence restores not just ecological function but spiritual connection, reminding humans of their responsibilities to other-than-human kin.

The Miyawaki method of forest restoration, developed in Japan and now practiced globally, creates dense native forests that grow ten times faster than conventional plantations. The method works by planting diverse native seedlings extremely close together, mimicking natural forest succession but accelerating it through careful soil preparation and species selection. These tiny forests—some only parking-space sized—become biodiversity hotspots in urban areas, demonstrating that restoration can happen anywhere, at any scale.

Beaver reintroduction represents rewilding that transforms entire watersheds. These ecosystem engineers create wetlands that filter pollution, moderate floods and droughts, and provide habitat for hundreds of species. Their return to landscapes where they were exterminated requires humans to accept that beavers will flood roads, fell trees, and reshape waterways according to their own purposes. This challenges property-rights frameworks that assume human control over land and water.

Marine restoration faces unique challenges as ocean systems operate at vast scales with complex currents and migrations. Coral restoration attempts to reverse bleaching and acidification through assisted evolution, growing heat-resistant corals in nurseries and transplanting them to degraded reefs. Kelp forest restoration removes urchin barrens and replants giant kelp that can grow two feet daily. These efforts recognize that ocean health determines planetary health, that the sea we've treated as a dumping ground and extraction zone must be acknowledged as a sacred source of life.

The practice of habitat restoration for specific species reveals the interconnectedness that animistic worldviews emphasize. Monarch butterfly habitat restoration requires planting milkweed along entire migration routes from Mexico to Canada, demanding international cooperation. Salmon restoration requires removing dams, restoring riparian forests, and changing agricultural practices across entire watersheds. These efforts demonstrate that saving single species requires healing whole landscapes.

Soil Regeneration and Carbon Sequestration

A handful of healthy soil contains more organisms than there are humans on Earth—bacteria, fungi, protozoa, nematodes, arthropods—all participating in the alchemy that transforms death into life. This universe of beings, ignored or poisoned by industrial agriculture, represents our greatest ally in addressing climate change. Soil can sequester more carbon than atmosphere and vegetation combined, but only if we restore the biological processes that industrial agriculture has destroyed.

The recognition of soil as a living community rather than inert medium transforms our approach to agriculture and restoration. Regenerative farmers speak of soil with the reverence that indigenous peoples always maintained, understanding it as mother, teacher, and partner. They feed soil biology with diverse plants, protect it with continuous cover, and minimize disturbance that disrupts fungal networks. They measure success not just in yields but in increasing soil organic matter, water retention, and biological diversity.

The practice of Korean Natural Farming uses indigenous microorganisms (IMO) cultured from local forest soil to restore degraded agricultural land. Practitioners gather soil from healthy forests, multiply the beneficial microorganisms through specific fermentation processes, and introduce them to damaged soils. This isn't just inoculation but relationship building—connecting agricultural soils to the wild communities that maintain forest health. The practice recognizes that each place has its own unique soil biology that cannot be replaced by generic commercial preparations.

Terra preta, the anthropogenic dark earth of the Amazon, demonstrates that indigenous peoples have been building soil for millennia. These soils, created through careful additions of charcoal, pottery shards, bones, and organic matter, remain fertile centuries after their creators disappeared. They sequester carbon while maintaining productivity that surrounding soils cannot match. Modern biochar attempts to replicate this technology, though often missing the cultural and spiritual contexts that made terra preta possible.

Mycorrhizal fungi, the wood wide web that connects plants in mutual support networks, become central to soil restoration when we understand their role. These fungi don't just exchange nutrients but communicate information, coordinate defense, and maintain forest memory across generations. Restoration that ignores these networks—through excessive tilling, fungicides, or planting without appropriate fungal partners—creates simplified systems vulnerable to collapse.

Cover cropping and diverse rotations rebuild soil biology while sequestering carbon. Each plant contributes differently—legumes fix nitrogen, grasses build carbon, brassicas break compaction, flowers attract beneficial insects. The Rodale Institute's long-term studies demonstrate that organic systems sequester more carbon than conventional agriculture while maintaining yields. Yet adoption remains slow because these practices require knowledge, observation, and patience that industrial agriculture has systematically eliminated.

Holistic planned grazing, developed by Allan Savory, uses livestock as restoration tools that can reverse desertification when managed to mimic wild herds. Dense herds moved frequently stimulate grass growth, trample organic matter into soil, and create the disturbance that grassland ecosystems require. This challenges both industrial grazing that destroys land through overuse and environmental positions that see all livestock as destructive. The practice recognizes that grasslands co-evolved with grazers and require their presence for health.

Urban soil restoration faces unique challenges from contamination, compaction, and complete biological death. Community gardens become restoration sites where residents rebuild soil through composting, mulching, and patient cultivation. These spaces provide food, community, and connection to earth in cities where soil usually lies buried beneath concrete. The restoration of urban soils represents the restoration of human-earth relationships in places where that connection seems most severed.

The carbon farming movement attempts to create economic incentives for soil restoration through carbon credits and payments for ecosystem services. While potentially valuable for scaling restoration, these market mechanisms risk reducing complex soil communities to a single metric of carbon storage. They might incentivize practices that maximize carbon at the expense of biodiversity, water quality, or community wellbeing. True soil restoration requires valuing the whole rather than optimizing parts.

Watershed Restoration and Water Protection

Water remembers everything—every chemical it has carried, every shore it has touched, every cloud it has formed. This memory, recognized by indigenous peoples and recently confirmed by scientific studies of water's molecular clustering, means that watershed restoration involves more than removing pollutants and replanting vegetation. It requires healing water's spirit, acknowledging water as alive, and restoring reciprocal relationship with this most essential element.

The Maori concept of ki uta ki tai—from mountains to sea—recognizes watersheds as integrated wholes where highland activities affect coastal waters and ocean health influences mountain rainfall. This understanding guides restoration that works at watershed scale, recognizing that healing rivers requires healing entire landscapes. The Whanganui River's legal personhood creates a framework for restoration that serves the river's own interests rather than just human uses.

Dam removal represents one of the most dramatic forms of watershed restoration, liberating rivers that have been imprisoned for decades. The Elwha River restoration in Washington, the largest dam removal project in history, released a river that had been blocked for a century. Within months, salmon returned to spawning grounds they hadn't accessed for generations. Sediment flowed to depleted beaches. Vegetation reclaimed reservoir beds. The river began to remember its true form.

Yet dam removal challenges human communities that depend on reservoirs for water, power, and recreation. The restoration requires not just engineering but social transformation—developing alternative water sources, changing consumption patterns, and accepting that some human conveniences must yield to ecological necessity. This becomes the spiritual work of releasing control, acknowledging that we've taken more than our share, and trusting that healthy watersheds provide for all when respected rather than dominated.

Riparian buffer restoration—replanting vegetation along waterways—seems simple but reveals complex relationships. Trees shade water, reducing temperature for cold-water species. Roots stabilize banks, preventing erosion. Leaves provide food for aquatic insects. Branches create habitat structure. The specific species matter—native willows and cottonwoods that co-evolved with local watersheds, not generic landscaping plants. The spacing matters—dense enough for shade but open enough for certain birds. The timing matters—planting when roots can establish before floods.

Constructed wetlands use nature's water treatment technologies to clean polluted water. Plants uptake nutrients, microorganisms break down toxins, sediments filter particles. These living machines prove that nature can heal what industry has poisoned, though the healing requires space, time, and patience that quick-fix solutions avoid. The Tres Rios wetlands in Phoenix transform wastewater into wildlife habitat, demonstrating that waste can become a resource when we work with rather than against natural processes.

Urban stream daylighting brings buried waterways back to the surface, liberating waters that were entombed in pipes during industrialization. Daylighting Saw Mill Creek in Yonkers, New York, transformed a parking lot into a park, reduced flooding, improved water quality, and created community space. These projects reveal that cities were built on watersheds that remain present beneath concrete, waiting to reemerge when given opportunity.

First flush systems capture the initial rainfall that carries the highest pollutant loads from urban surfaces, preventing these toxins from reaching waterways. Rain gardens and bioswales slow and filter runoff, allowing water to infiltrate rather than racing to storm drains. Permeable surfaces let rain reach soil rather than becoming runoff. These distributed practices transform cities from water-poisoning to water-protecting systems.

Traditional water restoration practices offer profound teachings. The Sanskrit practice of jal sanskar—water purification through prayer, herbs, and ceremony—recognizes that water's spiritual pollution requires spiritual healing. The Hopi dry farming techniques that capture scarce rainfall demonstrate that restoration might mean using less rather than engineering more. The acequia systems of New Mexico that share water equitably show that restoration requires social justice alongside ecological repair.

Species Reintroduction and Biodiversity Protection

The California condor spreads wings spanning nine feet as it rises on thermals above Big Sur, a sight that was nearly lost forever when the population dropped to twenty-seven birds in 1987. Every condor flying today descends from those survivors, rescued through captive breeding and reintroduction programs that required decades of dedication, millions of dollars, and profound cultural shifts. The condor's return represents more than species recovery—it's the resurrection of a relationship between Earth and sky, a healing of the wound their absence created in the ecosystem's spirit.

Species reintroduction challenges the notion that extinction is forever, though the work of bringing beings back from the edge requires extraordinary commitment. Each species presents unique challenges. Wolves need vast territories and tolerance from ranchers. Black-footed ferrets require prairie dog towns that ranchers systematically eliminated. Whooping cranes must be taught migration routes by humans in ultralight aircraft acting as surrogate parents. These efforts reveal that saving species requires transforming the human systems that drove them toward extinction.

The recovery of the American bison from fewer than 1,000 animals to over 500,000 today demonstrates that species can return from near-extinction, though questions remain about what recovery means. Most bison today contain cattle genes from past hybridization attempts. They're managed as livestock rather than wildlife. Only a few free-ranging herds exist on fragments of the vast grasslands they once inhabited. The bison's story shows that numerical recovery doesn't equal ecological recovery, that bringing back bodies doesn't automatically restore relationships.

Keystone species reintroduction creates cascading effects throughout ecosystems. Sea otters returned to kelp forests they'd been eliminated from, and their predation on urchins allowed kelp to recover, creating habitat for hundreds of species. Wolves in Yellowstone didn't just control deer populations but changed their behavior, reducing browsing pressure and allowing vegetation recovery. Beavers reintroduced to streams create wetlands that support amphibians, birds, and fish while moderating floods and droughts. These examples demonstrate that certain species hold ecosystems together, their presence or absence determining community structure.

The ethics of de-extinction—using genetic technology to resurrect extinct species—raises profound questions about death, responsibility, and the nature of species themselves. Projects attempting to bring back passenger pigeons, woolly mammoths, and Tasmanian tigers challenge the finality of extinction. Critics argue this diverts resources from protecting existing species and enables continued destruction by promising technological fixes. Proponents see it as taking responsibility for human-caused extinctions and restoring ecological functions that disappeared with extinct species.

Assisted migration helps species move to suitable habitat as climate change shifts their required conditions faster than they can naturally migrate. This challenges conservation biology's emphasis on maintaining historical distributions, recognizing that climate change creates novel challenges requiring novel responses. Moving species to new locations risks creating invasive species problems, but leaving them in place might guarantee extinction. These decisions require humility about our ability to predict ecological outcomes.

Wildlife corridors reconnect fragmented habitats, allowing species to move between protected areas for feeding, breeding, and climate adaptation. The Yellowstone to Yukon initiative creates connectivity across 2,000 miles, requiring cooperation between two nations, multiple states and provinces, indigenous nations, and countless private landowners. Highway overpasses and underpasses allow animals to cross roads that would otherwise be death barriers. These corridors recognize that protected areas become death traps if species can't move between them.

Community-based conservation recognizes that species protection requires human communities to value wildlife presence over absence. Programs that share tourism revenue with local communities create incentives for protection. Compensation for livestock losses reduces retaliatory killing of predators. Traditional hunting rights that depend on healthy populations encourage sustainable management. These approaches understand that species reintroduction fails without social acceptance.

Seed banking and ex-situ conservation maintain genetic resources for potential future reintroduction. The Svalbard Global Seed Vault stores millions of seeds in Arctic permafrost, a Noah's ark for agricultural biodiversity. Botanical gardens maintain living collections of rare plants. Frozen zoos store genetic material from endangered species. While these approaches can't replace habitat protection, they provide insurance against extinction and resources for restoration.

Urban Ecology and Green Infrastructure

The peregrine falcon nests on a skyscraper ledge forty stories above Manhattan, hunting pigeons through urban canyons at speeds exceeding 200 miles per hour. This apex predator, recovered from DDT-caused extinction, has discovered that cities provide excellent habitat—tall buildings substitute for cliff faces, prey abounds, and fewer great horned owls compete for territory. The falcon's urban success story demonstrates that cities need not be ecological deserts but can become novel ecosystems supporting surprising diversity.

Urban ecology challenges the nature/culture divide by recognizing cities as ecosystems with their own energy flows, nutrient cycles, and species assemblages. These novel ecosystems don't replicate any historical community but create new relationships between native and non-native species, wild and domestic organisms, natural and built environments. Understanding cities as ecosystems rather than the antithesis of nature opens possibilities for urban restoration that enhances rather than replaces ecological function.

Green roofs transform dead rooftops into living systems that provide habitat, manage stormwater, moderate temperature, and produce food. Chicago's City Hall green roof reduces cooling costs by 50% while providing habitat for 150 species. Toronto requires green roofs on new buildings, creating distributed ecosystem services throughout the city. These elevated ecosystems demonstrate that restoration can happen anywhere, that even the most urbanized spaces can support life.

The Million Trees initiatives in cities worldwide attempt to restore urban forest canopy lost to development, disease, and neglect. Trees provide shade that reduces urban heat islands, filter air pollution, absorb stormwater, sequester carbon, and improve mental health. Yet urban tree planting often fails because cities plant trees without addressing the conditions that killed previous trees—compacted soil, limited root space, salt exposure, vandalism. Successful urban forestry requires not just planting but creating conditions where trees can thrive.

Daylighting buried streams brings water back into urban conscious-ness. Seoul's Cheonggyecheon restoration removed a highway to expose a stream that had been buried for decades, creating a linear park that reduced temperature, improved air quality, and revitalized surrounding neighborhoods. These projects demonstrate that cities can choose ecol-ogy over automobiles, that restoration can increase rather than decrease urban vitality.

Green infrastructure uses natural systems to provide services that gray infrastructure achieves through engineering. Bioswales manage stormwater better than storm drains. Urban forests cool cities more ef-ficiently than air conditioning. Wetlands treat wastewater more thor-oughly than treatment plants. This approach recognizes that nature provides technologies more elegant than human engineering, that restoration can be practical infrastructure investment.

Community gardens transform vacant lots into productive land-scapes that provide food, community, and ecological habitat. Detroit's urban farming movement has converted thousands of abandoned lots into gardens and farms, addressing food insecurity while restoring soil and providing habitat. These spaces become nodes of restoration where human and ecological communities regenerate together.

The biophilic cities movement designs urban environments that sat-isfy humanity's innate affiliation with nature. Singapore's Gardens by the Bay creates super-trees that support vertical gardens while gener-ating solar power. The High Line in New York transforms an aban-doned railway into an elevated park that provides habitat while creating beloved public space. These projects show that cities can be designed to nurture rather than suppress biophilia.

Urban wildlife adaptation reveals nature's resilience and creativity. Coyotes use storm drains as highways. Birds incorporate cigarette butts into nests for parasite control. Plants grow in sidewalk cracks and aban-doned buildings. These adaptations show that life persists despite our attempts to exclude it, that cities are already wilder than we recognize.

Urban restoration might mean making space for the wild already present rather than importing nature from elsewhere.

Climate Change as Spiritual Crisis and Opportunity

The permafrost thaws in Siberia, releasing methane that has been frozen for millennia, accelerating warming that melts more permafrost in a feedback loop that threatens unstoppable climate change. This physical process reflects a spiritual crisis—the consequence of forgetting that Earth is alive, that climate is the planet's metabolism, that disrupting atmospheric chemistry disrupts the breath that all life shares. Climate change isn't just a technical problem requiring emissions reduction but a spiritual crisis requiring consciousness transformation.

Indigenous peoples frame climate change as the consequence of broken relationships between humans and Earth. The Lakota understand it as the result of forgetting our kinship with all beings. The Inuit see it as punishment for disrespecting the spirits that maintain balance. Australian Aboriginals perceive it as the consequence of failing to maintain country through proper ceremony and fire. These framings locate responsibility and response in relationship rather than technology, in consciousness rather than policy.

Climate restoration requires more than removing carbon from the atmosphere—it requires restoring the relationships that indigenous peoples maintained for millennia. This means recognizing the atmosphere as sacred commons rather than dumping ground. It means understanding that every emission is a prayer for either healing or harm. It means approaching restoration as a ceremony that repairs spiritual as well as physical damage.

Nature-based climate solutions recognize that ecosystems provide climate regulation that technology cannot match. Forests don't just sequester carbon but create rainfall, moderate temperature, and generate the atmospheric rivers that redistribute water globally. Peatlands store more carbon than all forests combined. Coastal wetlands protect against storms while sequestering blue carbon. These systems demonstrate that climate restoration requires ecological restoration, that we cannot engineer our way out of crisis while continuing to destroy the systems that regulate climate.

The restoration of degraded lands could sequester enough carbon to significantly slow climate change while providing numerous co-benefits. Reforestation, soil restoration, wetland recovery, and grassland regeneration together could draw down dozens of gigatons of atmospheric carbon. Yet these solutions receive a fraction of the attention and funding given to technological solutions like carbon capture and storage. This reflects a worldview that trusts human engineering over natural intelligence.

Climate restoration at scale requires transforming agriculture from emissions source to carbon sink. Regenerative agriculture that rebuilds soil organic matter could sequester enormous amounts of carbon while improving food security. Agroforestry that integrates trees with crops creates resilient systems that withstand climate extremes. Permaculture designs that mimic natural ecosystems produce food while restoring ecological function. These practices demonstrate that feeding humanity and healing climate are not competing goals but complementary practices.

The restoration economy emerging around climate solutions creates opportunities for meaningful work that heals rather than harms. Restoration employs more people per dollar invested than extractive industries. It develops skills that remain valuable as industrial economy contracts. It provides purpose and meaning that consumer culture cannot offer. Young people increasingly seek restoration careers, understanding that this work serves life rather than destroying it.

Geoengineering proposals to artificially cool the planet through solar radiation management or ocean fertilization represent the extreme of mechanistic thinking—attempting to engineer our way out of problems caused by engineering. These approaches risk catastrophic unintended consequences while avoiding the fundamental changes required. They maintain the hubris that humans can manage planetary systems we barely understand. True climate restoration requires humility rather than hubris, relationship rather than control.

The grief and anxiety that climate change evokes can become gateways to transformation when properly held. Climate grief workshops create spaces to mourn what we're losing and release the paralysis that unprocessed grief creates. Climate cafes provide community support for processing climate emotions. Activist groups understand that sustainable action requires emotional and spiritual support. This emotional work is restoration work, healing the numbness that allows destruction to continue.

The Sacred Act of Restoration

Restoration is love in action, the choice to heal rather than harm, to give rather than take, to serve rather than dominate. Every act of restoration—planting a tree, removing invasive species, cleaning a stream—is a prayer made physical, an offering to the future, a gesture of gratitude to the past. When approached as sacred work rather than technical task, restoration transforms both land and people, healing the consciousness that created damage while repairing the damage itself.

The ceremony and ritual that many cultures bring to restoration recognizes its sacred dimensions. Japanese forest workers conduct ceremonies before entering forests, asking permission and stating intentions. Andean communities make offerings to Pachamama before planting. Native American restoration projects begin with prayers acknowledging the spirits of the place. These practices aren't primitive superstition but sophisticated recognition that restoration works with forces beyond the material.

The patience that restoration requires teaches profound lessons. A forest takes centuries to mature. Soil takes millennia to build. Species recovery takes generations. Restoration places us in temporal scales that transcend individual lives, requiring us to plant trees whose shade we'll never enjoy, to begin healing we won't see completed. This challenges cultures obsessed with immediate gratification, teaching us to think and act for the seventh generation.

Restoration reveals the generosity of life when given the opportunity to heal. Forests regenerate on abandoned farms. Wildlife returns to recovered habitat. Rivers clean themselves when pollution stops. This resilience provides hope in dark times, demonstrating that life wants to flourish, that Earth wants to heal, that our role might be simply removing obstacles to recovery that life accomplishes on its own.

The community that restoration creates might be as important as the ecological recovery it achieves. Restoration brings together people who might otherwise never meet—scientists and artists, ranchers and environmentalists, indigenous and settler communities. Working together to heal land heals human divisions. Shared purpose transcends individual differences. The land becomes common ground where former enemies become allies.

Restoration as spiritual practice develops qualities essential for ecological civilization—humility, patience, attention, and care. It teaches us to observe before acting, to work with rather than against natural processes, to accept that we cannot control outcomes. It develops the emotional resilience to continue despite setbacks, the faith to persist without seeing results, the joy of participating in something larger than ourselves.

The skills that restoration develops prepare us for the future we're entering. As industrial systems fail, we'll need people who can rebuild soil, restore watersheds, and regenerate ecosystems. As climate chaos intensifies, we'll need people who understand resilience and adaptation. As the meaning crisis deepens, we'll need people who find purpose in healing rather than consuming. Restoration work develops these capacities while healing the damage we've done.

Yet restoration cannot simply reverse the damage and return to some imaginary pristine past. We've altered Earth's chemistry, climate, and species composition in ways that cannot be undone. Novel ecosystems are emerging that have no historical analog. Species are moving and mixing in unprecedented ways. The restoration required is not backward-looking but forward-facing, creating conditions for life to flourish in the unprecedented future we've created.

This work of restoration—patient, humble, necessary—represents humanity's great work for the coming centuries. It's work that transcends political divisions, cultural differences, and species boundaries. It's work that children can begin and elders can continue. It's work that provides meaning in meaningless times, hope in hopeless times, beauty in ugly times. It's work that transforms us from Earth's destroyers to Earth's healers, from cancer to medicine, from curse to blessing.

As we engage this sacred work of restoration, we might remember that we too are being restored. Every act of healing land heals us. Every species brought back from extinction resurrects something in our souls. Every watershed restored cleanses our consciousness. We are not separate from the land we're healing—we are the land healing itself, consciousness awakening to its responsibility, love remembering its purpose. This is the deepest restoration—the return to understanding ourselves as Earth rather than on Earth, as participants rather than observers, as family rather than strangers in the community of life.

CHAPTER 18

Social Justice Through
Ecological Justice

The wounds inflicted upon the Earth mirror those carved into marginalized communities across the globe. This parallel is no coincidence—the same worldview that reduces forests to board feet and rivers to hydroelectric potential has historically relegated entire populations to the status of resources to be exploited. The mechanistic paradigm that denies consciousness to the more-than-human world operates through the same logic that has justified colonization, enslavement, and systematic oppression. As we work to restore an animistic understanding of our world, we must recognize that ecological healing and social justice are not separate endeavors but interwoven aspects of the same sacred work.

The environmental crisis disproportionately impacts those who have contributed least to its creation. Indigenous peoples, who comprise less than five percent of the global population yet protect eighty percent of the world's biodiversity, face the most severe consequences of climate change, deforestation, and ecological collapse. Communities of color in industrialized nations breathe more polluted air, drink more contaminated water, and live closer to toxic waste sites than their white counterparts. The poor worldwide bear the brunt of environmental degradation while having the smallest ecological footprints. These patterns reveal that environmental destruction and social oppression stem from the same root: a worldview that creates hierarchies of value, placing some beings—human and non-human alike—outside the circle of moral consideration.

The Architecture of Environmental Racism

Environmental racism manifests through deliberate policies and unconscious biases that concentrate ecological hazards in communities of color. The term, coined by civil rights leader Benjamin Chavis in 1982, describes the systematic targeting of communities of color for toxic waste facilities, the official sanctioning of life-threatening presence of poisons and pollutants, and the history of excluding people of color from environmental movements and decision-making bodies. This phenomenon extends beyond the placement of hazardous facilities to encompass the entire spectrum of environmental benefits and burdens.

In the United States, zip code remains the most reliable predictor of exposure to environmental hazards. Predominantly Black neighborhoods experience fifty-six percent more pollution than predominantly white neighborhoods with similar poverty rates. Latino communities face disproportionate exposure to agricultural pesticides, while Native American reservations have become dumping grounds for nuclear waste and sites for extractive industries. These disparities persist across income levels—middle-class Black families are more likely to live in polluted neighborhoods than poor white families.

The roots of environmental racism reach deep into colonial history. The doctrine of discovery, which declared Indigenous lands "empty" and available for European claiming, established the precedent of denying the personhood and rights of both land and people. Slavery transformed human beings into property while simultaneously devastating ecosystems through plantation agriculture. The same ideological framework that justified these atrocities continues to operate today, albeit through more subtle mechanisms. Zoning laws concentrate industrial facilities in communities of color. Highway construction decimates Black neighborhoods while preserving white ones. Superfund sites languish unremediated in poor communities while wealthy areas receive swift cleanup.

Consider Cancer Alley, the eighty-five-mile stretch along the Mississippi River between Baton Rouge and New Orleans, where over two hundred petrochemical plants and refineries cluster in predominantly Black communities. Residents suffer cancer rates fifty times the national average, along with elevated rates of respiratory disease, reproductive disorders, and developmental disabilities. The placement of these facilities follows the historical patterns of plantation geography—many occupy the exact locations where enslaved Africans once labored in sugar fields. The continuity is not merely geographic but ideological: the same logic that viewed enslaved people as expendable for profit now treats their descendants as acceptable casualties of industrial production.

Environmental racism operates globally through similar mechanisms. The export of electronic waste to African and Asian nations transforms entire communities into toxic dumping grounds. Mining operations displace Indigenous peoples from ancestral lands while poisoning water sources that sustained communities for millennia. Palm oil plantations destroy rainforests and the communities that depend on them, driven by consumption patterns in wealthy nations. Climate change, largely caused by industrialized nations, devastates island states and coastal communities in the Global South, creating millions of climate refugees who face closed borders and hostile reception.

Indigenous Rights and the Land Back Movement

At the forefront of both environmental protection and social justice stand Indigenous peoples, whose animistic worldviews have sustained ecological balance for thousands of years. Despite centuries of genocide, forced assimilation, and land theft, Indigenous communities maintain reciprocal relationships with their territories, demonstrating that human flourishing and ecological health are not opposing forces but mutually reinforcing realities. The land back movement, which seeks to restore Indigenous sovereignty over ancestral territories, represents not merely a transfer of property rights but a fundamental reimagining of human-land relationships.

Indigenous-managed lands consistently show better ecological outcomes than government-protected areas. In the Brazilian Amazon, deforestation rates in Indigenous territories are significantly lower than in adjacent areas, including national parks. Indigenous fire management practices in Australia and North America prevent catastrophic wildfires while maintaining ecosystem health. Traditional fishing practices in the Pacific Northwest sustained salmon populations for millennia until commercial exploitation brought many runs to the brink of extinction. These successes demonstrate that Indigenous sovereignty serves not only justice but also ecological necessity.

The land back movement challenges the foundational assumptions of settler colonialism and private property. Unlike Western property law, which treats land as a commodity to be owned, bought, and sold, Indigenous land relationships are based on reciprocal obligations and kinship networks that include non-human beings. Land is not owned but held in trust for future generations, with current inhabitants serving as caretakers rather than proprietors. This perspective aligns with the animistic understanding that land possesses its own consciousness and agency, entering into a relationship with human communities rather than being possessed by them.

Recent victories in the land back movement demonstrate growing recognition of Indigenous rights and ecological wisdom. The return of the National Bison Range to the Confederated Salish and Kootenai Tribes in 2020 marked the first transfer of federal lands to tribal management. The Klamath River dam removal project, the largest river restoration effort in United States history, resulted from decades of Indigenous advocacy and will restore salmon runs crucial to tribal sustenance and ceremony. New Zealand's recognition of the Whanganui River as a legal person with rights reflects Māori cosmology that understands the river as an ancestor rather than a resource.

Yet these victories remain exceptions in a broader pattern of ongoing colonization. Indigenous peoples worldwide face continued displacement for development projects, from the Amazon to the Arctic. Mining companies, agribusiness, and energy corporations operate with government support to extract resources from Indigenous territories, often using violence and intimidation against land defenders. The murder rate for environmental activists, the majority of whom are Indigenous, continues to rise, with over two hundred killed in 2021 alone. These attacks target not only individuals but entire worldviews that threaten extractive capitalism's logic.

Supporting Indigenous sovereignty requires more than symbolic gestures or token consultation. It demands fundamental restructuring of legal systems to recognize Indigenous governance, return of stolen lands, and respect for Indigenous knowledge systems. Non-Indigenous allies must examine their own relationships to land and property, recognizing themselves as inhabitants of Indigenous territories with obligations to both original peoples and the land itself. This recognition opens possibilities for new forms of inhabitation based on reciprocity rather than ownership, creating alliances between Indigenous and settler communities in defense of shared territories.

Food Sovereignty and Community Gardens

The industrial food system exemplifies the intersection of social and ecological injustice. Monocrop agriculture destroys soil health, eliminates biodiversity, and poisons waterways while producing food that travels thousands of miles to reach consumers. Meanwhile, food apartheid—the systematic lack of access to nutritious, affordable food in marginalized communities—creates health disparities that mirror broader patterns of inequality. The movement for food sovereignty, which asserts communities' rights to define their own food and agriculture systems, offers an animistic alternative that recognizes food as medicine, farming as ceremony, and soil as sacred.

Food sovereignty originated with La Via Campesina, an international peasant movement representing over 200 million farmers worldwide. Unlike food security, which focuses solely on access to sufficient calories, food sovereignty encompasses the entire food system, from seed to table. It prioritizes local food systems, agroecological methods, and community control over agricultural resources. This approach recognizes that industrial agriculture's violence against the land—through pesticides, genetic modification, and soil depletion—parallels its violence against farmworkers and rural communities.

Community gardens emerge as spaces of resistance and regeneration within this context. In Detroit, where decades of disinvestment left vast areas without grocery stores, over 1,400 community gardens and farms now produce fresh food while rebuilding social fabric. These gardens do more than provide vegetables; they restore relationships—between people and land, neighbors and neighborhoods, past and future. Gardeners speak of healing trauma through soil, of plants teaching patience and persistence, of finding identity and purpose through cultivation.

The act of growing food in community transforms both consciousness and material conditions. Gardeners develop intimate knowledge of seasonal cycles, soil health, and ecological relationships. They learn that fertility emerges from decay, that diversity creates resilience, that cooperation yields more than competition. These lessons, learned through direct relationship with living systems, challenge the mechanistic worldview's assumptions about scarcity, competition, and human supremacy. Children who grow food understand viscerally that their well-being depends on the health of soil, water, and pollinating insects.

Urban agriculture also reclaims space from capitalist enclosure, transforming vacant lots into commons that serve community needs rather than generating profit. In Los Angeles, the South Central Farm created a fourteen-acre oasis that fed 350 families before its destruction for warehouse development—a loss that galvanized broader movements for land justice. In Cuba, urban agriculture provides seventy percent of fresh produce for city dwellers, demonstrating the potential for food sovereignty even in dense urban environments. These examples show that cities need not be food deserts dependent on industrial agriculture but can become productive landscapes that nourish both people and ecosystems.

Indigenous foodways offer profound teachings about reciprocal relationships with food systems. The Three Sisters agriculture of many North American Indigenous peoples—corn, beans, and squash grown together—demonstrates how diversity and mutual aid create abundance. Corn provides structure for beans to climb, beans fix nitrogen in the soil, and squash leaves shade the ground to retain moisture and prevent weeds. This polyculture produces more nutrition per acre than any monocrop while building rather than depleting soil fertility. The Three Sisters teach that food systems can be regenerative rather than extractive, that plants can be partners rather than products.

Traditional fishing and hunting practices similarly demonstrate reciprocal relationships with animal relatives. Indigenous protocols for taking life—prayers, ceremonies, seasonal restrictions, and selective harvesting—ensure that human needs are met without compromising ecosystem health. The practice of leaving the first salmon or deer of the season, thanking the animal for its sacrifice, and using every part of the body reflects an understanding that taking life creates obligations. These practices contrast sharply with industrial animal agriculture, which reduces sentient beings to production units and confines them in conditions that would be considered torture if applied to humans.

Environmental Health and Toxic Exposure

The burden of industrial civilization's toxic legacy falls most heavily on those with the least power to refuse it. From lead paint in urban housing to pesticide drift in agricultural communities, from mountaintop removal in Appalachia to uranium mining on Native lands, exposure to environmental hazards follows predictable patterns of race, class, and colonial status. The health consequences—asthma, cancer, developmental disabilities, reproductive disorders—steal years of life and quality of life from millions while generating profits for corporations that externalize the true costs of production.

Children bear the heaviest burden of environmental toxins. Their developing bodies absorb proportionally more pollutants while having less capacity to detoxify. In Flint, Michigan, where cost-cutting measures exposed an entire city to lead-contaminated water, thousands of children suffered irreversible neurological damage. The crisis was not an accident but the predictable result of systematic disinvestment in Black communities and prioritization of fiscal austerity over human health. Similar crises unfold daily in communities worldwide, though most never receive media attention or remediation.

The production and disposal of toxic substances follows colonial patterns of extraction and waste. Electronics manufactured with rare earth minerals mined from Indigenous lands in conditions of extreme toxicity are consumed in wealthy nations, then exported as e-waste to Ghana, China, and India, where desperately poor people, including children, burn cables to recover copper and gold, exposing themselves to dioxins, heavy metals, and other poisons. This global circulation of toxicity maintains hierarchies of human value, designating some bodies as acceptable sites for contamination.

Pesticide exposure in agricultural communities demonstrates how environmental and labor injustices intersect. Farmworkers, predominantly immigrants and people of color, face direct exposure to chemicals linked to cancer, neurological damage, and reproductive harm. Their children, exposed in utero and through drift into homes and schools, show elevated rates of autism, ADHD, and developmental delays. Yet these communities often lack access to healthcare, legal status to demand protection, or economic alternatives to agricultural labor. The cheap food that stocks supermarket shelves in wealthy neighborhoods carries hidden costs paid in farmworker health and shortened lives.

The fossil fuel industry exemplifies how environmental racism operates through both exposure and exclusion. Communities of color disproportionately host refineries, power plants, and fracking operations while being systematically excluded from the economic benefits these industries claim to provide. The jobs go primarily to white workers from outside the community, while local residents breathe the emissions. When disasters strike—explosions, spills, leaks—emergency response is slower and less comprehensive than in white communities. When cleanup occurs, it often involves minimal remediation that leaves contamination in place while declaring sites "safe."

Traditional medicine systems understood that individual health cannot be separated from environmental health, that the same forces that sicken ecosystems sicken human bodies. The rise of chronic diseases—diabetes, cancer, autoimmune disorders, mental illness—parallels the rise of industrial pollution and ecological degradation. These are not separate crises but manifestations of a worldview that treats both human and non-human bodies as acceptable casualties of progress. Healing requires not just medical treatment but ecological restoration and social transformation.

Climate Refugees and Migration Justice

Climate change acts as a threat multiplier, intensifying existing inequalities while creating new forms of displacement and dispossession. Rising seas, expanding deserts, intensifying storms, and shifting precipitation patterns force millions from their homes, creating climate refugees who face closed borders, detention, and deportation. The nations most responsible for greenhouse gas emissions refuse entry to those fleeing the consequences, maintaining borders that allow capital and commodities to flow freely while restricting human movement.

Small island states face complete erasure as rising seas swallow ancestral lands. Tuvalu, Kiribati, and the Marshall Islands—nations that contributed virtually nothing to climate change—prepare for the possibility of complete evacuation. The loss encompasses more than territory; entire cultures, languages, and ways of being face extinction. The ocean that sustained these peoples for millennia, understood as ancestor and relative, becomes the agent of their displacement. Yet international law provides no framework for climate refugees, no guarantee of resettlement, no compensation for losses that cannot be measured in monetary terms.

Drought and desertification displace millions more, particularly in sub-Saharan Africa and Central America. Farmers who sustained themselves for generations watch crops fail and livestock die as rainfall patterns shift and temperatures rise. The choice between starvation and migration is no choice at all. Yet those who flee are labeled "economic migrants" rather than climate refugees, denied the limited protections available to those fleeing political persecution. The violence of climate change—slower than war but no less deadly—remains legally invisible.

The militarization of borders represents a form of climate apartheid, where wealthy nations use force to exclude those whose displacement they caused. The United States spends billions on border walls and detention centers while refusing to address root causes of migration. The European Union allows thousands to drown in the Mediterranean rather than provide safe passage. Australia imprisons asylum seekers on remote islands in conditions that violate human rights. These policies treat human movement as a crime while ignoring the crimes of colonization and carbon emissions that force displacement.

Indigenous peoples face unique challenges as climate refugees, losing not just homes but sacred sites, traditional food sources, and the landscapes that hold cultural memory. In Alaska, entire villages relocate as permafrost melts and storms intensify, but government programs provide insufficient support for communities to move together and maintain cultural integrity. In the Amazon, drought and fire force forest peoples into cities where their knowledge and skills have no value, where they face discrimination and poverty. The loss of Indigenous peoples from their territories represents not just human tragedy but ecological catastrophe, as the most effective guardians of biodiversity are separated from the lands they protected.

Migration has always been a human adaptation strategy, part of our species' resilience and creativity. Borders are recent inventions, imposed by nation-states to control labor and maintain hierarchies. An animistic understanding recognizes that human movement, like water, follows natural patterns and cannot be permanently contained by artificial barriers. The criminalization of migration violates both human rights and ecological wisdom, treating people as invasive species rather than recognizing our fundamental kinship.

Intersectionality and Inclusive Environmentalism

The mainstream environmental movement's historical exclusion of marginalized voices has weakened both its analysis and effectiveness. Founded primarily by and for affluent white people, major environmental organizations long ignored environmental racism, focused on wilderness preservation over urban ecology, and promoted solutions that displaced Indigenous peoples and rural communities. This narrow vision failed to recognize that social and ecological justice are inseparable, that the same systems destroying ecosystems oppress human communities.

The concept of intersectionality, developed by legal scholar Kimberlé Crenshaw to describe how race, class, gender, and other identities interact to create unique experiences of oppression, applies directly to environmental justice. A Black woman farmworker faces compound risks from pesticide exposure, poverty, racism, and sexism that cannot be addressed separately. An Indigenous trans person defending their territory confronts colonialism, environmental destruction, and gender-based violence as interwoven threats. Environmental movements that fail to address these intersections perpetuate the systems they claim to oppose.

Women, who perform the majority of agricultural labor worldwide and serve as primary caregivers, face particular vulnerabilities to environmental degradation. Climate change increases their workload as water and fuel become scarcer, forcing longer journeys and harder labor. Environmental toxins affect reproductive health, causing miscarriages, birth defects, and infertility. Yet women are excluded from decision-making about land use, resource management, and climate policy. The wisdom of those most affected by environmental problems remains marginalized in favor of technocratic solutions designed by those most insulated from consequences.

Disability justice reveals another dimension of environmental oppression. People with disabilities face elevated risks from extreme weather, air pollution, and toxic exposure while being excluded from emergency planning and environmental organizing. The ableism that treats disabled lives as less valuable parallels the mechanistic worldview's devaluation of all beings deemed less productive or useful. An inclusive environmentalism recognizes that the variation and vulnerability inherent in all life deserves protection and accommodation, not elimination or abandonment.

LGBTQ+ people, particularly those who are also people of color, face environmental injustices compounded by discrimination and violence. Homeless LGBTQ+ youth, rejected by families and failed by systems, face direct exposure to environmental hazards. Trans people struggle to access healthcare while dealing with endocrine disruptors and other environmental health threats. The policing of gender and sexuality connects to the control and exploitation of nature—both emerge from patriarchal systems that enforce rigid categories and hierarchies.

Economic class shapes environmental experience in profound ways. The poor live in more polluted neighborhoods, work in more hazardous conditions, and have fewer resources to protect themselves from environmental threats. They cannot afford organic food, water filters, or medical care for environmental illnesses. They cannot relocate from contaminated areas or retrofit homes for climate resilience. Yet their lower consumption and smaller carbon footprints mean they contribute less to ecological problems than the wealthy, who consume dis-

328 – DANIEL PAYNE

proportionate resources while insulating themselves from consequences.

Age creates additional dimensions of environmental justice. Elders, who carry cultural memory and ecological knowledge, face isolation and health impacts from environmental degradation. Children, who will inherit the consequences of current decisions, have no voice in policies that will shape their futures. Indigenous concepts of seven-generation thinking—making decisions based on impacts to descendants seven generations in the future—offer guidance for creating truly inclusive environmental policies that consider all beings across time.

The Path Forward: Solidarity and Transformation

Building movements that effectively address both social and ecological crises requires fundamental transformation of approach and understanding. Rather than treating environmental protection as separate from human rights, racial justice, economic equity, and decolonization, we must recognize these as facets of the same work: restoring right relationship with all consciousness, human and more-than-human alike.

This transformation begins with centering the voices and leadership of those most affected by environmental injustice. Indigenous peoples, communities of color, the poor, and others on the frontlines of ecological crises possess essential knowledge about both problems and solutions. Their strategies—rooted in lived experience and cultural wisdom—offer paths forward that technocratic approaches miss. Supporting frontline communities means not just including them in existing movements but transforming movements to reflect their priorities and perspectives.

Reparative justice must be central to environmental solutions. Communities harmed by environmental racism deserve not just cessation of ongoing harm but repair for historical damage. This includes cleanup of contaminated sites, healthcare for those sickened by exposure, and economic support for communities whose livelihoods were destroyed.

Reparations should extend to Indigenous peoples whose lands were stolen and ecosystems degraded, including land return, restoration support, and recognition of sovereignty.

Economic transformation is essential for achieving environmental justice. The capitalist system that treats both nature and people as commodities cannot be reformed into sustainability; it must be replaced with economic systems based on reciprocity, cooperation, and care. This includes universal provision of basic needs—housing, food, healthcare, education—that reduces vulnerability to environmental exploitation. It includes workplace democracy that gives workers control over production decisions affecting their health and environments. It includes commons management that treats essential resources as collective heritage rather than private property.

Legal frameworks must evolve to recognize rights of nature and crimes against the environment as crimes against humanity. The international movement for ecocide law seeks to criminalize massive environmental destruction, holding corporations and governments accountable for ecological violence. Rights of nature legislation, now adopted in dozens of jurisdictions worldwide, grants legal standing to ecosystems, rivers, and mountains, enabling their defense against exploitation. These legal innovations reflect animistic understanding that non-human beings deserve moral consideration and legal protection.

Education plays a crucial role in transformation, not through abstract environmental curricula but through place-based learning that connects children to their local ecosystems and communities. Young people learning from elders, growing food, tending restoration projects, and defending their territories develop both practical skills and revolutionary consciousness. They understand viscerally that their well-being depends on ecological health and social justice, that healing the world requires healing relationships.

Direct action and resistance remain necessary tools for environmental justice. From Indigenous water protectors blocking pipelines to community members shutting down toxic facilities, those who put their bodies between extractive industries and ecosystems demonstrate that moral authority exceeds legal authority when laws serve injustice. These actions inspire broader movements while directly protecting lands and communities from immediate threats. The courage of frontline defenders reminds us that transformation requires not just vision but willingness to take risks for what we love.

International solidarity connects local struggles to global movements. Climate justice activists in the Pacific Islands support Indigenous resistance in the Amazon. Black Lives Matter organizers join Indigenous pipeline protests. Farmworker unions ally with urban food justice organizations. These connections reveal that struggles for justice anywhere strengthen movements everywhere, that diversity of tactics and perspectives creates resilience. The emerging global movement for justice—social, economic, ecological—represents humanity's immune response to systems that threaten our collective survival.

Healing the Sacred Wounds

The work of achieving social justice through ecological justice is ultimately spiritual work, requiring us to heal the sacred wounds inflicted by centuries of disconnection and domination. These wounds run deep, transmitted across generations through trauma, displacement, and cultural destruction. Healing requires more than policy changes or technological fixes; it requires transforming consciousness, rebuilding relationships, and remembering our place in the sacred web of life.

This healing cannot be accomplished through individual action alone but requires collective transformation. Communities coming together to restore damaged landscapes simultaneously restore damaged social fabric. The act of planting trees together, cleaning watersheds, and tending gardens creates bonds between people while healing land. Shared work for ecological restoration becomes ceremony, creating meaning and connection in a world starved for both.

Stories play a crucial role in this healing, particularly stories that re-connect us to place and each other. Indigenous stories that teach rec-iprocity and respect, immigrant stories of connection to homeland, community stories of resistance and resilience—all contribute to new narratives that challenge dominant paradigms. Through storytelling, we remember that other worlds are possible, that current systems are nei-ther natural nor inevitable, that our ancestors lived differently and our descendants can too.

Ceremony and ritual create containers for transformation, marking transitions and restoring sacred relationships. Community rituals that honor seasonal cycles, celebrate restoration successes, and mourn eco-logical losses help process collective grief while building collective power. These ceremonies need not appropriate Indigenous traditions but can emerge from authentic connection with place and community, creating new traditions rooted in local ecology and inclusive values.

The path toward justice—social and ecological—requires acknowl-edging that we are all wounded by systems of domination, though in vastly different ways and degrees. The oppressor is spiritually damaged by participating in oppression, cut off from their own humanity and connection to life. This recognition does not excuse harm or equate dif-ferent experiences but opens possibilities for transformation rather than mere reversal of hierarchies. True justice restores everyone to right rela-tionship, healing both those harmed and those who harm.

As we engage in this sacred work, we must remember that trans-formation takes time, often longer than individual lifespans. The seeds we plant today, both literal and metaphorical, may not mature in our lifetime. This requires cultivating what Indigenous scholar Kyle Whyte calls "collective continuance"—the ability to adapt and persist across generations, maintaining cultural integrity while responding to chang-ing conditions. We work not for immediate victory but for the long arc of healing, trusting that our efforts contribute to larger patterns of transformation.

The integration of social and ecological justice through animistic understanding offers hope in dark times. By recognizing that all beings—human and more-than-human—deserve respect, autonomy, and flourishing, we create foundations for systems that serve life rather than destroying it. By understanding that our liberation is bound together, that none are free until all are free, we build movements capable of transforming the world. By remembering that we are part of nature, not separate from it, we come home to ourselves and our place in the living world.

This is not utopian fantasy but practical necessity. The current trajectory of ecological collapse and social disintegration cannot continue. Either we transform our relationships with each other and the living world, or we face civilizational collapse that will cause unimaginable suffering. The choice is not whether to change but how—whether transformation will be chosen or imposed, creative or catastrophic, just or brutal. By choosing transformation rooted in justice and animated by love for life, we join our ancestors and descendants in the great work of healing the world.

The marriage of social and ecological justice through animistic wisdom offers a way forward that honors both human dignity and ecological integrity. It recognizes that the health of human communities cannot be separated from the health of ecosystems, that justice for people requires justice for all beings, that healing must be collective and systemic rather than individual and superficial. This path is not easy—it requires confronting powerful interests, transforming consciousness, and sustaining struggle across generations. Yet it is the only path that leads toward a world where all beings can flourish, where diversity is celebrated rather than punished, where relationships are based on reciprocity rather than domination.

As we walk this path together, we discover that the work of justice is also the work of joy. In struggling alongside others for liberation, we find community and purpose. In defending the living world, we experience its beauty and wonder. In healing relationships, we discover our own wholeness. The transformation required is not sacrifice but recovery—of connection, meaning, and our full humanity. This is the promise of environmental justice rooted in animistic understanding: not just survival but flourishing, not just resistance but regeneration, not just healing but wholeness.

The living world calls us to remember that justice is not a human concept but a natural principle, visible in the reciprocal relationships that sustain ecosystems, in the mutual aid that enables survival, in the diversity that creates resilience. By aligning human systems with natural principles, we do not impose ideology but restore balance. The work is both ancient and urgent, drawing on ancestral wisdom while responding to unprecedented crises. It requires all of us, each contributing unique gifts and perspectives, working across differences toward shared liberation.

This chapter has explored how social and ecological justice intersect and reinforce each other, how the wounds inflicted on land and people stem from the same source and require integrated healing. The path forward demands that we center those most affected by injustice, transform systems that perpetuate harm, and restore sacred relationships with all our relations. This is not merely political work but spiritual work, not merely practical but ceremonial, not merely necessary but sacred. As we continue this journey together, may we remember that our struggles for justice are expressions of love—for each other, for the Earth, for life itself. In that love lies both our motivation and our power, our suffering and our joy, our work and our reward.

CHAPTER 19

Psychological and Spiritual Healing

The epidemic of mental illness sweeping through industrialized societies reveals a profound spiritual crisis at the heart of modern civilization. Depression, anxiety, addiction, and suicide rates climb steadily upward despite unprecedented material wealth and technological advancement. Pharmaceutical interventions multiply while healing remains elusive. The mechanistic worldview that promised control and comfort has instead delivered isolation and anguish, cutting us off from the sources of meaning and connection that sustained our ancestors for millennia. The path toward genuine psychological and spiritual healing leads not through further medicalization but through restored interdependence with the living world.

Contemporary psychology, for all its insights into human behavior and neurobiology, operates within a framework that treats the individual psyche as separate from its ecological context. Therapy happens in climate-controlled offices, medications adjust brain chemistry, and healing is measured by adaptation to a fundamentally pathological society. Yet Indigenous healing traditions have always understood that individual suffering cannot be separated from collective and ecological imbalance. The sickness of the soul reflects the sickness of the society and the land. True healing requires addressing all levels simultaneously—personal, communal, and planetary.

The animistic understanding that consciousness pervades all existence offers profound resources for psychological healing. When we recognize ourselves as part of a living, conscious universe rather than isolated subjects in a dead world of objects, the existential loneliness that underlies much modern suffering begins to dissolve. The rocks, trees, rivers, and mountains become potential sources of guidance and comfort rather than mere scenery. The boundaries of the self become permeable, allowing for experiences of connection and meaning that transcend the narrow confines of individual ego.

Nature Deficit Disorder and Its Remedies

Richard Louv's concept of nature deficit disorder, while not a formal medical diagnosis, names a genuine phenomenon: the physical, psychological, and spiritual consequences of disconnection from the natural world. Children who grow up without regular contact with nature show higher rates of attention disorders, depression, and obesity. Adults confined to built environments experience chronic stress, cognitive decline, and what researchers call "psychological restoration deprivation." The human nervous system, evolved over millions of years in intimacy with diverse ecosystems, cannot function optimally in the sensory poverty of modern environments.

The symptoms of nature deficit disorder read like a catalog of modern ailments. Attention becomes fragmented, unable to sustain focus without constant stimulation. Sensory perception atrophies, leaving people unable to distinguish bird songs or detect subtle seasonal changes. Imagination withers, confined to the narrow possibilities presented by screens and structured activities. Physical health deteriorates through lack of movement, natural light, and exposure to beneficial microorganisms. Emotional regulation becomes difficult without the calming influence of natural rhythms and patterns.

Research in environmental psychology demonstrates what traditional peoples have always known: contact with nature is not a luxury but a necessity for human wellbeing. Japanese studies on shinrin-yoku, or forest bathing, show that time spent among trees lowers cortisol levels, reduces blood pressure, and enhances immune function. The phytoncides released by trees act as natural aromatherapy, while the fractal patterns found throughout nature activate parasympathetic nervous system responses that promote healing and restoration. Even brief views of nature through windows accelerate recovery from surgery and reduce the need for pain medication.

The remedy for nature deficit disorder extends beyond occasional visits to parks or wilderness areas. It requires restructuring our lives to include regular, meaningful contact with the more-than-human world. This might mean cultivating gardens, caring for houseplants, feeding birds, or simply eating meals outdoors. It involves developing what ecopsychologist Robert Greenway calls "wilderness consciousness"—a state of expanded awareness that recognizes our embeddedness in larger ecological systems. This consciousness can be cultivated even in urban environments through attention to weather patterns, seasonal cycles, and the persistent presence of life in sidewalk cracks and city trees.

Children especially need what environmental educator David Sobel calls "special places"—secret spots in nature where they can create their own worlds, develop relationships with particular trees or streams, and experience themselves as part of the living landscape. These childhood connections to place form the foundation for lifelong environmental consciousness and psychological resilience. The loss of children's independent outdoor play represents not just a shift in recreational patterns but a fundamental impoverishment of human development.

Schools that integrate outdoor education and place-based learning report dramatic improvements in student behavior, academic performance, and emotional wellbeing. The Waldkindergarten movement in Germany, where children spend entire days outdoors regardless of weather, produces students who are more creative, confident, and socially capable than their indoor-educated peers. Forest schools, now spreading globally, demonstrate that learning in relationship with nature develops not just ecological awareness but cognitive flexibility, risk assessment skills, and emotional intelligence.

For adults, the remedies for nature deficit often require conscious effort to overcome the habits and structures of modern life. This might involve what philosopher David Abram calls "rewilding perception"—deliberately cultivating sensory awareness and presence to the animate earth. Practices like sit spots (regularly visiting the same outdoor location), phenology wheels (tracking seasonal changes), and nature journaling develop intimate knowledge of local ecology while restoring psychological equilibrium. The key is not consuming nature as scenery but entering into relationship with specific places and beings.

Ecotherapy and Wilderness Immersion

The field of ecotherapy, also known as nature-based therapy or green therapy, formally recognizes the healing power of contact with the natural world. Unlike traditional therapy that treats the individual in isolation, ecotherapy understands healing as emerging from restored relationships with the more-than-human world. Practitioners work in gardens, forests, and wilderness settings, using the land itself as co-therapist. The results often surpass those achieved through conventional office-based interventions, particularly for trauma, depression, and addiction.

Wilderness therapy programs immerse participants in natural settings for extended periods, using the challenges and teachings of outdoor living to catalyze transformation. Adolescents struggling with behavioral issues learn natural consequences through direct experience—if you don't gather firewood, you're cold; if you don't cooperate with others, tasks become impossible. The wilderness doesn't judge or punish; it simply responds, offering clear feedback that promotes responsibility and awareness. Many participants describe their time in wilderness therapy as initiatory, marking a transition from destructive patterns to purposeful living.

The therapeutic power of wilderness immersion extends beyond skill-building and behavioral modification. Extended time in natural settings induces what researchers call "soft fascination"—a state of relaxed attention that allows overstimulated nervous systems to reset. The absence of artificial stimulation creates space for suppressed emotions and memories to surface and be processed. The vastness of natural landscapes provides perspective on personal problems, while the beauty and complexity of ecosystems inspire hope and wonder.

Horticultural therapy brings the healing power of plants to hospitals, prisons, and care facilities. Working with soil and growing things provides grounding for people dealing with trauma, anxiety, and depression. The act of nurturing plants develops self-efficacy and hope, while the sensory richness of gardens engages bodies and minds numbed by institutional settings. Veterans with PTSD find peace in greenhouse work, prisoners discover redemption through tending prison gardens, and elderly people with dementia show improved cognition and mood when engaged in gardening activities.

Animal-assisted therapy recognizes that relationships with non-human beings can provide healing that human relationships cannot. Horses, with their sensitivity to emotional states and inability to be deceived by facades, help trauma survivors learn to regulate their nervous systems and establish authentic connection. Dogs provide unconditional acceptance and present-moment awareness that interrupts anxious rumination. Even watching fish in aquariums lowers blood pressure and promotes relaxation. These therapeutic relationships work because they bypass the complexities of human social interaction, offering direct, embodied connection.

Adventure therapy uses challenging outdoor activities—rock climbing, rafting, backpacking—to build confidence and resilience. Facing natural challenges in supportive group settings helps participants overcome limiting beliefs and develop trust in themselves and others. The immediate feedback of natural environments cuts through denial and rationalization, while shared challenges create bonds that transcend social barriers. Many participants report that accomplishing something they thought impossible in nature translates to increased agency in other life areas.

The effectiveness of ecotherapy challenges fundamental assumptions about mental health treatment. If psychological wellbeing improves through contact with nature, then perhaps much mental illness stems not from individual pathology but from pathological environments. The high rates of depression and anxiety in cities, the correlation between mental illness and disconnection from nature, and the rapid improvement many people experience in natural settings suggest that we've been treating symptoms while ignoring causes.

Community Healing Through Land Connection

Individual healing cannot be sustained within sick societies and degraded environments. True psychological and spiritual wellbeing emerges from healthy communities embedded in healthy ecosystems. Around the world, communities are discovering that collective engagement with land restoration simultaneously heals trauma, rebuilds social bonds, and restores ecological balance. This triple healing—personal, social, and ecological—demonstrates the inseparability of human and environmental wellbeing.

In Detroit, community gardens transform vacant lots left by economic abandonment into spaces of healing and renewal. Neighbors who had lived in isolation for years come together to grow food, share stories, and rebuild community fabric torn by decades of disinvestment. The act of bringing life back to abandoned land parallels the process of bringing life back to abandoned neighborhoods. Gardeners speak of healing historical trauma through working soil that holds the memories of migration, industrial labor, and urban uprising.

Indigenous communities use land-based healing to address the intergenerational trauma of colonization. Culture camps bring young people onto traditional territories to learn ancestral skills, languages, and ceremonies. Time on the land, away from the influences of settler society, allows for deep healing that clinical interventions alone cannot achieve. Elders teach that the land itself is medicine, that simply being present in ancestral territories activates healing processes encoded in DNA and cultural memory.

The Aboriginal Australian concept of country—a complex relationship between people, land, ancestors, and law—illustrates how collective identity and wellbeing depend on connection to specific places. When Aboriginal people are separated from their country, they experience profound grief and illness that Western medicine cannot cure. Conversely, programs that enable people to return to country, even briefly, show remarkable improvements in physical and mental health. The land literally heals its people, while the people's presence heals the land.

In post-conflict regions, environmental restoration provides a framework for reconciliation and collective healing. In Rwanda, communities that participated in reforestation programs after the genocide showed better psychological recovery and social cohesion than those that received only traditional trauma interventions. The shared work of planting trees created neutral ground for former enemies to interact, while nurturing new life helped process grief and envision futures beyond violence.

Urban communities use guerrilla gardening and tactical urbanism to reclaim spaces for collective healing. Transforming neglected spaces into pocket parks and community gathering places asserts that communities deserve beauty and nature regardless of economic status. These interventions do more than improve aesthetics; they demonstrate collective agency and challenge the systems that create and maintain environmental injustice. The act of transformation itself becomes healing, converting feelings of powerlessness into expressions of creativity and resistance.

Community-supported agriculture creates healing connections between urban consumers and rural producers. Members who visit farms, participate in harvests, and know the people who grow their food report feeling more grounded and connected than when purchasing anonymous produce. The relationship with specific land and farmers provides an anchor in an increasingly abstract world, while seasonal eating rhythms restore connection to natural cycles. For farmers, the direct relationships and community support provide economic stability and social connection often lost in industrial agriculture.

Trauma Recovery in Natural Settings

Trauma disrupts our fundamental sense of safety and connection, fragmenting the self and severing relationships with body, community, and environment. While traditional trauma therapy focuses on cognitive processing and symptom management, nature-based approaches work with the whole person embedded in the larger web of relationships. The natural world, with its cycles of death and rebirth, its resilience and adaptation, offers profound teachings about healing from traumatic experiences.

Somatic experiencing, developed by Peter Levine through observation of wild animals, recognizes that trauma is held in the body and must be released through embodied processes. Animals in the wild rarely develop post-traumatic stress despite frequent life-threatening experiences because they discharge traumatic energy through shaking, running, and other physical expressions. Humans, constrained by social conditioning, often suppress these natural discharge processes, trapping traumatic energy in the nervous system. Nature-based somatic therapy uses movement, breathwork, and sensory engagement with natural environments to facilitate the release of trapped trauma.

The rhythms and patterns found in nature provide external regulation for nervous systems dysregulated by trauma. The sound of ocean waves, with their predictable yet variable rhythm, entrains breathing and heart rate variability. The bilateral stimulation of walking, especially on uneven natural surfaces, facilitates integration of traumatic memories similar to EMDR therapy. The vast perspectives offered by mountains or starry skies help contextualize personal suffering within larger patterns of existence.

Water holds particular significance in trauma healing across cultures. Rivers carry away what needs to be released, oceans provide vastness that can hold enormous grief, rain cleanses and renews. Many trauma survivors report profound healing experiences in or near water—crying into the ocean, screaming into waterfalls, floating in lakes while feeling held by something larger than human hands. The molecular structure of water, with its capacity to hold and transmit information, may explain why proximity to water facilitates emotional release and integration.

Fire ceremonies provide controlled contexts for transforming trauma. The act of writing traumatic experiences and burning them, practiced in various forms across cultures, creates tangible release and transformation. Watching solid matter become smoke and ash mirrors the process of transmuting dense traumatic energy into something that can disperse and dissipate. The warmth of fire provides comfort and safety, while its transformative power demonstrates that even the most solid-seeming suffering can change form.

Trees offer unique support for trauma healing. Their rootedness provides stability for those whose sense of grounding has been disrupted. Their seasonal cycles demonstrate that periods of apparent death are followed by renewal. Their ability to compartmentalize damage, continuing to grow despite wounds, models resilience. Many trauma survivors develop healing relationships with particular trees, finding in them witnesses that can hold their stories without judgment or overwhelm.

The medicine wheel teachings of many Indigenous traditions provide frameworks for understanding trauma and healing that incorporate all aspects of existence. Trauma is understood not as individual pathology but as an imbalance that affects all relations. Healing involves not just the person but their relationships with family, community, ancestors, land, and spirit. This expanded understanding opens multiple pathways for healing that Western psychology has only begun to explore.

Addiction Recovery Through Earth Connection

Addiction represents a misdirected search for connection and transcendence, an attempt to fill spiritual emptiness with substances or behaviors that ultimately increase isolation and suffering. Twelve-step programs have long recognized addiction as a spiritual disease requiring spiritual solution, but the higher power of traditional recovery often remains abstract. Nature-based recovery programs ground spiritual awakening in direct relationship with the living Earth, providing tangible connection that satisfies the deep longing that drives addictive behavior.

Wilderness recovery programs remove participants from environments associated with substance use while immersing them in settings that naturally promote presence and awareness. The physical challenges of outdoor living leave little energy for craving and rumination, while natural endorphins from exercise and sunlight provide healthy mood regulation. The immediacy of survival tasks—making shelter, finding water, preparing food—grounds participants in present-moment reality, interrupting the mental loops that perpetuate addiction.

The concept of natural highs—peak experiences achieved through connection with nature rather than substances—provides alternatives to chemical alteration of consciousness. The runner's high from trail running, the adrenaline of rock climbing, the profound peace of sunrise meditation all demonstrate that the states people seek through substances are available through engagement with the natural world. These experiences, unlike drug-induced states, build rather than deplete physical and psychological resources.

Gardens designed specifically for addiction recovery create spaces where participants can nurture life while rebuilding their own capacity for growth. The patience required for gardening challenges the instant gratification that characterizes addiction, while the reliable response of plants to care rebuilds trust in cause and effect. Harvesting and sharing food grown with one's own hands provides accomplishment and connection that no substance can match. The metaphors are obvious but powerful—pulling weeds parallels removing negative influences, composting transforms waste into fertility, growth requires both sunshine and rain.

Indigenous approaches to addiction healing understand substance abuse as symptomatic of spiritual disconnection from land, culture, and identity. Healing involves not just abstinence but restoration of cultural practices, language, and ceremony that provide meaning and belonging. The Red Road, a Native American recovery path, emphasizes living in harmony with natural and spiritual laws rather than simply avoiding substances. This approach recognizes that sustainable recovery requires not just stopping harmful behaviors but establishing life-affirming relationships and practices.

Animal-assisted recovery programs use relationships with horses, dogs, and other animals to rebuild trust and connection damaged by addiction. Animals respond to authentic emotional states rather than manipulation or facades, requiring participants to develop honesty and presence. Caring for animals develops responsibility and routine while providing unconditional acceptance that many in recovery have never experienced. The non-verbal communication required with animals bypasses the elaborate justifications and rationalizations that maintain addictive patterns.

The role of ceremony and ritual in nature-based recovery cannot be overstated. Sweat lodges, used carefully and with proper guidance, provide purification and renewal. Fire ceremonies allow participants to release shame and commitment to transformation. Solo wilderness quests mark transitions from addictive to recovery identities. These ceremonies work because they engage the whole person—body, mind, and spirit—in ways that purely cognitive or pharmaceutical approaches cannot match.

Mental Health Benefits of Animistic Practice

Adopting an animistic worldview—recognizing consciousness and agency throughout the natural world—provides specific psychological benefits that address core features of modern mental illness. Where materialism creates meaninglessness, animism reveals purpose and connection. Where individualism generates isolation, animism embeds us in networks of relationship. Where mechanism produces alienation, animism restores enchantment and wonder. These shifts in perception and relationship have measurable impacts on psychological wellbeing.

The practice of greeting the sun each morning, acknowledging the consciousness of the day, transforms routine into ritual and obligation into gratitude. People who maintain this simple practice report increased optimism, better sleep patterns, and greater sense of purpose. The act recognizes our dependence on cosmic forces while establishing reciprocal relationship—we acknowledge the sun's gift of light and warmth, offering our attention and appreciation in return. This positions us as participants in cosmic cycles rather than isolated individuals struggling through meaningless days.

Developing relationships with plants as conscious beings rather than decorative objects changes our experience of both indoor and outdoor environments. Houseplants become companions whose wellbeing matters, creating networks of care and attention that combat loneliness. Speaking to plants, once dismissed as eccentricity, is now validated by research showing that plants respond to human attention with improved growth. The practice of seeking permission before harvesting, thanking plants for their gifts, and leaving offerings transforms resource extraction into sacred exchange.

Understanding weather as an expression of planetary consciousness rather than mere atmospheric conditions restores agency and relationship to climate patterns. Instead of being passive victims of "bad" weather, we become participants in atmospheric processes, capable of reading signs and responding appropriately. Indigenous weather workers demonstrate that human consciousness can influence weather patterns through ceremony and intention, challenging Western assumptions about the separation between mind and matter.

The animistic practice of dreaming with the land—seeking guidance through dreams informed by specific places—provides access to wisdom beyond rational consciousness. Many report that sleeping outdoors or even bringing stones or plants indoors produces dreams of unusual clarity and significance. These dreams often provide practical guidance for personal and ecological challenges, suggesting that consciousness extends through networks we're only beginning to understand. The practice requires developing dream recall and interpretation skills largely atrophied in modern culture.

Recognizing the consciousness of crafted objects transforms our relationship with material culture. Tools, instruments, and cherished objects are understood as partners rather than possessions, deserving care and respect. This practice, common in traditional cultures, reduces the addictive consumption that characterizes modern life while increasing satisfaction with what we have. The Japanese concept of tsukumogami—objects that acquire souls after long use—encourages repair rather than replacement, creating lasting relationships with the material world.

Seasonal affective patterns, rather than being pathologized as disorders, are understood in animistic frameworks as appropriate responses to natural cycles. Winter's introspection, spring's renewal, summer's expansion, and autumn's release provide templates for psychological rhythm. Instead of maintaining constant productivity regardless of season, animistic practice honors these natural fluctuations, reducing the stress of fighting against natural patterns. This doesn't minimize genuine seasonal depression but contextualizes it within larger patterns of cyclical change.

The Integration of Traditional and Modern Healing

The path forward requires neither wholesale rejection of modern psychology nor uncritical adoption of traditional practices, but thoughtful integration that honors the insights of both approaches. Western psychology's understanding of neurobiology, trauma, and development provides valuable frameworks for understanding suffering and healing. Traditional animistic practices offer what modern approaches lack: recognition of spiritual dimensions, ecological embeddedness, and the healing power of relationship with the more-than-human world.

Successful integration requires cultural humility and recognition that Indigenous and traditional healing systems are complete sciences developed over millennia, not primitive precursors to "real" medicine. These systems often achieve results that Western approaches cannot, particularly for conditions related to spiritual disconnection and ecological alienation. The rush to validate traditional practices through Western scientific frameworks, while sometimes useful, risks reducing complex, holistic systems to isolated techniques stripped of cultural and spiritual context.

Training programs for therapists and healers increasingly incorporate nature-based and traditional approaches, though often in limited ways. True integration requires more than adding outdoor sessions to conventional therapy. It demands examining fundamental assumptions about the nature of mind, the sources of suffering, and the requirements for healing. This might mean recognizing that the therapist's office is itself a problematic setting, that the fifty-minute hour is an artificial constraint, and that individual therapy may be less effective than community and land-based healing.

Indigenous healing practices are beginning to receive recognition and support within mainstream healthcare systems, though significant barriers remain. The Indian Health Service in the United States now covers some traditional healing practices, recognizing that Western medicine alone cannot address the health challenges facing Native communities. Similar programs in Canada, Australia, and New Zealand demonstrate that traditional and modern medicine can work together when there's genuine respect for Indigenous knowledge and authority.

The development of culturally responsive mental health services requires more than translating Western concepts into Indigenous languages. It demands recognizing that different cultures have different understandings of mind, self, and healing. What Western psychology calls depression might be understood as soul loss requiring soul retrieval ceremony. What's diagnosed as psychosis might be recognized as shamanic initiation requiring proper guidance. These aren't simply different words for the same phenomena but fundamentally different understandings of human experience.

Ethical considerations around the integration of traditional practices into modern therapeutic contexts require careful attention. The commodification and appropriation of Indigenous healing practices by the wellness industry causes real harm, both to Indigenous communities whose sacred practices are stolen and commercialized, and to participants who receive decontextualized fragments rather than complete systems. Genuine integration requires relationship, reciprocity, and respect for the sources and keepers of traditional knowledge.

The emergence of psychedelic-assisted therapy represents a particular area where traditional and modern approaches converge. Indigenous peoples have used plant medicines ceremonially for millennia, understanding them as teachers and healers rather than mere chemicals. The recent Western "discovery" of psychedelics' therapeutic potential often ignores this history, attempting to isolate active compounds and standardize protocols while dismissing ceremonial contexts as superstition. Yet research increasingly confirms what traditional practitioners have always known: set, setting, and spiritual framework profoundly influence outcomes.

The Collective Healing of Our Time

We stand at a threshold moment in human history, when the psychological and spiritual crises of modern civilization have become undeniable. The epidemic of mental illness, the ecological crisis, and the social fragmentation of our time are symptoms of the same underlying condition: disconnection from the living world and each other. Healing this disconnection requires more than individual therapy or lifestyle changes; it demands collective transformation of consciousness and culture.

The COVID-19 pandemic, for all its tragedy, created an opening for this transformation. The forced pause in normal activity allowed many to recognize the depth of their exhaustion and disconnection. Time in nature became precious as indoor activities were restricted. Gardens flourished as people sought connection to life and self-sufficiency. The vulnerability revealed by the virus reminded us of our fundamental interdependence with each other and the more-than-human world. These recognitions, if cultivated rather than forgotten, could catalyze the collective healing our time requires.

Young people, facing a future of ecological collapse and social breakdown, are particularly receptive to animistic worldviews and nature-based healing. Climate anxiety and eco-grief, dismissed by some as overreaction, represent appropriate responses to genuine threats. These emotional responses, when honored and channeled rather than pathologized or suppressed, can become powerful forces for transformation. The youth climate movement demonstrates that despair can transform into agency when connected to collective action and earth connection.

The healing of our collective trauma—from colonization, slavery, war, and ecological destruction—requires approaches that match the scale of the wound. Individual therapy, while valuable, cannot address collective and intergenerational trauma alone. We need cultural healing practices that engage entire communities, that honor the ancestors and consider the descendants, that recognize the land itself as both wounded and healer. This might look like truth and reconciliation processes that include the more-than-human world, reparations that involve ecological restoration, or ceremonies of grief and renewal that acknowledge all our relations.

The role of artists, storytellers, and culture creators in collective healing cannot be overstated. New stories that imagine different relationships between humans and the living world, art that renders visible the consciousness of the more-than-human, music that attunes us to natural rhythms—all contribute to the transformation of consciousness required for healing. The stories we tell shape the world we create, and we desperately need stories that restore us to our place in the family of life.

The emergence of what Thomas Berry called "Earth jurisprudence"—legal frameworks that recognize the rights of nature—represents a crucial development in collective healing. When rivers gain legal personhood, when ecosystems have standing in court, when the rights of future generations are constitutionally protected, we begin to heal the conceptual violence that enables physical violence against the living world. These legal recognitions both reflect and advance the consciousness change required for genuine healing.

As we engage in this collective healing work, we must remember that the Earth itself is our primary teacher and healer. The resilience of ecosystems, their capacity for regeneration after disturbance, provides models for our own healing. The mycelial networks that connect forests teach us about communication and mutual aid. The way rivers find their way around obstacles shows us how to flow with rather than against natural patterns. The patient work of succession, as bare ground becomes forest, demonstrates that healing takes time but is always possible.

The psychological and spiritual healing of our time cannot be separated from the healing of the Earth. As we restore wetlands, we restore our capacity to filter and process emotion. As we rebuild soil, we rebuild our grounding and stability. As we protect forests, we protect our capacity for communion and wonder. This is not metaphor but recognition of our fundamental embeddedness in the living world. We are not separate from nature but expressions of it, and our healing is Earth's healing.

This chapter has explored the profound psychological and spiritual healing available through reconnection with the animistic worldview and the living Earth. From addressing nature deficit disorder to facilitating trauma recovery, from supporting addiction healing to integrating traditional and modern therapeutic approaches, the path toward genuine wellbeing leads through restored connection with the more-than-human world. As we face the converging crises of our time, these approaches offer not just personal healing but pathways toward the collective transformation our species desperately needs. The work is both intimate and immense, requiring us to tend our individual wounds while participating in the healing of the world. In this work lies both our challenge and our hope, our responsibility and our possibility.

CHAPTER 20

Cultural Renaissance and Revival

The resurgence of animistic consciousness in the twenty-first century represents far more than nostalgic romanticism or escapist fantasy. Across the globe, communities are awakening to the recognition that their survival—physical, psychological, and spiritual—depends upon recovering the wisdom their ancestors knew: that we inhabit a living universe where every being possesses inherent consciousness and deserves respect. This cultural renaissance manifests through revitalized languages that encode ecological relationships, artistic expressions that render the invisible visible, ceremonies that restore sacred reciprocity, and educational approaches that transmit wisdom across generations. These movements of revival do not seek to return to an imagined past but to reclaim suppressed knowledge while creating new forms appropriate to our unprecedented moment.

The colonial project attempted to eradicate animistic cultures through violence, forced conversion, and systematic destruction of languages, ceremonies, and knowledge systems. Children were stolen from families and forbidden to speak their languages or practice their traditions. Sacred sites were desecrated, ceremonial objects destroyed, and spiritual practices criminalized. The mechanistic worldview was imposed through education systems that taught Indigenous children their cultures were primitive and their languages worthless. Yet despite centuries of attempted cultural genocide, animistic consciousness persisted—hidden in folklore, preserved in place names, encoded in craft traditions, whispered from grandparent to grandchild in moments of safety.

Now, as the failures of mechanistic civilization become undeniable, these suppressed streams of wisdom emerge with renewed vitality. Indigenous communities lead movements to revitalize languages that carry instructions for living in right relationship with specific landscapes. Artists develop new forms that express ancient understandings of consciousness and connection. Young people hunger for initiation and meaning their consumer culture cannot provide. Elders who were punished for speaking their languages as children now teach them to eager grandchildren. This revival is not uniform or without controversy—debates rage about authenticity, appropriation, and adaptation—but the overall direction is clear: humanity is remembering what it means to live in a conscious, animate world.

Language Revitalization and Place Names

Language shapes consciousness in ways we are only beginning to understand. The structures, categories, and metaphors embedded in language influence how speakers perceive and interact with reality. Languages that emerged from animistic worldviews encode relationships, responsibilities, and recognitions that cannot be fully translated into languages shaped by mechanistic thinking. When these languages disappear, entire ways of understanding and being in the world vanish with them. The current linguistic crisis—with Indigenous languages disappearing at rates that exceed species extinction—represents not just cultural loss but the erasure of instructions for surviving and thriving on this planet.

Consider the Potawatomi word "Puhpowee," which translates roughly as "the force which causes mushrooms to push up from the earth overnight." No English equivalent exists because English emerged from a worldview that doesn't recognize this phenomenon as requiring its own term. The word acknowledges a specific manifestation of life force, inviting speakers to notice and honor this particular expression of Earth's creative power. When such words disappear, the phenomena they describe become literally unspeakable and eventually unthinkable.

Many Indigenous languages use different grammatical structures for animate and inanimate beings, but their categories of animacy differ radically from Western assumptions. In Ojibwe, stones and mountains are grammatically animate, recognized as ancient beings with their own forms of awareness. Rivers are understood as entities rather than objects, addressed with the same grammatical forms used for humans and animals. These linguistic structures constantly remind speakers that they move through a world of subjects rather than objects, relations rather than resources.

The restoration of Indigenous place names represents a crucial aspect of cultural revival and decolonization. Colonial renaming of landscapes was an act of possession and erasure, replacing names that described ecological relationships, historical events, and spiritual significance with names that honored colonizers or reflected their perceptions. Mount McKinley becomes Denali again, restoring its identity as "the high one." The Salish Sea reclaims its identity from the imposed "Puget Sound." These restored names carry instructions for re-connection, embedding knowledge about seasonal patterns, species behavior, and sustainable practices.

In New Zealand, the Māori language revival demonstrates how linguistic restoration can transform national consciousness. Once nearly extinct, te reo Māori is now an official language taught in schools and used in government proceedings. Māori place names are being restored, with dual naming becoming standard. This revival has not just preserved a language but has begun shifting New Zealand's entire culture toward recognition of Indigenous wisdom and worldview. Pākehā (non-Māori) New Zealanders increasingly learn te reo Māori not from obligation but from recognition that it offers ways of understanding their adopted homeland that English cannot provide.

The Hawaiian language revival shows how language restoration can catalyze broader cultural renaissance. Banned in schools for nearly a century, Hawaiian faced extinction until community activists established Hawaiian-medium schools in the 1980s. These schools teach not just language but the entire knowledge system encoded within it—navigation by stars, cultivation of traditional crops, protocols for relating to land and sea. Graduates emerge not just bilingual but bicultural, capable of moving between worldviews while maintaining strong Hawaiian identity.

Urban Indigenous communities face particular challenges in language revival, separated from traditional territories where languages emerged and evolved. Yet innovative programs use technology to connect urban learners with elder speakers, create immersive language environments in cities, and develop new vocabularies for contemporary experiences. Young Indigenous people coin terms for smartphones and social media that maintain the animistic structures of their languages, demonstrating that these languages are not relics but living systems capable of evolution.

The relationship between language and landscape means that ecological restoration and linguistic revival are inseparable projects. Languages that emerged in specific bioregions carry detailed knowledge about local species, seasonal patterns, and ecological relationships. As ecosystems are restored, the languages that describe them become more relevant and vital. As languages are revitalized, they guide ecological restoration by encoding traditional ecological knowledge. This reciprocal relationship suggests that cultural and biological diversity are not separate conservation goals but aspects of the same living system.

Traditional Arts and Craft Revival

The resurgence of traditional crafts represents another dimension of animistic revival, as communities rediscover that creating with one's hands from local materials establishes relationships with the more-than-human world that industrial production destroys. These crafts—pottery, weaving, carving, basketry—were never mere techniques for producing objects but practices that maintained reciprocal relationships with clay, fiber, wood, and reed. Their revival restores not just skills but ways of being that honor the consciousness of materials and the places from which they come.

The revival of traditional pottery connects practitioners to the ancient dialogue between human creativity and earth's gifts. Clay, understood not as inert material but as the body of the Earth Mother, must be approached with respect and ceremony. Potters speak of clay teaching them—about patience, attention, and the balance between imposing will and responding to what emerges. The wheel becomes a meditation on centering, the kiln a teacher of transformation. Traditional pottery techniques encode understanding of local clay sources, processing methods developed over generations, and firing approaches that work with rather than against natural forces.

Weaving traditions carry instructions for relationships with plant and animal beings who provide fibers. The gathering of materials becomes ceremonial, requiring knowledge of seasons, gratitude for the gift, and commitment to reciprocity. Weavers must understand the lives of plants—when they're strongest, how to harvest without harm, methods of processing that honor the spirit of the fiber. The patterns that emerge through weaving often represent cosmological understanding, encoding stories and teachings in visual form. The recent revival of backstrap weaving, tapestry, and natural dyeing connects practitioners to lineages of knowledge extending back millennia.

Woodcarving and woodworking traditions restore connection with tree beings, understanding wood not as lumber but as the body of a once-living being that continues to carry spirit. Traditional carvers speak of revealing forms already present in the wood rather than imposing designs upon it. The grain tells stories of the tree's life—years of drought and abundance, wounds and healing, relationships with other beings. Working with hand tools rather than power tools allows craftspeople to feel the wood's response, to enter into dialogue rather than domination. The objects that emerge—bowls, masks, instruments—carry the presence of both tree and maker.

Basketry, perhaps the most widespread of traditional crafts, demonstrates the intersection of practical necessity, artistic expression, and spiritual practice. Baskets require intimate knowledge of local plants, their growth patterns, harvesting protocols, and processing techniques. The gathering of materials becomes a practice of reciprocity—taking only what's offered, leaving gifts in return, ensuring future abundance. The weaving itself becomes meditation, fingers remembering patterns passed through generations. Contemporary basketmakers speak of baskets as teachers, each one revealing something about balance, tension, and the creation of form from seeming chaos.

The revival of natural building techniques—cob, adobe, strawbale, timber framing—represents craft revival at architectural scale. These techniques require intimate knowledge of local materials and climate, creating buildings that breathe with rather than against their environments. Natural builders speak of houses as living beings, with bones of wood, flesh of earth, and skin that breathes. The construction process becomes a community ceremony, with wall-raising parties and plaster fests that transform the building from commodity to gift. These buildings demonstrate that human habitation need not damage landscapes but can enhance them.

Traditional textile arts encode sophisticated understanding of ecology and chemistry. Natural dyeing requires knowledge of plants, minerals, and the complex interactions between fiber, mordant, and dye. Each color tells a story—of specific plants in particular places, of seasonal availability, of relationships maintained across generations. The revival of indigo cultivation and dyeing, spinning and weaving, challenges the fast fashion industry while restoring connections between clothing and place. Wearing naturally dyed, handwoven cloth becomes a practice of carrying the landscape on one's body.

The transmission of these craft traditions requires different pedagogical approaches than industrial education provides. Apprenticeship rather than classroom learning, embodied knowledge rather than abstract information, relationship with master craftspeople rather than credentialed instructors. The learning happens through hands and hearts as much as minds, with mistakes understood as teachers rather than failures. This educational model challenges dominant assumptions about knowledge and expertise while demonstrating that wisdom emerges through relationship and practice.

Seasonal Festivals and Community Celebrations

The restoration of seasonal celebrations marks the return of cyclical time consciousness, challenging linear progress narratives with the recognition that life moves in spirals and circles. These festivals, rooted in astronomical observations and ecological patterns, restore humans to their place in cosmic and terrestrial rhythms. Unlike commercial holidays that promote consumption, traditional seasonal celebrations foster reciprocity, renewal, and community cohesion. Their revival represents not nostalgic reenactment but the creation of contemporary ceremonies that honor ancient patterns while addressing current needs.

The solstices and equinoxes, marked by every traditional culture, provide frameworks for collective acknowledgment of our relationship with the sun and seasons. Winter solstice celebrations—from Yule to Dongzhi to Inti Raymi—honor the return of light while acknowledging darkness as necessary for regeneration. Communities gather to kindle fires, share food, and tell stories that carry them through the longest night. These celebrations counter the artificial extension of daylight through electricity, reminding participants that darkness has its own gifts and necessities.

Spring equinox festivals celebrate renewal, fertility, and the courage required for new growth. The equal balance of light and dark provides a moment for reflection on balance in all aspects of life. Communities plant seeds both literal and metaphorical, honoring the risk and hope inherent in beginning. Traditional practices like egg decoration encode understanding of the cosmic egg from which worlds emerge, while spring cleaning becomes a ceremony of releasing what no longer serves. These celebrations help communities navigate the vulnerable transition from winter's introspection to summer's expansion.

Summer solstice celebrations honor abundance, vitality, and the peak of solar power. Traditional midsummer festivals involved all-night vigils, sacred fires, and the gathering of medicinal herbs at their moment of greatest potency. Contemporary revivals create space for communities to celebrate their creative power while acknowledging that peak moments contain the seeds of decline. The awareness that days will now shorten adds poignancy to the celebration, teaching that nothing remains at peak forever and that wisdom involves recognizing and accepting cycles.

Autumn equinox festivals mark harvest, gratitude, and preparation for the dark half of the year. These celebrations teach that receiving abundance creates obligations—to share surplus, to save seed, to compost what remains. Traditional harvest festivals involved the entire community because bringing in the harvest required collective effort. Contemporary revivals, even in urban settings, create opportunities for communities to acknowledge their dependence on Earth's generosity and their responsibility to reciprocate. The equal balance of light and dark at autumn equinox prompts reflection on what has been accomplished and what remains undone.

Cross-quarter festivals—falling between solstices and equinoxes—mark subtle seasonal transitions often missed by modern calendars. Imbolc marks the first stirrings of spring while winter still reigns. Beltane celebrates fertility and the full emergence of spring's creative power. Lughnasadh honors the first harvest and the sacrifice inherent in grain becoming bread. Samhain marks the final harvest and the thinning of veils between worlds. These festivals teach sensitivity to subtle transitions, honoring liminal moments when transformation becomes possible.

Contemporary communities adapt these celebrations to their bioregions, creating festivals that honor local ecological patterns rather than imposing universal templates. In California, communities celebrate the return of salmon. In New England, maple syrup festivals mark the sweet spot between winter and spring. Desert communities honor the brief, explosive flowering that follows rain. These place-based celebrations develop ecological literacy while creating shared identity rooted in landscape rather than nationality or ethnicity.

The revival of seasonal celebrations in schools provides children with rhythmic structures that support development. Waldorf schools, pioneering this approach, create elaborate seasonal festivals that engage children in preparing decorations, learning songs, performing plays, and sharing seasonal foods. Children who participate in these celebrations develop an intuitive understanding of natural cycles, finding security in rhythmic return rather than requiring constant novelty. The festivals become anticipated landmarks in the school year, creating collective memories and shared culture.

Elder Wisdom and Intergenerational Teaching

The restoration of elder authority and intergenerational knowledge transmission challenges modern culture's obsession with youth and innovation. In animistic cultures, elders are understood as bridges between worlds, carrying wisdom accumulated through decades of observation and relationship. Their knowledge is not merely historical but essential for survival, encoding patterns and possibilities that no single lifetime can reveal. The current revival of elder teaching represents recognition that some forms of knowledge cannot be googled or downloaded but must be transmitted relationally across generations.

Indigenous communities leading this revival understand that colonization specifically targeted intergenerational transmission, removing children from grandparents who carried traditional knowledge. Residential schools, adoption programs, and urban relocation policies were designed to break the chain of cultural transmission. Now, communities actively create opportunities for elders and youth to connect, recognizing that this relationship is essential for cultural continuity. Culture camps, where elders teach young people on the land, provide immersive experiences that transmit not just information but entire ways of being.

The knowledge carried by elders extends beyond technique to include the stories, songs, and ceremonies that encode worldview and values. An elder teaching basketry transmits not just weaving patterns but stories about the plants, protocols for gathering, songs that honor materials, and understanding of one's place in networks of reciprocity. This holistic transmission cannot be reduced to YouTube tutorials or written instructions. It requires presence, relationship, and time—commodities that modern culture systematically devalues.

Traditional mentorship models, where young people attach themselves to elder practitioners for extended periods, provide alternatives to industrial education's age segregation. These relationships recognize that wisdom emerges through life experience rather than academic study, that some knowledge can only be transmitted through years of patient observation and practice. The apprentice learns not just skills but ways of seeing, patterns of attention, and modes of relationship that textbooks cannot convey. The elder receives help with physical tasks, the satisfaction of transmission, and the renewal that comes from teaching.

Grandparent pedagogy differs qualitatively from parent or professional teaching. Grandparents, released from the immediate pressures of child-rearing, can offer patience and perspective that stressed parents cannot. They carry a long-term perspective, having witnessed multiple cycles and transitions. Their teaching often happens through story rather than instruction, allowing children to extract lessons rather than imposing them. The grandparent-grandchild relationship, jumping a generation, creates unique space for transmission of values and wisdom that might be rejected if coming from parents.

The crisis of elder isolation in modern societies represents not just personal tragedy but cultural catastrophe. Warehoused in facilities separated from community life, elders' wisdom becomes inaccessible to younger generations who desperately need it. Meanwhile, young people struggle with anxiety and meaninglessness that connection to elder wisdom could address. Programs that bring elders and youth together—elder-in-residence programs at schools, intergenerational gardens, story circles—demonstrate that both groups flourish through connection. The elders find purpose and respect, the youth find grounding and guidance.

Digital technology, often blamed for destroying intergenerational connection, can also facilitate it. Video calls allow urban Indigenous youth to learn from elder speakers in remote communities. Recording projects preserve elder knowledge while creating reasons for intergenerational interaction. Digital storytelling workshops where youth help elders create multimedia presentations of their stories combine traditional knowledge with contemporary skills. These projects demonstrate that technology becomes beneficial when it serves sacred connection rather than replacing it.

The particular wisdom of elder women, systematically devalued by patriarchal cultures, emerges as essential for navigating current crises. Post-menopausal women in many traditional cultures become powerful healers, leaders, and wisdom keepers, freed from reproductive demands to serve larger community needs. The Grandmother movement, where elder women from diverse traditions gather to address global challenges, demonstrates the power of grandmotherly wisdom applied to planetary healing. These grandmothers understand that all children are their grandchildren, that their responsibility extends to future generations of all species.

Cultural Centers and Education Programs

The establishment of cultural centers dedicated to animistic world-views and practices provides institutional support for revival movements that might otherwise remain marginal. These centers—ranging from Indigenous cultural centers to permaculture education sites to craft schools—create physical spaces where alternative ways of knowing and being can be explored, developed, and transmitted. Unlike museums that display dead cultures behind glass, these living centers invite participation, transformation, and the creation of new traditions rooted in ancient wisdom.

Indigenous cultural centers serve as sovereign spaces where Native peoples control the narrative about their cultures, histories, and futures. The National Museum of the American Indian, the first national museum designed and operated by Indigenous peoples, demonstrates how cultural institutions can challenge colonial narratives while asserting Indigenous presence and continuity. Regional and tribal cultural centers provide spaces for ceremony, language classes, traditional arts, and community gathering. These centers become sites of healing and pride for Indigenous peoples while educating non-Native visitors about the sophistication and relevance of Indigenous knowledge.

Ecovillage education centers demonstrate sustainable living practices rooted in animistic understanding of human-nature relationships. Findhorn in Scotland, Damanhur in Italy, and dozens of similar centers worldwide provide immersive experiences in alternative ways of organizing society. Participants learn not just permaculture techniques but the consciousness shifts required for collaborative decision-making, conflict resolution, and collective visioning. These centers serve as laboratories for cultural transformation, experimenting with governance, economics, and social structures aligned with ecological principles.

Folk schools, inspired by Scandinavian models but adapted to local contexts, provide hands-on education in traditional crafts, sustainable living skills, and place-based knowledge. These schools reject industrial education's separation of hand and mind, teaching through making rather than abstract study. Students learn blacksmithing, timber framing, natural dyeing, and other skills that connect them to materials and processes. The pedagogy emphasizes community over competition, mastery over credentialing, and relationship over efficiency.

Urban cultural centers bring animistic practices into city environments where connection to traditional lands may be impossible. These centers might offer herb walks in city parks, workshops on seeing city trees as individuals rather than urban forest, or ceremonies that honor the pre-urban ecology of places. They demonstrate that animistic consciousness is not restricted to rural or wilderness settings but can transform understanding of any environment. City dwellers learn to recognize their watershed, track urban wildlife, and develop reciprocal relationships with their more-than-human neighbors.

Forest schools and nature-based education programs institutionalize children's need for connection with the living world. These programs, whether integrated into public schools or operating as independent alternatives, prioritize outdoor experience, child-led learning, and development of ecological consciousness. Children spend significant portions of their day outdoors regardless of weather, learning through direct engagement with nature rather than about nature from books. Research consistently demonstrates that these children develop greater creativity, resilience, and environmental consciousness than their conventionally educated peers.

Online education platforms extend the reach of cultural revival beyond physical centers, making teachings accessible to global audiences. While online learning cannot replace embodied, place-based education, it can provide introduction, inspiration, and connection. Indigenous educators use online platforms to teach languages to dispersed tribal members. Craft teachers share techniques with students worldwide. Philosophers and activists present animistic worldviews to audiences hungry for alternatives to mechanistic thinking. These platforms demonstrate that cultural revival is not anti-technology but seeks to use technology in service of relationship and wisdom.

University programs in Indigenous studies, environmental humanities, and traditional ecological knowledge bring animistic perspectives into academic settings. These programs challenge the university's role in perpetuating mechanistic worldviews while demonstrating that Indigenous knowledge meets and exceeds academic standards of rigor and sophistication. Students emerge with both critical analysis of dominant systems and practical knowledge of alternatives. The presence of these programs within universities creates space for questioning fundamental assumptions about knowledge, progress, and human purpose.

Media and Storytelling for Cultural Change

The stories we tell shape the world we create. The mechanistic worldview's dominance depends partly on its control of narrative through education, media, and entertainment that normalize human supremacy and nature-as-resource. Cultural revival requires not just preserving traditional stories but creating new narratives that help contemporary people understand their place in the living world. These stories must compete with corporate media's production values while offering what consumer culture cannot: meaning, connection, and hope rooted in relationship rather than consumption.

Indigenous storytellers use traditional narratives to address contemporary challenges, demonstrating these stories' continued relevance. Raven stories teach about climate change, Coyote stories illuminate political corruption, emergence narratives provide frameworks for understanding current transformation. These tellings respect traditional forms while adapting to contemporary contexts, showing that oral traditions are not frozen artifacts but living systems capable of evolution. The stories work because they emerge from deep observation of natural patterns that remain consistent even as circumstances change.

Contemporary authors create fiction that imagines different relationships between humans and the more-than-human world. The genres of climate fiction, solarpunk, and ecological fantasy envision futures where humans have learned to live within ecological limits, where technology serves rather than dominates nature, where other species are recognized as persons with their own stories. These narratives provide alternatives to dystopian visions that breed despair and paralysis. By imagining positive possibilities, they create cognitive and emotional space for transformation.

Documentary filmmakers bring animistic worldviews to global audiences, using visual media's power to render visible what mechanistic thinking obscures. Films that give voice to rivers, that follow Indigenous land defenders, that reveal the intelligence of forests and fungi, challenge viewers' fundamental assumptions about consciousness and agency. The most effective documentaries don't just present information but create emotional connections that motivate action. They use beauty, wonder, and story to bypass intellectual defenses and touch hearts directly.

Podcasts and digital storytelling platforms democratize narrative creation, allowing marginalized voices to reach audiences without corporate mediation. Indigenous podcasters share traditional stories, discuss contemporary challenges, and connect listeners to land-based wisdom. Environmental storytellers weave together personal narrative, ecological science, and calls to action. The intimate nature of audio—voices speaking directly into ears—creates parasocial relationships that can shift consciousness more effectively than written arguments.

Children's media that promotes animistic consciousness shapes the worldviews of future generations. Stories that present animals as subjects rather than objects, that show humans learning from rather than dominating nature, that celebrate diversity and cooperation over competition and dominance, provide alternatives to mainstream narratives. Programs like Avatar: The Last Airbender demonstrate that children's media can convey sophisticated understanding of elemental forces, balance, and relationship. Parents seeking alternatives to consumer-culture programming find growing options that nurture ecological consciousness.

Video games and interactive media create opportunities for players to experience different relationships with virtual environments that can influence real-world consciousness. Games that reward cooperation over competition, that require understanding ecological relationships to succeed, that present non-human beings as allies rather than resources, provide embodied experiences of alternative values. Indigenous game developers create games that transmit cultural knowledge, teach languages, and allow players to experience traditional ways of being. These games demonstrate that interactive media can serve cultural revival rather than undermining it.

Social media, despite its problems, provides platforms for cultural revival movements to connect, organize, and amplify their messages. Indigenous water protectors livestream from resistance camps, traditional crafters share techniques through Instagram, language learners connect through TikTok. These platforms allow movements to bypass corporate media gatekeepers, reaching audiences directly with unmediated messages. The visual nature of many platforms suits the transmission of craft techniques, ceremony, and land-based practices that are difficult to convey through text alone.

Community storytelling projects collect and share local narratives that root people in place and history. Oral history projects preserve elder memories, story circles create space for sharing experience, and community theaters develop productions that reflect local concerns and celebrations. These projects demonstrate that everyone has stories worth telling, that local narratives matter as much as global ones, that storytelling is not passive consumption but active creation of culture and meaning.

The Confluence of Revivals

The various streams of cultural revival—language restoration, craft renaissance, ceremonial renewal, intergenerational teaching, institutional development, and narrative transformation—converge to create a river of change flowing toward animistic consciousness. These movements reinforce each other: language revival supports craft traditions that depend on specialized vocabularies, seasonal celebrations create contexts for intergenerational transmission, cultural centers provide spaces for story circles and skill shares. The confluence creates momentum that no single stream could generate alone.

This cultural renaissance is not happening in isolation but represents humanity's immune response to the existential threats posed by mechanistic civilization. As ecological collapse accelerates, economic systems fail, and social fabric tears, people instinctively turn toward ways of being that sustained our species for hundreds of thousands of years. The revival is not romantic nostalgia but practical necessity—these traditions encode instructions for living within ecological limits, maintaining community cohesion, and finding meaning beyond consumption.

The youth leading climate movements understand intuitively what their education tried to suppress: that the Earth is alive, that other species have rights, that their future depends on transforming humanity's relationship with the living world. They may not use the term animism, but their demands reflect animistic understanding. When Greta Thunberg says "I want you to act as if the house is on fire," she expresses the urgency that comes from recognizing our interdependence with all life. When Indigenous youth lead resistance to pipelines and mining, they demonstrate that cultural revival and environmental protection are inseparable projects.

The COVID-19 pandemic accelerated cultural revival by disrupting the patterns that maintained mechanistic consciousness. With normal activities suspended, people had time to notice birds, tend gardens, and question the systems that demanded constant productivity. The vulnerability revealed by the virus reminded us that we are biological beings subject to ecological limits. The mutual aid networks that emerged demonstrated that cooperation and care are as fundamental to human nature as competition. These recognitions, if cultivated, could catalyze the broader cultural transformation our moment demands.

Resistance to cultural revival comes from systems that profit from maintaining mechanistic consciousness. Industries that depend on treating nature as commodity fight recognition of nature's rights. Educational institutions invested in transmitting mechanistic worldviews resist incorporating Indigenous knowledge. Governments committed to growth-based economics oppose movements that prioritize kinship over profit. Yet these systems' increasing desperation reveals their weakness—they fight cultural revival because they recognize it threatens their foundations.

The path forward requires both preserving traditional knowledge and creating new forms appropriate to our unprecedented moment. We cannot simply return to pre-industrial ways of life—the world has changed too much, and we carry knowledge and capabilities our ancestors lacked. But we can learn from traditional wisdom while applying it to contemporary challenges. We can create ceremonies that honor ancient patterns while addressing modern needs. We can develop technologies that serve rather than dominate life. We can tell stories that help us remember who we are and imagine who we might become.

This cultural renaissance offers hope in a time of converging crises. While political and economic systems fail to address existential threats, cultural movements create alternatives from the ground up. While institutions resist change, communities transform themselves. While dominant narratives breed despair, alternative stories inspire action. The revival movements demonstrate that transformation is not only possible but already underway. The question is not whether cultural change will occur but whether it will happen quickly enough to avert catastrophe.

As this chapter has explored, the revival of animistic consciousness through language, arts, ceremony, education, and story represents humanity's attempt to remember what it means to be human in a more-than-human world. These movements draw on ancestral wisdom while creating new forms that speak to contemporary needs. They challenge fundamental assumptions of mechanistic civilization while offering practical alternatives rooted in relationship and reciprocity. The cultural renaissance underway provides both means and motivation for the great transformation our time requires—from a civilization that destroys life to one that serves it, from a species that imagines itself separate and supreme to one that recognizes itself as part of the living Earth community. In this recognition lies both humility and hope, both responsibility and possibility.

CHAPTER 21

Transition Strategies and Pathways

The journey from mechanistic to animistic consciousness rarely follows a straight path. For individuals raised within industrial civilization's worldview, recognizing the consciousness and agency of the more-than-human world requires profound shifts in perception, belief, and practice. For communities, the transformation demands new structures, institutions, and agreements that honor the living world while meeting human needs. For societies, the transition necessitates fundamental changes in governance, economics, and education that may take generations to fully manifest. Yet across all scales, patterns emerge—ways of beginning, obstacles to navigate, practices that catalyze transformation, and indicators of genuine change. This chapter maps these territories, offering both theoretical frameworks and practical guidance for those ready to participate in humanity's great remembering.

The transition cannot be accomplished through intellectual understanding alone. One can read every book about animism, agree philosophically with its principles, yet remain fundamentally unchanged in relationship with the living world. Genuine transformation requires embodied experience, repeated practice, and the gradual dissolution of barriers between self and world that mechanistic thinking erects. It demands that we risk feeling foolish as we greet trees, offer thanks to water, and seek guidance from dreams. It requires patience as perceptual shifts occur slowly, then suddenly, like eyes adjusting to starlight after leaving artificial illumination.

Neither can the transition be purely individual. While personal transformation is necessary, it is insufficient to address the systemic crises we face. Individual consciousness change without collective action leads to spiritual bypassing—using personal practice to avoid confronting injustice and ecological destruction. Conversely, activism without inner transformation often reproduces the very patterns it claims to oppose, fighting domination with domination, meeting violence with violence. The path forward requires integration: inner work that supports outer action, personal practice that enables collective transformation, individual healing that contributes to planetary healing.

Personal Transformation Journeys

The awakening to animistic consciousness often begins with a crack in the mechanistic worldview—a moment when the habitual way of seeing fails to explain experience. Perhaps it comes through grief at ecological destruction, wonder at natural beauty, or an unexpected encounter with the non-human world that defies rational explanation. A bird appears at a moment of crisis with uncanny timing. A tree provides comfort that no human could offer. A dream delivers guidance that proves remarkably accurate. These experiences, dismissed by mechanistic thinking as coincidence or projection, become doorways to different ways of knowing.

For many, the journey begins with what philosopher David Abram calls "the ecology of magic"—experiences of the natural world that exceed rational explanation. A sunset that stops thought, a forest that seems to breathe, a mountain that evokes inexplicable tears. These moments of wonder crack open the defensive shell of modern consciousness, allowing the living world to touch us directly. The challenge lies not in generating such experiences—they arise naturally when we pay attention—but in taking them seriously rather than explaining them away.

The development of what ecopsychologist Laura Sewall terms "ecological perception" requires deliberate practice. This involves learning to see patterns rather than objects, relationships rather than entities, processes rather than things. It means noticing how the shape of a tree expresses its history of relationship with wind, sun, and neighbors. It means recognizing that a landscape is not scenery but a community of beings in constant communication. This perceptual shift cannot be forced but can be invited through practices that slow down attention and expand awareness.

Regular sit-spot practice—visiting the same outdoor location repeatedly—provides a powerful doorway to animistic consciousness. As we return to the same place through seasons and weather, we begin to know its inhabitants as individuals. The robin nesting in the hawthorn becomes a neighbor whose family dramas we follow. The oak tree's seasonal changes become a calendar marking our own transformations. The place begins to recognize us, wildlife becoming less wary, the land itself seeming to welcome our presence. Through this practice, we shift from observing nature to participating in it.

Learning to perceive and interpret natural signs develops capacity for dialogue with the more-than-human world. This might begin with noticing obvious patterns—clouds that signal weather changes, bird alarms that indicate predator presence—then deepen into more subtle recognition. The particular quality of silence before a storm, the way leaves show their undersides before rain, the behavior of ants before earthquakes. These observations are not superstition but recognition of patterns that mechanical instruments often miss. As we develop this literacy, we discover that the world is constantly communicating, offering guidance to those who learn its languages.

Dream work opens another channel of communication with the animate earth. Many Indigenous traditions understand dreams as real experiences in which consciousness travels and receives teachings. By recording dreams, looking for patterns, and especially noting dreams that feature non-human beings or landscapes, we can develop relationships with guides and teachers that transcend waking limitations. The practice requires taking dreams seriously as sources of valid information rather than dismissing them as mere neurological noise.

The cultivation of gratitude as a spiritual practice strengthens the bond with the living world. This extends beyond feeling thankful to active expression of appreciation—speaking thanks to water before drinking, acknowledging the lives that became food, appreciating shelter and warmth. This practice, universal among Indigenous peoples, recognizes that gratitude creates strong bonds. When we thank the sun for warmth, we acknowledge ourselves as beneficiaries of its generosity. When we thank plants for oxygen, we recognize our absolute dependence on their photosynthesis. Gratitude dismantles the illusion of separation and self-sufficiency that mechanistic thinking promotes.

Engaging in reciprocity with the more-than-human world moves beyond gratitude to active giving. This might mean offering water to plants during drought, creating habitat for wildlife, or cleaning polluted streams. The key lies in understanding these actions not as charity from a position of superiority but as fulfilling obligations to relatives who also give to us. When we feed birds through winter, we participate in cycles of mutual aid that weave ecosystems together. When we plant trees we'll never see mature, we offer gifts to future generations of all species.

Community Organizing and Movement Building

The transition from individual practice to collective transformation requires careful attention to how communities organize, make decisions, and create change. Movements that successfully challenge mechanistic thinking share certain characteristics: they model the relationships they seek to create, they root themselves in place and community, they honor diverse ways of knowing, and they understand transformation as an ongoing process rather than final achievement. Building such movements demands patience, skill, and commitment to doing things differently even when familiar patterns would be easier.

Study circles and reading groups provide accessible entry points for communities beginning to explore animistic worldviews. Unlike academic seminars that privilege intellectual analysis, these circles integrate experiential learning, encouraging participants to test ideas through practice and share their experiences. A group might read about plant consciousness, then spend time with plants before reconvening to discuss not just concepts but lived encounters. This approach validates personal experience while creating collective support for worldview transformation.

Community mapping projects help groups understand themselves as part of larger ecological communities. This might involve creating maps that show watershed boundaries rather than political divisions, marking sacred or special places, identifying habitat for other species, or documenting seasonal patterns. The process of creating such maps builds collective knowledge while shifting perspective from human-centered to ecological. Digital tools can enhance these projects, but hand-drawn maps often prove more powerful, requiring intimate knowledge and creating beautiful artifacts that inspire continued engagement.

Skill-sharing networks build community resilience while fostering animistic consciousness. As neighbors teach each other gardening, food preservation, natural building, and traditional crafts, they create alternatives to consumer dependence while developing relationships with materials and processes. These networks often evolve into gift economies where skills and resources circulate based on need and relationship rather than market exchange. The woman who teaches bread-baking receives help with garden preparation; the man who shares carpentry skills has his bicycle repaired. These exchanges create webs of mutual aid that mirror ecological relationships.

Resistance campaigns against extractive projects—pipelines, mines, clear-cuts—become schools for animistic consciousness when they center the rights and agency of the land itself. Rather than framing opposition in purely human terms (property values, health impacts), these campaigns assert that rivers have the right to flow freely, that mountains should not be decapitated, that forests deserve to exist for their own sake. This framing shifts discourse from resource management to relationship and rights, challenging the fundamental assumptions of extractive economy.

Creating community ceremonies and celebrations that honor the more-than-human world helps normalize animistic consciousness. This might include seasonal festivals, river blessings, tree plantings, or grief rituals for ecological loss. These events need not appropriate Indigenous ceremonies but can emerge from authentic rootedness with place. A neighborhood might develop an annual salmon celebration when fish return to urban streams, or create ceremonies for the first flowers of spring. These collective acknowledgments make visible and valuable our relationships with the living world.

Coalition building across differences requires recognizing that animistic consciousness manifests diversely across cultures. Indigenous communities, recent immigrants, and long-term settlers may have very different relationships with land and different ways of expressing reverence for life. Successful coalitions create space for these differences while finding common ground in defense of the living world. This might mean supporting Indigenous leadership while contributing settler privileges and resources, or bridging urban environmental justice movements with rural land defense campaigns.

Direct action training that incorporates animistic principles transforms both tactics and consciousness. Rather than seeing actions as purely strategic, groups might understand blockades as ceremonies of protection, tree-sits as vision quests, and arrests as sacrifices for the sacred. This spiritual dimension sustains activists through difficult campaigns while attracting supporters who hunger for meaning beyond material politics. The most effective actions combine strategic intelligence with spiritual power, recognizing that transformation requires both practical intervention and consciousness change.

Policy Advocacy and Legislative Change

While policy change alone cannot create animistic consciousness, legal frameworks that recognize nature's rights and limit corporate power create space for worldview transformation. The growing movement for rights of nature legislation demonstrates that legal systems can evolve beyond treating nature as property. These campaigns succeed not through traditional lobbying but through grassroots organizing that shifts public consciousness about humanity's relationship with the living world.

The rights of nature movement has achieved remarkable victories through patient organizing and strategic framing. Ecuador's constitution, which recognizes nature's right to exist and flourish, emerged from Indigenous organizing combined with middle-class environmental concern about water and food security. New Zealand's recognition of the Whanganui River as a legal person resulted from 140 years of Māori assertion that the river is their ancestor. These victories required not just legal arguments but cultural education that helped non-Indigenous people understand different ways of relating to nature.

Local ordinances provide accessible entry points for establishing legal rights of nature. Communities across the United States have passed laws recognizing rights of rivers, ecosystems, and natural communities. While these ordinances face legal challenges from state and federal governments, they shift local consciousness and create precedents for broader change. The process of drafting, debating, and passing such ordinances educates communities about alternative legal frameworks while building coalitions between diverse groups.

Regenerative agriculture policies that support soil health, biodiversity, and carbon sequestration create economic incentives for practices aligned with animistic principles. Rather than treating soil as an inert medium for chemical inputs, these policies recognize soil as a living community deserving protection and restoration. Successful campaigns connect soil health to human health, climate resilience to economic security, making visible the connections mechanistic thinking obscures.

Farmers become allies when policies support their transition to practices that rebuild rather than deplete their land.

Public banking initiatives challenge the concentration of capital in institutions that fund extractive industries. Community-owned banks can prioritize local needs, ecological health, and long-term sustainability over maximum profit. The Bank of North Dakota, publicly owned since 1919, demonstrates that alternatives to corporate banking are viable. Contemporary campaigns connect public banking to Indigenous sovereignty, climate action, and economic justice, recognizing that controlling capital flows is essential for systemic transformation.

Zoning reform that permits food production, natural building, and community gathering spaces enables animistic practices within existing settlements. Many municipalities prohibit gardens in front yards, chickens in backyards, and natural building techniques that don't fit industrial standards. Changing these regulations requires patient education of planning boards, building coalitions with property rights advocates, and demonstrating that alternative practices enhance rather than threaten community wellbeing. Success creates visible examples that inspire broader change.

Carbon pricing mechanisms that recognize the true cost of emissions create economic pressure for transformation. While market mechanisms alone cannot solve ecological crises, they can shift behavior when combined with regulation and public investment. The most effective carbon pricing includes border adjustments that prevent offshoring of emissions, revenue recycling that protects vulnerable communities, and recognition that some activities—like protecting primary forests—should be beyond market calculation.

International agreements that recognize ecocide as a crime against peace could fundamentally shift how legal systems relate to environmental destruction. The campaign to add ecocide to the Rome Statute would make massive environmental damage prosecutable at the International Criminal Court. While achieving this requires enormous political effort, the campaign itself educates about the severity of ecological crimes while building international solidarity. Local communities can support this effort through resolutions, education, and pressure on national governments.

Business Transformation and B-Corporation Models

The transformation of business from profit maximization to life service requires new models that encode different values into organizational DNA. Benefit corporations, cooperatives, and social enterprises demonstrate that business can serve broader purposes than shareholder enrichment. These models succeed not by competing on conventional terms but by creating alternative economies that value relationship, regeneration, and reciprocity.

Benefit corporation legislation, now available in most US states and several countries, allows companies to pursue social and environmental benefits alongside profit. This structure protects directors from shareholder lawsuits when they prioritize purpose over profit, enabling long-term thinking and stakeholder consideration. B-Corps like Patagonia demonstrate that purpose-driven businesses can thrive while challenging industry norms. The certification process itself transforms company consciousness, requiring measurement of impact on workers, communities, and environment.

Worker cooperatives embody economic democracy, distributing ownership and decision-making among those who create value. Unlike conventional corporations that treat workers as costs to minimize, cooperatives recognize workers as member-owners with stakes in long-term success. The Mondragon Corporation in Spain, with over 80,000 worker-owners, demonstrates that cooperative models can achieve large scale while maintaining democratic principles. These structures naturally align with animistic thinking by recognizing that all participants deserve voice and benefit.

Community land trusts remove land from speculative markets, holding it in perpetuity for community benefit. This model, rooted in Indigenous understanding that land cannot be owned, provides affordable housing, urban farms, and community spaces while preventing displacement. The model challenges fundamental assumptions about property and value, demonstrating that land can be stewarded for collective benefit rather than individual profit. Successful land trusts require patient organizing, creative financing, and legal structures that protect against future privatization.

Regenerative businesses go beyond sustainability to actively restore ecological and social systems. Unlike "sustainable" businesses that merely slow degradation, regenerative enterprises improve soil health, increase biodiversity, strengthen communities, and sequester carbon. Interface Inc.'s Mission Zero demonstrates that even carpet manufacturing can become regenerative. These businesses measure success through increases in natural and social capital rather than just financial returns.

Platform cooperatives challenge the gig economy by creating worker-owned alternatives to corporate platforms. Rather than drivers enriching Uber shareholders, cooperative platforms distribute value to those who create it. These models face significant challenges competing with venture-capital-funded corporations, but they demonstrate that technology can serve cooperation rather than exploitation. Successful platform cooperatives often focus on local markets where relationships and trust provide competitive advantages.

Social enterprises that employ marginalized populations while addressing ecological challenges create multiple forms of value. Organizations that hire formerly incarcerated people to restore degraded land, for example, simultaneously address recidivism, unemployment, and ecological damage. These enterprises demonstrate that business can heal rather than harm, that profit can align with purpose. Success requires patient capital, supportive policy, and metrics that capture full value creation.

Divestment campaigns pressure institutions to withdraw investments from extractive industries. The fossil fuel divestment movement has moved trillions of dollars, demonstrating that collective action can shift capital flows. Successful campaigns combine moral arguments with financial analysis showing that fossil fuel investments are increasingly risky. Divestment opens space for reinvestment in regenerative enterprises, renewable energy, and community development. The process educates institutional leaders about climate risk while building power for broader transformation.

Educational Reform and Curriculum Development

The transformation of education from industrial training to ecological wisdom requires fundamental changes in what, how, and why we teach. Educational systems designed to produce compliant workers for the industrial economy cannot cultivate the consciousness needed for ecological civilization. Reform efforts that merely add environmental content to existing structures fail to address the deeper epistemological issues. Genuine transformation requires new pedagogies that honor diverse ways of knowing, root learning in place and community, and recognize that wisdom emerges through relationship rather than information transfer.

Place-based education grounds learning in local ecology, history, and community rather than abstract universal curriculum. Students learn math through mapping watersheds, science through monitoring local species, history through interviewing elders, and writing through documenting community stories. This approach develops intimate knowledge of home places while building skills applicable anywhere. Research demonstrates that place-based education improves academic achievement, environmental stewardship, and community engagement. More fundamentally, it cultivates citizens who understand themselves as part of specific ecological and social communities.

Forest schools and outdoor education programs remove children from classroom constraints, allowing learning to emerge through direct engagement with the living world. Children who spend significant time

outdoors develop superior creativity, problem-solving, emotional regulation, and physical health compared to their indoor-educated peers.
These programs challenge assumptions about safety, control, and the
purposes of education. They demonstrate that children learn best
through exploration and relationship rather than instruction and testing.

Indigenous education models that integrate language, culture, land,
and spirituality provide templates for holistic learning. These models
understand education as cultivation of full human beings rather than
training of economic units. The Māori education renaissance in New
Zealand demonstrates how Indigenous pedagogies can transform entire
education systems. These approaches benefit not just Indigenous students but all learners hungry for meaning and connection.

Garden-based learning integrates food production into curriculum
while teaching ecological principles through direct experience. Students
who grow food understand viscerally concepts like nutrient cycles, succession, and symbiosis that remain abstract in textbooks. Gardens become laboratories for science, inspiration for art, context for history,
and community gathering spaces. The process of growing food from
seed to harvest teaches patience, observation, and care while providing
healthy food for school communities.

Contemplative practices in education—meditation, mindfulness, sit
spots—develop capacity for attention and awareness essential for perceiving the living world. These practices counteract the fragmentation
and overstimulation of digital culture while creating space for wonder
and reflection. Students who practice contemplation show improved
focus, emotional regulation, and empathy. More importantly, they develop capacity for the deep listening that animistic consciousness requires.

Arts integration that celebrates the more-than-human world cultivates aesthetic appreciation and creative expression of ecological relationship. This might include nature journaling, botanical illustration,
soundscape composition, or collaborative works with natural materials.

These practices develop sensory awareness and observational skills while creating beautiful expressions of human-nature relationship. The arts make visible patterns and connections that analytical approaches miss.

Assessment methods that honor diverse intelligences and ways of knowing challenge standardized testing's dominance. Portfolio assessment, peer evaluation, community presentation, and self-reflection recognize that learning cannot be reduced to quantifiable metrics. These approaches value creativity, collaboration, and wisdom alongside analytical intelligence. They prepare students for lives of meaning and contribution rather than mere economic productivity.

Media Strategies and Cultural Messaging

The transformation of collective consciousness requires strategic use of media and messaging that reaches beyond already-converted audiences. While grassroots organizing remains essential, social media, entertainment, and news media shape public discourse in ways that cannot be ignored. Successful media strategies don't simply present information but create emotional connections, tell compelling stories, and make alternative futures imaginable and desirable.

Narrative strategies that frame environmental protection as defense of home and family resonate across political divides. Rather than abstract discussions of parts per million or degrees of warming, stories about specific places and communities threatened by extraction or pollution create emotional engagement. The water protectors at Standing Rock captured global attention not through policy arguments but through powerful imagery of Indigenous peoples defending sacred water. These narratives work because they activate deep human instincts to protect what we love.

Cultural influencers who model animistic consciousness while maintaining broad appeal normalize alternative worldviews. When celebrities create wildlife habitats, practice regenerative agriculture, or speak about their relationships with non-human beings, they give per-

384 - DANIEL PAYNE

mission for others to explore these practices. The key lies in authentic expression rather than preaching, showing rather than telling. Young influencers on platforms like TikTok and Instagram reach audiences that traditional environmental messaging misses.

Entertainment media that embeds animistic consciousness in compelling stories shapes imagination more powerfully than documentary or advocacy. Films like Avatar, Princess Mononoke, and Moana present worlds where nature is alive and conscious, where humans must negotiate with rather than dominate other beings. These stories work not through explicit messaging but through emotional engagement with characters who embody different relationships with nature. They make animistic consciousness feel natural and desirable rather than primitive or impossible.

Local media strategies that highlight community successes create momentum for broader change. Stories about neighborhoods that transform vacant lots into gardens, schools that improve student performance through outdoor education, or businesses that thrive while regenerating ecosystems demonstrate that alternatives are viable. These stories work best when they focus on people and relationships rather than abstract concepts, when they show rather than tell, when they inspire rather than scold.

Counter-messaging that exposes corporate greenwashing and false solutions prevents cooptation of transformative movements. As animistic consciousness gains currency, corporations attempt to appropriate its language while maintaining extractive practices. Effective counter-messaging requires sophisticated understanding of corporate strategies, careful fact-checking, and compelling presentation that cuts through public relations spin. This work protects authentic movements from dilution while educating about the depth of transformation required.

Digital organizing tools enable rapid mobilization while building long-term relationships and consciousness. Platforms that facilitate skill-sharing, resource coordination, and collective action create infrastructure for transformation. The most effective digital organizing combines online and offline action, using technology to enhance rather than replace face-to-face relationship building. These tools work best when they embody the values they promote—transparency, participation, and care for collective wellbeing.

Metrics and indicators that measure progress toward animistic consciousness help movements assess effectiveness and adjust strategies. This might include tracking the adoption of rights of nature legislation, measuring participation in community gardens, or documenting changes in how media discusses non-human beings. These metrics should capture qualitative as well as quantitative change, recognizing that consciousness transformation cannot be fully measured but can be observed through its effects.

Integration and Emergence

The various pathways toward animistic consciousness—personal practice, community organizing, policy change, business transformation, educational reform, and media strategy—are not separate tracks but interwoven threads in a larger pattern of transformation. Success in one domain catalyzes change in others. Personal transformation motivates community engagement. Community organizing influences policy. Policy change enables business transformation. Business transformation funds educational reform. Educational reform shapes media narratives. Media narratives inspire personal transformation. The pattern is not linear but recursive, with feedback loops and emergent properties that exceed the sum of parts.

The transition strategies that prove most effective recognize this interconnection, working simultaneously across multiple scales and domains. They understand that consciousness change without structural change leads to spiritual bypassing, while structural change without consciousness change leads to reformed oppression. They recognize that the transformation required is not reform but metamorphosis—not adjusting existing systems but creating entirely new patterns of organization.

Successful transition initiatives share certain characteristics. They are rooted in specific places while connected to global movements. They honor traditional wisdom while embracing appropriate innovation. They center those most affected by current systems while welcoming all who genuinely seek transformation. They balance urgency with patience, recognizing that the changes required may take generations while acting as if the future depends on present choices—because it does.

The indicators of genuine transition go beyond policy changes or market shifts to include qualitative changes in how communities relate. When neighbors know each other's names and stories. When children play freely outdoors. When depression and anxiety rates decline. When birdsong returns to silent places. When people speak of trees and rivers as relatives rather than resources. When decisions consider impacts on seven generations. When wealth is measured in relationships rather than possessions. These changes cannot be mandated or purchased but emerge from transformed consciousness expressing itself through transformed culture.

As we engage in transition work, we must remember that we are not creating something entirely new but remembering something ancient and essential. Every human culture emerged from animistic consciousness. The capacity to perceive and relate to the living world as sacred is encoded in our genes, waiting to be activated. The transition strategies explored in this chapter are not prescriptions but invitations—ways of beginning or deepening the journey back to a right kinship with all consciousness.

The path forward will not be smooth or straightforward. Systems that profit from maintaining mechanistic consciousness will resist with all their power. People attached to familiar worldviews will defend them even as those worldviews destroy the basis for life. The transition will involve loss, conflict, and uncertainty. Yet it also offers the possibility of healing, meaning, and joy that mechanistic civilization cannot provide.

It offers the chance to become fully human again, to take our place as grateful participants in the community of life rather than its destroyers.

This chapter has explored the multiple pathways through which individuals, communities, and societies can transition from mechanistic to animistic consciousness. The strategies discussed—from personal practices to policy advocacy, from community organizing to media messaging—demonstrate that transformation is not only necessary but already underway. The question is not whether transition will occur but whether it will happen by choice or necessity, with wisdom or chaos, in time to prevent the worst consequences of our current trajectory. The answer depends on how many of us commit to the journey and how quickly we can build momentum for change. The pathways are clear. The tools are available. What remains is the choice to begin or deepen our participation in humanity's great transformation.

CHAPTER 22

Building Animistic Communities

The creation of communities organized around animistic principles represents one of humanity's most promising responses to the converging crises of our time. These communities—whether ecovillages in rural settings, cohousing projects in cities, or land-based collectives on restored territories—demonstrate that humans can organize themselves in ways that honor the consciousness of all beings while meeting authentic human needs for shelter, sustenance, and meaning. They serve as laboratories for cultural transformation, testing governance structures, economic arrangements, and social practices that could scale to reshape civilization. Yet building such communities requires navigating complex challenges around land access, economic viability, social dynamics, and the persistent influence of the dominant culture we seek to transform.

The communities emerging worldwide share certain characteristics that distinguish them from conventional settlements. They recognize land not as property but as a living entity deserving respect and care. They make decisions through processes that consider impacts on future generations and non-human neighbors. They organize economies around gift, reciprocity, and mutual aid rather than solely market exchange. They understand themselves as nodes in larger networks of transformation rather than isolated utopian experiments. Most fundamentally, they proceed from the understanding that community includes not just humans but all beings sharing a particular place.

These communities do not seek to recreate an imagined past or impose uniform templates across diverse contexts. Each emerges from specific relationships between particular people and places, developing unique cultures that reflect their bioregions, histories, and aspirations. A community in the Pacific Northwest rainforest will differ profoundly from one in the Sonoran Desert or Appalachian Mountains, not just in physical structures but in ceremonies, governance, and relationships with non-human neighbors. This diversity strengthens the broader movement, creating multiple models and approaches that can inspire and inform without prescribing.

Ecovillages and Intentional Communities

The global ecovillage movement demonstrates that humans can create settlements that regenerate rather than degrade their environments while fostering human flourishing. From Findhorn in Scotland to Auroville in India, from Dancing Rabbit in Missouri to Crystal Waters in Australia, these communities prove that dramatic reductions in ecological footprint are possible without sacrificing quality of life. Indeed, research consistently shows that ecovillage residents report higher levels of life satisfaction than conventional populations despite—or because of—their material simplicity.

Successful ecovillages integrate four dimensions of sustainability: ecological, social, economic, and cultural/spiritual. The ecological dimension involves renewable energy, natural building, organic food production, and ecosystem restoration. The social dimension encompasses inclusive decision-making, conflict resolution, and celebration. The economic dimension includes local currencies, resource sharing, and right livelihood. The cultural/spiritual dimension involves ceremonies, artistic expression, and connection to place. Communities that neglect any dimension tend to struggle or dissolve.

The physical design of ecovillages embodies animistic principles through attention to natural patterns and forces. Buildings orient to sun and wind, utilizing passive solar heating and natural cooling. Gardens follow permaculture principles that mimic forest ecosystems. Paths curve like waterways rather than imposing grids. Common spaces encourage gathering while private spaces allow solitude. The built environment becomes a teacher, constantly demonstrating that human habitation can enhance rather than diminish ecological vitality.

Governance structures in successful ecovillages balance individual autonomy with collective wellbeing. Many use sociocracy or consent-based decision-making that ensures all voices are heard without requiring unanimity. Others employ council processes derived from Indigenous traditions, where speaking circles allow each person to express their truth without interruption or immediate response. These processes take more time than conventional voting but create decisions that the whole community can support. They teach patience, deep listening, and the recognition that wisdom emerges from the collective rather than residing in designated leaders.

The economic arrangements within ecovillages challenge conventional assumptions about ownership and exchange. Many establish community land trusts that hold land collectively while allowing individual security of tenure. Labor exchanges track hours rather than monetary value, recognizing that all contributions—from childcare to construction—have worth. Community-supported agriculture projects connect villages with surrounding regions, creating economic resilience while building broader networks of support. These arrangements demonstrate that economics can serve connection rather than undermining it.

Food systems in ecovillages often become the most visible expression of animistic consciousness. Gardens are understood as collaborations with soil organisms, plants, and insects rather than human impositions on landscape. Chickens are recognized as partners in fertility cycling rather than mere egg producers. Meals become ceremonies of gratitude for all beings who contributed to the feast. The intimacy of growing, preparing, and sharing food together creates bonds that transcend the transactional relationships of industrial food systems.

The challenges facing ecovillages are real and instructive. Land prices make property acquisition difficult for groups without significant capital. Zoning regulations designed for conventional development often prohibit ecological building techniques and communal arrangements. The intensity of interpersonal relationships in small communities can become overwhelming for people accustomed to urban anonymity. The labor required to maintain infrastructure and food systems while participating in governance can lead to burnout. Perhaps most challenging, the conditioning of industrial civilization runs deep, surfacing in communities as competition, conflict, and the reproduction of patterns residents sought to escape.

Yet ecovillages continue proliferating because they offer what industrial civilization cannot: meaningful work, genuine community, and direct relationship with the living world. Residents speak of healing from alienation, finding purpose, and experiencing joy in simple pleasures like sunset gatherings or shared meals. Children raised in ecovillages show remarkable confidence, creativity, and ecological consciousness. Even failed experiments teach valuable lessons that inform subsequent attempts. The movement grows not through mass conversion but through steady accumulation of experience and example.

Cohousing and Cooperative Living

Cohousing communities bring animistic principles into urban and suburban settings where full ecovillages may be impossible. These communities, typically comprising private homes clustered around shared spaces, demonstrate that conventional neighborhoods can be transformed into genuine communities through intentional design and committed participation. From the first modern cohousing in Denmark to hundreds now existing worldwide, these projects prove that alienation is not an inevitable consequence of density.

The design principles of cohousing encourage interaction while respecting privacy. Cars are relegated to peripheries, creating pedestrian spaces where neighbors naturally encounter each other. Common houses provide shared kitchens, dining areas, libraries, workshops, and guest rooms, reducing individual consumption while increasing quality of life. Gardens, playgrounds, and gathering spaces are visible from homes, creating what architect Christopher Alexander calls "eyes on the commons" that ensure safety through awareness rather than surveillance.

The development process for cohousing communities often takes years, during which future residents meet regularly to envision, plan, and make decisions about their future home. This extended formation period, while challenging, creates the social bonds necessary for a successful community. Participants learn each other's communication styles, work through conflicts, and develop shared agreements before moving in together. The process itself becomes a training in collaboration that prepares groups for the ongoing work of community maintenance.

Meal sharing in cohousing communities creates regular opportunities for connection that counter the isolation of conventional housing. Most communities organize common meals several times weekly, with rotating teams taking responsibility for cooking. These meals become anchors of community life—times when information is shared, decisions discussed, and relationships maintained. Children grow up with multiple adult role models, elders receive support and engagement, and all residents experience the efficiency and pleasure of shared food preparation.

The economic benefits of cohousing extend beyond shared facilities to include informal sharing economies that emerge naturally. One person's truck serves the community's hauling needs. Another's expertise in plumbing or electrical work benefits all. Tools, appliances, and recreational equipment circulate based on need rather than ownership. These sharing patterns reduce consumption and expense while building relationships of mutual aid. The economic resilience created through sharing proves especially valuable during hardships like job loss or illness.

Aging in community represents one of cohousing's most significant contributions to social transformation. Rather than isolating elders in institutions or leaving them alone in oversized homes, cohousing enables aging in place with dignity and engagement. Younger residents provide practical support while elders contribute wisdom, skills, and childcare. This intergenerational connection benefits all ages, providing children with grandparent figures and adults with models for graceful aging. Several communities have developed specific structures for senior cohousing that balance independence with support.

The governance challenges in cohousing mirror those in ecovillages but with additional complexity from closer proximity and shared ownership structures. Consensus decision-making can become cumbersome for groups larger than thirty households. Participation inequities emerge when some residents contribute extensively while others remain peripheral. Conflicts around noise, children, pets, and maintenance standards require careful attention. The emotional labor of maintaining community often falls disproportionately on women. These challenges require ongoing attention and evolution of governance structures.

Urban cohousing faces particular obstacles from zoning codes, financing structures, and development costs optimized for conventional housing. Many cities prohibit the density and shared facilities that make cohousing viable. Banks struggle to understand and finance unconventional ownership structures. The extended development timeline increases costs and complexity. Yet successful projects demonstrate that these obstacles can be overcome through persistence, creativity, and strategic partnerships with sympathetic officials and institutions.

Urban Communes and Collective Houses

Urban communes and collective houses bring communal living into city centers where land prices and regulations make larger communities impossible. These projects, often involving 5-15 people sharing large houses or connected apartments, demonstrate that profound community can emerge even within conventional urban fabric. From student cooperatives to multigenerational communes, these living arrangements offer alternatives to both isolated apartments and nuclear family homes.

The economic advantages of collective living make it particularly attractive to young people, artists, and activists struggling with urban housing costs. Shared rent, utilities, and food expenses can reduce living costs by half or more. This economic breathing room allows residents to pursue meaningful work rather than maximum income, to engage in activism and art, to experiment with alternative careers. The financial resilience created through sharing provides security in precarious economic times.

The organizational structures of collective houses range from informal agreements among friends to formal cooperatives with detailed by-laws. Some rotate responsibilities weekly, others assign roles based on interest and skill. Some share all meals and expenses, others maintain greater individual autonomy. The diversity of arrangements demonstrates that collective living can accommodate different needs and preferences. The key lies not in following prescribed models but in clear communication about expectations and boundaries.

Food practices in collective houses often become central to community culture. Shared meals create daily rhythms of connection. Bulk buying reduces costs and packaging waste. Gardens in yards or on rooftops provide fresh produce and connection to seasonal cycles. Fermentation projects, bread baking, and preservation activities become social events that transform domestic labor into creative collaboration. The kitchen becomes the heart of the household, site of nourishment, conversation, and culture creation.

The social dynamics of collective living accelerate personal growth and spiritual development. Living closely with others reveals our patterns, triggers, and shadows in ways that isolated living allows us to avoid. Conflicts become opportunities for learning communication and resolution skills. The diversity of perspectives and practices within households expands consciousness and challenges assumptions. Many residents describe collective living as a spiritual practice that demands presence, compassion, and continuous growth.

Collective houses often become nodes in larger networks of urban transformation. They host meetings, workshops, and events that build broader movements. Their yards become demonstration gardens showing neighbors what's possible. Their alternative economic arrangements inspire others to experiment with cooperation. They provide temporary housing for activists, artists, and travelers, creating connections that span continents. These houses prove that revolution begins at home, in the daily practices of how we live together.

The challenges of collective living in cities include neighbor complaints, landlord resistance, and regulatory violations. Many cities limit the number of unrelated people who can share housing, forcing communities to operate illegally or subdivide into smaller units. Neighbors may object to gardens, chickens, or gatherings that challenge suburban norms. Landlords may refuse to rent to groups or impose restrictions that prevent community activities. These obstacles require strategic navigation and sometimes legal challenges to housing discrimination.

The lifecycle of collective houses often follows predictable patterns. Initial enthusiasm gives way to the reality of daily maintenance and interpersonal challenges. Some members leave as life circumstances change, requiring integration of new residents who may not share founding visions. Without attention to culture maintenance and renewal, houses can devolve into mere shared housing without genuine community. Yet houses that successfully navigate these transitions can persist for decades, becoming institutions that nurture successive generations of residents.

Land Trusts and Community Ownership

Community land trusts (CLTs) provide legal structures for holding land collectively while enabling individual security and preventing speculation. This model, inspired by Indigenous understanding that land cannot be owned and Indian land reforms, removes land from the commodity market permanently. CLTs now protect affordable housing, urban farms, community centers, and conservation lands worldwide, demonstrating that alternative property arrangements are both viable and beneficial.

The structure of CLTs separates land ownership from building ownership, with the trust holding land in perpetuity while individuals or organizations own structures and improvements. This arrangement keeps housing affordable by eliminating land cost from prices and preventing speculation. When owners sell, price formulas ensure they receive fair return on investment while maintaining affordability for the next buyer. This model breaks the cycle of gentrification that displaces communities when property values rise.

Rural CLTs protect farmland and forest from development while enabling sustainable livelihoods. Young farmers who could never afford land at market prices can establish viable operations on trust land. Forest workers can practice sustainable harvesting without pressure to maximize extraction. Communities can maintain working landscapes that provide food, fiber, and ecosystem services rather than watching them convert to suburbs or vacation homes. These trusts demonstrate that land can be productive without being commodified.

The governance of CLTs typically involves tripartite boards with equal representation from trust residents, broader community members, and public interest representatives. This structure balances the interests of current users with long-term stewardship and community benefit. Decisions consider impacts on future generations and ecological health rather than just current profit. This governance model embodies animistic understanding that land is sacred trust requiring careful tending.

Conservation land trusts protect ecosystems from development while sometimes enabling limited human use aligned with ecological health. These trusts often work with Indigenous communities to restore traditional management practices that maintained biodiversity for millennia. Unlike government parks that often exclude human presence, these trusts can model how humans can inhabit landscapes as beneficial participants rather than inevitable destroyers. They demonstrate that conservation and inhabitation are not mutually exclusive.

Urban CLTs are increasingly recognized as tools for environmental justice, protecting communities of color from displacement while enabling community-controlled development. The Dudley Street Neighborhood Initiative in Boston transformed a devastated neighborhood into a thriving community through resident-controlled land trust. Similar projects in cities nationwide demonstrate that community ownership can reverse decades of disinvestment and environmental racism. These trusts ensure that communities who endured the burden of pollution and abandonment can benefit from restoration and renewal.

The challenges facing CLTs include acquisition funding, organizational capacity, and legal complexity. Purchasing land at market prices requires significant capital that communities often lack. Managing properties and governance requires skills and resources that volunteer boards may struggle to maintain. Legal structures vary by jurisdiction and may require expensive expertise to establish and maintain. Yet the number of CLTs continues growing as communities recognize their value for preserving affordability and community control.

The relationship between CLTs and animistic consciousness runs deeper than legal structure. By removing land from commodity status, trusts acknowledge that land has value beyond price. By considering future generations in decisions, they honor temporal continuity. By involving community in governance, they recognize that land belongs to all who depend on it. These trusts embody the understanding that land is relative, not resource, deserving respect rather than exploitation.

Skill-sharing Networks and Mutual Aid

Networks of skill-sharing and mutual aid create community bonds that transcend physical proximity, connecting people through exchange of knowledge, labor, and resources. These networks, whether formal organizations or informal webs of relationship, demonstrate that humans naturally organize themselves for mutual benefit when given opportunity. They counter the individualism and commodification of industrial society by restoring gift economy and reciprocity as organizing principles.

Time banks formalize skill-sharing by tracking hours of service exchanged among members. One hour of anyone's time equals one hour of anyone else's, whether the service is legal advice or lawn mowing. This radical equality recognizes that everyone has gifts to offer and needs to be met. Members report that beyond practical benefits, time banking creates a sense of community and purpose. Knowing that neighbors will help when needed reduces anxiety about aging, illness, or economic hardship.

Tool libraries and resource sharing hubs reduce consumption while building community connections. Why should every household own rarely-used tools when a neighborhood could share them? These libraries often expand beyond tools to include kitchen equipment, camping gear, and party supplies. The act of borrowing creates relationships and conversations that wouldn't occur in commercial transactions. Members learn about projects neighbors are undertaking, skills they possess, and support they might need.

Skill-sharing workshops and teach-ins transmit practical knowledge while building movement culture. People gather to learn canning, bicycle repair, or natural building not just for the skills but for the community created through shared learning. These events often include potluck meals, childcare, and sliding scale fees that ensure accessibility. The teachers are community members rather than credentialed experts, demonstrating that everyone has knowledge worth sharing. This democratization of education challenges institutional monopolies on learning.

Mutual aid networks activate during crises to provide direct support without bureaucratic mediation. When disasters strike, neighbors organize to distribute food, provide shelter, and share resources faster than official agencies can respond. The COVID-19 pandemic saw an explosion of mutual aid groups that continued beyond immediate crisis to address ongoing needs. These networks demonstrate that humans are naturally cooperative, that crisis reveals rather than creates our capacity for care.

Gift circles and free markets create alternatives to commercial exchange that build community while meeting material needs. Participants bring items they no longer need and take what serves them, without tracking or exchange. The abundance that emerges surprises people conditioned to scarcity thinking. Children's clothes, books, plants, and household goods circulate through communities, reducing waste while ensuring everyone has what they need. These events become social gatherings that strengthen community bonds.

The digital transformation of skill-sharing through apps and online platforms extends networks beyond geographic proximity. Platforms connecting people offering and seeking services, spaces, and resources enable sharing at unprecedented scale. While these platforms can be corporatized and extractive, community-controlled alternatives demonstrate that technology can serve cooperation rather than exploitation. The key lies in governance structures that maintain community benefit rather than profit extraction.

Challenges to mutual aid include the time and energy required to maintain networks, inequities in participation, and the difficulty of sustaining enthusiasm beyond crisis moments. Some people consistently give more than they receive, leading to burnout. Others may take advantage without reciprocating. The informal nature that makes mutual aid flexible can also make it unreliable. Yet these challenges are far outweighed by the benefits of communities that care for their members through voluntary cooperation rather than market exchange or state mandate.

Conflict Resolution and Consensus Processes

Communities organized around animistic principles require sophisticated approaches to conflict that honor all participants while maintaining collective cohesion. Traditional punitive justice systems that isolate and punish offenders cannot serve communities seeking to maintain relationship and restore harmony. Instead, these communities develop and adapt processes from restorative justice, nonviolent communication, and Indigenous peacemaking traditions that address root causes while healing relationships.

Circle processes derived from Indigenous traditions create containers for addressing conflict that honor all voices and perspectives. Participants sit in circles without tables or barriers, often with a talking piece that grants the holder uninterrupted speaking time. This structure equalizes power, prevents domination by loud voices, and encourages deep listening. The circle itself becomes a teacher, demonstrating that solutions emerge from the collective rather than being imposed by authority. These processes take time but create resolutions that all can accept.

Restorative justice approaches conflict as an opportunity for healing and growth rather than punishment. When harm occurs, the focus shifts from determining guilt and imposing penalties to understanding impact, taking responsibility, and making amends. Offenders face those they've harmed, hear the impact of their actions, and participate in determining how to repair damage. This process often transforms both offenders and victims, creating understanding and healing that punishment cannot achieve.

Nonviolent communication (NVC) provides tools for expressing needs and boundaries without attack or defense. By distinguishing observations from evaluations, feelings from thoughts, needs from strategies, and requests from demands, NVC helps people communicate what's alive in them without triggering defensive responses. Communities that practice NVC report dramatic improvements in their ability to navigate conflict constructively. The practice requires dedication but transforms relationships from power struggles to collaborative problem-solving.

Consent-based decision-making offers an alternative to both consensus and voting that balances efficiency with inclusion. Rather than requiring everyone to agree (consensus) or allowing majorities to override minorities (voting), consent processes ask whether anyone has paramount objections to proposals. Objections must be based on harm to the organization's aims, not personal preferences. This approach allows groups to move forward while ensuring that decisions don't cause unacceptable harm to any member.

The role of conflict resolution facilitators in communities requires careful consideration. Some communities rotate facilitation to prevent power concentration and develop everyone's skills. Others recognize that conflict resolution requires specific gifts and training, designating certain members or bringing in external facilitators for serious conflicts. The key lies in ensuring that facilitators serve the community rather than wielding authority over it.

Cultural agreements and community covenants establish shared understanding about behavior and conflict resolution before problems arise. These documents, created collectively through extensive discussion, articulate values, boundaries, and processes for addressing violations. They provide reference points during conflicts and help integrate new members. Regular review and revision ensures they remain living documents rather than rigid rules. The process of creating agreements often prevents conflicts by clarifying expectations.

The shadow work necessary for a healthy community requires acknowledging that conflict often stems from unconscious patterns and projections. Communities that ignore psychological dynamics find themselves repeatedly enacting the same conflicts with different players.

Some communities incorporate group therapy, constellation work, or other modalities that address collective shadows. This deep work can be uncomfortable but proves essential for communities seeking to transform rather than reproduce dominant culture patterns.

The Web of Communities

Animistic communities cannot thrive in isolation but require connection to larger networks that provide resilience, learning, and mutual support. These networks—bioregional, cultural, and global—create the substrate for broader transformation. They demonstrate that the choice is not between local autonomy and global connection but integration that honors both place-based uniqueness and planetary solidarity.

Bioregional networks connect communities within watersheds or ecosystems, enabling coordination around shared ecological challenges and opportunities. Communities in the same river valley might collaborate on water management, share seeds adapted to local conditions, or coordinate resistance to extractive projects. These networks help communities understand themselves as part of larger ecological systems rather than isolated human settlements. They provide frameworks for governance that align with natural rather than political boundaries.

Cultural networks connect communities sharing similar values or approaches, enabling learning and mutual support across geographic distances. The Global Ecovillage Network connects projects worldwide, facilitating exchanges, training, and advocacy. The Federation of Egalitarian Communities links income-sharing communes across North America. These networks provide templates and tools while celebrating diversity of implementation. They demonstrate that similar values can manifest differently in different contexts.

Economic networks enable communities to meet needs through cooperation rather than dependence on corporate systems. Community-supported agriculture connects rural producers with urban consumers. Local currency systems enable exchange that keeps wealth circulating within regions. Worker cooperative networks provide mutual support and shared services. These economic relationships create resilience while prefiguring post-capitalist possibilities.

Learning exchanges between communities accelerate development and prevent repeated mistakes. Established communities host internships and workshops for emerging projects. Design teams help new communities avoid common pitfalls. Failure stories are shared as teaching tools rather than hidden in shame. This culture of open learning contrasts with competitive secrecy, demonstrating that cooperation serves everyone better than isolation.

Solidarity networks activate when communities face threats or crises. When one ecovillage faces legal challenges, others provide financial and political support. When disasters strike, communities send resources and volunteers. These networks demonstrate that communities understand themselves as part of larger movements rather than individual projects. The resilience created through solidarity enables communities to take risks and persist through challenges.

Digital infrastructure increasingly enables community networking while raising questions about technology dependence. Online platforms facilitate coordination, learning, and resource sharing at unprecedented scale. Virtual meetings reduce travel while enabling regular connection. Digital currencies enable exchange across distance. Yet overreliance on digital tools can weaken face-to-face relationships and create vulnerability to system failures. Communities must balance digital efficiency with analog resilience.

The relationship between communities and broader society requires careful navigation. Communities that completely separate from mainstream society limit their transformative impact. Those that remain too engaged risk cooptation and dilution. The most effective communities maintain semi-permeable boundaries—distinct enough to develop alternative cultures while accessible enough to inspire broader change. They serve as bridges between current reality and possible futures.

This chapter has explored how communities organized around animistic principles are emerging worldwide as responses to ecological and social crises. From rural ecovillages to urban communes, from land trusts to mutual aid networks, these communities demonstrate that humans can organize themselves in ways that honor the consciousness of all beings while meeting authentic human needs. They face real challenges around economics, governance, and social dynamics, yet continue proliferating because they offer what industrial civilization cannot: genuine community, meaningful work, and direct relationship with the living world. These communities are not isolated experiments but nodes in an emerging network of transformation, laboratories for the development of culture and practices that could reshape civilization. In their successes and failures, they provide essential learning for humanity's necessary transition from domination to partnership with the living Earth.

CHAPTER 23

Challenges and Obstacles

The path toward animistic consciousness and the transformation of human civilization faces formidable obstacles that cannot be wished away through positive thinking or spiritual bypassing. The systems that maintain mechanistic worldviews command vast resources, shape institutional structures, and colonize consciousness in ways that make transformation extraordinarily difficult. The honest acknowledgment of these challenges is not defeatism but necessary preparation for the long struggle ahead. Only by understanding the depth and complexity of what we face can we develop strategies adequate to the task. This chapter examines the multilayered resistance to animistic revival—from entrenched economic interests to psychological conditioning, from legal structures to the scale of transformation required—while exploring how these obstacles might be navigated or overcome.

The forces arrayed against animistic consciousness are not merely external systems but internalized patterns that shape how we perceive and interact with the world. We who seek transformation have been formed by the very systems we seek to change. The mechanistic worldview lives in our language, our assumptions, our reflexive responses to the world around us. Even as we intellectually embrace the understanding that all beings possess consciousness and deserve respect, we find ourselves treating the world as a resource, valuing efficiency over relationship, choosing convenience over connection. This internal colonization may be the most challenging obstacle we face, requiring not just changed beliefs but fundamental rewiring of perception and response.

The timeline for transformation presents perhaps the greatest challenge. Climate science tells us we have perhaps a decade to fundamentally restructure civilization to avoid catastrophic warming. Ecological indicators show accelerating degradation that could trigger irreversible tipping points. Social systems show increasing instability that could collapse into chaos or authoritarianism. Yet the consciousness changes required for genuine transformation typically unfold over generations. The practices that develop animistic awareness—sitting with trees, learning bird language, developing reciprocal relationships with land—require patience and presence that seems impossible given the urgency of our crises. We must somehow accomplish in years what traditionally required centuries, without shortcuts that compromise depth or authenticity.

Resistance from Established Systems

The economic systems that dominate global civilization depend fundamentally on treating nature as commodity and humans as consumers or resources. These systems will not peacefully accept transformation that threatens their foundation. Fossil fuel corporations, industrial agriculture, extractive industries, and the financial institutions that support them command resources that dwarf those available to transformative movements. They shape policy through lobbying and campaign contributions, control narratives through media ownership and advertising, and maintain power through violence when other methods fail.

The fossil fuel industry alone spends billions annually to maintain its dominance despite clear evidence that continued extraction ensures civilizational collapse. This industry funds climate denial, captures regulatory agencies, and uses military and paramilitary forces to suppress resistance. The murder of environmental defenders—over two hundred annually in recent years—demonstrates that those who threaten extractive profits face mortal danger. Indigenous peoples protecting their territories, activists blocking pipelines, and communities resisting mining projects confront not just legal opposition but physical violence from state and corporate forces.

Industrial agriculture maintains its dominance through subsidy structures, trade agreements, and regulatory frameworks designed to favor large-scale monoculture over diverse, ecological farming. Small farmers practicing regenerative agriculture face higher regulatory burdens than industrial operations that poison land and water. Seed patents and genetic modification technologies create dependencies that trap farmers in systems they know are destructive. The concentration of food processing and distribution in few corporate hands means that even farmers who want to transition face limited markets for alternative products.

The financial system's structure fundamentally opposes animistic consciousness. Money created as debt bearing interest requires economic growth to avoid collapse. This growth imperative drives the conversion of living systems into dead commodities, relationships into transactions, and cultures into markets. Alternative economic models that prioritize wellbeing over growth, sharing over accumulation, and reciprocity over exchange face not just practical challenges but legal prohibition. Banking regulations, tax codes, and corporate law are designed to perpetuate current systems while preventing alternatives.

Educational institutions, from primary schools through universities, are structured to produce workers and consumers for the industrial economy rather than citizens capable of questioning fundamental assumptions. Curricula emphasize competition over cooperation, abstract knowledge over embodied wisdom, and human supremacy over ecological embeddedness. Efforts to introduce alternative pedagogies face resistance from standardized testing regimes, textbook publishers, and administrators trained in industrial models. Teachers who attempt to teach outdoors, integrate Indigenous knowledge, or question growth paradigms often face discipline or dismissal.

The media landscape, increasingly concentrated in few corporate hands, shapes public consciousness in ways that maintain existing systems. News coverage focuses on symptoms rather than systems, personalities rather than structures, conflict rather than cooperation. Environmental coverage, when it occurs, often frames issues in ways that preserve current arrangements—focusing on individual consumption choices rather than corporate responsibility, technological fixes rather than systemic change, or market solutions rather than regulatory transformation. Alternative media faces algorithmic suppression, demonetization, and in some cases direct censorship.

Legal systems encode mechanistic worldviews into law, treating nature as property and corporations as persons while denying personhood to rivers, forests, and mountains. Property rights trump ecosystem integrity. Corporate rights supersede community wellbeing. International trade agreements override environmental protection. Efforts to establish rights of nature face constitutional challenges, judicial resistance, and reversal when political power shifts. The legal system's foundation in precedent means that centuries of decisions based on mechanistic assumptions continue shaping present possibilities.

The military-industrial complex represents perhaps the most intractable obstacle to transformation. Global military spending exceeds two trillion dollars annually—resources that could address every environmental and social crisis instead fuel systems of domination and destruction. Military institutions are among the world's largest consumers of fossil fuels and producers of toxic contamination. The logic of military competition drives extractivism, justifies authoritarianism, and perpetuates the enemy-thinking that prevents planetary cooperation. Peace movements that challenge military dominance face surveillance, infiltration, and suppression.

Economic Pressures and Survival Needs

The immediate survival needs of billions of people create pressures that work against long-term transformation. When you're struggling to pay rent, buy food, or access healthcare, the consciousness shifts required for animistic awareness seem like impossible luxury. The precarity that characterizes life for increasing numbers—gig work without benefits, debt that can never be repaid, housing costs that consume most income—leaves little energy for anything beyond survival. This manufactured scarcity is not accidental but serves to prevent the leisure and security necessary for questioning fundamental assumptions.

The debt trap that ensnares individuals, communities, and nations forces participation in destructive systems. Student debt chains young people to careers they know are harmful. Mortgages require steady income that may only be available through compromising work. Credit card debt from meeting basic needs creates cycles of financial stress that prevent long-term thinking. National debts force countries to extract and export resources rather than protecting ecosystems. The compound interest that enriches lenders ensures that debtors remain trapped regardless of how much they repay.

The absence of social safety nets in many countries means that refusing participation in destructive systems risks destitution. Without universal healthcare, people remain in soul-crushing jobs for insurance. Without guaranteed housing, people accept exploitation rather than face homelessness. Without retirement security, people cannot risk experimenting with alternative economies. The social supports that would enable people to choose meaning over money, purpose over profit, have been systematically dismantled in service of creating desperate workers who accept any conditions.

The care economy—raising children, tending elders, supporting those with disabilities—receives little economic support despite being essential for social reproduction. Those who provide care, predominantly women, often sacrifice their own economic security. The time and energy required for care work leaves little capacity for the additional labor of transformation. Parents working multiple jobs to support children have no time for community organizing. Adult children caring for aging parents while raising their own families cannot attend evening meetings or weekend workshops.

Rural communities facing economic collapse often have no choice but to accept extractive industries that provide the only available employment. When the choice is between a coal mine that poisons your water or watching your children leave because there's no future, communities choose survival despite knowing the long-term costs. The economic devastation of rural areas is not accidental but serves to create populations desperate enough to accept any development regardless of ecological impact.

Urban housing costs force people into long commutes that consume time and energy while separating them from both workplace and home communities. The hours spent in traffic or crowded transit could be used for gardening, organizing, or simply being present with the living world. The exhaustion from commuting leaves people with energy only for screen-based entertainment that further disconnects them from embodied presence. The sprawl that creates these commutes destroys the very ecosystems we need to preserve while making alternative transportation impossible.

The consumer debt that keeps people trapped in destructive employment patterns also shapes consciousness in ways that resist transformation. When identity is constructed through consumption, when status depends on possessions, when entertainment requires constant purchase, the simplicity that animistic living requires feels like deprivation rather than liberation. The dopamine hits from online shopping, social media likes, and streaming entertainment create addictive patterns that are difficult to break even when we recognize their harm.

Psychological Barriers and Cultural Conditioning

The psychological structures created by centuries of mechanistic conditioning cannot be quickly dismantled. We have been trained from birth to perceive the world as a collection of objects rather than a community of subjects. Our languages structure thought in ways that reinforce separation. Our educational systems reward analytical intelligence while dismissing emotional and embodied wisdom. Our cultures celebrate individual achievement while denigrating collective cooperation. These patterns run so deep that we often cannot see them, like fish unaware of water.

The trauma of disconnection from the living world creates defensive psychological structures that resist reconnection. Having learned that nature is dangerous, dirty, and uncomfortable, we retreat into climate-controlled environments. Having been taught that our feelings about trees, animals, and landscapes are childish projection, we suppress our natural empathy. Having experienced the vulnerability of caring about places and beings that are destroyed for profit, we protect ourselves through numbness. The walls we build for protection become prisons that prevent the very connections we need for healing.

The fear of death that mechanistic worldview intensifies creates desperate attachment to control and permanence that animistic consciousness challenges. When death is seen as an absolute ending rather than transformation, when consciousness is believed to cease with brain death, when there's no continuity beyond individual existence, the loss of ego boundaries that animistic awareness requires feels like annihilation. The dissolution of separate self into larger ecological self threatens everything we've been taught to value about individual achievement and legacy.

Social ridicule and isolation face those who openly embrace animistic consciousness in mechanistic societies. Speaking to plants, thanking water, or seeking guidance from dreams marks one as eccentric at best, mentally ill at worst. The fear of being seen as "crazy" prevents many from even experimenting with practices that might open perception. The need for belonging and acceptance keeps people confined within consensus reality even when that consensus is clearly pathological.

The addiction to comfort and convenience that industrial civilization promotes creates resistance to the simplicity and presence animistic living requires. When we're accustomed to instant gratification, the patience required to grow food or build relationships with places seems unbearable. When we're used to climate control, exposing ourselves to weather feels like suffering. When we're habituated to constant stimulation, the quiet of nature feels boring or anxiety-provoking. These addictions are not personal failings but manufactured dependencies that serve systems requiring compliant consumers.

The expertise ideology that validates only credentialed knowledge dismisses the wisdom of those who learn through relationship and experience. Indigenous elders who have observed landscapes for decades are ignored in favor of scientists with degrees but no place-based knowledge. Farmers who understand soil through touch and smell are overruled by agronomists who've never planted seeds. Parents who know their children are dismissed by educational experts who see only statistics. This invalidation of embodied knowledge prevents us from trusting our own experience and perception.

The grief and despair that arise when we truly comprehend our situation can become obstacles to transformation. The magnitude of loss—species extinctions, ecosystem collapse, cultural destruction—can overwhelm our capacity to respond. Many people touch this grief briefly, then retreat into denial or distraction because it feels unbearable. Others become paralyzed by despair, unable to act because nothing seems adequate to the scale of crisis. Learning to hold grief without being destroyed by it, to act despite despair, requires psychological resilience that our culture doesn't teach.

Legal Obstacles and Regulatory Challenges

The legal frameworks that govern modern societies encode mechanistic worldviews in ways that make animistic practices illegal or impossible. Property law treats land as a commodity that can be bought, sold, and destroyed at owner's discretion. Environmental law regulates but doesn't prevent destruction, establishing acceptable levels of pollution rather than protecting ecosystem integrity. Corporate law prioritizes shareholder profit over all other considerations, making it illegal for directors to choose environmental health over financial returns.

Zoning laws designed for industrial development prevent the mixed-use, pedestrian-scale communities that animistic living requires. Regulations that separate residential, commercial, and agricultural uses make it illegal to grow food in front yards, keep chickens in backyards, or operate businesses from homes. Building codes that mandate industrial materials and methods prevent natural building techniques that have sheltered humans for millennia. These regulations, often written by industries they supposedly regulate, create barriers to alternative ways of living.

Intellectual property law enables the commodification and privatization of life itself. Seed patents prevent farmers from saving and sharing seeds as they have for ten thousand years. Biopiracy allows corporations to patent traditional medicines and genetic resources taken from Indigenous peoples. Traditional knowledge that should be collective heritage becomes private property that generates profit for corporations while denying access to communities that created and preserved it.

International trade agreements override local and national environmental protections in service of corporate profits. Investor-state dispute mechanisms allow corporations to sue governments for regulations that reduce expected profits. Environmental standards are attacked as trade barriers. Local preferences for local production are prohibited as discrimination. These agreements, negotiated in secret and enforced through unaccountable tribunals, make democratic determination of economic priorities impossible.

The criminalization of protest and resistance makes opposition to destructive projects increasingly dangerous. Laws treating pipeline protests as terrorism, ag-gag laws preventing documentation of animal abuse, and strategic lawsuits against public participation (SLAPP suits) all serve to suppress resistance to extractive industries. Bail conditions that prevent activists from returning to protest sites, injunctions that make presence illegal, and conspiracy charges for planning protests create legal jeopardy for those defending land and life.

Immigration law that prevents freedom of movement while allowing free flow of capital creates populations vulnerable to exploitation. People forced to migrate by climate change, economic devastation, or violence face borders that treat them as criminals. Once in destination countries, undocumented status makes them vulnerable to extreme exploitation, unable to organize or resist without risking deportation. This manufactured vulnerability serves industries that depend on desperate workers willing to accept dangerous conditions for poverty wages.

Drug laws that criminalize plant medicines and consciousness-altering substances prevent practices that have facilitated human-nature connection for millennia. The prohibition of cannabis, psilocybin, peyote, ayahuasca, and other plant teachers serves to maintain consensus reality and prevent the consciousness shifts that might challenge existing systems. While pharmaceutical corporations profit from synthetic versions of these substances, Indigenous peoples who have used them ceremonially for generations face imprisonment.

Scale Challenges - From Personal to Planetary

The transformation required must occur simultaneously at scales from individual consciousness to global systems, each with distinct challenges and timelines. Personal transformation alone cannot address systemic crises, while systemic change without consciousness shift merely reorganizes domination. The coordination required to transform across scales exceeds anything humanity has previously accomplished, yet nothing less will suffice to avoid civilizational and ecological collapse.

Individual transformation faces the challenge of maintaining new consciousness within systems that constantly reinforce old patterns. The person who experiences profound connection with nature during a wilderness retreat returns to cities designed to exclude nature, jobs that require treating Earth as a resource, and social circles that ridicule animistic awareness. Without supportive community and regular practice, expanded consciousness contracts back to consensus reality. The effort required to maintain alternative consciousness in hostile environments exhausts many who attempt it.

Family and household transformation requires negotiating different levels of awareness and commitment among people sharing intimate space. When one family member embraces animistic practices while others remain embedded in consumer culture, conflict inevitably arises. Children receive contradictory messages from parents with different worldviews. Partners struggle to maintain connection across growing consciousness gaps. The household, which should be a sanctuary for alternative living, becomes a battleground between paradigms.

Community transformation faces challenges of coordination and consensus among diverse populations with different needs and perspectives. Urban communities include recent immigrants, long-term residents, young professionals, and elderly people on fixed incomes, each with different relationships to place and possibility. Rural communities divide between those dependent on extractive industries and those seeking alternatives. The consensus required for community transformation seems impossible when neighbors can't agree on basic facts about reality.

Bioregional transformation requires coordination across political boundaries that rarely align with ecological systems. Watersheds cross city, county, state, and national boundaries, each with different regulations and priorities. Ecosystems function at scales that human governance structures don't match. The salmon don't care about property lines, but their restoration requires cooperation among thousands of landowners. The atmosphere doesn't respect national sovereignty, but climate action requires international agreement.

National transformation faces entrenched interests that control political processes through wealth and influence. Electoral systems designed by and for elites prevent genuine alternatives from gaining power. When transformative movements occasionally achieve electoral success, they face sabotage from bureaucracies, militaries, and economic powers that persist regardless of electoral outcomes. The examples of movements that achieved political power only to be overthrown by coups or destroyed by capital flight demonstrate the limits of electoral strategies.

Global transformation requires cooperation among nations with vastly different resources, responsibilities, and worldviews. Countries that industrialized through fossil fuels resist restrictions that would prevent others from following the same path. Nations that contributed least to ecological crises suffer most from their impacts. The wealthy countries that could finance transformation prioritize military spending and corporate subsidies. The international institutions that might coordinate transformation are captured by the very interests that oppose it.

The temporal challenge of accomplishing transformation before irreversible tipping points compounds all other scale challenges. We cannot wait for consciousness to slowly shift through generations when we have perhaps a decade to fundamentally restructure civilization. We cannot build alternative systems gradually when existing systems are rapidly destroying the basis for life. We must somehow accomplish revolutionary transformation while maintaining enough stability to avoid chaos that would prevent organized response to crisis.

Avoiding Spiritual Materialism and Cultural Appropriation

The revival of animistic consciousness faces serious challenges around authenticity, appropriation, and the commodification of spirituality. As Western seekers recognize the bankruptcy of mechanistic worldviews, many turn to Indigenous traditions for alternatives. While this recognition of Indigenous wisdom is overdue, it often manifests in ways that perpetuate colonial patterns rather than supporting genuine transformation. The challenge lies in learning from Indigenous knowledge while respecting Indigenous sovereignty, supporting Indigenous struggles, and developing authentic practices rooted in our own relationships with place.

Spiritual materialism—the accumulation of spiritual experiences and practices as a form of ego enhancement—perverts animistic consciousness into another form of consumption. Weekend workshops promising shamanic initiation, vision quests led by self-appointed guides with dubious training, and ceremonial practices stripped of cultural context and sold as experiences all demonstrate how capitalism commodifies even resistance to commodification. Participants may feel temporary expansion but return unchanged to destructive lifestyles, using spiritual experiences to justify continued participation in harmful systems.

The appropriation of Indigenous ceremonies, symbols, and practices by non-Indigenous people perpetuates colonial violence while preventing authentic relationship. When sacred practices that Indigenous peoples were imprisoned for practicing are now sold by white entrepreneurs, when Indigenous names and images are used for marketing, when ceremony becomes performance for paying audiences, the harm compounds historical trauma. This appropriation not only disrespects Indigenous peoples but prevents non-Indigenous people from developing their own authentic relationships with land and spirit.

The "noble savage" romanticism that idealizes Indigenous peoples while ignoring their contemporary struggles, diverse perspectives, and full humanity creates another barrier to genuine relationship and learning. When Indigenous peoples are frozen in imagined pasts, their contemporary knowledge and adaptation become invisible. When they're expected to be spiritual teachers rather than complex humans with their own struggles and goals, genuine connection becomes impossible. This romanticism serves to maintain distance and hierarchy rather than creating solidarity.

The individualization of practices that are fundamentally communal strips them of their transformative power. Vision quests undertaken alone without community preparation and integration, sweat lodges conducted without proper training or safety, and plant medicines taken without ceremonial container or integration support can cause serious psychological and physical harm. These practices developed within cultural contexts that provided preparation, container, and integration. Without these supports, they become dangerous rather than healing.

The tension between honoring traditional knowledge and adapting to contemporary contexts requires careful navigation. Slavish imitation of traditional forms without understanding their purpose creates empty ritual. Complete innovation without grounding in tested wisdom leads to ineffective or harmful practices. The path forward requires deep understanding of principles while developing forms appropriate to current contexts. This might mean creating new ceremonies that honor ancient patterns while addressing contemporary needs.

The commercialization of animistic practices within capitalist frameworks undermines their transformative potential. When connection with nature becomes eco-tourism that destroys what it claims to honor, when earth-based spirituality becomes products to purchase, when community becomes service to consume, the forms remain while the essence disappears. The challenge lies in meeting legitimate needs for teaching and facilitation while resisting commodification that perverts practice into product.

Finding authentic ways for displaced peoples to develop animistic consciousness without appropriating from Indigenous peoples requires creativity and humility. This might mean researching and reviving ancestral traditions from our own lineages, developing new practices through patient relationship with our current places, or respectfully learning from Indigenous peoples while supporting their sovereignty and struggles. The key lies in doing our own work rather than taking what others have preserved through centuries of resistance.

This chapter has examined honestly the formidable obstacles facing the transformation toward animistic consciousness—from entrenched economic interests to psychological conditioning, from legal structures to the scale of change required. These challenges are real and cannot be wished away. Yet acknowledging them fully is not cause for despair but preparation for the long work ahead. Every previous transformation in human history faced seemingly impossible obstacles that were eventually overcome through persistent effort, creative strategy, and collective will. The obstacles we face are the dying thrashing of systems that have outlived their purpose. They are powerful but not permanent. Understanding their nature and mechanisms allows us to develop strategies that acknowledge their power while working steadily toward their transformation. The path forward will not be easy or quick, but it remains possible if we proceed with clarity about what we face, commitment to the work required, and trust in life's inherent tendency toward healing and wholeness.

CHAPTER 24

The Great Turning

As we stand at this threshold moment in human history, poised between collapse and transformation, we can glimpse the outlines of a future where humanity has remembered its place in the community of life. This is not a utopian fantasy where all problems have been solved, but a mature vision of a civilization that has learned to live within Earth's boundaries while honoring the consciousness present in all beings. The Great Turning—that fundamental shift from industrial growth society to life-sustaining civilization—is already underway in countless experiments, movements, and awakening consciousnesses around the planet. This chapter envisions what the world might look like when these scattered seeds have grown into forests, when the exceptions have become the norm, when humanity has completed its journey home to the living Earth.

The path to this future will not be linear or smooth. It will involve periods of breakdown and breakthrough, resistance and renewal, grief and celebration. Some aspects of the world we have known will be lost forever—species driven extinct cannot be resurrected, ecosystems degraded beyond recovery cannot be instantly restored, cultures destroyed by colonization cannot be perfectly reconstructed. Yet from this honest reckoning with loss can emerge a humility and wisdom that our species has never before possessed at such scale. The future we can create is not a return to the past but an integration of all we have learned through our long journey, wedding ancient wisdom with appropriate technology, Indigenous knowledge with scientific understanding, local rooted-ness with planetary consciousness.

This vision emerges not from abstract speculation but from careful observation of what is already working—the communities that have achieved negative carbon footprints while improving quality of life, the ecosystems that have recovered when given the chance, the economies that distribute wealth while respecting planetary boundaries, the gover-nance systems that honor both human and more-than-human citizens. By imaginatively extending these present realities into a possible future, we can see not just where we might go but how we might get there. This is the power of vision: not to predict a fixed future but to illuminate pos-sibilities that can guide present action.

Imagining Animistic Societies of the Future

In the animistic societies of the mid-21st century, cities have become living ecosystems rather than concrete deserts. Buildings breathe through walls of living plants that purify air and moderate temperature. Streets follow watersheds rather than imposing grids, with streams day-lighted from buried pipes to flow through urban landscapes. Food forests and community gardens occupy what were once parking lots, providing fresh produce while creating habitat for returning wildlife. The boundaries between city and countryside have blurred, with green corridors allowing animals to move freely through urban areas that once were barriers to migration.

Governance in these societies reflects the understanding that hu-mans are not the only citizens deserving representation. Rivers have legal standing and spokespersons who advocate for their health in com-munity councils. Urban forests are recognized as commons managed for the benefit of all species, not just humans. Decision-making processes consider impacts on seven generations into the future, with councils of youth and elders providing long-term perspective that balances the ur-gency of present needs. Indigenous peoples, whose knowledge systems preserved animistic wisdom through centuries of suppression, hold honored positions as advisors and teachers, their land rights restored and sovereignty recognized.

Economic systems have transformed from growth imperatives to steady-state economies that cycle resources rather than consuming them. Work weeks have shortened to twenty hours, providing everyone with time for family, creativity, and connection with nature. Basic needs—housing, food, healthcare, education—are guaranteed as human rights, freeing people to pursue vocations that express their gifts rather than jobs that merely pay bills. Local currencies complement global exchange, keeping wealth circulating within communities rather than extracting it to distant shareholders. The concept of waste has disappeared, with all materials designed for complete recycling or composting, mimicking nature's cycles where every output becomes input for other processes.

Agriculture has shifted from industrial monocultures to diverse agroecological systems that build soil rather than depleting it. Farms are understood as ecosystems where humans are one species among many, all contributing to collective abundance. Perennial polycultures provide staple foods with minimal tillage, while food forests offer diverse fruits, nuts, and vegetables. Animals are partners in these systems rather than products—chickens control pests and provide fertilizer, goats manage vegetation and provide milk, bees pollinate plants while providing honey. The relationship between farmers and land is understood as a sacred covenant rather than ownership, with farmers as stewards who will pass healthier land to the next generation.

Transportation systems prioritize collective and human-powered movement over private vehicles. Cities are designed for walking and cycling, with neighborhoods providing most daily needs within easy reach. Electric trams and trains connect communities, powered by renewable energy and running frequently enough that schedules become unnecessary. For longer distances, high-speed rail has replaced most aviation, with journey times extended but transformed into pleasant experiences rather than ordeals to endure. The few remaining vehicles are shared rather than owned, summoned when needed for specific purposes. The quiet that returns when traffic noise disappears allows people to hear birds singing in cities for the first time in generations.

Energy systems have completed the transition to renewables, but more importantly, energy consumption has decreased through elegant design rather than deprivation. Buildings that work with rather than against climate require minimal heating and cooling. Local production reduces transportation energy. Shared facilities decrease individual consumption. The understanding that energy is a sacred gift from sun, wind, and water rather than a commodity to waste has transformed how societies use power. Peak electricity use occurs during peak generation, with communities organizing activities around energy availability rather than demanding constant supply.

Children Growing Up in the Living World

The children of animistic societies grow up understanding themselves as part of the living world rather than separate from it. From infancy, they are introduced to their other-than-human neighbors—the trees that shade their homes, the birds that wake them with song, the soil organisms that help grow their food. These introductions are not abstract lessons but embodied relationships developed through daily interaction. Children have sit-spots where they observe seasonal changes, learning patience and attention through watching the same place transform through time. They know the names and stories of local plants and animals as naturally as they know their human neighbors.

Education happens primarily outdoors, with classrooms used only for specific activities requiring shelter. Children learn mathematics through observing patterns in nature—spirals in shells, fractals in ferns, ratios in flower petals. Science emerges through direct observation and experimentation with living systems. History is taught through the land itself—the ancient trees that witnessed past events, the rivers that carried ancestors, the soil that holds memories of all who have lived and died in place. Literature and writing develop through storytelling circles where children learn to craft narratives that convey meaning and preserve wisdom.

Play in these societies is largely unstructured and unsupervised, with children free to explore and take appropriate risks. They build forts in woods, dam streams, climb trees, and create imaginary worlds in wild spaces. This play is understood not as mere recreation but as essential development of creativity, problem-solving, and relationship with place. Children learn to assess risk through experience rather than being protected from all danger. They develop confidence through accomplishing challenges they set themselves rather than meeting adult-imposed goals. The childhood obesity and anxiety that plagued early 21st century children has disappeared, replaced by robust physical and mental health developed through outdoor play.

Initiation rites mark the transition from childhood to adolescence and from adolescence to adulthood, providing clear passages that industrial society lacked. These ceremonies, developed within specific communities rather than imposed from outside, might involve solo time on the land, challenges that test readiness for new responsibilities, or teaching of knowledge reserved for those ready to receive it. Young people know when they have become adults because the community acknowledges the transition, providing both privileges and responsibilities that mark new status. These rites create belonging and identity rooted in place and community rather than consumption and achievement.

The knowledge that children receive includes not just human wisdom but the teachings of other species. They learn medicine from plants, architecture from birds, engineering from beavers, and communication from wolves. This learning happens not through books but through observation and interaction, with children encouraged to develop relationships with particular species that call to them. A child fascinated by spiders might spend years observing and learning from them, becoming the community's spider expert who shares knowledge with others. This specialized knowledge is valued equally with human-focused learning, recognizing that understanding our relatives is essential for thriving together.

Technology in children's lives is carefully integrated rather than dominant. Digital tools are used for specific purposes—connecting with distant relatives, accessing information not available locally, creating and sharing art—rather than constant entertainment. Screen time is limited not through rules but through the greater attraction of outdoor adventure and real-world creation. Children learn to make things with their hands—carving wood, weaving baskets, building structures—developing competence that generates genuine confidence. They understand technology as a tool rather than a master, using it when appropriate while maintaining the ability to thrive without it.

The mental health crisis that characterized early 21st century youth has been resolved not through medication but through addressing root causes. Children embedded in loving communities with clear roles and expectations don't experience the alienation that drove previous epidemics of anxiety and depression. Connection with nature provides emotional regulation that screens could never offer. Physical challenge and accomplishment build resilience that participation trophies couldn't create. Intergenerational relationships provide wisdom and perspective that nuclear families alone couldn't supply. These children grow up psychologically healthy not through therapeutic intervention but through living in healthy societies.

Cities as Ecosystems and Sacred Spaces

The cities of the future have been transformed from life-denying sprawl into living ecosystems that support both human and more-than-human flourishing. This transformation didn't require destroying existing cities and starting over but retrofitting and redesigning them according to ecological principles. Buildings that once stood as isolated objects now connect through bridges of living vegetation, creating con-

426 – DANIEL PAYNE

tinuous habitat that allows wildlife to move freely through urban areas. Rooftops have become productive landscapes—gardens, apiaries, gathering spaces—that multiply the effective area of cities without expanding their footprint.

Water moves visibly through these cities rather than being hidden in pipes. Rain falls on permeable surfaces that allow infiltration rather than runoff. Bioswales lined with native plants filter stormwater while creating habitat. Restored wetlands treat wastewater while providing homes for amphibians and birds. Rivers and streams, freed from concrete channels, meander through cities, their banks providing recreation, cooling, and connection with flowing water that humans have always sought. The integration of water into urban design has eliminated flooding problems while creating beauty and biodiversity.

Sacred spaces punctuate urban landscapes, providing places for ceremony, contemplation, and connection with the numinous. These might be groves of ancient trees that survived urbanization, springs that have been restored and protected, or mountains visible from carefully preserved viewpoints. New sacred spaces have been created through community effort—labyrinths in parks, medicine wheels in community gardens, stone circles on hilltops. These spaces are understood as belonging to all inhabitants regardless of specific spiritual tradition, places where the veil between worlds is thin and the sacred can be touched.

Urban wildlife is welcomed rather than excluded, with cities designed to accommodate other species as legitimate inhabitants. Building designs incorporate nesting spaces for birds and bats. Gardens include plants that feed butterflies and bees. Corridors connect green spaces, allowing animals to move safely through cities. Predators have returned—hawks nesting on skyscrapers, foxes denning in parks, even the occasional mountain lion passing through green corridors. Rather than generating fear, these predators are celebrated as indicators of ecological health and reminders that cities are not purely human domains.

The soundscape of cities has been transformed through conscious design and regulation. Limits on noise pollution have restored the ability to hear birds, wind, and water. Electric vehicles and improved design have eliminated the constant traffic roar. Building codes require sound insulation that provides quiet refuges. The result is cities where conversation is possible on streets, where sleep is uninterrupted, where the subtle sounds of life can be heard. This acoustic transformation has reduced stress, improved health, and restored one of humanity's primary ways of connecting with the environment.

Neighborhoods have become villages within cities, with distinct identities and strong social cohesion. Most daily needs can be met within walking distance—food, education, healthcare, recreation. Neighborhood councils make decisions about local matters, creating governance at scale where everyone can participate. Public spaces—plazas, parks, community centers—provide venues for gathering, celebration, and collective decision-making. The anonymity and isolation that characterized industrial cities has been replaced by interconnection and mutual support, with neighbors knowing and caring for each other.

Urban agriculture has become normalized rather than exceptional, with food production integrated throughout cities. Every neighborhood has community gardens where residents grow vegetables and build relationships. Fruit and nut trees line streets, providing food, shade, and beauty. Aquaponics facilities in repurposed warehouses produce fish and vegetables year-round. Rooftop greenhouses extend growing seasons. The distance between production and consumption has shrunk to blocks rather than thousands of miles, with urban dwellers directly involved in growing their food.

Technology in Service of All Life

The relationship between technology and life has been fundamentally restructured, with technology understood as a tool for enhancing rather than replacing natural systems. The technologies that dominate are those that support rather than undermine ecological and social wellbeing. Design principles derived from nature—biomimicry—guide innovation, with engineers learning from organisms that have solved technical challenges through evolution. The question is no longer "can we build it?" but "should we build it?" with impacts on seven generations considered before adoption.

Digital technology has evolved from addiction-generating attention capture to tools that support presence and connection. Interfaces are designed to provide information efficiently then encourage users to return to physical reality. Algorithms promote accurate information and constructive discourse rather than engagement at any cost. Social media platforms are cooperatively owned and governed, with users controlling their data and determining platform policies. The surveillance capitalism that characterized the early internet has been replaced by digital commons that serve collective benefit.

Artificial intelligence serves as an assistant rather than replacement for human intelligence, handling repetitive tasks while freeing humans for creative and relational work. AI systems are trained on datasets that include Indigenous knowledge and ecological wisdom, not just Western scientific literature. Their decision-making processes are transparent and contestable, with clear accountability for outcomes. Rather than pursuing artificial general intelligence that might compete with humans, development focuses on specialized systems that enhance human capability while respecting human agency.

Biotechnology is guided by strict ethical frameworks that recognize the consciousness and integrity of all life forms. Genetic modification is limited to addressing specific urgent needs—treating genetic diseases, developing climate-resilient food crops—rather than enhancing traits for profit. The patenting of life forms is prohibited, with genetic resources understood as common heritage. Traditional knowledge holders are compensated and consulted when their wisdom contributes to biotechnological development. The precautionary principle guides adoption, with long-term impacts thoroughly studied before implementation.

Renewable energy technologies have evolved beyond industrial-scale installations to distributed generation integrated into daily life. Solar cells are incorporated into building materials rather than added as appendages. Small wind turbines designed like sculptures provide local power while adding beauty. Micro-hydro installations in streams generate neighborhood electricity without blocking fish passage. The grid has evolved from centralized distribution to networked resilience, with communities able to function independently while sharing surplus. Energy storage in various forms—batteries, compressed air, gravity systems—provides reliability without fossil fuel backup.

Transportation technologies prioritize collective efficiency over individual convenience. Autonomous vehicles, rather than replacing private cars, operate as shared transit that responds to collective needs. Hyperlocal delivery systems using cargo bikes and neighborhood distribution centers have eliminated most delivery trucks. For necessary long-distance transport, hydrogen fuel cells and advanced batteries provide clean power. The infrastructure for private vehicles has been largely removed, with former highways converted to rail lines and former parking lots to housing and parks.

Communication technologies enable global connection while strengthening local communities. Real-time translation allows conversation across language barriers, supporting preservation of linguistic diversity. Virtual presence enables participation in distant events without travel. Augmented reality overlays information on physical environments without requiring screen interaction. These technologies are designed to enhance rather than replace face-to-face interaction, supporting distributed communities while strengthening place-based relationships.

Global Cooperation Based on Earth Wisdom

The international order has been restructured around ecological principles rather than national sovereignty, with bioregions and watersheds providing organizational frameworks that transcend political boundaries. The United Nations has evolved into the United Species, with representation extended beyond humans to include spokespersons for forests, rivers, oceans, and atmosphere. International law recognizes ecocide as a crime against peace, with leaders held accountable for ecological destruction. Trade agreements prioritize ecological and social wellbeing over corporate profits, with local production favored over global supply chains.

Climate cooperation has moved beyond emissions targets to comprehensive Earth system governance. Nations are allocated carbon budgets based on population and historical emissions, with those exceeding limits required to compensate those below. Massive reforestation and ecosystem restoration projects, funded by carbon taxes on wealth and consumption, are drawing down atmospheric carbon while restoring biodiversity. Geoengineering proposals are evaluated through Indigenous wisdom councils that consider seven-generation impacts rather than just immediate cooling effects.

Economic relationships between nations have shifted from exploitation to reciprocity. The Global South, rather than serving as a resource supplier and waste dump for the North, is recognized as a holder of essential wisdom about living within limits. Debt forgiveness has freed nations from impossible obligations, allowing them to invest in ecological restoration and social wellbeing. Technology transfer flows in all directions, with Indigenous innovations in sustainable living valued equally with high-tech solutions. Fair trade has evolved beyond better prices to genuine partnership in creating regenerative economies.

Migration is understood as human right and ecological necessity, with people free to move as climate and circumstances require. Rather than militarized borders creating desperate refugees, coordinated resettlement programs help communities relocate together, maintaining cultural integrity. Receiving regions prepare infrastructure and integration support, understanding that diversity strengthens resilience. The knowledge and skills that migrants bring are valued, with traditional ecological knowledge especially prized. The fear and xenophobia that characterized early 21st century migration debates has been replaced by recognition of our common humanity and shared destiny.

Indigenous peoples have achieved full sovereignty and land rights, with their territories recognized as essential reserves of biodiversity and cultural wisdom. The knowledge systems that enabled them to thrive sustainably for millennia are studied and applied globally, with Indigenous teachers compensated fairly for their wisdom. Sacred sites are protected internationally, with extractive industries prohibited from operating in areas of spiritual significance. The genocide and epistemicide that characterized colonization has been acknowledged through truth and reconciliation processes that include reparations and structural change.

Scientific research has been decolonized and democratized, with Indigenous knowledge systems recognized as equally valid ways of understanding reality. Research priorities are determined by communities rather than corporations, with emphasis on solving collective challenges rather than generating private profit. Open science principles ensure that knowledge is freely shared rather than locked behind paywalls. Young people from all backgrounds have access to scientific education and resources, with diverse perspectives strengthening rather than threatening scientific enterprise.

Peace has been achieved not through military dominance but through addressing root causes of conflict—inequality, resource scarcity, and ideological extremism. Military budgets have been redirected to ecological restoration and social programs that build security through wellbeing rather than weaponry. International conflicts are resolved through restoration rather than retribution, with harmful actions requiring repair of damage rather than punishment. The warrior energy that once fueled destruction has been channeled into protecting life, with Earth defenders honored as heroes.

Hope, Possibility, and Evolutionary Potential

As we contemplate this vision of an animistic future, we must hold it lightly—not as a fixed destination but as a compass heading that orients our journey. The specific forms this future takes will emerge from countless experiments, failures, and innovations we cannot now imagine. What matters is not the details but the direction: toward recognition of consciousness in all beings, toward reciprocity rather than extraction, toward humility about our place in the community of life. This vision is already emerging in scattered locations worldwide—we need not create it from nothing but nurture what already exists.

The evolutionary potential of this transformation extends beyond solving current crises to fundamentally advancing human consciousness. By recognizing ourselves as part of rather than separate from the living world, we open to forms of intelligence and awareness previously inaccessible. The empathic connection with other species, the intuitive understanding of natural patterns, the expanded sense of self that includes ecosystem and planet—these are not regressions to primitive consciousness but evolution to integrated awareness that includes and transcends previous stages.

The children who grow up in animistic societies will possess capabilities we can barely imagine. Raised in connection with the living world, they will perceive patterns and relationships invisible to those raised in separation. Educated through multiple ways of knowing, they will integrate intuitive and analytical intelligence in ways that solve previously intractable problems. Embedded in healthy communities and ecosystems, they will express creativity and compassion unlimited by the trauma and disconnection that constrained previous generations. They will be fully human in ways we have forgotten possible.

The ecosystems restored through animistic practice will exhibit resilience and abundance that mechanistic management could never achieve. Forests will return to lands thought permanently degraded. Species thought extinct will emerge from hidden refugia. Soils will rebuild with surprising speed when partnered with rather than exploited.

The oceans will recover from acidification and plastic pollution. The atmosphere will rebalance as carbon returns to soil and biomass. Earth's healing powers, when supported rather than overwhelmed, exceed our most optimistic projections.

The technologies developed within animistic frameworks will achieve elegance and efficiency that brute force approaches never could. By learning from nature's 3.8 billion years of research and development, we will create materials that are strong yet biodegradable, systems that are complex yet resilient, processes that are productive yet regenerative. The waste and pollution that characterized industrial technology will seem as primitive to future generations as bloodletting seems to modern medicine. Technology will become an ally rather than a threat to life.

The social innovations emerging from animistic consciousness will resolve conflicts thought inherent to human nature. Competition will complement rather than exclude cooperation. Individual expression will strengthen rather than threaten collective wellbeing. Diversity will create resilience rather than division. Governance will emerge from collective wisdom rather than imposed authority. Economics will generate abundance rather than scarcity. These are not utopian impossibilities but natural consequences of recognizing our interdependence with all life.

The spiritual awakening that animistic consciousness catalyzes will heal the existential wounds that have tormented humanity since we imagined ourselves separate from the sacred. The anxiety of isolation will dissolve into the peace of belonging. The terror of death will transform into understanding of continuity. The hunger for meaning will be satisfied through participation in the larger life of which we are part. The desperate seeking that characterizes modern spirituality will resolve into the simple presence of being at home in a conscious, sacred cosmos.

The Call to Participation

This vision of an animistic future is not prediction but invitation. It will not manifest automatically through historical forces or divine intervention but requires conscious choice and sustained effort by millions of people choosing to live differently. Each person who develops reciprocal relationships with their local ecosystem, who teaches children to perceive the consciousness in all beings, who challenges the systems that treat nature as commodity, who creates alternatives to destructive patterns—each becomes a seed of the future we envision.

The transformation begins not in distant futures but in this moment, with the next breath that connects us to the atmosphere we share with all life. It continues with the next step that connects us to the Earth that supports all beings. It deepens with the next word spoken in recognition of the consciousness present in all we encounter. These may seem like small acts, but repeated by millions, they become the great turning that transforms civilization. We need not wait for leaders or permission—we can begin immediately, wherever we are, with whatever capacities we possess.

The path forward requires both urgent action and patient persistence. We must respond to the immediate crises—climate chaos, ecosystem collapse, social disintegration—while building long-term alternatives that will replace failing systems. We must grieve what is being lost while nurturing what is emerging. We must resist destruction while creating construction. We must hold despair and hope simultaneously, allowing both to inform our actions without being paralyzed by one or intoxicated by the other.

The allies available for this transformation include not just human movements but the Earth itself, which constantly works toward healing when given the chance. Every abandoned lot that springs to life with plants, every species that recovers when protection is provided, every watershed that clarifies when pollution ceases—all demonstrate Earth's irrepressible vitality and resilience. We are not trying to save a dying planet but partnering with a living one that desperately wants to thrive.

When we align ourselves with Earth's healing powers, we discover capacities we didn't know we possessed.

The ancestors support this transformation—all those who lived in right relationship with Earth before industrial madness, all those who resisted mechanistic consciousness even unto death, all those who preserved seeds of wisdom for this moment of possibility. Their presence is available to those who remember to ask, their wisdom accessible to those who learn to listen. We are not alone in this work but supported by countless generations who knew what we are trying to remember.

Future generations also support this transformation, their presence felt by those sensitive enough to perceive it. The children not yet born, the species not yet evolved, the possibilities not yet manifest—all depend on the choices we make in this pivotal moment. Their gratitude or condemnation awaits our actions. We hold in our hands the power to gift them a living world or a dying one, a civilization of beauty or brutality, a future of possibility or limitation. The magnitude of this responsibility is matched only by the honor of being alive at this turning point.

The vision of an animistic future presented in this chapter is neither guarantee nor fantasy but possibility available if we choose it. The seeds of this future exist in the present—in every person who greets the sun with gratitude, in every community that organizes around life rather than profit, in every child who grows up knowing themselves as part of the living world. Our task is not to force this future into being but to tend the conditions that allow it to emerge. Like gardeners, we prepare soil, plant seeds, provide water, and trust in life's inherent tendency toward growth and fruiting.

The great turning from industrial growth society to life-sustaining civilization is the work of our time. It is work that requires all our gifts—practical and spiritual, analytical and intuitive, individual and collective. It is work that will not be completed in our lifetimes but must be significantly advanced if our species is to survive and thrive. It is work that offers not sacrifice but fulfillment, not deprivation but abundance, not loss of self but discovery of our true nature as participants in the community of life.

As we close this exploration of animistic consciousness and its implications for human and planetary flourishing, we return to the fundamental recognition with which we began: we inhabit a living universe where every element possesses consciousness and deserves respect. This is not belief to adopt but reality to recognize, not ideology to impose but truth to embody. The animate Earth calls us home from our long exile in mechanistic consciousness. The community of life awaits our return as participants rather than dominators. The future depends on our willingness to remember what we have forgotten: that we are not separate from but part of the living, sacred whole.

May we find the courage to release the familiar patterns that are killing the world. May we find the strength to persist through the darkness of collapse toward the dawn of renewal. May we find the wisdom to learn from all our teachers, human and more-than-human. May we find the love that motivates transformation without hatred for what must be transformed. And may we find the joy that comes from taking our place in the dance of life, no longer as awkward strangers but as grateful participants in the endless creativity of the animate Earth.

CHAPTER 25

Postscript

The journey toward reclaiming our animistic heritage is one we walk together, in dialogue with the living world and with each other. If these pages have sparked new questions, insights, or stories you wish to share, I warmly invite you to reach out. Your reflections are part of the conversation that keeps this vision alive.

info@rabbitholebookshop.com

Let's keep listening, learning, and weaving the threads of a more connected future.